Microsoft®

W9-AHS-247

Step by Step

Microsoft
SQL Server™ 2000
Analysis Services

OLAP Train
Reed Jacobson

PUBLISHED BY
Microsoft Press
A Division of Microsoft Corporation
One Microsoft Way
Redmond, Washington 98052-6399

Library of Congress Cataloging-in-Publication Data
Jacobson, Reed.
   The Microsoft SQL Server 2000 Analysis Services Step by Step / Reed Jacobson.
    p. cm.
   Includes index.
   ISBN 0-7356-0904-7
    1. OLAP technology.

  QA76.9.D343 J33   2000
  005.74--dc21   99-086771

Printed and bound in the United States of America.

1 2 3 4 5 6 7 8 9   QWTQWT   5 4 3 2 1 0

Distributed in Canada by Penguin Books Canada Limited.

A CIP catalogue record for this book is available from the British Library.

Microsoft Press books are available through booksellers and distributors worldwide. For further information about international editions, contact your local Microsoft Corporation office or contact Microsoft Press International directly at fax (425) 936-7329. Visit our Web site at mspress.microsoft.com. Send comments to *mspinput@microsoft.com*.

Acquisitions Editor: David Clark
Project Editor: Devon Musgrave
Technical Editor: Jack Beaudry

Contents

Part 2

Multidimensional Expressions

Part 3

Advanced Administration

Preface

Who Should Read This Book?

Analysis Services is a powerful but easily overlooked component of Microsoft SQL Server 2000. By using Analysis Services, you can create fast, flexible, interactive reports based on information locked in huge corporate databases. By using Analysis Services, you can add spreadsheet-like analytical capabilities to large, shared data sources. By using Analysis Services, you can create *multidimensional* views of numeric data.

A person who retrieves information from a multidimensional database typically finds the interaction to be simple, logical, and intuitive. The person charged with designing and creating a multidimensional database, however, often initially finds the concepts to be complex, challenging, and unfamiliar. Books that explain Analysis Services (or OLAP Services, as it was called in the previous version of SQL Server) often assume that the reader is already familiar with multidimensional concepts. For many people, reading a book on Analysis Services feels similar to how a nonswimmer would feel diving into the deep end of a swimming pool.

This book will give you a safe, gradual introduction to multidimensional concepts in general and to the Analysis Services component of SQL Server 2000 in particular. The book uses simple, concrete examples to explain multidimensional terminology and concepts, stripping away the confusion and inherent complexity. The book also guides you through the tools available in Analysis Services, beginning with the simplest possible solutions and progressing to sophisticated techniques for handling unusual situations and optimizing large databases.

This book provides an effective resource to a wide variety of readers:

- If you are a database administrator with the responsibility of creating and managing an Analysis Services database, this book will give you the foundation you need.

- If you're a decision maker with the responsibility of determining the role Analysis Services might play in your organization, this book will give you the perspective you need.

- If you're an analyst with the responsibility of converting spreadsheet models into a shareable, scalable form, this book will give you the techniques you need.

What Does This Book Cover?

The book is organized into three parts. Part 1, "Administration Fundamentals," provides the conceptual framework for multidimensional analysis and then describes all the tools necessary to create a functional Analysis Services database. Part 2, "Multidimensional Expressions," introduces the language that adds powerful analytical capabilities to a database. Part 3, "Advanced Administration," deals with issues that arise in real-world situations—when databases become large enough to require optimization or when access to the database needs to be secured.

Analysis Services is a powerful and extensive product, and this book is intended as a solid introduction, not as a comprehensive reference. Following are some advanced topics that are beyond the scope of this book:

- **Data mining**   The ability to search for patterns and relationships in large databases. This topic is extensive and requires an entire book of its own.

- **Actions**   The ability for an administrator to preassign actions—such as opening a custom Web page—that a user browsing a report can trigger. Actions are largely a tool for application developers, and this book is focused on tasks performed by database administrators.

- **Extreme scalability**   The ability to spread a database over multiple servers or to link data from one server to another. These are specialized tasks that will be undertaken by relatively few corporations using Analysis Services.

What Do You Need to Use This Book?

To use this book, you'll need to install the Analysis Services component of SQL Server 2000. The full installation of SQL Server 2000 is required only for the section "Automating the Processing of a Database" in Chapter 9, "Processing Optimization." For most of the book, you can install Analysis Services from the Standard Edition of SQL Server 2000. Installing Analysis Services from the Enterprise Edition of SQL Server 2000 is required only for the section "Working with Partitions," also in Chapter 9.

This book does not require any system requirements in addition to the following requirements for SQL Server 2000:

- Intel (or compatible) Pentium, Pentium Pro, or Pentium II processor running at 166 MHz or faster

- Minimum 64 MB RAM, with 128 MB recommended for the Enterprise Edition

- Minimum 50 MB free disk space, with 130 MB required for the typical installation of Analysis Services

- Minimum 800 x 600 resolution monitor

- Microsoft Mouse or compatible, and CD-ROM drive (or access to network source)

- Microsoft Internet Explorer 5.0 or later

For the operating system, you must have at least the Workstation Edition of Microsoft Windows NT 4.0 Service Pack 5 or later, or the Professional Edition of Microsoft Windows 2000. To carry out the actions of the section "Working with Partitions" in Chapter 9, which requires the Enterprise Edition of SQL Server 2000, you'll need the Server Edition of Windows NT 4.0 or the Advanced Server Edition of Windows 2000.

To carry out the tasks of Chapter 5, "Office 2000 Analysis Components," you'll need Microsoft Excel 2000. For some of the tasks in Chapter 5, you'll need Microsoft FrontPage 2000, which is available alone or with the Premium Edition of Microsoft Office 2000.

You'll also need to install the sample files from the CD that accompanies this book. See the next section for information on using the companion CD.

How Do I Use the Companion CD?

The Readme.txt file on the CD includes instructions for installing the sample files. Each chapter uses separate sample files, so it is not necessary to complete earlier chapters to carry out the tasks of a later chapter. If you choose to install the sample files to a folder other than the default, carry out the following steps each time you restore an OLAP database:

1. Start Analysis Manager by clicking Start, selecting Programs, Microsoft SQL Server, Analysis Services, and then clicking Analysis Manager.

2. In the console tree, expand the Analysis Servers folder. Right-click the server, and click Restore Database.

3. Navigate to the folder where you installed the sample files from the companion CD. Select a chapter .cab file, and click Open.

4. Click Restore, and then close the Restore Database Progress dialog box when processing has completed.

5. In the console tree, expand the restored OLAP database folder and the Data Sources folder.

6. Right-click the data source in the console tree, and then click Edit. Enter the correct path to the data source on the Connection tab and click OK.

For more complete information about using the companion CD, consult the Readme.txt file on the CD.

Acknowledgments

Thanks to the great team at Microsoft Press who made this book happen: Eric Stroo for first recognizing the potential for this book, Ben Ryan for seeing the book through to completion from the acquisitions end, Devon Musgrave for keeping the project moving and the text flowing, Jack Beaudry for conscientiously checking the technical accuracy, Sandra Haynes for simplifying incomprehensible and convoluted sentence structures, and Elizabeth Hansford for making the pages look beautiful in print.

Thanks to the great team at OLAP Train and Aspirity for breaking ground in understanding and teaching the concepts in this book: Tom Chester for being the first to plunge into the brave new world of what was then called OLAP Services, Sara Bergseth for being a superb role model and teacher, Hilary Feier for willingly plunging into experiments and arguments to find out how things really work, and Rand Heer for his wisdom when difficult decisions needed to be made.

Special thanks to the Plato dev team for their insights and support, especially to Corey Salka, Amir Netz, Ariel Netz, Mosha Pasumansky, Thierry D'Hers, and Marin Bezic.

Part 1

Administration Fundamentals

Chapter 1

A Data Analysis Foundation

In this chapter, you will learn

- The purpose and structure of a data warehouse.

- What multidimensionality means in a database.

- The vocabulary of Analysis Services.

- Where Analysis Services stores information.

- How Analysis Manager communicates with the Analysis server.

- How client applications communicate with the Analysis server.

Microsoft SQL Server 2000 Analysis Services is advertised as a *multidimensional* database server. The term *multidimensional* conjures up images of Albert Einstein's curved space-time, parallel universes, and mathematical formulas that make solving for integrals sound soothingly simple. And yet the buzz is that Analysis Services is supposed to make analyzing huge amounts of data fast, flexible, and easy.

In H. G. Wells' story *The Time Machine,* life was easy and beautiful for the city dwellers of the future because all the hard and dirty work was being done by mysterious beings hidden underground (who, incidentally, harvested the simple-minded surface people for food). One might fear that in a similar way Analysis Services makes it easy for an analyst to manipulate data because it pushes complex and confusing administrative tasks onto the less visible database administrator.

The real story is neither as dramatic nor as frightening as the H. G. Wells story. The bottom line is that calling a database multidimensional is really a bit of a lie. It's a snazzy term, but when applied to databases it has nothing in common with the multidimensional behavior of particles accelerating near the speed of light or even with the multidimensional aspects of Alice's adventures down the rabbit hole. This chapter will help you understand what multidimensionality really means in a database context and how Analysis Services can help simplify your data analysis needs.

Understanding Data Warehousing

Suppose that you are the president of a small, new company. Your company needs to grow, but you have limited resources to support the expansion. You have decisions to make, and to make those decisions you must have particular information. Much of the information you need comes from outside the organization. That's why you read the *Wall Street Journal* and keep a bookmark in your browser pointed at *www.bloomberg.com*. But much of the information you need also comes from inside the organization, and much of that information is numerical. A data warehouse is a tool for storing and analyzing numerical information.

Ralph Kimball, perhaps the preeminent apostle of data warehousing philosophy, describes a data warehouse simply as "the place where people can access their data." He lists six critical requirements for a data warehouse:

- Warehouse retrievals must be fast.

- Warehouse values must be internally consistent.

- Users must be able to slice and dice—that is, extract a single item (slice) and compare items in a cross-tabulated table (dice)—warehouse data.

- A warehouse must include easy-to-use browsing tools.

- Warehouse data must be complete and reliable.

- Quality warehouse data requires quality data-gathering processes.

Analysis Services can play an integral part in the data warehousing strategy of a corporation, but it does not satisfy all the needs of a data warehouse. In fact, Analysis Services facilitates only two of the six requirements: Analysis Services does help make retrieval from a warehouse fast (Requirement 1), and it does make it easier to slice and dice the data (Requirement 3). Analysis Services does not directly provide easy-to-use browsing tools (Requirement 4)—although, as described in Chapter 5, "Office 2000 Analysis Components," you can use the Microsoft Excel 2000 PivotTable report tool as a simple browser for an Analysis Services warehouse.

Kimball's remaining three requirements—all of which have to do with making the data in the warehouse consistent, reliable, and trustworthy—must be done *before* your use of Analysis Services enters the picture. In other words, Analysis Services assumes that you already have a valid, functional data warehouse created using a relational database management system such as SQL Server.

Analysis Services creates a new layer on top of an existing relational warehouse. The purpose of that new layer is to make access to the data very fast and very flexible (two of Kimball's data warehouse requirements).

Note Even though Analysis Services is bundled with SQL Server 2000, it does not require that you use SQL Server as your relational database management system. You can use Analysis Services with Oracle, DB2, Informix, or any other relational database tool, including Microsoft Access.

The Purpose of a Data Warehouse

A data warehouse stores stable, verified data values. You might find it helpful to compare a data warehouse with a transaction database:

- A transaction database helps people carry out activities, and a data warehouse helps people make decisions. For example, a transaction database might show which seats are available on an airline flight so that a travel agent can book a new reservation. A data warehouse, on the other hand, might show the historical pattern of empty seats by flight so that an airline manager can decide whether to adjust flight schedules in the future.

- A transaction database is volatile; its information constantly changes as new orders are placed or cancelled, as new products are built or shipped, or as new reservations are made. A data warehouse is stable; its information is updated at standard intervals—perhaps monthly, weekly, or even hourly—and, in an ideal world, an update would add values for the new time period only, without changing values previously stored in the warehouse.

- A transaction database focuses on the details: the travel agent booking a flight reservation doesn't want to know the average number of empty seats, and the parent purchasing the latest Harry Potter book doesn't care about inventory levels for the Juvenile Fiction product line. A data warehouse focuses on high-level aggregates: the manager updating flight schedules doesn't care which specific seats were empty but does want to see the big picture. The implication of this difference is that the key values in a data warehouse must be numeric values that can be summarized.

- A transaction database typically provides the data values that are then stored in a data warehouse.

Dimensions in Data Analysis

In the world of data warehousing, a summarizable numerical value that you use to monitor your business is called a *measure*. When looking for numerical information, your first question is which measure you want to see. You could look at, say, Sales Dollars, at Shipment Units, at Defects Per Hour, or at Ad Campaign Responses. Suppose that you ask to see a report of your company's Units Sold. Here's what you get:

113

Looking at the one value doesn't tell you much. You want to break it out into something more informative. For example, how has your company done over time? You ask for a monthly analysis, and here's the new report:

January	February	March	April
14	41	33	25

Your company has been operating for four months, so across the top of the report you find four labels for the months. Rather than the one value you had before, you now find four values. The months subdivide the original value. The new number of values equals the number of months. This is analogous to calculating linear distances in the physical world: the length of a line is simply the length.

You're still not satisfied with the monthly report. Your company sells more than one product. How did each of those products do over time? You ask for a new report by product and by month:

	January	February	March	April
Colony Blueberry Muffins			6	17
Colony Cranberry Muffins	6	16	6	8
Sphinx Bagels	8	25	21	

Your young company sells three products, so down the left side of the report are the three product names. Each product subdivides the monthly values. Meanwhile, the four labels for the months are still across the top of the report. You now have 12 values to consider. The number of values equals the number of products times the number of months. This is analogous to calculating the area of a rectangle in the physical world: area equals the rectangle's length times its width. The report even looks like a rectangle.

The Term *OLAP* in Analysis Services

The previous version of Analysis Services was named OLAP Services. The name was changed in SQL Server 2000 to avoid the use of an unfamiliar acronym and also because Analysis Services now includes data mining tools, which are outside the realm of OLAP technology. The term *OLAP* still appears frequently in the product documentation, and you should understand what it means. Understanding the history of the term can help you understand its meaning.

In the 1980s, E. F. Codd coined the term *online transaction processing* (OLTP) and proposed 12 criteria that define an OLTP database. His terminology and criteria became widely accepted as the standard for databases used to manage the day-to-day operations (transactions) of a company. In the 1990s, Codd came up with the term *online analytical processing* (OLAP) and again proposed 12 criteria to define an OLAP database. This time his criteria did not gain wide acceptance, but the term *OLAP* did, seeming perfect to many for describing databases designed to facilitate decision making (analysis) in an organization.

Some people use *OLAP* simply as a synonym for data warehousing. Usually, however, the term *OLAP* describes specialized tools that make warehouse data easily accessible. It is in that specialized sense that the term *OLAP* is used in SQL Server 2000 Analysis Services.

The comparison to a rectangle, however, applies only to the arithmetic involved, not to the shape of the report. Your report could be organized differently—it could just as easily look like this:

Colony Blueberry Muffins	January	
Colony Blueberry Muffins	February	
Colony Blueberry Muffins	March	6
Colony Blueberry Muffins	April	17
Colony Cranberry Muffins	January	6
Colony Cranberry Muffins	February	16
Colony Cranberry Muffins	March	6
Colony Cranberry Muffins	April	8
Sphinx Bagels	January	8
Sphinx Bagels	February	25
Sphinx Bagels	March	21
Sphinx Bagels	April	

Whether you display the values in a list like the one above (where the numerical values form a line) or display them in a grid (where they form a rectangle), you still have the potential for 12 values if you have four monthly values for each of three products. Your report has 12 potential values because the products and the months are independent. Each product gets its own sales value—even if that value is zero—for each month.

Back to the rectangular report. Suppose that your company sells in two different states and you'd like to know how each product is doing each month in each state. Add another set of labels indicating the states your company uses, and you get a new report, one that looks like this:

		January	February	March	April
WA	Colony Blueberry Muffins			3	10
	Colony Cranberry Muffins	3	16	6	
	Sphinx Bagels	4	16	6	
OR	Colony Blueberry Muffins			3	7
	Colony Cranberry Muffins	3			8
	Sphinx Bagels	4	9	15	

The report now has two labels for the states, three labels for products (each shown twice), and four labels for months. It has the potential for showing 24 values, even if some of those value cells are blank. The number of potential values equals the number of states times the number of products times the number of months. This is analogous to calculating the volume of a cube in the physical world: volume equals the length of the cube times its width times its height. Your report doesn't really look like a cube—it looks more like a rectangle. Again, you could rearrange it to look like a list, and the beginning of the list would look like this:

WA	Colony Blueberry Muffins	January	
WA	Colony Cranberry Muffins	January	3
WA	Sphinx Bagels	January	4
OR	Colony Blueberry Muffins	January	
OR	Colony Cranberry Muffins	January	3
OR	Sphinx Bagels	January	4
WA	Colony Blueberry Muffins	February	
WA	Colony Cranberry Muffins	February	16
WA	Sphinx Bagels	February	16

Whichever way you lay out your report, it has three independent lists of labels, and the total number of potential values in the report equals the number of unique items in the first independent list of labels (for example, two states) times the number of unique items in the second independent list of labels (three products) times the number of unique items in the third independent list of labels (four months). Because the phrase *independent list of labels* is wordy, and because the arithmetic used to calculate the number of potential values in the report is identical to the arithmetic used to calculate length, area, and volume—measurements of spatial extension—in place of *independent list of labels,* data warehouse designers borrow the term *dimension* from mathematics. Remember that this is a borrowed term. A data analysis dimension is very different from a physical dimension. Thus, your report has three dimensions—State, Product, and Time—and the report's number of values equals the number of items in the first dimension times the number of items in the second dimension, and so forth. Using the term *dimension* doesn't say anything about how the labels and values are displayed in a report or even about how they should be stored in a database.

Each time you've created a new dimension, the items in that dimension have conceptually related to one another—for example, they are all products, or they are all dates. Accordingly, items in a dimension are called *members* of that dimension.

Now complicate the report even more. Perhaps you want to see dollars as well as units. You get a new report that looks like this:

		January		February		March		April	
		U	$	U	$	U	$	U	$
WA	Colony Blueberry Muffins					3	7.44	10	24.80
	Colony Cranberry Muffins	3	7.95	16	42.40	6	15.90		
	Sphinx Bagels	4	7.32	16	29.28	6	10.98		
OR	Colony Blueberry Muffins					3	7.44	7	17.36
	Colony Cranberry Muffins	3	7.95					8	21.20
	Sphinx Bagels	4	7.32	9	16.47	15	27.45		

U=Units; $=Dollars

Because units and dollars are independent of the State, Product, and Time dimensions, they form what you can think of as a new, fourth dimension, which you could call a Measures dimension. The number of values in the report still equals the product of the number of members in each dimension: 2 times 3 times 4 times 2, which equals 48. But there is not—and there does not need to be—any kind of physical world analogue. Remember that the word *dimension* is simply a convenient way of saying *independent list of labels*, and having four (or twenty or sixty) independent lists is just as easy as having three. It just makes the report bigger.

In the physical world, the object you're measuring changes depending on how many dimensions there are. For example, a one-dimensional inch is a linear inch, but a two-dimensional inch is a square inch, and a three-dimensional inch is a cubic inch. A cubic inch is a completely different object from a square inch or from a linear inch. In your report, however, the object that you measure as you add dimensions is always the same: a numerical value. There is no difference between a numerical value in a "four-dimensional" report and a numerical value in a "one-dimensional" report. In the reporting world, an additional dimension simply creates a new, independent way to subdivide a measure.

Although adding a fourth or fifth dimension to a report is not a metaphysical act, that's not to say that adding a new dimension is trivial. Suppose that you start with a report with two dimensions: 30 products and 12 months, or 360 possible values. Adding three new members to the product dimension increases the number of values in the report to 396, a 10 percent increase. Adding a third dimension with three new members, however, increases the number of values in the report to 1080, a 300 percent increase. Consider this extreme example: with 128 members in a single dimension, a report has 128 possible values, but with those same 128 total members split up into 64 dimensions—with two members in each dimension—a report has 18,446,744,073,709,551,616 possible values!

Hierarchies in Data Analysis

When an organization is small or hasn't been around for a long time, it's easy to understand the business simply by looking at the detailed numbers. For example, if you have a company that has been in business for only four months and it has only three products, you can comfortably analyze data at the lowest level of detail. Psychological studies indicate that most people can easily comprehend about seven items—or seven groups of items. Grouping—*aggregating*—is the way that humans deal with numerous items. Once your company has sold products for more than six months, you'll undoubtedly want to start looking at the values by quarter as well as by month. Likewise, once your company has more than a dozen products, you'll probably want to group the products into product lines or product groups. But how do aggregations such as quarters and product lines fit into dimensions?

Generally, you think of members in a dimension as "belonging together." January and February naturally seem to belong together and clearly should reside in the same dimension. January and Colony Blueberry Muffins don't naturally belong together and clearly should not reside in the same dimension. But what about the members January and Qtr1? Do they belong together?

Remember that a dimension is really an independent list of labels for the report. To decide whether new members belong in a new dimension or in an existing dimension, imagine the new members as the column headings of a report, with the members of the existing dimension forming the row headings. If the new members are independent, you should—at least potentially—have a value each time they intersect. But look at a report that shows months on the rows and quarters on the columns:

	Qtr1	Qtr2
January	14	
February	41	
March	33	
April		25
May		29
June		39

Half the cells are empty, and it's not coincidental. There is no such thing as a January in Qtr2, just as there's no April in Qtr1. The report looks silly. Putting the two quarters in a dimension other than the Time dimension multiplies the total number of values by two but also guarantees that half of the values will always be empty. So the number of true potential values has not changed. In fact, the report with quarters on the columns never shows you what you want to see, which is the total for each quarter.

The report you want looks more like this:

Qtr1	88
January	14
February	41
March	33

Qtr2	93
April	25
May	29
June	39

Months and quarters are not completely independent members and should not appear in separate dimensions. The quarter totals are simply *aggregations* of the month totals, and they belong in the same dimension. There is, however, something different between Qtr1 and January. For one thing, you probably want the *January* label to be indented more than the *Qtr1* label. And there's something similar about the labels *Qtr1* and *Qtr2*.

Even though the words *Month* and *Quarter* don't appear in the report, you naturally refer to the labels *January*, *February*, and so forth as months, and you refer to the labels *Qtr1*, *Qtr2*, and so forth as quarters. Months and quarters form a *hierarchy* within the Time dimension, and each degree of summarization is referred to as a *level*. For example, in this Time dimension, January and February are members of the Month level, and Qtr1 and Qtr2 are members of the Quarter level. As time goes on and you add more months and quarters, you'll eventually add a Year level to the dimension's hierarchy. A dimension containing more than a few members almost always breaks into a hierarchy, and a hierarchy, by definition, contains levels.

When you have a hierarchy in a dimension, sometimes you'll want to see the entire hierarchy, sometimes you'll want to see only the top one or two levels, and sometimes you'll want to see only the lowest level. You can use the term *members* to describe either all the members in the entire dimension or only the members of a specific level within the dimension. For example, the members of the Time dimension include years and quarters as well as months, and the members of the Months level within the Time dimension do not include any years or quarters. The members at the lowest level of detail are called *leaf members*. A dimension cannot exist without leaf members, but it is possible to have a dimension with nothing but leaf members—that is, with only one level. For example, in the Measures dimension, it doesn't make sense to sum the total of Units and Dollars.

Some hierarchies, such as Time, are *balanced*: if there are months under Qtr1, there will also be months under Qtr2, Qtr3, and Qtr4. In a balanced hierarchy, it's easy to give names to levels. For example, the levels in a typical Time hierarchy might have the names Year, Quarter, and Month.

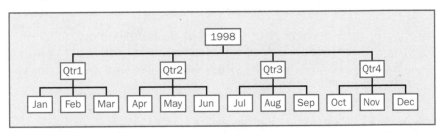

Some hierarchies are *unbalanced*. An organization chart is often unbalanced. For example, in many companies, there might be many more people—and thus many more levels of management—in the Manufacturing organization than in Human Resources. In an unbalanced hierarchy, it's often difficult to give names to specific levels, but leaf members are always the ones that have no children below them.

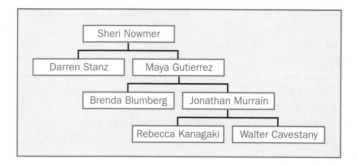

Some hierarchies appear to blur the distinction between unbalanced and balanced. For example, in a geographic hierarchy, you might have easily named levels—Country, Region, and State—but skip the Region level for certain States. This really is a balanced hierarchy (because there are easily named levels), but the parents of some of the members are missing or invisible. A hierarchy that hides some of the parent members is called a *ragged* hierarchy.

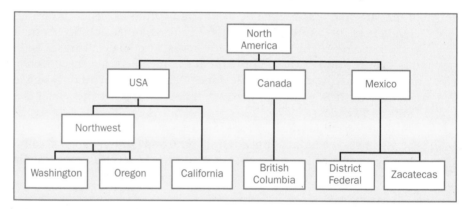

Analysis Services gives you a great deal of flexibility in defining balanced or unbalanced hierarchies, whether ragged or not. A dimension always has leaf members. The hierarchy simply defines how (and whether) the values for leaf members are summarized.

The Structure of a Data Warehouse

Analysis Services makes it easy for a client application to create reports that use multiple dimensions, but the values displayed in the report ultimately come from a relational data warehouse. Because Analysis Services assumes that you already have a relational data warehouse, this book does not deal with the often agonizing issues involved in gathering clean data into a relational warehouse but simply includes sample relational data warehouses to work from. Whether you create your own relational warehouse, get a corporate database administrator to build one for you, or use one that already exists, at some point you will need to link Analysis Services to the relational warehouse. So, to use Analysis Services successfully, you must know what Analysis Services expects the data warehouse to look like. Analysis Services requires a data warehouse with a very specific form—a form characterized by a *fact table*.

A Fact Table

A fact table is a table in the relational data warehouse that stores the detailed values for measures, or *facts*. A fact table that stores Dollars and Units by State, by Product, and by Month has five columns, conceptually similar to those in the following sample:

In a database table, a column is sometimes called a field, *and a row is sometimes called a* record.

State	Product	Month	Units	Dollars
WA	Colony Cranberry Muffins	January	3	7.95
WA	Sphinx Bagels	January	4	7.32
OR	Colony Cranberry Muffins	January	3	7.95
OR	Sphinx Bagels	January	4	7.32
WA	Colony Cranberry Muffins	February	16	42.40

In these sample rows from a fact table, the first three columns—State, Product, and Month—are key columns. The remaining two columns—Units and Dollars—contain measure values. Each column in a fact table should be either a key or a measure.

To be usable by Analysis Services, the fact table must contain a column for each measure. A Sales warehouse might contain two measure columns—one for Dollars and one for Units. A shop-floor warehouse might contain three measure columns—one for Units, one for Minutes, and one for Defects. In a report, you can think of the measures as forming a separate dimension. That is, you can put Units and Dollars side by side as column headings, or you can put Units and Dollars as row headings. In the fact table, however, each measure appears as a separate column.

To be usable by Analysis Services, the fact table must contain rows at the lowest level of detail you might want to retrieve for a measure. In other words, the fact table contains rows only for leaf members of each dimension. Analysis Services cannot use a fact table that stores aggregates, such as quarter and year totals. For example, if a State dimension includes a hierarchy, consisting of State, Region, and Country, only the members from the State level appear in the fact table. Analysis Services will create all the summarized values. In the fact table, specifying a single leaf member for each dimension should identify a single row.

The sample rows in the preceding table illustrate the conceptual layout of a fact table. Actually, a fact table almost always uses an integer key for each member, rather than a descriptive name. Because a fact table tends to include an incredible number of rows—in a reasonably large warehouse, the fact table might easily have millions of rows—using an integer key can substantially reduce the size of the fact table. The key column for a date dimension might be either an integer key or a Date value. The actual layout of a fact table might look more like that of the following sample rows:

STATE_ID	PROD_ID	Month	Sales_Units	Sales_Dollars
1	589	1/1/1998	3	7.95
1	1218	1/1/1998	4	7.32
2	589	1/1/1998	3	7.95
2	1218	1/1/1998	4	7.32
1	589	2/1/1998	16	42.40

Dimension Tables

The fact table contains only the lowest level of detail. If you have eight products grouped into two product lines, the fact table does not contain any rows for the product lines, only rows for the products. Likewise, the fact table does not contain any rows for quarter totals or year totals, only values for the months, the lowest level of detail. The information necessary to create summaries— that is, the information relating to a dimension's hierarchies—is stored in the warehouse in separate dimension tables.

A dimension table contains one row for each leaf member of the dimension. A Product dimension table with three products will have three rows. A dimension table contains one column containing the names of the members. In most cases, a dimension table also contains a numeric key column that uniquely identifies each member. If the dimension is involved in a balanced hierarchy, the dimension table will also have an additional column that gives the parent for each member. For example, if you have three products in a Product dimension, the dimension table might look something like this:

PROD_ID	Product_Name	Subcategory
589	Colony Cranberry Muffins	Muffins
592	Colony Blueberry Muffins	Muffins
1218	Sphinx Bagels	Bagels

In the data warehouse, the key column for a dimension table must contain a unique value for each member of the dimension. This column containing unique key values is called a *primary key column*, and it should be indexed. The primary key column of each dimension table must match one of the key columns in the related fact table. Each key value that appears once in the dimension table will appear multiple times in the fact table. For example, the Product ID 589, for Colony Cranberry Muffins, appears in only one dimension table row, but it will appear in many fact table rows. This is called a *one-to-many* relationship. In the fact table, a key column (which is on the many side of the one-to-many relationship) is called a *foreign key column*. The relational database uses the matching values from the primary key column (in the dimension table) and the foreign key column (in the fact table) to *join* a dimension table to a fact table.

One reason for using an integer key for dimension members is to reduce the size of the fact table. Also, an integer key allows seemingly duplicate members to exist in a dimension table. In a Customer dimension, for example, you might have two different customers named John Smith, but each one will be assigned a unique Customer ID, guaranteeing that each member key will appear only once in the dimension table.

If the dimension includes a balanced hierarchy, its dimension table will contain a column for the parent of the member. In a typical hierarchy, the same parent name appears for more than one member. For example, both Colony Cranberry Muffins and Colony Blueberry Muffins have Muffins as a parent in the preceding table. If the hierarchy continues—for example, if each Product Subcategory is itself part of a Product Category—the dimension will include an additional table where the parent occurs as a unique value:

Product_Subcategory	Product_Category
Muffins	Bread
Bagels	Bread

This process repeats for as many levels as there are in the hierarchy. Each level of a dimension's hierarchy corresponds to a new table in which each member of the hierarchical level appears as a unique value. Of course, as at the lowest level of the dimension, the text name column for a member can be accompanied by a numeric key column, either to guarantee uniqueness or to reduce storage space in a one-to-many relationship. A hierarchy forms a chain of one-to-many relationships. A single Product Category corresponds to multiple Product Subcategories; a single Product Subcategory corresponds to multiple Products; and a single Product corresponds to multiple rows in the fact table.

In some warehouses, the separate tables that make up each level of a dimension hierarchy are merged into a single table, similar to this one:

PROD_ID	Product_Name	Product_Subcategory	Product_Category
589	Colony Cranberry Muffins	Muffins	Bread
592	Colony Blueberry Muffins	Muffins	Bread
1218	Sphinx Bagels	Bagels	Bread

Whether each dimension is stored in a single table or whether a dimension is split up into separate tables mapping to the various levels of the dimension's hierarchy, the relevant portion of a warehouse has the general form of a single fact table—with a key column for each dimension and a numeric column for each measure—accompanied by a dimension table (or a chain of dimension tables) for each dimension. The fact table is in the center, with dimension tables shooting out like the points of a star.

In fact, when each dimension is stored in a single table, the database's organization is called a *star* design. When a database's dimensions are stored in a chain of tables, the database organization is called a *snowflake* design because a snowflake looks somewhat like a star with branching points. Of course, even within a single data warehouse, some dimension tables can use a star design while others use a snowflake design.

Usually, the reason for combining the hierarchy tables for a dimension into a single table is to make reports extracted directly from the relational data warehouse run faster. A relational database must perform time-consuming joins each time a report executes, and a star design for a dimension requires fewer joins than a snowflake design. Analysis Services stores all the dimension information in its own internal structures, so a star design does not create faster reports than a snowflake design.

Note   If a client application creates a report directly from a relational data warehouse, a snowflake design for dimensions can significantly hinder performance. However, if the warehouse will be used only as a data source for Analysis Services, the trade-offs between a snowflake design's clarity and maintainability and a star design's performance become more complex. Chapter 10, "Dimension Optimization," explains how to minimize performance issues related to dimension table design.

Alternative Dimension Table Structures

"Create a dimension from a date column" in Chapter 2, "Analysis Manager from 500 Feet," describes how to create a time hierarchy from a single date column.

In an idealized form, each dimension in a warehouse has a separate dimension table, and each lowest-level member appears only once in a dimension table. Analysis Services can, however, work with other warehouse arrangements. This section previews some of the most important variations.

Most data warehouses include a Time dimension. Sometimes the fact table will store a key for the Time dimension as a Date rather than as an integer key to a dimension table. In that case, no dimension table for the Time dimension exists. Analysis Services can still use the Date column from the fact table as the source for the Time dimension because it extracts unique values to create the effect of a dimension table. Analysis Services can even extract an entire hierarchy from a single Date column.

A dimension with an unbalanced hierarchy—such as an Employee dimension—also requires a slight variation of the snowflake dimension table design. In an Employee dimension, the leaf members are all employees. Each employee's manager, however, is also an employee. Unlike a standard snowflake, where the parent member is in a new level and gets a new table, in an Employee dimension, the parent member simply points back to a new row of the original dimension table. This is called a *parent-child* dimension because both the parent member and the child member are in the same table. A parent-child dimension provides a great deal of flexibility in how a hierarchy is organized.

Chapter 3 explains how to create multiple hierarchies within a single dimension.

You might want to create two different hierarchies for the same leaf member. Suppose, for example, that your company uses a matrix management organization in which each employee reports to two separate management hierarchies—one corresponding to the employee's skill set and one corresponding to the employee's current project assignment. A single Employee dimension table—or a series of snowflaked tables chained to a single lowest-level dimension table—undoubtedly includes columns for both hierarchies. In Analysis Services, you can create separate hierarchies, both of which use the same leaf members but which then aggregate using different parent members.

Chapter 10 explains how to make a multiple hierarchy more efficient.

A dimension table can also include additional columns that do not participate directly in a hierarchy. For example, a Product dimension table might contain a Price column that does not fit into a Product, Subcategory, and Category hierarchy. A column that does not enter into a hierarchy is called a *member property*. A member property can appear at any level of a hierarchy. For example, in a product hierarchy, you might have a manager assigned to each Product Subcategory, so the Manager member property would apply to the members at the Product Subcategory level. Some client applications will display member properties, and you can use member properties in calculations.

Using member properties in calculations will be discussed in Chapter 6, "MDX Values."

Understanding Analysis Services

As mentioned earlier, a data warehouse is a "place for people to access their data." Without Analysis Services, a data warehouse reporting system consists of a relational database at one end that stores data values, and a reporting application at the other end that displays those values. Analysis Services fits between the relational database and the reporting application. It functions as an intermediate layer that converts relational warehouse data into a form that makes it fast and flexible for creating analytical reports.

The primary component of Analysis Services is the Analysis server. Running as a service on Microsoft Windows 2000 or Microsoft Windows NT, the Analysis server extracts information from the data warehouse and creates what's called a *cube,* once again borrowing terminology from the description of physical space. The term *cube* is somewhat plausible because the number of values in the cube is the product of the number of members on each dimension, just as the number of units in a cube is the product of the number of units on each edge of the cube. In the physical world, however, the term *cube* refers to an object with three dimensions. In Analysis Services, a *cube* is simply the storage location for the pool of possible values that you might want to include in a specific report and does not imply anything about the number of dimensions it contains. A cube can have as few as 1 dimension and as many as 64 dimensions (if you count Measures as a dimension). Remember that the word *dimension* merely indicates an independent way that data values can be subdivided.

Conceptualizing a Cube

A cube in Analysis Services is a logical construct. It allows a client application to retrieve values *as if* every possible summarized value existed in the cube. Conceptually, a cube is similar to a fact table but with a few significant differences. Like a fact table, a cube contains one column for each dimension and one column for each measure. Also like a fact table, a cube contains a row for each possible combination of members for all dimensions. Unlike a fact table, however, which contains only the lowest level members of each dimension, a cube contains members from all the levels of each dimension. Assuming a cube with three dimensions—State, Product, and Time—a few sample rows from a cube might be conceptualized like this:

State	Product	Time	Units	Dollars
All	All	All	113	251.26
WA	All	All	64	146.07
WA	Muffins	All	38	98.49
WA	Colony Blueberry Muffins	All	13	32.24
WA	Colony Blueberry Muffins	Qtr1	3	7.44
WA	Colony Blueberry Muffins	Mar	3	7.44

The bottom row of the example corresponds to the row that would be in the fact table—it contains the leaf member of each dimension. None of the other rows would appear in a fact table—each has at least one member from a summary level of a dimension's hierarchy. These sample rows illustrate only a tiny sample of the possible values in even this small cube.

Conceptually, the cube contains all the detail values stored in the fact table, but that doesn't mean that the cube physically copies the detail values from the fact table. The cube can dynamically retrieve values as needed from the fact table. To improve performance, the cube usually copies the detail values into a proprietary structure that allows for extremely fast retrieval. Analysis Services allows the cube designer to decide whether to store the leaf level values in the proprietary structure or retrieve them from the fact table. Aside from performance differences, where the detail values are physically stored is completely invisible to a user of a cube.

Storage design will be covered more fully in Chapter 8, "Storage Optimization."

The cube—again, conceptually—also contains a value for each measure summarized at each possible hierarchy level for each dimension, but, again, that doesn't mean that the cube actually stores all those possible summarized values. The cube can calculate any value by dynamically summarizing leaf-level values. However, to improve performance, the cube can also precalculate selected aggregations and store them. Analysis Services allows the cube designer to control how many aggregations are physically created. Aside from performance differences, whether or not the cube physically stores a particular summarized value is completely invisible to a user of a cube.

Chapter 8 discusses designing aggregations in detail.

When prestoring values in a cube, Analysis Services stores values for only simple aggregations—summing, counting, and taking the minimum or maximum value. You can, however, create *calculated members* that perform calculations on aggregated values. Calculated members make it easy to create values such as average prices or weighted averages. In addition to including sophisticated built-in tools for creating calculated members, Analysis Services allows you to access external functions from Microsoft Visual Basic for Applications (VBA) or Excel, or even write your own external functions.

Chapter 3 introduces calculated members. Chapter 6 and Chapter 7, "MDX Sets," explain how to create sophisticated calculated members.

If you create multiple cubes that are similar to one another—that is, cubes that have dimensions in common—you can group those cubes into an *OLAP database*. When you define a dimension, you can put the dimension in a *library* where it can be used by any cube within the database, or you can make the dimension *private*—that is, specific to and usable by only a single cube.

Sometimes you might want to compare values from multiple cubes. For example, a Sales cube might contain Sales Dollars by Product, by Time, and by Customer. A Cost cube might contain Cost Dollars by Product, by Time, and by Cost Center. You can't put Cost Dollars directly into the Sales cube because you don't have Cost Dollar information at the Customer level. Analysis services allows you to create a *virtual cube* that combines measures from cubes that share at least one common dimension.

Chapter 4, "Advanced Dimensions and Cubes," explains how to create and use virtual cubes.

In the Analysis Services world, a report gets its information from a cube and a cube gets its information from a data warehouse. A cube is a way of packaging, or presenting, the values from a data warehouse. The Analysis server is the component that creates cubes and ultimately provides values to client applications from the cubes.

Analysis Services Administrator Tools

When you interact with the Analysis server, you do so in one of two roles: as an administrator who gives instructions for creating cubes from warehouses or as a user who gives instructions for creating reports from cubes.

When you interact with the Analysis server as an administrator, you use the Analysis Manager application. Analysis Manager allows you to define and populate cubes. The Analysis Manager application communicates with the Analysis server by using a layer named Decision Support Objects (DSO). DSO is a set of programming instructions that allows an application to control Analysis Services. Analysis Manager is simply an application that Microsoft created that uses DSO to control Analysis services. You could use DSO to write your own applications to manage the Analysis server, and, in fact, there are certain aspects of the Analysis server that are available through DSO but that aren't included in the Analysis Manager application. The following figure illustrates the administrative access to the Analysis server. The thin black lines represent instructions; the thick blue lines represent data flows.

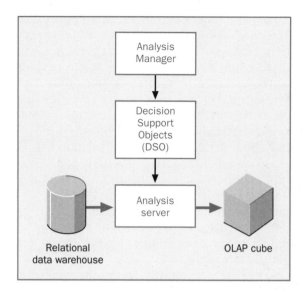

Analysis Services User Tools

Chapter 5 dis-
cusses Office
2000 client
features in more
detail. Chapter 7
discusses MDX
and the MDX
Sample applica-
tion.

When interacting with the Analysis server as a user rather than an administrator, you make requests to retrieve data from a cube into a report by using a client browser application. The Analysis Manager tool used by administrators has a simple browser tool included within it. Microsoft Office 2000 includes PivotTable reports in Excel and a PivotTable list ActiveX control as part of the Office Web Components. Both of these tools are capable of browsing an Analysis Services cube. Analysis Services also includes an application named MDX Sample that allows you to query a cube by using multidimensional expressions (MDX). In addition, you can purchase client applications from any of several third-party companies.

All client applications must communicate with the Analysis server through a client process named PivotTable Service, which must reside on the client computer. PivotTable Service is automatically installed on a computer when you install Analysis Services (server or client components) or when you install Office 2000. PivotTable Service can run on any Microsoft Windows operating system beginning with Windows 95. It's impossible to retrieve values from a cube without using PivotTable Service to communicate with the Analysis server. In fact, even when you use Analysis Manager to administer a cube and use the browser to view the cube, Analysis Manager communicates with PivotTable Service and PivotTable Service retrieves the data from the Analysis server.

Chapter 5
explains how
to create local
cubes.

In many ways, PivotTable Service overlaps the functionality of the Analysis server. You can use PivotTable Service to create, load, and browse a local cube on a client machine, even with no connection to a server.

PivotTable Service works closely with the Analysis server to make retrievals as fast and flexible as possible. For example, both the Analysis server and PivotTable Service maintain storage buffers—called *caches*—that retain recently

Data Transformation Services

Analysis Services assumes that the data warehouse already exists and does not include any tools to help create a data warehouse. SQL Server, however, does include a tool that can help manage the tasks of getting data into a data warehouse. Data Transformation Services (DTS) is a feature built into SQL Server that moves and transforms data. You can use DTS to automate the transfer of data from operational systems into a data warehouse.

DTS supports additional plug-ins, and Analysis Services provides a plug-in that allows DTS to manage updating an Analysis server cube.

The Analysis Services DTS plug-in will be discussed in Chapter 9, "Processing Optimization."

When you use Analysis Manager to define OLAP structures, the information about how to create those structures is called *metadata*. Analysis Manager stores metadata in a *repository*. When the Analysis server creates OLAP structures such as databases, cubes, and dimensions, it creates several files and folders that are stored in an Analysis Services data folder. You can specify the Analysis Services data folder at the time you install Analysis Services, and you can change the location later using Analysis Manager. All the data files managed by the Analysis server reside in a single folder tree. Both the repository and the data files are extremely important. You should frequently back up the repository while developing a database, and you should frequently back up the data files once you begin loading them.

By default, the metadata repository is an Access database file named msmdrep.mdb that is stored in the Bin folder in the Analysis Services folder on the Analysis server machine. The default repository is in Access format so that all users, including those that don't use SQL Server for relational data, can use Analysis Services. Analysis Services comes with a wizard that enables you to migrate the repository to SQL Server. Unfortunately, there's no way to migrate the repository to databases other than SQL Server.

If you do use SQL Server, you should probably migrate the repository. Once you migrate the repository, you cannot move it back, but if an error occurs during the migration process, Analysis Services discards any changes and continues to use the original repository. Migrating the repository does not remove the original Access database, but you can delete it after the migration has completed.

If you do keep the repository in the Access database, be sure to use Access to compact it frequently. The repository is a readable database. However, you should avoid reading or writing to it using tools other than Analysis Manager (or DSO). There is no guarantee that the repository design won't change in future versions of Analysis Services.

retrieved values. PivotTable Service is very intelligent about using its own cache before making a request of the Analysis server. For example, if a report requests values for January and February and then later requests values for the entire first quarter, PivotTable Service will request only the March value from the server, retrieving the data for the other two months from its own cache. The cache on the server, meanwhile, improves performance for multiple users who make similar requests. PivotTable Service communicates with the server every few seconds to make sure that the values in its cache are still valid.

In the same way that an administrative program such as Analysis Manager uses DSO to communicate with the Analysis server, a client application such as Excel 2000 uses OLE DB for OLAP to communicate with PivotTable Service. OLE DB for OLAP is a set of methods added to OLE DB to provide efficient access to multidimensional data and is typically used by programmers developing commercial applications with tools such as C++. To assist programmers developing corporate applications, OLE DB for OLAP comes with a wrapper layer called Microsoft ActiveX Data Objects (Multidimensional), or ADO MD, which is a simpler set of instructions commonly used by tools such as Microsoft Visual Basic. The following graphic illustrates client-side interaction with the Analysis server. The thin black lines represent instructions, and the thick blue lines represent data flows.

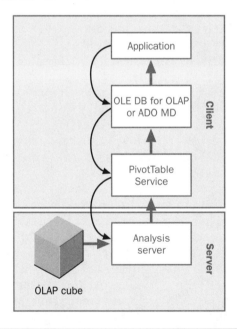

Note OLE DB for OLAP and ADO MD are not proprietary to Microsoft. Any developer can create a data warehouse or OLAP database that supports OLE DB for OLAP, and any developer can create a client that works with any OLE DB for OLAP data source. Any third-party client application that works with OLE DB for OLAP will work with the Analysis server. In contrast, DSO is a Microsoft proprietary tool and will work to administer the Analysis server only.

Unfortunately, the current version of Analysis Services does not provide a mechanism for creating a client that can browse an Analysis server cube without having PivotTable Service installed on the client machine. This means that it's impossible to create a simple browser-based client application. Analysis Services does, however, now make it possible to connect to a server using Internet protocols. Some third-party clients pass Internet client requests to an intermediate computer that does have PivotTable Service installed. The intermediate computer then passes the request on to the Analysis server and relays the resulting report to the Internet browser.

Chapter Summary

This term	Means this
Data warehouse	A relational database designed to store management information
Online transaction processing (OLTP)	A database system used to manage transactions such as order processing
Online analytical processing (OLAP)	A database system optimized to support decision-making processes
Measure	A summarizable numerical value used to monitor business activity
Dimension	A list of labels that can be used to cross-tabulate values from other dimensions
Member	A single item within a dimension
Aggregation	Summarized values of a measure
Hierarchy	Levels of aggregation within a single dimension
Level	A layer of aggregation within a dimension hierarchy
Leaf member	A member at the lowest level of a hierarchy
Fact table	The relational database table that contains values for one or more measures at the lowest level of detail for one or more dimensions
Primary key column	A column in a database dimension table that contains values that uniquely identify each row
Foreign key column	A column in a database table that contains many values for each value in the primary key column of another database table
Join	The processes of linking the primary key of one table to the foreign key of another table
Star design	A database arrangement where multiple levels of a dimension hierarchy are included in a single dimension table

(continued)

(continued)

This term	Means this
Snowflake design	A database arrangement where each level of a dimension hierarchy is in a separate dimension table
Member property	Information about a member that is not part of the dimension hierarchy
Virtual dimension	A single-level alternate hierarchy for a dimension that is based on a member property
Cube	The conceptual container of detail values from a single fact table, along with all possible aggregations for one or more dimension hierarchies
Calculated member	A mechanism for aggregating measures using formulas more complex than those stored in a cube.
OLAP database	A collection of one or more related cubes and their associated dimensions
Metadata	Instructions for creating OLAP structures such as cubes and dimensions
Repository	Physical storage location for OLAP metadata
Cache	Storage locations on both the server and the client that enhance query performance

Chapter 2

Analysis Manager from 500 Feet

Estimated time: 1 hour

In this chapter, you'll learn how to

- Navigate objects using Analysis Manager.

- Create a new OLAP database.

- Use the Dimension Wizard to define a dimension.

- Use the Cube Wizard to define a cube.

- Process and browse an OLAP cube.

A few weeks ago, I was driving due south on Interstate 5 in Washington when I saw the moon begin to rise immediately in front of me. Although I know that Seattle is farther north than Nova Scotia, making most celestial objects appear farther south than they might otherwise, I also knew that the moon could not be rising in the south. But I saw it rise, right before my eyes.

The next day I dug out a map and traced the flow of Interstate 5. Sure enough, through the region I had been driving, the freeway bends strongly to the east. In my mental map, Interstate 5 is a vertical line running straight from Vancouver, British Columbia to Tijuana, Mexico. My mental map—good enough for most practical purposes—is not suitable for evaluating celestial landmarks.

One of the best ways to get a good mental map of a town or city is to fly over it and compare visible landmarks to a good map. The view without a map is beautiful but meaningless; the map without the view is informative but sterile. The combination is enlightening. In this chapter, you'll take a low-altitude flight over the Analysis Manager. You won't be poking around for antiques inside the stores, or smelling the begonias, or even kicking through the broken bottles and cans in dirty alleys—that'll come in later chapters—but you will get an overall picture of how cubes, measures, dimensions, and facts all fit together within Analysis Manager.

Previewing Analysis Manager

Analysis Manager, one of the components of Microsoft SQL Server 2000 Analysis Services, is the tool you use to administer the Analysis server. Analysis Manager is a snap-in application within Microsoft Management Console (MMC), a common framework for hosting administrative tools. If you've used the Microsoft SQL Server Enterprise Manager or another MMC application, Analysis Manager should appear familiar. If not, you might find that an MMC application bears some resemblance to Windows Explorer, with a tree view in the left pane and detailed information in the right pane.

Explore the console tree

Before creating a database of your own, you can use Analysis Manager to explore the FoodMart 2000 sample database that is installed as part of the Analysis Services sample files.

1. To start Analysis Manager, click the Microsoft Windows Start button, point to Programs, point to the Microsoft SQL Server group, point to the Analysis Services group, and then click Analysis Manager. (If you did not choose the default installation options, your path to Analysis Manager might be different.)

The tree view in the left pane of the MMC is called the console tree and is the primary means for navigating Analysis Manager. Each level of the tree contains folders, OLAP objects, or both. The Analysis Servers folder displays a list of servers that are available to you. Each server displays the name of the computer running it, since only one server can run on a single computer. The server name acts as a folder for OLAP databases on that server.

2. Expand and select the Analysis server you want to browse—most likely the computer where Analysis Manager is running. (To expand the folder, click the plus sign to the left of the icon.)

A list of databases appears; FoodMart 2000 is probably the only one you see. In Analysis Services, a database acts as a container for related cubes, dimensions, and other analysis objects.

3. Expand and select the FoodMart 2000 database in the console tree to see the main folders: Data Sources, Cubes, Shared Dimensions, Mining Models, and Database Roles.

A single OLAP database can interact with more than one relational database, and the Data Sources folder stores the list of connected relational databases. Likewise, an OLAP database can contain multiple cubes and dimensions, so each of these objects has its own folder. The Mining Models folder is used for the data mining functionality that is new in SQL Server 2000. The Database Roles folder is used to support client security. Most of the time, you'll work in the Cubes and Shared Dimensions folders.

Security is discussed in Chapter 11, "Security."

4. Expand and select the Cubes folder to see the six cubes already created in the FoodMart 2000 sample database. As discussed in Chapter 1, "A Data Analysis Foundation," a cube is the storage location for values that can be included in an analytical report.

Explore menu commands

An MMC snap-in application, such as Analysis Manager, has two levels of menus. The top-level menus—Console, Window, and Help—belong to MMC itself and do not apply to the current snap-in application. The second level of menus is actually a toolbar. This toolbar contains the Action, View, and Tools menus, which are specific to the current MMC snap-in application—in this case, Analysis Manager. The Action menu is context-sensitive—that is, the commands that appear on the menu change depending on the object you select in the left pane—in the console tree. The same commands that appear on the Action menu also appear on a shortcut menu if you right-click an object in the console tree. Using the FoodMart 2000 database as an example, explore the different menu commands available to different objects.

The Server Action menu contains a Migrate Repository command, which moves the repository from Microsoft Access to SQL Server, as explained in Chapter 1.

1. Click the server object, and then select the Action menu. A list of commands related specifically to the server appears. Press the Escape key to close the menu.

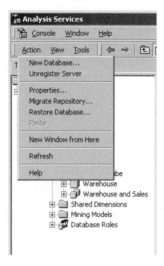

2. Right-click the Sales cube in the FoodMart 2000 database.

A shortcut menu containing commands related specifically to a cube appears. The View menu that appears on the shortcut menu corresponds to the View menu on the toolbar.

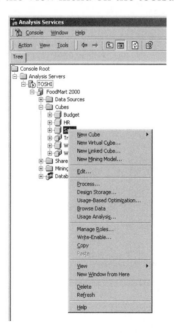

Because different commands are available for different objects, you can't simply scan through all the menus on the menu bar, hoping to recognize the command you want as you can in most Windows applications. Rather, you must think of the object the command applies to, select that object, and then look for the command on the menu.

Explore the detail pane

The right pane in Analysis Manager displays detailed information that changes depending on the object you've selected in the console tree. It has up to three tabs—Getting Started, Meta Data, and Data—each of which displays a possible view. The Getting Started tab is available regardless of which object is currently selected; it displays links to the online tutorials and to important Microsoft Web sites. The Meta Data tab is available for every object under the Analysis Servers folder; it displays *meta data* for the selected object. Meta data means *data about data*—that is, data that describes the nature of the database, as opposed to the data contained in the database itself. The Data tab is available only when a cube is selected in the console tree; it displays a simple browser for reviewing data in the cube.

Note   The right pane displays the Getting Started, Meta Data, and Data tabs only when HTML mode is enabled. To enable or disable HTML mode, click the View menu on the toolbar and then click HTML.

---

1. Click the FoodMart 2000 database object, and select the Meta Data tab at the top of the right pane.

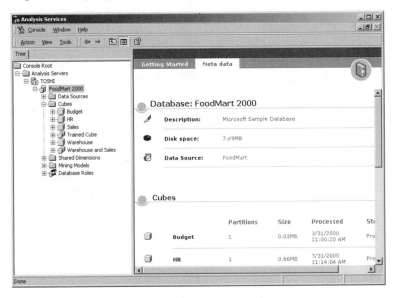

The Meta Data tab displays information about the FoodMart 2000 database. The Meta Data tab is context-sensitive. The information it displays depends on the object you select in the console tree.

2. Click the Sales cube, and watch the Meta Data tab change.

With a cube selected, the Data tab becomes available in the right
pane.

You'll learn how
to use the simple
browser later in
this chapter after
you create your
own cube.

3. With the Sales cube selected, click the Data tab at the top of the right
pane. The right pane changes to show a simple cube browser displaying
the data in the FoodMart 2000 Sales cube.

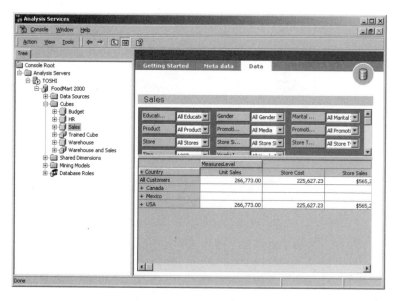

In addition to using the Data tab on the right pane, you can display
the simple browser by selecting a cube and clicking Browse Data from the
Action menu.

4. Collapse the FoodMart 2000 database to avoid distractions as you create
your own database and cube.

Preparing to Create a Cube

In this chapter, you'll use cube and dimension wizards to create a new cube. Creating a cube by using the wizards is remarkably quick, but before you begin you need to make a few preparations.

Review the data warehouse structure

The cube you'll create in this chapter is based on a simple Microsoft Access warehouse database supplied on this book's companion CD. The database file (Chapter2.mdb) is an extremely simplified version of the FoodMart 2000 database. The sample Chapter2 warehouse database is small enough that you should be able to clearly understand its structure, but it illustrates the basic dimension types described in Chapter 1.

The following diagram shows the structure of the Chapter2 warehouse database, which consists of a single fact table: SalesFact. The SalesFact table has four dimension keys—Month, State_ID, Product_ID, and Employee_ID—and two measures—Sales_Units and Sales_Dollars. The State_ID key is joined to a single dimension table (star schema), the Product_ID key is joined to a chain of dimension tables (snowflake schema), and the Employee_ID key is joined to the Employee dimension table (parent-child). The Month key will show you how the Dimension Wizard can create an entire hierarchy from a single date column.

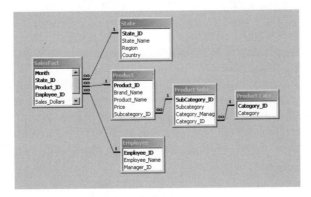

Create a new OLAP database

In Analysis Manager, before creating a cube, you must first create an OLAP database in which to store it. An OLAP database can contain more than one cube, but a cube cannot exist outside a database. You will create an OLAP database named Chapter 2 to store your first cube.

1. Right-click the server in the console tree, and click New Database to display the Database dialog box.

2. Type **Chapter 2** as the database name, and type **Market Database** as the description.

You cannot re-name an existing database, so type carefully.

A database name can be up to 50 characters long. The name can include spaces and numbers but not special characters, and the first character must be a letter. Unfortunately, you cannot rename an existing database, so type carefully.

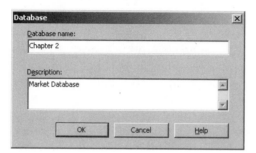

3. Click OK to close the dialog box and to create the database. When you first define a database, its folders are empty.

Specify a data source

Technically, you can use more than one data source with a cube if you create partitions, as explained in "Working with Partitions" in Chapter 9, "Processing Optimization."

A cube must retrieve its data values from the fact table in a relational data warehouse. That data warehouse must be defined within the OLAP database as a data source. Different cubes within an OLAP database can retrieve values from different data warehouses, so an OLAP database can contain multiple data sources, but a single cube will always use only a single data source.

The data source must be supplied by an OLE DB provider. OLE DB is an industry-standard technology that is a generalized replacement for the ODBC (Open Database Connectivity) standard used for many years. Some relational database systems, such as Access and SQL Server, function as native OLE DB providers. Some relational systems might support the older ODBC standard but not OLE DB. In that case, you can use the generic Microsoft OLE DB provider for ODBC drivers. A native OLE DB provider can be up to twice as fast as using OLE DB provider for ODBC drivers, so whenever possible, use the native OLE DB provider. Because the Chapter2 warehouse database is an Access database, you can use the Access (Jet) OLE DB provider.

1. Expand the Chapter 2 database folder. Right-click the Data Sources folder, and on the shortcut menu, click New Data Source.

2. Select Microsoft Jet 4.0 OLE DB Provider, and click Next.

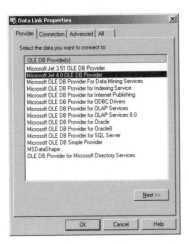

3. On the Connection tab of the Data Link Properties dialog box, click the
    ellipsis button (…), navigate to the folder containing the Chapter2.mdb
    (the default is C:\Analysis) warehouse database, and double-click the
    database.

4. Click Test Connection to make sure the data source definition is correct.
    Then click OK to close the dialog box. Expand the Data Sources folder to
    see the new data source.

    The name of the data source reflects the file location of the Access
    database. As with many objects in Analysis Manager, you can't rename
    the data source directly. The only way to "rename" a data source is to
    copy the data source and attempt to paste it back to the same database.

5. Right-click the new data source, and click Copy on the shortcut menu.
    Right-click the Chapter 2 database, and click Paste on the shortcut menu.
    When asked for a new name, type **Market** and press Enter. Right-click
    the original data source, click Delete on the shortcut menu, and click Yes
    to confirm.

When you copy an object—such as a data source, a database, a cube, or a dimension—and attempt to paste the object back into the same container, Analysis Manager prompts for a new name. This is the only way to "rename" an object. Once you've copied and pasted the object, you can delete the original. If you want to "rename" a data source, you must do so before using it as the source for a cube or dimension.

Note Renaming a data source is essentially impossible, but you can easily edit the definition of the data source. For example, you can change the location of the database file or even change the type of OLE DB provider. To edit a data source, right-click its name in the Data Sources folder and click Edit. You use the same dialog box to edit the data source as you used to create it. If you make a modification to the database—for example, if you rename a column in a table— you must refresh the connection to see the changes in the Analysis Manager. To refresh the connection, right-click the data source name and click Refresh on the shortcut menu.

Once you've created a data source for a database, you can then use that data source when you create new dimensions or cubes.

Designing a Cube by Using the Cube Wizard

Once you've created an OLAP database and specified at least one data source within the database, you can build a cube. A cube consists of one or more measures (such as Sales or Cost) from a fact table, and one or more dimensions (such as Product or Time) from dimension tables. When you build a cube, you must specify a fact table, select the measures to extract from the fact table, and also specify any dimensions you want to use, creating the dimensions if they don't already exist. The Cube Wizard bundles all these steps into one sequential process.

Select the fact table and the measures

Each cube has one fact table, which in turn determines the contents of the cube. In a cube, there is a very close relationship between a fact table and measures. Measures are the numeric values that will be summarized in the cube. All the measures in a cube come from a single fact table. When you begin to design your cube, the Cube Wizard first asks you to select a fact table and then asks you to select measures from that fact table.

1. Right-click the Cubes folder under the Chapter 2 database, point to New Cube, and then click Wizard to start the Cube Wizard. On the welcome screen, click Next.

2. Select SalesFact from the list of tables.

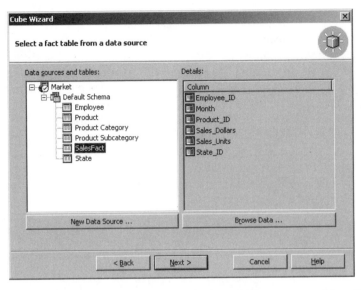

3. If you want to confirm that you've selected the correct table, click Browse Data to review the records in the table. Then close the Browse Data window to continue with the wizard.

4. After selecting the fact table, click Next to move to the next step of the wizard.

5. Add the Sales_Dollars and Sales_Units column as measures by double-clicking each in turn. You can also select a measure and click the right arrow button (>).

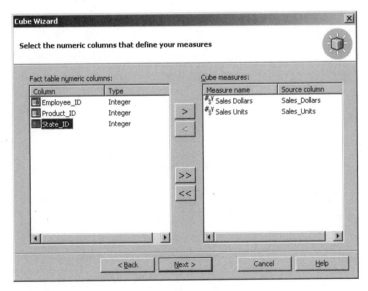

6. After adding both measures, click Next.

When the Cube Wizard prompts you for a fact table, it shows all the tables available in the data source, rather than trying to guess which table is the fact table. That's because a data source can contain more than one fact table, and, in fact, the same table might be used as a dimension table for one cube and a fact table for a different cube. For example, assuming that a Product dimension table contained a Price column, you could create a cube that summarizes prices, using the Product table as a fact table. Remember, however, that your cube can use only a single table as a fact table. If you need to create a cube that combines measures from two source tables, you must either create two cubes and combine them later using a virtual cube—as described in Chapter 4, "Advanced Dimensions and Cubes"—or you must use the relational database tool to create a *query* or *view* that combines the tables. Analysis Services can use the query or view as if it were a table.

Create a dimension from a star schema table

The SalesFact table in the Chapter2 warehouse database contains four dimension key columns: Month, State_ID, Product_ID, and Employee_ID. Each of the four dimension keys in the SalesFact table lends itself to creating a dimension in a different way.

The State_ID key is joined to a single dimension table named State. The State dimension table includes columns suitable for creating a three-level hierarchy—State_Name, Region, and Country. All the levels are contained in a single star schema dimension table. The Cube Wizard understands how to work with a star schema table.

After you specify the measures, you have an opportunity to select—or create—dimensions. To create a new dimension within the Cube Wizard, you launch a second wizard, the Dimension Wizard.

1. Click New Dimension in the wizard to start the Dimension Wizard. Select the option to skip the welcome screen, and then click Next.

2. Click the option Star Schema: A Single Dimension Table, and then click Next.

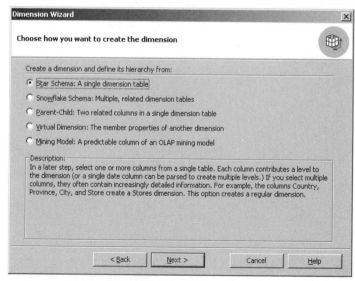

3. In the Select The Dimension Table screen, select State from the Available Tables list.

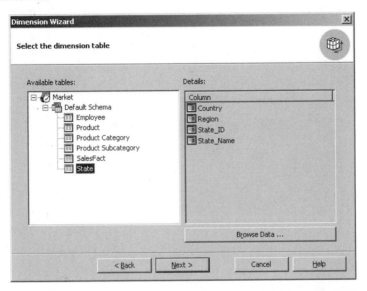

If you want to confirm that you've selected the correct table, click Browse Data to review the records in the table. Then close the Browse Data window to continue with the wizard.

4. After selecting the dimension table, click Next to move to the next step of the wizard.

5. On the Select The Levels For Your Dimension screen, double-click Country, Region, and State_Name—in that order. You select levels from the most summarized to the most detailed.

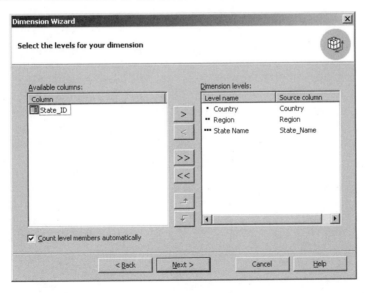

Member keys and advanced options will be covered in Chapter 3, "Dimension and Cube Editors."

6. Click Next three times: once after selecting the levels, once to bypass the member keys step, and once to bypass the advanced options step. Type **State** as the name of the dimension. Before closing the wizard, you can preview the dimension hierarchy.

7. In the Preview box, expand the All New Dimension member and the USA member. Then click Finish. (When the wizard creates the dimension, it uses the dimension name you enter in the top-level member name. In this case, All New Dimension will be replaced with All State.)

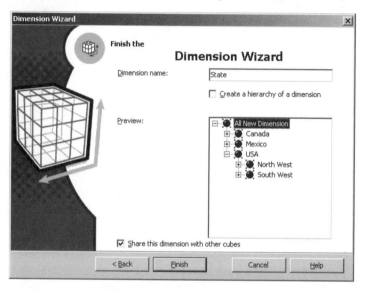

The Dimension Wizard returns you to the Cube Wizard, which automatically puts the new dimension in the Cube Dimensions list.

Create a dimension from snowflake schema tables

The Product_ID key of the SalesFact table is joined to a series of dimension tables: Product, Product Subcategory, and Product Category. Each dimension table contains the columns for a single level of a three-tier hierarchy. This is a classic snowflake schema dimension. The Dimension Wizard makes creating a dimension from snowflake schema tables almost as easy as creating a dimension from a star schema table.

1. Click New Dimension in the Cube Wizard to again launch the Dimension Wizard.

2. Click the option Snowflake Schema: Multiple, Related Dimension Tables, and click Next.

3. Double-click the dimension tables in the following order: Product, Product Subcategory, and Product Category.

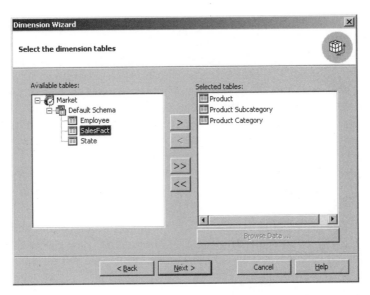

4. Click Next to move to a step that allows you to confirm the relationships between the dimension tables.

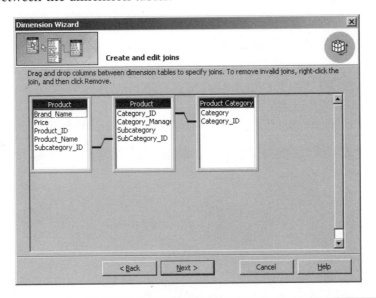

Caution   The Dimension Wizard looks *only* at the column names in suggesting joins between tables. The wizard does not check the data types of the columns or relationships established in the relational database. If the two columns with matching names are of incompatible data types (for example, if one is a Long Integer and another is a String), the Dimension Wizard will suggest a join, but you will see an error later when you try to retrieve the dimension information from the tables. The wizard also looks for joins one table at a time: the most recent table compared to the next most recent. The bottom line is that you should very carefully inspect the joins in the Create And Edit Joins screen. To remove an invalid join, select the join line and press Delete. To add a new join, drag a column from one table to the corresponding column in the other table.

5. Review the joins between the tables. Provided that you added the tables in the correct order, the wizard suggests the proper relationships. If necessary, add joins between the two Subcategory_ID columns and the two Category_ID columns, and click Next to continue.

The next step allows you to select the levels for your dimension. This process is identical to the process for a star schema dimension, except that there are extra key columns you can ignore. You should add levels starting from the most aggregated level, making sure each level has more members than the previous level. The appropriate order for levels in this dimension is: Product_Category, Product_Subcategory, and Product_Name. The Dimension Wizard warns you if you attempt to add them in the wrong order.

6. Double-click Category (*not* Category_ID), Product_Name, and Subcategory (*not* Subcategory_ID)—intentionally reversing the order of the last two levels. The Dimension Wizard displays a message suggesting that you rearrange the levels.

Unless you're building the dimension from a sample database that doesn't accurately represent the real product hierarchy, you should accept the wizard's recommendation.

7. Click Yes to put the Product_Name level below the Subcategory level.

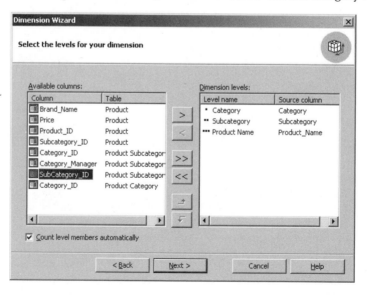

8. Click Next three times: once after specifying the levels, once to bypass the member keys step, and once to bypass the advanced options step.

9. Type **Product** as the name of the dimension, expand items in the Preview window as desired, and click Finish.

Member keys and advanced options will be covered in Chapter 3.

There are only two differences between creating a dimension from a star schema table and creating one from snowflake schema tables: the step to select a dimension table is changed to allow multiple tables, and the step to validate the joins between the tables is added. When populating the dimension, Analysis Services will treat the snowflake schema tables as if they were joined into a single table.

Chapter 10, "Dimension Optimization," discusses the performance differences between a star schema dimension and a snowflake schema dimension.

Create a dimension from a parent-child table

The Employee_ID key of the SalesFact table is joined to the Employee dimension table. Each Employee_ID in the SalesFact table corresponds to an employee record in the Employee table. Each record in the Employee table also has a Manager_ID column, which—if this were a snowflake schema dimension— would join to the table for the next level of the hierarchy. But a manager is also an employee, so the Manager_ID column actually joins back to the Employee_ID column of the Employee table. The Employee table is called a *parent-child* table, and it allows a dimension to have an unbalanced hierarchy—some branches of the hierarchy contain more levels than other branches. A parent-child dimension is similar to a snowflake schema dimension in that each join creates a new level; the only difference is that the higher levels in the hierarchy come from the same table as the leaf level. The Dimension Wizard makes it easy to create a parent-child dimension.

1. Click the New Dimension button in the Cube Wizard to again launch the Dimension Wizard.

2. Click Parent-Child: Two Related Columns In A Single Dimension Table, and click Next.

3. Select Employee as the dimension table, and click Next.

4. In the Member Key drop-down list, select Employee_ID. This is the column that is joined to the fact table. In the Parent Key drop-down list, select Manager_ID. In the Member Name drop-down list, select Employee_Name.

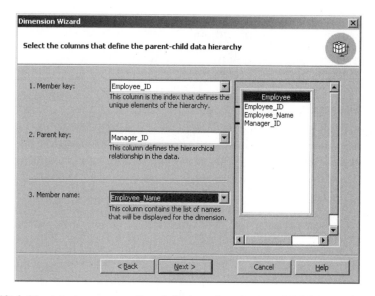

5. Click Next twice: once after defining the parent-child hierarchy, and once to bypass the advanced options step.

6. Type **Employee** as the name of the dimension, and in the Preview box expand each member in the Preview window that has a plus sign to the left of the icon.

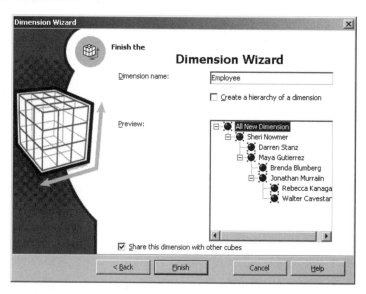

7. Click Finish.

In "Create a ragged hierarchy" in Chapter 3, you'll learn how to make a standard dimension appear to be unbalanced.

A standard dimension—whether based on a star schema table or on snowflake schema tables—is always balanced and could never have a member with children (such as Maya Gutierrez) as the sibling of a member without children (such as Darren Stanz). A parent-child dimension allows for flexible, unbalanced dimensions.

Create a dimension from a date column

You can even create a dimension with no separate dimension table at all. In the Chapter2 warehouse database, there is no separate dimension table for the Time dimension; there is only a column named Month in the fact table. Analysis Services can use the fact table itself as a dimension table; it simply extracts unique values from the column you select. Normally, you need a dimension table to define a hierarchy. The Dimension Wizard, however, can generate an entire hierarchy from a single Date/Time column. The wizard, in fact, offers to generate any of several date-related hierarchies and lets you choose the one you want.

1. Click the New Dimension button in the Cube Wizard to again launch the Dimension Wizard.

2. Click Star Schema: A Single Dimension Table, and then click Next.

3. Select SalesFact as the Dimension table, and click Next. Because the SalesFact table contains a Date/Time column, the wizard displays a screen offering to create a Time dimension based on that column.

4. On the screen that asks you to select the dimension type, click Time Dimension. The Date Column drop-down list allows you to choose which date column to use if there is more than one in the table. In this case, there is only one Date/Time column, so Month is already correctly selected. Click Next.

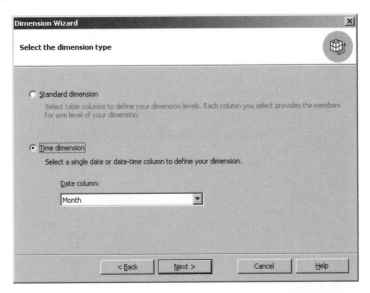

5. On the screen that asks you to create the Time dimension levels, you can select the type of time dimension hierarchy you want. You can even specify the day and month for the year to start—useful for dealing with fiscal years. In the Select Time Levels drop-down list, click Year, Quarter, Month, and then click Next.

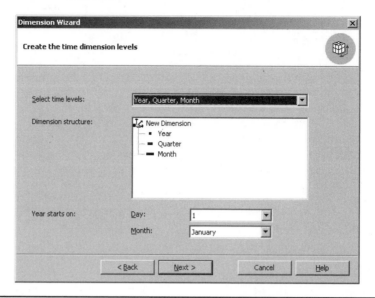

Note The wizard will probably appear much slower when you attempt to retrieve values for the Time dimension than it did for the Product or State dimensions. This is not because creating the hierarchy level definitions is slow, but because the wizard is scanning the entire fact table to find unique dates. With a large fact table, you might want to use an integer key for the Time dimension and store the Time dimension information in a separate, small, dimension table. Issues involved in creating a separate Time dimension table are covered in Chapter 3.

6. When you use the wizard to generate date-related levels, you do not select columns to use for the levels. Click Next to bypass the Advanced Options screen.

7. In the final screen of the Dimension Wizard, type **Time** as the dimension name and expand the hierarchy in the Preview box to see the Year, Quarter, and Month levels of the hierarchy.

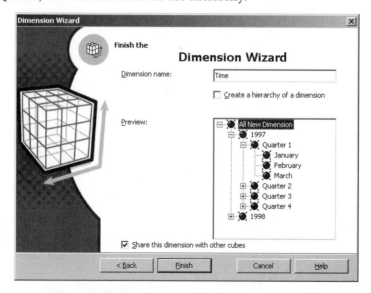

8. Click Finish to return to the Cube Wizard.

Remember that measures and dimensions define a cube. Once you've specified the measures (and the fact table that supplies them) and specified any dimensions, you have given the Cube Wizard everything it needs to create the cube.

Name and save a cube

Once you've completely defined the cube, you can give it a name.

1. In the Cube Wizard, click Next. Click Yes when asked if you want to count the fact table rows.

2. Type **Sales** as the name of the cube, and click Finish.

The Cube Wizard opens the Cube Editor, in case you want to review or refine the definition of the cube.

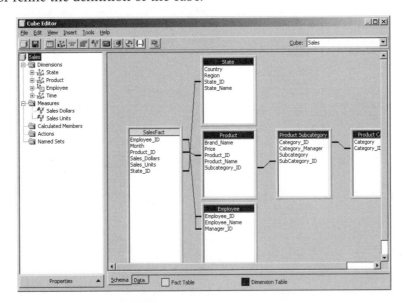

3. Click Exit on the File menu to close the Cube Editor. Click No when asked if you want to set storage options.

Storage options are covered in Chapter 8, "Storage Optimization."

The cube is now fully defined, named, and saved. (The Cube Wizard saves the definition of the cube.) Saving the cube definition stores that definition in the OLAP repository database but does not create the actual cube files or load values from the data warehouse. To use the cube, you must first process it.

Processing and Browsing a Cube

Processing a dimension and processing a cube are two separate tasks. When you process a dimension, Analysis Services reads in the information from the dimension tables and constructs a map of the dimension. Within the map, each member is stored, fully qualified, using all levels of the hierarchy for the dimension. For example, suppose that Washington is a member in the State dimension. It's a unique state; no other state has the same name. The map, however, still stores the entire hierarchy for the state: All State→USA→North West→Washington. By storing the entire hierarchy for each member in the dimension map, Analysis Services can use the map to quickly find relationships between members when you query the cube. Of course, the dimension map is compressed and very efficient.

"How the Analysis Server Processes a Dimension" in Chapter 9 explains the creation of a dimension map in detail.

When you process a cube, Analysis Services first combines the dimension maps from all the dimensions used in the cube into a multidimensional cube map. It then reads the detail records from the warehouse fact table, storing detail values in a data storage area. The data storage area is efficiently organized and does not take up any room for key combinations that do not contain a value.

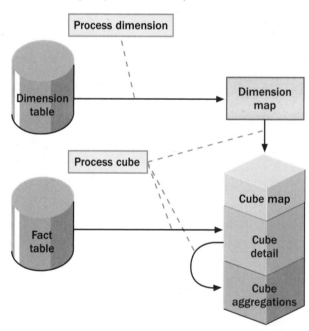

Process a cube

When you process a cube, the Analysis server automatically processes any dimensions that are used in the cube that have not yet been processed. So, to process the cube and all its dimensions, you need to execute only one command.

1. Expand the Cubes folder of the Chapter 2 database, right-click the newly created Sales cube, and click Process.

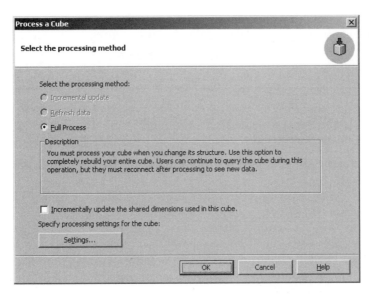

The Process A Cube dialog box shows you that the only available option is to completely process the cube.

2. Click OK to begin processing. A log appears showing the progress. As each dimension is processed, a group of entries appears in the log. As the cube is processed, another group of entries appears in the log.

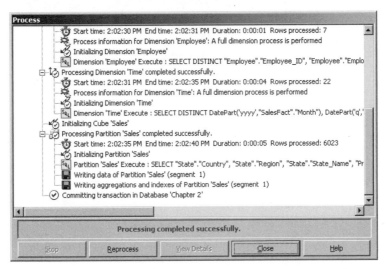

3. Scroll up and down the log to see the steps involved in processing dimensions and a cube. To see the full text of an entry in the log, select the line and click View Details. (If you do view an entry, close the small window before continuing.)

4. Click Close to close the Process log window.

Chapter 8 will explain in detail how to design and create aggregations.

When you processed the cube, Analysis Services copied the detail values from the fact table into a proprietary data structures. It did not store any aggregated values. For a small cube such as this one, the lack of aggregations will not hinder your ability to browse the cube.

Browse cube data

You can use the simple browser provided by Analysis Manager to view the values in the Sales cube.

1. Right-click the Sales cube in the Chapter 2 database, and click Browse Data.

You can maximize the Cube Browser window by double-clicking the caption bar, or you can resize the window by dragging any edge of it. The Cube Browser window displays a *data grid* with measures across the top in the *column area,* and the first dimension (sorted alphabetically by name) down the left side in the *row area.* Remaining dimensions appear at the top of the browser in the *slicer area.* Cube slicers are sometimes called *filters* or *page fields.*

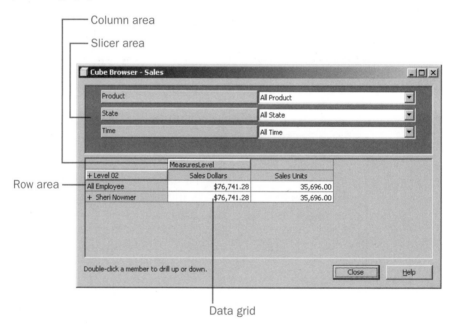

2. In the row or column areas, a plus sign (+) indicates that you can expand the hierarchy and view more detail, and a minus sign (–) indicates that you can collapse the hierarchy to view less detail. Double-click the Sheri Nowmer label to see her subordinates.

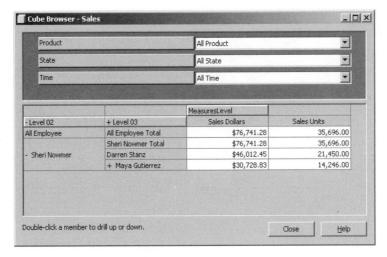

3. Double-click the Sheri Nowmer label again to collapse the hierarchy.

4. Drag the State button from the slicer area over the top of the Level 02 label in the row area. When the mouse pointer icon includes a double-headed arrow, release the mouse button. The browser swaps, or *pivots*, the two dimensions.

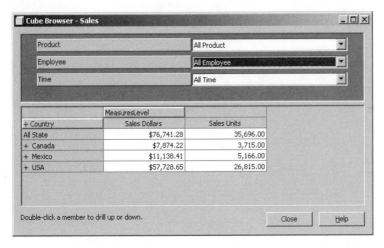

5. Then double-click the Country label (the column heading) to expand all three countries at one time.

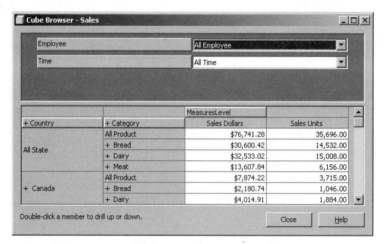

You can change the size of the slicer area by dragging its bottom border.

6. Double-click the Country label again to collapse the countries.

7. Drag the Product button from the slicer area over the top of the Canada label. When the mouse pointer icon does *not* include a double-headed arrow, release the mouse button. The browser combines both dimensions within the row headings.

8. Click the drop-down arrow next to the Time button in the slicer area. In the dimension tree, click the plus sign next to All Time, click the plus sign next to 1997, and then click Quarter 3. Clicking a plus or minus sign expands or contracts the tree. Clicking a label selects that member.

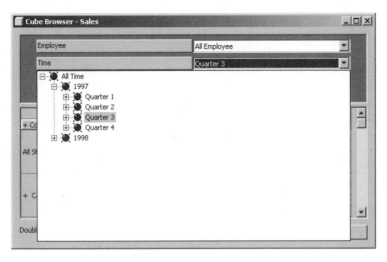

9. Click Close or press Escape to close the Cube Browser window.

Now you have used the Analysis Manager to create an OLAP database, dimensions, and a cube. With a cleanly designed data warehouse, you can use the Cube Wizard and the Dimension Wizard to easily create cubes and dimensions. The cubes and dimensions you create by using the wizards, however, might not be precisely what you need. In Chapters 3 and 4, you'll learn how to use advanced properties to get complete control over the design of new or existing objects.

Chapter Summary

To	Do this
View metadata information for an object in Analysis Manager	Select the object in the console tree, and click the Meta Data tab in the right pane.
Run a menu command in Analysis Manager	Either select an object in the console tree and click the Action menu, or right-click an object in the console tree.
Create a new database	Right-click the server in the console tree, and click New Database. Type a name for the database, and click OK.
Create a new data source	Right-click the Data Sources folder in the library of a database, and click New Data Source. Select the OLE DB provider. Activate the Connection tab, and specify a data source. Then click OK.

(continued)

(continued)

To	Do this
Create a cube by using the Cube Wizard	Right-click the Cubes folder in a database, point to New Cube, and click Wizard.
Create a new dimension from within the Cube Wizard	On the add dimension screen of the Cube Wizard, click the New Dimension button.
Add a join between snowflaked dimension tables	Drag the column name from one table to another.
Delete a join between two tables	Select the join, and press Delete.
Add a new level to a dimension in the Dimension Wizard	Double-click the name of a column in the dimension table.
Create a dimension hierarchy from a Date/Time column	Select a dimension table that contains at least one Date/Time column. Select Time as the dimension type, and select the Date/Time column.
Process a cube	In the console tree, right-click the cube and click Process.
Browse data in a cube	In the console tree, right-click the cube and click Browse Data.

Chapter 3

Dimension
and Cube Editors

In this chapter, you'll learn how to

- Use the Dimension Editor to create shared dimensions.

- Use the Cube Editor to create cubes and private dimensions.

- Modify dimension and level properties.

- Use specialized features of Time and parent-child dimensions.

- Create expressions for member keys, member names, and measures.

- Create calculated members.

A friend of mine designs autopilot software for a large commercial airplane manufacturing company. He once told me that the autopilot software could perform an instrument landing just fine, completely without a pilot, but that the FAA requires the pilot to be in control anyway. Somehow, I'm thankful for that FAA regulation.

Creating an OLAP cube is nowhere near as complex as piloting an airplane. And the Cube and Dimension Wizards are nowhere near as sophisticated as autopilot software. But as with landing a plane, when creating dimensions and cubes, you'll come across some situations where automatic solutions aren't a good match for a human sensibility. The Dimension and Cube Editors contain manual controls. Often, you might want to use the editors exclusively—without using the wizards at all—or you can create a dimension or cube by using a wizard and then make modifications using the editor.

In Analysis Manager, the main console, the Dimension Editor, and the Cube Editor are the three main windows. Everything else is a dialog box or a wizard. In this chapter, you'll create a new OLAP database and then use the Dimension Editor to create State, Product, and Time dimensions and the Cube Editor to create a Sales cube, new measures, and a private Employee dimension. At the end of the chapter, you'll have a Sales cube similar to the one that you created in Chapter 2, "Analysis Manager from 500 Feet," but this time you'll use the editors rather than the wizards and the resulting cube will be much more sophisticated.

Note You can set several of the properties described in this chapter by using the Advanced Options screen of the Dimension Wizard. The Advanced Options screen also allows you to set optimization properties that will be explained in Part 3, "Advanced Administration." Once you've learned how to use the Dimension and Cube Editors to specify all the available properties, you will be able to easily utilize the Advanced Options screen of the wizard.

Start the lesson

1. In Analysis Manager, right-click the server object, click New Database, type **Chapter 3** as the database name, type **Advanced Market Database** as the description, and then click OK.

2. Follow the instructions in "Specify a data source" in Chapter 2 to create a data source in the Chapter 3 OLAP database, but select the Chapter3 relational database instead of the Chapter2 database.

Working with a Standard Star Schema Dimension

A cube must contain at least one dimension, and the dimension must exist before you create the cube. As you saw in Chapter 2, the Cube Wizard can spawn the Dimension Wizard to make it possible for you to create dimensions as part of the process of creating a cube. If you are using only the editors, you will probably create dimensions before creating a cube.

A star-schema dimension has only one dimension table, which makes it a convenient place to become familiar with the Dimension Editor.

Use the Dimension Editor

The Dimension Editor allows you to manipulate both dimensions and levels within a dimension (as shown in the following steps) and is a key component of Analysis Manager. The Dimension Editor opens up in a separate window from the main Analysis Manager console. The Dimension Editor works only with *shared dimensions*.

1. In the Chapter 3 database, right-click Shared Dimensions, point to New Dimension, and click Editor.

2. Select State as the dimension table in the Tables list box, and click OK.

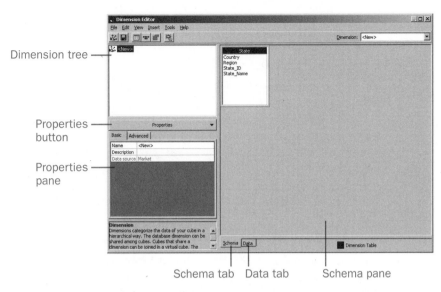

Dimension tree

Properties button

Properties pane

Schema tab   Data tab   Schema pane

The left side of the Dimension Editor is divided into two panes. The upper left pane contains the dimension tree, a tree-view control that displays levels as you design the dimension. The lower left pane is the Properties pane. If you click the Properties button at the top of the Properties pane, the pane disappears, leaving only the button at the bottom of the Editor window. Clicking the button again restores the pane. To resize the Properties pane, drag the top edge of the Properties button.

To expand or collapse the Properties pane, click Properties on the View menu. To change the size of the Properties pane, drag the top edge of the pane.

3. In the Properties pane, the current name of the dimension is <New>. Type **State** as the value of the Name property, and press Enter. The name of the dimension will appear in the dimension tree. Once you save a shared dimension, you can no longer rename it.

4. Drag State_Name from the State table in the Schema pane onto the name of the dimension in the dimension tree. This creates a new level in the tree.

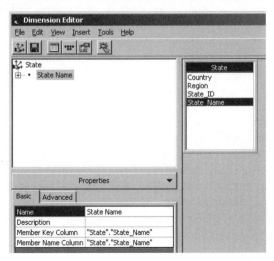

The default name for a level is the same as the name of the database column—with underscore characters converted to spaces. The name of a level appears as a heading label in most browsers. You can change the name in the Properties pane.

5. Select the State Name level in the dimension tree, and in the Properties pane, type **State** as the new name. Press Enter. You now have a relational table, a dimension, and a level each with the name *State*. The State table is the warehouse source for dimension member information, the State dimension will contain the entire hierarchy, and the State level contains only the names of the individual states.

Tip   You can rename a level by selecting the level name in the dimension tree and then clicking it. (Don't double-click the name; select it, wait a moment, and then click it once.)

---

6. Within the Dimension Editor, you can browse the members of the dimension. At the bottom of the Schema pane, click the Data tab. This switches from the Schema pane to the Data pane. Then click the plus sign next to All State to show the individual states.

Choose how to sort members of a level

Chapter 9, "Processing Optimization," explains performance implications of the Member Key Column and Member Name Column properties.

A member name is the text that appears in a heading row or column on a report, so you want to make these names meaningful and descriptive. Many times, however, a source table for a dimension contains one column that contains a descriptive name for each member and another column that has an integer key for each member. This is particularly true at the lowest level of a dimension. Each level of a dimension has two properties: Member Key Column references the column that contains integer keys for the members, and Member Name Column references the column that contains the labels that should appear in a browser. As a default, an OLAP dimension uses the same column for the member keys and for the member names. You can, however, specify a key for each member that's separate from the member name.

Separating the member name from a member key gives you control over how you sort the list of members. By default, Analysis Services sorts members alphabetically by name. If the member key differs from the member name, you can choose whether to sort by name or by key. For example, perhaps the standard in your company is to sort state names not alphabetically but by the order that products were first sold in that state. If the values in the State_ID key column of the relational dimension table are in the desired sort order, you can tell Analysis Services to display the name for the state, while sorting the list using the integer key.

1. In the Dimension Editor, select the State level in the dimension tree and click the Basic tab in the Properties pane.

   The Member Name Column property has the value *"State"."State_Name"*, which identifies the names of the table and the column that provide the member names for this level. The Dimension Editor always places double quotation marks around table and column names. If you ever need to delimit an ordinary string, you must use apostrophe characters. The Member Key Column property has the same *"State"."State_Name"* value.

2. Click in the Member Key Column property box, and click the ellipsis (...) button.

   The Select Column dialog box appears and shows a list of the columns in the State dimension table. Select State_ID from the tree, and click OK. The value of the Member Key Column property changes to *"State".* *"State_ID"*, but the member names displayed in the Data pane don't change.

3. Switch to the Advanced tab in the Properties pane, and scroll to the bottom of the list of properties.

4. Change the value of the Order By property from *Name* to *Key*, and press Enter.

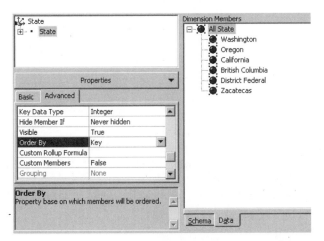

The list of member names in the Data pane changes to reflect the ordering of the keys. An uninitiated person might think that something had gone wrong with the sort order, but company employees know that this simply reflects the standard ordering for the states.

Add additional levels in the Dimension Editor

Within the Dimension Editor, you add additional levels to a dimension simply by dragging a column for the dimension from the dimension table onto the dimension tree. Dropping the column onto the dimension name adds the column as the lowest level of the dimension. Dropping a column onto an existing level name adds the column as a new level just above the existing level.

1. In the Dimension Editor, click the Schema tab at the bottom of the right pane to switch to the Schema pane.

2. Drag the Country column from the State table onto the State level of the dimension tree (not onto the dimension name).

A new level, Country, appears just above the existing State level.

```
State
  ⊞  •   Country
  ⊞  ••  State
```

Next you'll create a level based on the Region column. The new level should appear between the Country level and the State level, but first try putting it in the wrong location.

3. Drag the Region column from the State table onto the name of the dimension. When warned that Region contains fewer members than the State level, click No to put the new level at the bottom of the dimension tree anyway.

```
State
  ⊞  •    Country
  ⊞  ••   State
  ⊞  •••  Region
```

4. In the dimension tree, drag and drop the Region level on top of the State level.

This moves the level just above the State level. The same rules apply when dragging a level within the dimension tree as when dragging a column from the dimension table onto the tree: If you drop the level on the name of the dimension, it's put at the lowest level. If you drop the level onto an existing level, it becomes that level's parent.

5. At the bottom of the right pane, click the Data tab. Then expand all the nodes of the State dimension tree.

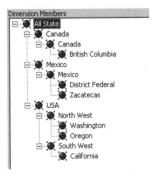

The top level—or *All* level—of a dimension does not have a Member Key Column or Member Name Column property. The name for that one member does not come from the relational data warehouse. The default name for the All level is the word *All* followed by the name of the dimension. You can, however, change the name of the dimension.

6. In the dimension tree, select the State dimension. On the Advanced tab of the Properties pane, change the All Caption property value to **North America** and press Enter. Then expand the North America node to redisplay the dimension hierarchy.

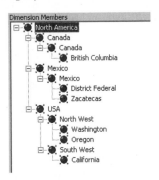

Create a ragged hierarchy

An Analysis Services dimension retrieves its member names and keys from a dimension table. Each level in a standard dimension corresponds to a column in the dimension table (or to an expression based on a column). Under normal circumstances, this means that each member of a dimension hierarchy has the same number of members above it as any other member at the same level. In OLAP terminology, the levels of a standard dimension are *balanced*. In some situations, however, a balanced hierarchy is not appropriate.

For example, the State dimension has levels for Country, Region, and State, and the countries Canada and Mexico have only a single region each. Expanding through the region to get to the state seems unnecessarily complicated. In a dimension, you can hide unnecessary members. To hide a member, either it must have the same value as the parent (as is the case in the State dimension) or it must be blank.

1. In the Dimension Editor, select the Region level of the State dimension and click the Advanced tab of the Properties pane.

2. Select the Hide Member If property, select *Only Child With Parent's Name* from the option list, and press Enter.

The dimension preview changes to hide the Canada and Mexico regions.

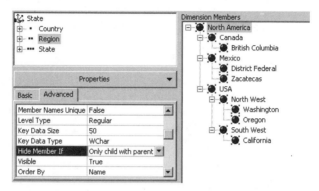

3. Click the Save button to save the dimension.

Internally, the dimension is still balanced, as it was before. To the person using the dimension, however, it appears that British Columbia has fewer ancestors than Washington. This is called a *ragged* hierarchy.

Working with a Standard Snowflake Dimension

The Product dimension comes from a set of dimension tables, one for each level of the Product hierarchy. The Dimension Wizard asks you directly if you have multiple (snowflake) tables for the dimension. In the Dimension Editor, you must add the additional dimension tables yourself. In this section, you'll create a new version of the Product dimension you created in Chapter 2. This time, however, you'll use the Dimension Editor exclusively and you'll utilize properties of a dimension that are not available by using the Dimension Wizard.

You can also create a new dimension by using the menu bar. On the File menu in the Dimension Editor, point to New Dimension and click Editor.

Create a dimension from multiple tables

From within the Dimension Editor, you can create a new dimension in two ways: by using the Dimension Wizard or by using multiple dimension tables. You can click the New Dimension button to launch the Dimension Wizard. To create a new dimension without using the wizard, follow these steps:

1. In the Dimension Editor, select <new> from the Dimension drop-down list box on the toolbar.

The Dimension Editor displays a dialog box that allows you to choose only one table at this time.

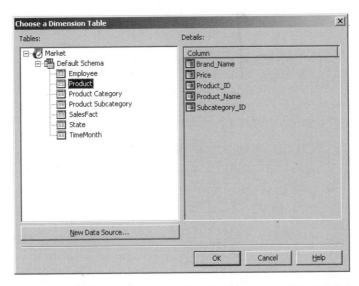

2. Select the Product table, and click OK. When specifying the first table for a snowflake dimension, select either the table for the lowest level or the one for the highest level. If you select a table in the middle of the chain, the Dimension Editor might not create joins properly as you add additional tables.

3. To add the additional tables, click Tables on the Insert menu. Double-click the Product Subcategory table and the Product Category table, and then click Close. The Dimension Editor automatically joins tables if a column with the same name appears in both tables. To remove a join, select the join line and press Delete. To add a join, drag a column from one table to the corresponding column of another table.

You can also click the Insert Table button on the toolbar to add additional tables.

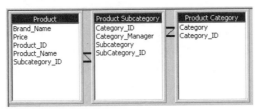

4. On the Basic tab of the Properties pane, type **Product** as the name of the dimension and press Enter.

Creating a dimension from multiple dimension tables is not much more difficult in the Dimension Editor than it is using the Dimension Wizard.

Allow duplicate names in a dimension

In the Dimension Editor, you can browse the first 1000 rows of a warehouse table. Sometimes it's instructive to compare the contents of a dimension table with the properties of a level in the Dimension Editor. For example, the Product table contains 200 products, with 200 unique Product_ID values. The

Product_Name column, however, contains only 40 unique names since there might be more than one brand for a product name.

1. Right-click the caption bar of the Product table, and click Browse Data.

Products at row 3 and 43 both have Jack Cheese as the Product Name and 2 (Cheese) as the Subcategory_ID. Only the Brand Name differs between the products. Similarly, products at row 18 and 58 are both named Blueberry Yogurt.

Browse Data: "Product" (First 1000 rows)					
	Product_ID	Brand_Name	Product_Name	Price	Subcategory_ID
1	44	Club	Low Fat Sour Cream	3.22	11
2	45	Club	Sour Cream	0.55	11
3	46	Club	Jack Cheese	3.58	2
4	47	Club	Muenster Cheese	2.78	2
5	48	Club	String Cheese	1.9	2
6	49	Club	Low Fat String Cheese	3.68	2
7	50	Club	Havarti Cheese	4.19	2
8	51	Club	Head Cheese	1.48	2
9	52	Club	Cheese Spread	2.26	2
10	53	Club	Sharp Cheddar Cheese	3.68	2
11	54	Club	Mild Cheddar Cheese	2.99	2
12	56	Club	2% Milk	0.72	8
13	57	Club	Buttermilk	0.66	8
14	58	Club	Chocolate Milk	2.4	8
15	59	Club	1% Milk	1.4	8
16	60	Club	Whole Milk	2.74	8
17	61	Club	Strawberry Yogurt	0.74	12
18	62	Club	Blueberry Yogurt	3.93	12
19	63	Red Spade	Chicken Hot Dogs	3.19	7
20	67	Red Spade	Turkey Hot Dogs	1.9	7
21	68	Red Spade	Foot-Long Hot Dogs	3.92	7
22	71	Red Spade	Roasted Chicken	2.79	4
23	72	Red Spade	Corned Beef	2.79	3

2. Close the Browse Data window, and double-click the Product_Name column in the Product table.

Double-clicking a column name in a table is equivalent to dragging the column name onto the dimension name in the dimension tree—that is, it adds the column as a new bottom level.

3. Drag the Subcategory column from the Product Subcategory table onto the Product Name level in the dimension tree. Then drag the Category column from the Product Category table onto the Subcategory level.

Dragging a column from a warehouse table onto an existing level inserts the new level above the existing level.

4. Select the Category level in the dimension tree, and switch to the Advanced tab of the Properties pane.

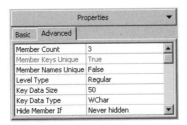

The Member Count for the level is *3* because there are three unique category names in the Category table. The Member Keys Unique property is *True* and is also disabled because the top level of a dimension must always have unique key values. The Member Names Unique property is *False*. For the Category level, the Member Name Column is the same as the Member Key Column, so the level really does have unique member names. Leave the property set to *False* for now. In "Specify a default member" later in this chapter, you'll see the effect of changing the Member Keys Unique and Member Names Unique properties.

5. Select the Subcategory level in the dimension tree, and look at the advanced property values.

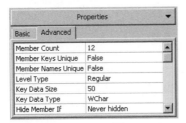

The Member Count for the level is *12*—this corresponds to the number of rows in the Product Subcategory table. Both the Member Keys Unique and Member Names Unique properties should be *False* (the default value). If either property is *True*, change it to *False*.

6. Select the Product Name level, and look at the advanced property values.

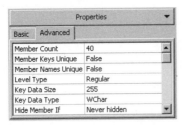

The Member Count for the level is *40*, even though there are 200 rows in the Product dimension table. Each group of identically named products is being treated as a single member. The Member Keys Unique and Member Names Unique properties should both be *False*. If either property is *True*, change it to *False*.

7. At the bottom of the Schema pane, click the Data tab to preview the dimension. Expand All Product, Bread, and Muffins.

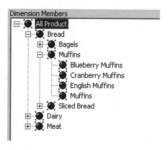

There are four muffin products listed. Each of these products represents several entries in the Product table because there are different brands for each product. For example, all the Blueberry Muffin products are lumped into a single member because the Member Key Column property for the Product name level points to the Product_Name column in the warehouse.

Create an expression for a member name

You can keep the Analysis server from grouping the products together by setting the Member Key Column property to the Product_ID column, which is unique for each product, but first you must set a dimension property that allows the dimension to have duplicate names.

1. In the dimension tree, select the Product dimension. On the Advanced tab of the Properties pane, change the Allow Duplicate Names property to *True*.

2. In the dimension tree, select the Product Name level. On the Basic tab of the Properties pane, select the Member Key Column property, click the ellipsis button, select the Product_ID column in the Product table, and click OK.

The dimension preview changes to show each of the individual products as separate, identically named members.

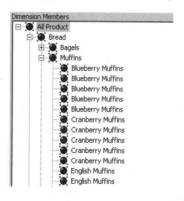

3. In the Properties pane, select the Advanced tab. The Member Count property value changed to *200*, reflecting the total number of products in the dimension table.

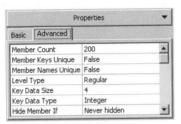

The dimension is technically correct, but a person viewing a report that shows five seemingly identical Blueberry Muffin entries might be confused or frustrated by the report. If you could prefix each product name with the name of the product's brand, the labels wouldn't be confusing. Typically, it's a good idea *not* to have members with duplicate names in a dimension. That's why the Dimension has *False* as the default value for the Allow Duplicate Names property. If you could only combine the brand name with the product name, there would be no duplicates.

The values for the Member Key Column and Member Name Column properties can consist of more than a single column name. You can use any structured query language (SQL) expression that the relational data source understands, provided that the expression returns a number or a string. You can use expressions to avoid what would otherwise be duplicate member names.

4. Click the Basic tab, and change the value of the Member Name Column property to **"Product"."Brand_Name"** + ' ' + **"Product"."Product_ Name"**. Press Enter.

Tip Clicking the ellipsis button displays the Select Column dialog box, which allows you to select only a single column; you must enter expressions by yourself. When working with a long expression, you can increase the size of the property box by dragging the right edge of the property pane, but there's no "zoom" window that shows the entire expression. Also, if you make a mistake, the Dimension Editor puts the entire expression back to what it was before you started editing. When you create a complex expression, select the entire expression and press Ctrl+C to copy it to the clipboard before pressing Enter. Then, if there is an error in the expression, you can easily use Ctrl+V to paste the copied expression so that you can find and fix the problem. For a particularly difficult expression, you might want to get the syntax of the expression correct within your relational database system and copy the expression to the property box. Within the Dimension Editor, all table and column names must be enclosed in double quotation marks, regardless of whether they contain spaces or special characters.

---

5. Expand the tree to the children of the Muffins member in the Data pane to see the unique product names.

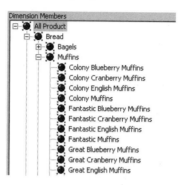

Each level of a dimension has a member key and a member name. The member key internally distinguishes one member from another. The member name appears on report captions. As a default, the member key is the same as the member name. If you make the member key different from the member name, you should make sure that the member names appear distinct on reports.

Specify a default member

Each dimension has a default member. This is the member that is used if the dimension is not included in a query. In the simple browser included in Analysis Manager, all dimensions are always included in a query—either as part of the data grid or as filter dimensions. In more sophisticated browsers, such as the PivotTable list browser you'll learn about in Chapter 5, "Office 2000 Analysis Components," you can omit a dimension from a query.

The standard default member is the All level member, but you can specify any default member you want. In this section, you'll learn how to create a constant default member. You'll also see how Member Keys Unique and Member Names Unique property settings for a level affect the way you specify a member. Suppose, for example, that you want the default member of the product dimension to be Colony Bagels—the first entry at the product level.

1. In the dimension tree, select the Product dimension, and switch to the Advanced tab of the Properties pane.

2. Select the Default Member property, and click the ellipsis button. Expand the members All Product, Bread, and Bagels; select the Colony Bagels member; and click OK.

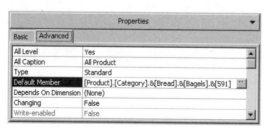

The description *[Product].[Category].&[Bread].&[Bagels].&[591]* appears as the value of the Default Member property. This is an elaborate way to specify a unique name for the Colony Bagels member. Shortly, you'll learn how to get a simpler unique member name. First take a tour of the full, elaborate name.

The name consists of individual dimension, level, and member names enclosed in brackets and separated by periods. *[Product]* is the name of the dimension. *[Category]* is the lowest level in the dimension that a value of *True* for either the Member Keys Unique property or the Member Names Unique property. *[Bread]* is the name of Colony Bagel's ancestor on the Category level. The ampersand (&) in front of the name indicates a key value, rather than a name. For the Category level, the name and the key are the same, but only the key is flagged as unique, so Analysis Manager uses the ampersand to designate the member key. *[Bagels]* is the child of Bread. The ampersand again indicates the key (even though the key and the name are the same). Finally, *[591]* is the key value (from the Product_ID column) for Colony Bagels.

This is much more complicated than it needs to be. The keys at the Product Name level are unique. If you change the Member Keys Unique property for the level to *True*, Analysis Manager can create a simpler unique member name for Colony Bagels.

3. In the dimension tree, select the Product Name level, and on the Advanced tab of the Properties pane, change the Member Keys Unique property to *True*.

4. In the dimension tree, select the Product dimension, select the Default Member property, and click the ellipsis button. Again select Colony Bagels, and click OK.

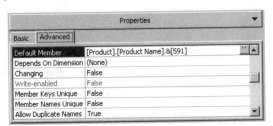

The unique name is now *[Product].[Product Name].&[591]*. The Product Name level is now the lowest level with a value of *True* for either Member Keys Unique or Member Names Unique. The unique name still uses the *[591]* to designate Colony Bagels because Member Names Unique is set to *False*. In fact, the member names for the Product Name level *are* unique. See what happens when you specify that the names are unique.

5. Select the Product Name level, and change the Member Names Unique property to *True*. Then select the Product dimension, select the Default Member property, click the ellipsis button, select Colony Bagels, and click OK.

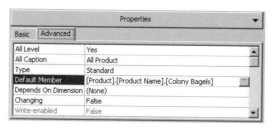

The unique member name changes to *[Product].[Product Name].[Colony Bagels]*. This is a much simpler name than the first one, but you can make it simpler still. The Product dimension happens to have unique names for the entire dimension. In other words, no category has the same name as a subcategory or a product. You can tell Analysis Manager that keys and names are unique within the entire dimension.

6. Select the Product dimension, change the Member Keys Unique property to *True*, and press Enter. Click Yes when informed that this will change the property for all levels. Change the Member Names Unique property to *True*, press Enter, and again click Yes when informed that this will change the property for all levels.

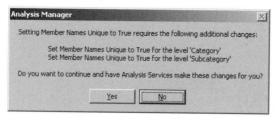

7. Select the Default Member property, click the ellipsis button, select Colony Bagels, and click OK.

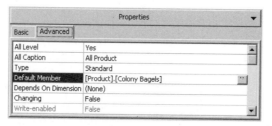

The unique name changes to *[Product].[Colony Bagels]*. This is the simplest possible unique member name. It is valid only if the Member Names Unique property is *True* for the entire dimension. If Member Keys Unique were *True* for the dimension but Member Names Unique were false, the simplest possible name would be *[Product].&[591]*. Some dimensions have unique members, some have unique keys, and some have neither. In general, if you specify that member names and member keys are unique as much as is true within a dimension, you'll be able to use simpler unique member names when referring to a member in an expression.

Create a detail-level member property

In the Market data warehouse, the Product table contains a Price column, which contains the list price of the product. The price of the product doesn't make sense as a level in the product's hierarchy; it's simply an additional piece of information that's available about the product. You can include this information within a dimension as a *member property* of the Product level.

1. In the Dimension Editor, click the Schema tab to convert the right pane into the Schema pane.

2. In the dimension tree, expand the Product Name level so that you can see the Member Properties folder below it.

3. Drag the Price column from the Product table onto the Member Properties folder for the Product Name level. You can see the member property as you browse the dimension.

4. Click the Data tab, and expand All Product, Bread, and Bagels. Select the Colony Bagels member to see its price displayed in the Member Properties list.

A client application can determine how it will make use of member properties. In "Create a single-level virtual dimension" in Chapter 10, "Dimension Optimization," you'll learn how to make a member property appear as a dimension by creating a *virtual dimension*. In "Use an external function to convert a string to a number" in Chapter 6, "MDX Values," you'll learn how to use member properties in a formula for a *calculated member*.

Create a summary-level member property

A member property can exist at any level of the hierarchy. In the Market warehouse, the Product Subcategory table contains a Category_Manager column. This is the name of the person assigned to manage sales for the products in that category. The category manager's name doesn't make sense as a new level in the hierarchy, but it can be a member property of the Subcategory level.

1. In the dimension tree, select the Subcategory level.

2. On the Insert menu, click Member Property.

3. In the Insert Member Property dialog box, double-click Category_Manager.

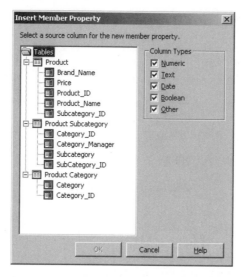

4. In the Data pane, expand the All Product and Bread members and select Bagels. You can see the manager name in the Member Properties list.

5. Click the Save button to save the Product dimension.

You can create a member property at any level, and a member property applies to only a single level. If products and families also had managers, you'd need to create a separate member property for each level.

Tip   In the source table or tables for a dimension, you can easily identify potential member properties: any column that isn't a member name or a member key is a potential member property. When the dimension tables appear in a snowflake schema, where each level of the hierarchy has its own table, you can also easily identify the appropriate level for a member property: it's simply the level that corresponds to the members from the same source table. When the dimension table is organized in a star schema, where all levels are combined into a single table, it can be tricky to identify the level for a member property. The best approach is to imagine breaking the table into a snowflake, with one table for each level, and to assign each member property to the highest possible table without having more than one value for a single key. The appropriate level for the property corresponds to the level of the imaginary snowflake table.

Working with Time Dimensions

There's practically no such thing as an OLAP database without a Time dimension. Often, a Time dimension contains months as the lowest level of detail—aggregated into quarters and years. Sometimes, a Time dimension will contain days as the lowest level of detail. On occasion, particularly if you're monitoring a manufacturing operation, you might create a dimension with minutes or even seconds as the lowest level of detail. Whatever the level of detail, a Time dimension has certain unique qualities.

For example, time typically occurs in regular intervals. Each hour contains 60 minutes, each day contains 24 hours, each quarter contains 3 months, and each year contains 4 quarters. This repetitive nature of time encourages certain questions, such as "How does this month compare to the same month of last year?" The multidimensional expressions (MDX) language, which you'll learn about in Part 2, "Multidimensional Expressions," has functions that make it easy to answer this type of question. By flagging certain dimensions as Time dimensions, and certain levels within a dimension as specific units of time, you can make those functions easy to use.

Of course, time isn't completely uniform because the 365 days in a year aren't evenly divisible by the 7 days in a week or the 12 months in a year. Some months have 30 days; some have 31, or 28, or occasionally 29. Months begin on different days of the week. Irregularities are a fact of life in Time dimensions, and when working with time, you need to be prepared for both the regularities and the irregularities.

Create a calendar date hierarchy

One irregularity that frequently arises when dealing with time is that many organizations use a fiscal year—where the starting day of the year isn't January 1. Sometimes, a company uses a fiscal year for internal purposes but must still use a calendar year when communicating with certain customers. The same lowest level date—for example, March 1, 1998—could be the first month of a fiscal year and the third month of the calendar year. To choose which way to display that lowest level date, you must use two different hierarchies. Analysis Services allows you to do that when you create the dimension. Since you can't rename an existing shared dimension, you must plan for multiple hierarchies before creating the dimension.

As you saw in Chapter 2, the Dimension Wizard can construct an entire hierarchy from a single Date/Time column. In this chapter, you'll re-create the Time dimension, again using the Dimension Wizard to create the hierarchy of levels. This time, however, you'll create a calendar hierarchy within the Time dimension. You'll also see how the Dimension Wizard uses expressions in the Member Name Column and Member Key Column properties to create a hierarchy from a single date value.

Using a Separate Dimension Table for Dates

The Chapter3 warehouse database used in this chapter has a separate date dimension table named TimeMonth. In the Chapter2 warehouse database from Chapter 2, the Month key of the SalesFact table was a date value and you used the fact table as the dimension table. Generally, when you design a data warehouse to use with Analysis Services, you should create a separate dimension table for dates rather than use a Date/Time column in the fact table. As with other dimension tables, you would then use an integer key to join the date dimension table with the fact table. Creating a separate date dimension table has certain advantages over storing a Date/Time column in the fact table.

For example, a date dimension table can contain additional properties for a date, such as the season for a month or a holiday flag for a day. Also, some organizations define fiscal months and quarters by arbitrarily assigning four weeks to the first two months of a quarter and five weeks to the third month (or five weeks to the first month of a quarter and four weeks to the second and third months). In that case, an expression can't derive the fiscal month or quarter from a Date/Time column, but a date dimension table could easily store the fiscal month and quarter values.

Also, a separate date dimension can usually reduce total storage space for a warehouse. A Date/Time column requires 8 bytes, while an integer key is typically 4 bytes. If a fact table contains millions, or even thousands, of records, the savings from a smaller key column in the fact table more than offsets the size of a date dimension table containing only a few hundred records. In addition, designing and processing a dimension based on a table with only a few records is much faster than extracting dimension values from a large fact table.

Finally, a separate date dimension table can be used with more than one fact table. This allows you to create a single, shared date dimension for multiple cubes. A shared dimension allows you to create a virtual cube to compare measures from multiple cubes.

Shared dimensions and virtual cubes are discussed in "Creating Virtual Cubes" in Chapter 4, "Advanced Dimensions and Cubes."

You can also click the New Dimension button on the toolbar to launch the Dimension Wizard.

1. In the Dimension Editor, click the File menu, point to New Dimension, and click Wizard to launch the Dimension Wizard.

2. When asked how you want to create the dimension, click the single table option and click Next. Select TimeMonth as the dimension table, and click Next. Click the Time Dimension option, and click Next. Select Year, Quarter, Month for the time levels, and click Next. Click Next to skip the Advanced Options screen.

3. On the finish screen, type **Time** as the name of the dimension, select the check box labeled Create A Hierarchy Of A Dimension, and type **Calendar** in the Hierarchy Name box that appears.

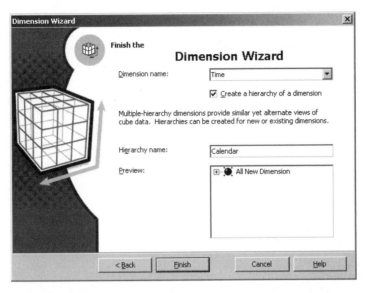

4. Click Finish to create the dimension.

The Dimension Wizard leaves you in the Dimension Editor with a new dimension named Time.Calendar. Because the wizard already created and saved the dimension, you can't change its name in the Properties pane.

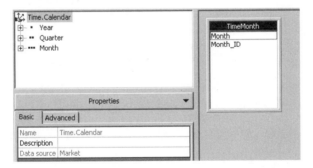

When you create an explicit hierarchy in a dimension, Analysis Services creates a compound name, with the dimension name followed by a period, which is followed by the hierarchy name. A dimension with an explicit hierarchy is simply an ordinary dimension. Technically, all dimensions have at least one hierarchy. If you create a dimension name without a period, the dimension has one unnamed hierarchy. The only effect of creating multiple hierarchies for a dimension is that Analysis Services makes it possible for a client application to indicate that the hierarchies are somehow related.

You can't include more than one period in a dimension name.

Set Time dimension properties

For the time being, the Time dimension contains only a single hierarchy. Before creating a second hierarchy for the dimension, look at some of the special time-related properties that the Dimension Wizard sets for you.

1. In the Dimension Editor, select the Time.Calendar dimension in the dimension tree and click the Advanced tab in the Properties pane. The value of the Type property is *Time*. The Type property has many possible values, but the only ones automatically set by the wizards are *Time* and *Standard*.

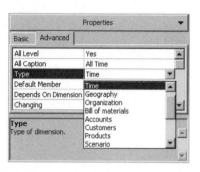

Note A dimension's Type property has no direct effect on Analysis server. The Type property is available for a client application to inspect—and certain MDX functions, as explained in Part 2, do behave differently based on the Type property of a dimension—but the server does not. You could change the Type property of the Time.Calendar dimension to *Standard* or that of the Product dimension to *Time*, and it would make no difference to the server.

The Dimension Wizard gives standard names to the levels of a Time dimension when it constructs the levels from a single Date/Time column. Level names often appear above row headings in cube browsers. If you're going to add a second hierarchy to the Time dimension, level names that are specific to the hierarchy might be less confusing when browsing the cube.

2. Change the name of the Year level to **Calendar Year**, the name of the Quarter level to **Calendar Quarter**, and the name of the Month level to **Calendar Month**. After renaming the levels, switch to the Advanced tab and notice the value of the Level Type property as you select the levels in turn. The Dimension Wizard sets the value of each Level Type to match the type of time data stored in the level.

Note   As with the Type property of the dimension, the Level Type property has no effect on the server; it's available only as information to a client application and to certain MDX functions. You can assign one of the time-related values to the Level Type, even if the dimension is not flagged as a Time dimension. Likewise, you can change the Level Type for a level to Regular, even if it is within a Time dimension.

3. Select the Calendar Year level, and click the Basic tab of the Properties pane. Compare the values of the Member Key Column and the Member Name Column properties.

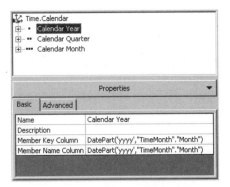

Both are the same, and both contain the expression *DatePart('yyyy', "TimeMonth"."Month")*. This expression extracts the four-digit year from a Date/Time column. The *DatePart* function is meaningful in the Microsoft Access dialect of SQL. (Analysis Manager generates a different expression if the relational data source doesn't recognize the *DatePart* function.) In essence, the Dimension Wizard creates levels from a Date/Time column by constructing expressions for the key and name columns at each level.

4. Select the Calendar Month level, and compare the values of the Member Key Column and the Member Name Column properties.

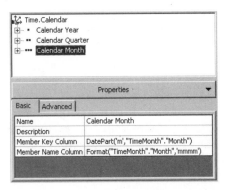

The expression for the member key is *DatePart('m',"TimeMonth"."Month")*, and the expression for the member name is *Format("TimeMonth". "Month",'mmmm')*. The member key is the month number, and the name is the descriptive name of the month. The Dimension Wizard also sets the Order By property (on the Advanced tab) to *Key*. This sorts the month names in calendar order as opposed to alphabetical order.

5. You can easily modify the member name expression to display the three-character abbreviation for a month. Change the formatting string portion of the Member Name Column property from *'mmmm'* to *'mmm'*. Press Enter, and browse the dimension to see the shortened names.

6. Select the Calendar Quarter level, and look at the expression for the Member Name Column.

It is *'Quarter ' + Format$(DatePart('q',"TimeMonth"."Month"))*. Suppose that you want the quarter label to display only *Qtr* as a prefix instead of *Quarter*.

7. In the expression for the Member Name Column of the Calendar Quarter level, change the prefix string from *'Quarter '* to *'Qtr'*. (Be sure to remove the space at the end of the string.) Press Enter, and browse the dimension to see the revised labels.

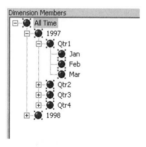

8. Click the Save button to save the Time.Calendar dimension.

The Type property of a dimension and the Level Type property of a level are significant only when dealing with a Time dimension. Even in a Time dimension, however, these properties are not critical. When the Dimension Wizard constructs a hierarchy from a Date/Time column, it creates expressions for the member name and the member key of each level. You can modify those expressions or even add new levels of your own, inventing appropriate expressions for the levels.

Create a fiscal date hierarchy

Many organizations use fiscal dates in addition to calendar dates. The Dimension Wizard can create a fiscal date hierarchy from a Date/Time column, but you might need to adjust some of the properties to get the dimension to work properly, particularly if the dimension is created as the second hierarchy of a single parent dimension.

1. In the Dimension Editor, click the File menu, point to New Dimension, and click Wizard.

2. Click the single table option, and click Next. Select TimeMonth as the dimension table, and click Next. Click the Time Dimension option, and click Next.

3. Select Year, Quarter, Month for the time levels, but select March as the starting month for the year. Then click Next twice.

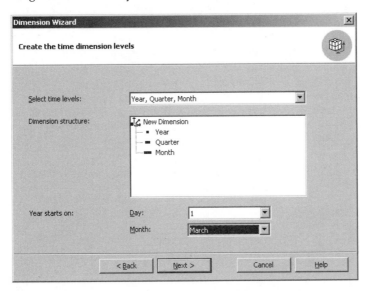

4. On the finish screen, type **Time** as the name of the dimension, select the check box for an explicit hierarchy, type **Fiscal** as the name of the hierarchy, and click Finish. This creates a second hierarchy for the Time dimension.

Whenever the Dimension Wizard constructs a time dimension from a Date/Time column, it always sets the Type property of the dimension to *Time*. Both the Time.Calendar dimension and the Time.Fiscal dimension have *Time* as the value of the Type property. The purpose of the Type property, however, is merely to allow certain MDX functions to identify the default Time dimension. If you have two Time dimensions, only one of them can be the default.

When you add dimensions to a cube, you add them in a particular order. The default Time dimension for an MDX function is the *first* dimension in the cube that has *Time* as the value of its Type property. One way to explicitly determine the default Time dimension is to explicitly determine the order of dimensions in a cube, as explained in "Add a shared dimension by using the Cube Editor" later in this chapter. Another, perhaps more straightforward, approach is to change the Type of one of the dimensions to *Standard*. Suppose you want Time.Calendar to be the default Time dimension. You would need to change the Type of the Time.Fiscal dimension.

Even though you change the Time.Fiscal dimension's Type property to Standard, leaving the levels flagged with the appropriate Level Type will still allow using default values for some MDX functions.

5. In the dimension tree, select the Time.Fiscal dimension. On the Advanced properties tab, change the Type property to *Standard*.

6. Change the names of the levels—from Year to **Fiscal Year**, from Quarter to **Fiscal Quarter**, and from Month to **Fiscal Month**.

Note   The expression generated for the Member Key Column of the Fiscal Year level is *DatePart('yyyy',iif (Month("TimeMonth"."Month") < 3 or (Month("TimeMonth"."Month") = 3 and Day("TimeMonth"."Month") < 1), "TimeMonth"."Month",DateAdd('yyyy', 1, "TimeMonth"."Month")))*. The Quarter level has similar expressions. While you can simply be grateful that the wizard created the expression so that you don't have to, this expression is also much more complicated than it needs to be. A fiscal date is simply a calendar date that has been shifted by a certain number of months (and, possibly, days). You could equally well convert to a fiscal year beginning in March with the formula *DatePart('yyyy',DateAdd('m', -2, "TimeMonth"."Month"))*.

---

7. In the Data pane, expand All Time, 1998, and Quarter 4. The months of the quarter appear, with December correctly preceding January.

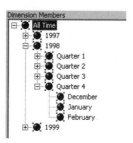

8. In the dimension tree, select the Fiscal Month level and look at the Member Key Column property.

Note   The expression generated by the wizard is *(DatePart('yyyy',"TimeMonth"."Month") * 100) + DatePart('m',"TimeMonth"."Month")*. There's no adjustment for the fiscal time shift, but the year is included with the month and December of 1997 will always precede January of 1998, regardless of the fiscal year. The same effect would be achieved by simply using the Date/Time column "TimeMonth"."Month" as the member key.

---

9. Click the Save button to save the Time.Fiscal dimension, and close the Dimension Editor to return to Analysis Manager's console view.

Building a Date Hierarchy from a String

You don't always have control of dimension tables in the relational warehouse. If a dimension table contains a Date/Time column, Analysis Manager can create expressions to build date hierarchy levels. Suppose, however, that in your data warehouse, dates are stored as strings. You can create your own expressions to build date hierarchy levels from a date string.

For example, suppose that your relational warehouse contains a DateDim table that contains a DateString column where dates are stored in the MM-DD-YYYY format, such as 04-01-2000 for April 1, 2000. To create a Year level, use the expression *Right("DateDim"."DateString",4)* for the Member Key Column property. To create a Month level, use the expression *Left("DateDim". "DateString",2)* for the Member Key Column property. The Member Key Column and Member Name Column properties can contain any SQL column expression supported by your relational warehouse.

Working with a Cube

Dimensions are useful only when incorporated into a cube. A cube uses dimension hierarchies to summarize measures from a fact table. A cube must always have at least one dimension, at least one measure, and one (and only one) fact table.

To create a cube that combines measures from multiple fact tables, you can use a virtual cube, as explained in "Creating Virtual Cubes" in Chapter 4.

Use the Cube Editor

The Cube Wizard makes it easy for you to quickly put together a cube. But a cube has many properties that aren't available when you use the wizard. So even if you use the wizard to create a cube, you'll undoubtedly use the Cube Editor to refine it. In fact, it isn't much harder to create a cube by using the Cube Editor than it is to use the Cube Wizard. In the following example, you'll use the Cube Editor to create the simplest possible cube from a fact table.

1. In the Chapter 3 database, right-click the Cubes folder, point to New Cube, and click Editor.

    Since each cube requires a fact table, you're immediately presented with a choice of tables to use.

2. Select SalesFact, and click OK. Click Yes when cautioned about counting rows in the fact table.

    The Cube Editor window appears. The Cube Editor window is similar to that of the Dimension Editor. The left pane has a tree view at the top, a *cube tree,* which shows the components of the cube. The left pane also has a Properties pane at the bottom. As in the Dimension Editor, if the Properties pane is collapsed, you can click the Properties button to display the pane. The right pane displays either the Schema tab that shows the tables that make up the cube or the Data tab that shows either actual or sample data for the cube.

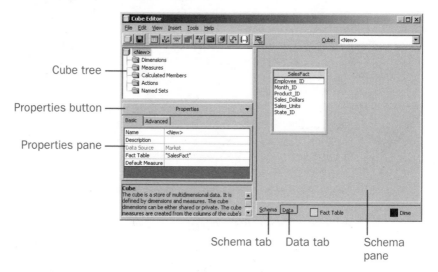

3. A cube must contain at least one measure from the fact table, so drag the Sales_Dollars column from the SalesFact table onto the Measures folder. The folder expands to show the new measure in the cube.

A cube must also contain at least one dimension related to a key column in the fact table. You can actually use a key column in the fact table to create a simple private dimension.

4. Drag the State_ID column from the SalesFact table onto the Dimensions folder.

The folder expands to show the new dimension, which is named after the column from the fact table, with any underscore characters converted to spaces. The icon to the left of the dimension doesn't include a hand, indicating that this is a new private dimension.

5. Change the All Caption property to **All State**. Expand the State ID dimension, and rename both the dimension and its solitary level from State ID to **State**.

One measure and one dimension are the minimal requirements for a cube. You can now look at sample data for the cube.

You can rename a private dimension, even after saving the cube.

6. Click the Data tab to see the structure of the cube, displaying sample values. To see actual values within the structure, you must process the cube.

	MeasuresLevel
State	Sales Dollars
All State	$9.60
1	$1.60
2	$1.60
3	$1.60
4	$1.60
5	$1.60
6	$1.60

7. Click the Process Cube button, and click Yes to save the cube. Type **Simple Sales** as the name of the cube, click OK, and click No when asked whether you want to design aggregates. Click OK when asked to choose the processing method. Close the Process log window.

The Preview pane now shows the actual values in the cube.

	MeasuresLevel
State	Sales Dollars
All State	$76,741.28
1	$30,147.54
2	$13,986.14
3	$13,594.97
4	$7,874.22
5	$5,930.26
6	$5,208.15

In this procedure, you created a simple cube—the smallest possible cube from the sample database. The cube has only one measure, and the one dimension has only a single, nondescriptive, level. The values you see in the Preview pane constitute the entire contents of the cube.

Note   With a private dimension, you use the Cube Editor, not the Dimension Editor, to edit all the dimension properties discussed earlier in this chapter. For example, for a private dimension, you can use the Cube Editor's Properties pane to change the dimension name and the dimension type and to choose whether to allow duplicate names. And for a level in a private dimension, you can use the Cube Editor's Properties pane to change the level Name, the Member Name Column, the Order By property, and so forth. You can also use the Cube Editor to add member properties to a private dimension.

Add a shared dimension by using the Cube Editor

When you have shared dimensions already created, you can create a substantial new cube very quickly, even using the Cube Editor. From within the Cube Editor, you can create a new cube by using either the editor or the wizard. When using the wizard, you click the New Cube button. To create a new cube using the Cube Editor, select <New> from the Cube drop-down list. Use the Cube Editor to create a new Sales cube that uses all the shared dimensions you created earlier in this chapter.

1. In the Cube drop-down list, select <New>.

2. Select SalesFact as the fact table, and click OK. Click Yes when cautioned about counting the rows in the fact table.

3. Drag the Sales_Dollars and Sales_Units columns from the SalesFact table into the Measures folder.

4. Right-click the Dimensions folder, and click Existing Dimensions. Click the Add All Dimensions button (>>), and click OK.

The four existing shared dimensions all appear in the Cube Editor. As discussed earlier in "Create a fiscal date hierarchy," if you have two Time dimensions in a cube, you might want to control which dimension comes first. To change the order of dimensions in a cube, you simply drag the dimension name in the cube tree.

5. In the Dimension folder, drag the Time.Fiscal dimension on top of the Time.Calendar dimension.

The dimensions trade places within the dimension folder. The default measure for a cube is the first measure listed in the Measures folder. To change the order of measures, simply drag the measure name.

6. Drag the Sales Units measure on top of the Sales Dollars measure to swap the order.

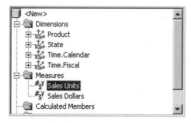

7. Click the Process Cube button, and click Yes when asked to save the cube. Type **Sales** as the name of the cube, and click OK. Click No when asked to design aggregations, click OK to accept a full process method, and close the Process log window.

Because the shared dimensions have not already been processed, processing the cube automatically process them.

8. Click the Data tab, and collapse the Country heading.

Product	Colony Bagels	▼
Time.Calendar	All Time	▼
Time.Fiscal	All Time	▼

	MeasuresLevel	
+ Country	Sales Units	Sales Dollars
North America	264.00	$308.88
+ Canada	33.00	$38.61
+ Mexico	6.00	$7.02
+ USA	225.00	$263.25

Note that Colony Bagels appears as the value for the Product dimension. That's because you specified it as the default member of the dimension in "Specify a default member," earlier in this chapter.

Working with Measures in a Cube

A cube must contain at least one dimension and at least one measure. The simplest measures are columns straight from the fact table, but it's possible to use expressions to add additional measures to a cube. In many ways, measures in a cube behave like a dimension with a single level. Because of this, in some contexts you might see Measures presented as if it were simply one of the dimensions of a cube.

Create a derived measure

When you select a measure, a Source Column property appears on the Basic tab of the Properties pane. The Source Column property is similar to the Member Key Column and Member Name Column properties of a dimension level. As with those properties, it contains the name of a table and column from the relational data source. And as with those properties, you can enter a SQL expression acceptable to your data source.

Suppose, for example, that you pay a standard commission rate of 15 percent on total dollar sales. You could create what can be called a *derived measure* that calculates the commission at the lowest level.

1. In the Sales cube, right-click the Measures folder and click New Measure. Select the Sales_Dollars column, and click OK.

The measure is added with the name Sales Dollars 1.

2. Change the Source Column property to **"SalesFact"."Sales_Dollars" * 0.15**, and type **Commission** for the Name property.

3. On the Tools menu, click Process Cube, agree to save the cube, decline to design aggregates, and click OK when asked to specify the processing method. Close the Process log window, and browse the data.

4. Scroll the grid as needed to see the new Commission measure.

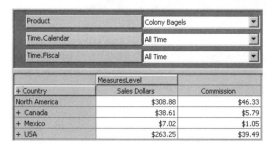

Perhaps you find it annoying that the Commission displays accuracy to the penny, when it's really an estimated value. You can get Analysis Services to round the values to integers by changing the measure's Display Format property.

5. Click the Advanced tab of the Properties pane, type **$#,#** as the Display Format, and press Enter. (You need to type the format string; it does not appear in the drop-down list.) The Preview pane generates sample values, but you can see that the numbers are rounded.

	MeasuresLevel	
+ Country	Sales Dollars	Commission
North America	$8,000.00	$8,000
+ Canada	$1,333.33	$1,333
+ Mexico	$2,666.67	$2,667
+ USA	$4,000.00	$4,000

The Display Format property does not change the way the values are stored, simply the way they are displayed.

The Commission measure is stored in the cube file, the same as if it were a numeric column that came directly from the fact table. In effect, if you have control over the relational data warehouse, you can create a view that adds the Commission column to the other columns of the fact table and, in Analysis Services, use the view as the fact table. You can always think of a derived measure as a column that might have been in the fact table itself.

Including Multiple Tables in a Derived Measure

A derived measure can include only columns from the fact table. This can cause complications in certain situations. For example, the Market sample warehouse includes Sales_Dollars and Sales_Units in the fact table. The Sales_Dollars in the fact table are *net* dollars—that is, dollars after discounts. The Price column in the Product table contains the list price for each product. Multiplying the Sales_Units column in the fact table by the Price column from the Product table gives you the Gross Dollars for each record.

The Gross Dollars measure would be an excellent candidate for a derived measure because it should be calculated before aggregating the dollar values. Unfortunately, even if both the fact table and the Product table are included in the cube definition, Analysis Services requires that all columns in a derived measure come from the fact table. The only way to create a derived measure that includes columns from multiple tables is to create a view in the relational data source and use that view as the fact table.

Specify the aggregation function for a measure

As you move up a hierarchy, a cube browser displays aggregated values. The default aggregation function is *Sum*, which adds lower level values to get higher level values. With some derived measure expressions, however, you get incorrect values if you use the *Sum* function to aggregate the values. See what happens when you attempt to calculate and aggregate an average price measure.

1. Click the Insert Measure toolbar button, and double-click the Sales_Units column. This creates a measure named Sales Units 1. Type **Bad Price** for the measure's Name property, and change the value of the Source Column property to **"SalesFact"."Sales_Dollars"/"SalesFact"."Sales_Units"**. This is a derived measure. It uses the default aggregation function: *Sum*.

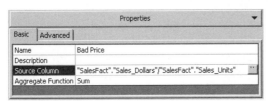

2. Process the cube—that is, click the Process Cube button, save the cube, don't design aggregates, and choose the full process method. Close the Process log window, and browse the data.

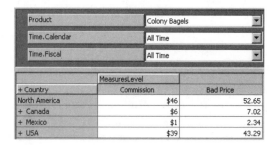

The values in the Bad Price column are clearly wrong. At the level of a fact table row, the price calculation is correct, but summing individual prices doesn't give a valid price for a state or country. If, rather than summing the prices, you found the minimum price, the derived measure would work properly.

3. Change the name of the Bad Price measure to **Min Price**, and change the value of the Aggregate Function to *Min*.

4. On the Tools menu, click Process Cube. Save the cube, don't design aggregates, and select the full process method. Close the Process log window, and click the Data tab to see the values in the cube. Scroll as necessary to see the new Min Price measure.

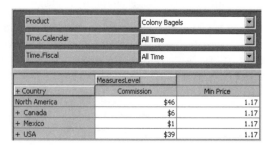

Derived measures calculate as part of the SQL statement that retrieves values from the fact table. The expression always calculates before any aggregations are performed. If you want to calculate a true average price, you must calculate after the units and dollars are summed. To do that, you must create a calculated measure.

Create a calculated measure

Creating a derived measure is one of two methods you can use to create measures that don't exist as columns in the fact table. The other method is to create a *calculated measure*. (You can actually create a calculated member for any dimension. A calculated member that's in the Measures dimension is a calculated measure.) The difference between a derived measure and a calculated measure is when the calculation is performed. A derived measure is calculated before aggregations are created, and the values of the derived measure are stored in the cube. A calculated measure is calculated after aggregations are created, and the values of a calculated measure aren't stored in the cube.

You'll learn how to create advanced calculated members in Part 2.

The primary criterion for choosing between a derived measure and a calculated measure is not efficiency, but accuracy. For example, in calculating a Price measure, it makes all the difference in the world whether you calculate the Price before aggregating the Dollars and Units (a derived measure) or whether you do it afterward (a calculated measure).

1. In the cube tree, right-click the Calculated Members folder, and click New Calculated Member. In the Calculated Member Builder dialog box, type **Net Price** as the new member name.

2. In the Data tree, fully expand the Measures dimension and double-click the Sales Dollars measure to make the member name appear in the Value Expression box. Click the slash (/) on the right side of the dialog box, and then double-click Sales Units in the Data tree.

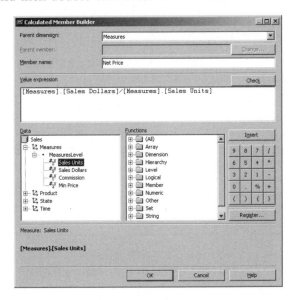

3. Click OK.

The Net Price measure appears in the Calculated Members folder. This is a calculated measure.

4. In the Data pane, scroll as needed to see the Net Price field, and select All Product in the Product dimension.

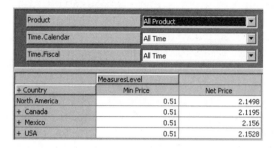

After adding a derived measure, you must process the cube to see the new values. After adding a calculated measure, you do not need to process the cube.

5. Select the Net Price measure, and look at the Properties pane. In addition to the Name property, it has a Parent Dimension property with the value of Measures and a Parent Member property that's empty. A calculated measure (that is, a calculated member that's in the Measures dimension) never has a parent member. Finally, you see a Value property. The Value property corresponds to the Source Column property for a derived measure, but this is an MDX expression based on members in the cube.

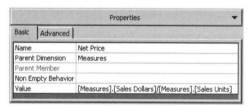

6. Select the Advanced tab, and for the Format String property, choose *Currency* from the drop-down list.

Note   For a regular measure, the name of the formatting property is Display Format. For a calculated measure, the name of the formatting property is Format String. Other than the name, the two properties are equivalent. Also, some browsers—such as the PivotTable list control you'll learn about in Chapter 5— allow you to format the value within the browser and consequently ignore the Format String and Display Format properties.

Most measures aggregate by using a *Sum* function—adding detail values to get the aggregation. If a calculation contains only addition or subtraction, you can chose whether to create a derived measure or a calculated measure based purely upon convenience or efficiency, since addition and subtraction can be done in any order. For example, you could create a Gross Profit measure by subtracting a Cost Of Goods Sold measure from a Net Sales Dollars measure. Since this calculation involves only subtraction, the values will be the same whether you choose to make it a derived measure—using columns from the fact table—or a calculated measure—using measures in a cube. If the measure will be used frequently, make it a derived measure; if infrequently, make it a calculated measure.

If a calculation involves multiplication by a constant, as in the Commission example given earlier, you'll get the same value regardless of whether you use a calculated or a derived measure. Again, base the decision on how frequently the measure will be accessed.

If a calculation involves multiplying or dividing one column by another—as in calculating a price or a ratio—the choice between a calculated measure and a derived measure is important. If you want to aggregate by summing and the expression for the measure involves multiplication or division, you'll almost always want to create a calculated measure. If, however, you use a *Min* or *Max* aggregation function, you might want to create a derived measure that calculates before the aggregation takes place.

Create a measure that calculates an average

The Aggregate Function property of a measure determines how the measure will be aggregated. The Aggregate Function property allows five possible aggregation types: *Sum*, *Min*, *Max*, *Count*, and *Distinct Count*. You can create any other aggregated value you might want—for example, an average or a ratio—by using a calculated measure. Calculating an average is a particularly interesting option, and it requires a measure that uses the *Count* function. First consider how the *Count* function operates. You can use the *Sum*, *Min*, and *Max* functions to create a measure from a *numeric* column in a fact table. You can use the *Count* function to create a measure from *any* column in the fact table. The *Count* function counts each row in the fact table. It doesn't count unique occurrences of a key. To count unique occurrences, you use the *Distinct Count* function, which is covered in the section "Calculate distinct counts for a dimension" in Chapter 4.

One of the most important uses of the *Count* function is to allow you to create a calculated measure that properly calculates an average. Use a measure with the *Count* function as the basis for a calculated measure that creates an average.

When you create a measure using the Count *function, you can use any column from the fact table.*

1. Click the Insert Measure toolbar button, and double-click the Employee_ID column. Type **Count** for the Name property of the new measure, and change the value of the Aggregate Function property to *Count*.

2. Click the Process Cube button. Save the cube, don't design aggregations, and accept the proposed Processing Method. Close the Process log window, and scroll the Data pane to see the values in the cube. Because Count is a regular measure, not a calculated measure, the cube must be processed after adding it.

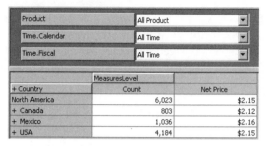

The *6,023* value for North America corresponds to the 6023 rows in the SalesFact table. The *Count* aggregation function simply counts the rows in the fact table.

3. Click the Insert Calculated Member toolbar button. In the Calculated Member Builder dialog box, type **Average Units** in the Member Name box.

4. Fully expand the Measures dimension. Double-click the Sales Units measure, click the slash button (/), and double-click the Count measure. Then click OK.

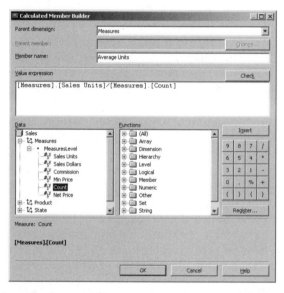

5. Select the Average Units measure in the Calculated Members folder, and for its Format String property, select #,# from the list. Press Enter, and scroll to see the values in the Data pane.

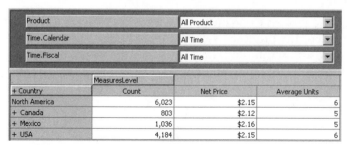

When calculating an average, you almost always want a true, weighted average. The *Count* aggregation function allows you to aggregate the row count from the fact table in parallel with the value you want to average. You can then create a calculated member to create the proper weighted average at each level of the hierarchy.

Hide an internal measure

In some cubes, you might want to use a measure such as Count as an intermediate value for creating a calculated measure such as Average Units, but you might not want it to appear in the list of available measures in client applications. A measure has a property that allows it to be hidden.

1. Select the Count measure in the cube tree, and click the Advanced tab of the Properties pane.

2. Change the value of the Visible property to *False*, and press Enter. (You won't see the change in the browser until you process the cube.)

   A measure might not behave exactly the way you expect after you change the Visible property to *False*. Client applications that explicitly specify the internal measure can still access it; the measure simply doesn't appear in lists of measures. Surprisingly, the measure even disappears from the list of measures in the Calculated Member Builder dialog box, even though you can manually type it into the expression for a calculated member.

3. Right-click the Average Units measure, and click Edit to open the Calculated Member Builder. Fully expand the Measures dimension in the Data tree. The Sales Units and Sales Dollars measures are still visible, but the Count measure is not. You can still use the Count measure in an expression—look at the Value Expression box—but you would have to type it yourself. You might want to wait to set the Visible property for measures until after you have created calculated measures.

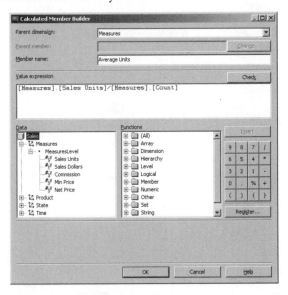

4. Click Cancel to close the Calculated Member Builder.

In addition to measures, most OLAP objects—dimensions, levels, calculated members—have a Visible property. Setting the Visible property of an object to *False* does not keep the object from being used in expressions or queries; it just keeps the object from appearing in client applications.

Working with a Parent-Child Dimension

The Employee dimension you created in Chapter 2 is an unbalanced, parent-child dimension. The levels of the dimension hierarchy come from recursive columns in a single table, rather than from individual columns in star schema or snowflake schema tables. The Dimension Editor does not allow you to create a parent-child dimension. You must always use the Dimension Wizard to create a new parent-child dimension. Once the dimension is created, you can use the Dimension Editor (if the dimension is shared) or the Cube Editor (if the dimension is private) to modify its properties.

Create a parent-child dimension

The most interesting properties of a parent-child dimension are visible only within the context of a cube. Now that you have a Sales cube in the Chapter 3 database, you can add a private Employee parent-child dimension and learn about advanced parent-child dimension properties.

You can also launch the Dimension Wizard by pointing to New on the Insert menu and clicking Dimension.

1. In the Cube Editor, right-click the Dimensions folder and click New Dimension to launch the Dimension Wizard.

2. Select the parent-child option, and click Next.

3. Select the Employee dimension table, and click Next.

4. Select Employee_ID in the Member Key list, Manager_ID in the Parent Key list, and Employee_Name in the Member Name list. Then click Next.

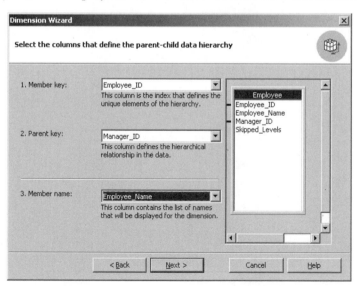

5. Click Next to skip the Advanced Options screen. Type **Employee** as the dimension name, clear the check box that allows you to share the dimension with other cubes, and click Finish.

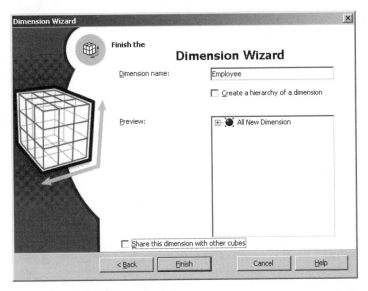

6. Click the Data tab, if necessary, to see the Data pane, and drag the Employee dimension down to the row area, replacing the existing dimension. The cube will display sample data because it hasn't been processed, but you can see the dimension members.

7. Expand the Sheri Nowmer, Maya Gutierrez, and Jonathan Murraiin members so that you can see the entire Employee hierarchy.

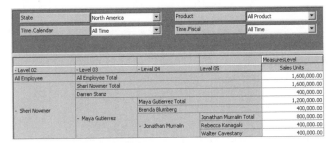

The labels for the row headings begin with Level 02. That's because the All level (with All Employee as its member) is in the same column as Sheri Nowmer.

Allow data for non-leaf-level members

In a standard dimension, only the leaf-level members can correspond to values in the fact table. For example, in a Time dimension, you can't have some rows in the fact table with monthly values and other rows with quarterly values. In a parent-child dimension, on the other hand, it's common to have values in the fact table at both the leaf level and at a parent level. For example, in the Market database, Sheri Nowmer is the CEO of the company, but she was directly responsible for many of the sales in the SalesFact table, as well as being indirectly responsible for the sales of all those below her in the organization. Before processing a cube that has data for non-leaf-level members, you must change a property of the dimension.

1. In the cube tree, select the Employee dimension, switch to the Advanced tab of the Properties window, and display the drop-down list for the Members With Data property.

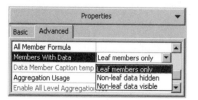

The Members With Data property is available only for a parent-child dimension, and it has three possible values: *Leaf Members Only* (the default) will display an error message if you process a cube where the fact table contains values for non-leaf-level members. *Non-Leaf Data Hidden* does not display an error message, but the total for a member may be greater than the sum of its visible children. The final option, *Non-Leaf Data Visible*, creates a new member for each parent. That new member can display the values linked to that member. The third option is appropriate for the Sales cube, so that you can directly compare Sheri Nowmer's sales with those of her subordinates.

2. Select *Non-Leaf Data Visible* as the value of the Members With Data property, and press Enter.

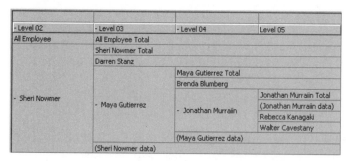

The Data pane refreshes to include new members for the managers' data. The new member names are in parentheses. Since the total rows for the managers clearly include the word "Total," you might want to simply display the employee name for the new data fields. You can change the template for how the new member name is generated.

3. Clear the Data Member Caption Template property, and press Enter. (You could also leave the property with only an asterisk.)

- Level 02	- Level 03	- Level 04	Level 05
All Employee	All Employee Total		
	Sheri Nowmer Total		
	Darren Stanz		
		Maya Gutierrez Total	
		Brenda Blumberg	
- Sheri Nowmer			Jonathan Murraiin Total
	- Maya Gutierrez		Jonathan Murraiin
		- Jonathan Murraiin	Rebecca Kanagaki
			Walter Cavestany
		Maya Gutierrez	
	Sheri Nowmer		

The managers' data members now look very similar to those of the other members.

4. Click the Process Cube button, click Yes to save the cube, No to design storage, and OK to fully process the cube. Then close the Process log window, and expand all the levels of the Employee dimension.

You can now easily compare Sheri Nowmer's individual sales with those of her entire group and with those of other managers and employees.

Manage levels within a parent-child dimension

The hierarchy for a parent-child dimension is derived from a single dimension table. As the person building the OLAP dimension, however, you still have a great deal of control over how to display the levels for the dimension. For example, in the Employee dimension, there's only one manager at the top level of the hierarchy. In consequence, the values for All Employee and Sheri Nowmer are identical. There's no need to have an All level in this dimension.

1. In the cube tree, select the Employee dimension; on the Advanced tab of the Properties window, change the value of the All Level property to *No*; and press Enter.

- Level 01	- Level 02	- Level 03	Level 04
	Sheri Nowmer Total		
	Darren Stanz		
		Maya Gutierrez Total	
		Brenda Blumberg	
- Sheri Nowmer			Jonathan Murraiin Total
	- Maya Gutierrez		Jonathan Murraiin
		- Jonathan Murraiin	Rebecca Kanagaki
			Walter Cavestany
		Maya Gutierrez	
	Sheri Nowmer		

The preview window refreshes to show a hierarchy with no All level. You can remove the All level from any dimension, not just a parent-child dimension. The Level names now begin with Level 01, and there is no redundant data. Perhaps you don't want to show Level 01, Level 02, and so forth as the names of the levels. You can assign specific names to as many levels of a parent-child dimension as you like.

2. Expand the Employee dimension, and select the Employee Id level. On the Advanced tab of the Properties window, select the Level Naming Template property and click the ellipsis button.

3. Click in the box to the right of the asterisk (*), and type **CEO**. Do not press Enter. As soon as you begin typing, the asterisk changes to a 1, and a new row, with asterisk, appears.

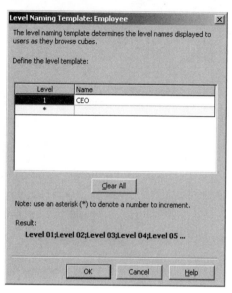

4. Click in the box in the second row, and type **Manager**. (You might need to click the box more than once before you can start typing.) In the box of the third row, type **Supervisor**, and in the box of the fourth row, type **Individual Contributor**.

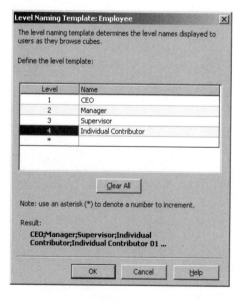

As you enter values into the level naming template grid, the result is displayed at the bottom of the grid. Any levels that are automatically created below the lowest level specified in the template are given sequentially incremented numbers.

Rather than use the Level Naming Template dialog box, you could simply type a string of labels separated by semicolons as the value of the Level Naming Template property.

5. Click OK to accept the template. In the preview pane, double click the CEO, Manager, and Supervisor headings so that you can again see the entire hierarchy.

- CEO	- Manager	- Supervisor	Individual Contributor
	Sheri Nowmer Total		
	Darren Stanz		
		Maya Gutierrez Total	
		Brenda Blumberg	
- Sheri Nowmer	- Maya Gutierrez		Jonathan Murraiin Total
		- Jonathan Murraiin	Jonathan Murraiin
			Rebecca Kanagaki
			Walter Cavestany
		Maya Gutierrez	
	Sheri Nowmer		

Darren Stanz and Brenda Blumberg are actually individual contributors. They simply report directly to the CEO and Manager, respectively. Ideally, you would like these employees to appear in the Individual Contributor column. For Darren, that would require skipping two levels, and for Brenda, it would require skipping one level. You skip levels in a parent-child hierarchy, provided that the dimension table contains a column indicating how many levels to skip.

6. Click the Schema tab to display the source tables for the cube. Right-click the heading of the Employee table, and click Browse Data. The Employee table contains a Skipped_Levels column containing 2 for Darren Stanz, 1 for Brenda Blumberg, and 0 for all other employees.

	Employee_ID	Employee_Name	Manager_ID	Skipped_Levels
1	1	Sheri Nowmer	1	0
2	2	Darren Stanz	1	2
3	3	Maya Gutierrez	1	0
4	4	Brenda Blumberg	3	1
5	5	Jonathan Murraiin	3	0
6	6	Rebecca Kanagaki	5	0
7	7	Walter Cavestany	5	0

Browse Data: "Employee" (First 1000 rows)

7. Close the Browse window, select the Skipped Levels Column property of the Employee Id level, and click the ellipsis button. Select the Skipped_Levels column, and click OK. This property has no effect until you process the cube.

8. Click the Process Cube button, click Yes to save the cube, No to design storage, and OK to fully process the cube. Then close the Process log window, click the Data tab, and expand all the levels of the Employee dimension.

- CEO	- Manager	- Supervisor	Individual Contributor
	Sheri Nowmer Total		
		Maya Gutierrez Total	
			Jonathan Murraiin Total
		- Jonathan Murraiin	Jonathan Murraiin
- Sheri Nowmer	- Maya Gutierrez		Rebecca Kanagaki
			Walter Cavestany
			Brenda Blumberg
		Maya Gutierrez	
			Darren Stanz
	Sheri Nowmer		

Darren and Brenda now appear on the Individual Contributor level, even though they report directly to higher level managers. Within a parent-child dimension, skipping levels creates a ragged hierarchy. In the "Create a ragged hierarchy" section earlier in this chapter, you learned how to create such a hierarchy within a standard dimension. In both a standard and a parent-child dimension, the term *ragged* means that some members have unusual relationships with their parents. In a ragged standard dimension, a parent is hidden and extra space is *removed*. In a ragged parent-child dimension, extra space is *added* in the place of one or more parents. In both cases, Analysis Services gives you a great deal of flexibility in creating dimensions that appropriately describe your business.

Chapter Summary

To	Do this
Create a new shared dimension by using the Dimension Editor	In the console tree, expand the desired database and the Library folder. Right-click the Shared Dimensions folder, point to New Dimension, and click Editor.
Add a new bottom level to a dimension	In the schema pane of the Dimension Editor, double-click the column for the dimension in the appropriate source table. Or drag the column name to the dimension name in the dimension tree.
Add a new level above an existing level	Drag the column name for the level onto the existing level.
Browse the rows in a dimension source table	Right-click the caption bar of a source table, and click Browse Data.
Browse the members of a dimension	Click the Data tab to activate the Preview pane.
Remove the All Level from a dimension	Select the dimension in the dimension tree, and activate the Advanced tab of the Properties pane. Change the All Level property value to *No*.

(continued)

(continued)

To	Do this
Use a different source column for a member key than for the member name	Change the Member Key Column property on the Basic tab of the Properties pane.
Sort the members of a level by the Member Key Column rather than by the Member Name Column	In the dimension tree, select the level. On the Advanced tab of the Properties pane, change the Order By property value to *Key*.
Process a dimension from within the Dimension Editor	Click the Process Dimension button on the toolbar.
Add multiple (snowflake) tables for a dimension	Add the first table when you create the dimension. Then click the Insert Table toolbar button to add additional tables.
Create a member name that combines values from two columns in the source table	Select the level, and activate the Advanced tab of the Properties pane. Enter a valid SQL expression in the Member Name Column property box.
Add a member property to a level	Expand the level in the dimension tree to see the Member Properties folder. Drag a column from a source table onto the Member Properties folder.
Create two hierarchies in the same dimension	Select the Create A Hierarchy For A Dimension check box at the end of the Dimension Wizard. Or give each dimension a name that consists of the shared dimension name followed by a period followed by the hierarchy name.
Process all the shared dimensions of a database at one time	In Analysis Manager, right-click the Shared Dimension folder in the console tree and click Process All Dimensions.
Create a cube by using the Cube Editor	In Analysis Manager, right-click the Cubes folder, point to New Cube, and click Editor. Choose a fact table, add measures and dimensions, and then name and save the cube.
Add or delete a measure	Start the Cube Editor, right-click a measure, and click New Measure or Delete.
Edit measure properties	Start the Cube Editor, click a measure in the cube tree, and edit measure properties on the Basic and Advanced tabs of the Properties pane.

(continued)

(continued)

To	Do this
Create a derived measure	Start the Cube Editor, right-click the Measures folder in the cube tree, and click New Measure. On the Basic tab of the Properties pane, under Source Column, enter an expression for the derived measure.
Edit dimension properties	Start the Cube Editor, right-click a dimension or dimension level in the cube tree, and edit the dimension properties in the Properties pane.
Create a parent-child dimension	Use the Dimension Wizard, and select the parent-child option.
Allow data for non-leaf members of a parent-child dimension	In the Dimension Editor, select the parent-child dimension. On the Advanced tab, change the value of the Members With Data property to *Non-Leaf Data Visible*.
Create a ragged standard dimension	In the Dimension Editor, select a standard dimension and click the level that you want to optionally hide. On the Advanced tab, change the value of the Hide Member If property to *Only Child With Parent's Name*.
Create a ragged parent-child dimension	In the Dimension Editor, select the one level of the parent-child dimension and click the Advanced tab. Assign the Skipped Levels Column property to a column in the dimension table that includes the number of levels to skip for each member.

Chapter 4

Advanced Dimensions and Cubes

Chapter Objectives   Estimated time: 2.5 hours

In this chapter, you'll learn how to

- Create custom member and rollup formulas.

- Manage very large, flat dimensions.

- Add drillthrough capabilities to a cube.

- Disable levels of a shared dimension.

- Prepare dimensions and cubes to allow dynamic changes.

- Create virtual cubes to combine or simplify cubes.

My brother works as a draftsman for an architectural firm. He told me recently that much of the challenge of modern home architecture comes from building unique, creative houses using nothing but prefabricated parts. I compared that to when one semiretired carpenter single-handedly framed our entire house 20 years ago. The carpenter didn't use any prefabricated trusses or walls. We would often see him pull out a piece of a shingle and a pencil to calculate cuts he needed to make to get a roof section to fit properly.

The Sales cubes in Chapters 2 and 3 are based on standard, simple star schema warehouse tables. They were like building a "typical" house by using "typical" prefabricated parts. The cubes you'll build in this chapter are more complex and require more special handling. The cubes relate to realistic situations, however, so you'll be glad to know that Microsoft SQL Server 2000 Analysis Services provides the custom tools you need to create cubes like these.

Start the lesson

1. In the Analysis Manager console tree, right-click the Server and click Restore Database.

2. Navigate to the Analysis folder installed from the CD that came with this book, select Chapter 4.cab, and click Open. Click Restore, and then close the Restore Database Progress dialog box.

3. If you did not install the files into the default location, expand the Chapter 4 database and the Data Sources folder. Right-click the Market data source, and click Edit. Click the ellipses (...) button next to the database name, navigate to the folder containing the sample files from this book, select Chapter4.mdb, and then click OK.

Creating a Finance Cube

A finance department often deals in terms of financial reporting—profit and loss statements, balance sheets, and so forth. Creating an OLAP cube for use in financial analysis is tricky because of the way account values aggregate: sometimes accounts sum to a parent, sometimes an account is subtracted from its parent, and sometimes an account does not aggregate into the parent value at all. Consider, for example, a profit and loss report.

- Level 01	- Level 02	- Level 03	Level 04	MeasuresLevel
				Amount
		Net Profit Total		11,074
		Gross Profit Total		46046.61
	- Gross Profit	Revenue		$76,741.28
		Cost of Goods		30,695
- Net Profit		Expenses Total		34,972
		Administrative		6,562
	- Expenses		Labor Total	28,410
		- Labor	Head Count	54
			Salary	18,900
			Benefits	9,510

The components of Net Profit are Gross Profit and Expenses. Both are positive numbers. But, to calculate Net Profit Total, you must subtract the Expenses Total value from the Gross Profit Total value. Likewise, to calculate Gross Profit Total, you must subtract the Cost Of Goods value from the Revenue value. Often, a Labor section of the report contains a line for Head Count, but the values from the Head Count line are for information only; they should not be added into the Labor Total value. In this section, you'll learn how to create a simple finance cube.

Create an initial finance cube

The process for creating the initial finance cube is similar to the process you used to create a Sales cube in earlier chapters; it doesn't require much elaboration.

1. In the Chapter 4 database, right-click the Cubes folder, point to New Cube, and click Wizard.

2. Click Next to skip the welcome screen. Select FinanceFact as the fact table, and click the Browse Data button.

The FinanceFact table has two columns containing dimension keys and one column containing measure values. The Month_ID column is suitable for use with the Time dimensions you created in "Working with Time Dimensions" in Chapter 3, "Dimension and Cube Editors." The Account_ID column will require a new dimension. You can create the Account dimension as a private dimension, since no other cubes in the database will need to use it. The values in the Amount column are all positive values, regardless of whether they will be added or subtracted within the report.

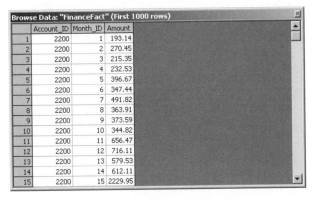

3. Close the Browse Data window, and click Next. Double-click Amount as the measure column, and click Next.

4. Double-click the Time.Calendar shared dimension to include it in the new cube. Then click the New Dimension button.

5. Select parent-child as the dimension type, and click Next. Select Account as the dimension table, and click Next. Select Account_ID as the member key, Parent_ID as the parent key, and Account as the member name. Then click Next twice.

6. Type **Account** as the name of the dimension, clear the check box that creates a shared dimension, and click Finish to close the Dimension Wizard.

7. Back in the Cube Wizard, click Next. Click Yes when warned about counting fact table rows, type **Finance** as the name of the cube, and click Finish.

8. Click the Process Cube button, decline the offer to design storage, and accept the default processing method. Close the Process log window, click the Data tab, and expand all the levels of the Account dimension.

- Level 02	- Level 03	- Level 04	Level 05	MeasuresLevel Amount
All Account	All Account Total			65,720.98
	Net Profit Total			65,720.98
		Expenses Total		35,026.31
		Administrative		6,562.31
	- Expenses		Labor Total	28,464.00
- Net Profit			Benefits	9,510.00
		- Labor	Head Count	54.00
			Salary	18,900.00
		Gross Profit Total		30,694.67
	- Gross Profit	Cost of Goods		30,694.67
		Revenue		

The initial cube layout looks roughly like a profit and loss report, but the numbers in the Amount column are all wrong—they're added when they should be subtracted—and the order of the accounts seems a little nonstandard.

Refine the formatting of an Account dimension

For a moment, ignore the values in the Amount column and look only at the Account member labels. The All Account member is redundant with the Net Profit member, and Gross Profit should appear before Expenses in the report. You can refine the formatting of the dimension while reviewing skills you learned in Chapter 3.

1. In the Dimensions folder, select the Account dimension, and click the Advanced tab of the Properties pane. Change the All Level property to *No*.

2. Select the Type property, and choose *Accounts* from the drop-down list.

The dimension type has no effect on the Analysis server, but a client application might be able to take advantage of the information.

Typically, an account dimension is based on codes that provide the appropriate order for the dimension. Provided that the Member Key Column property for the Account dimension gives the proper order for the dimension members—which it does in this warehouse—you can sort by key to put the accounts in the proper order.

3. Expand the Account dimension, and select the Account Id level. Change its Order By property to *Key*, and press Enter.

- Level 01	- Level 02	- Level 03	Level 04	MeasuresLevel
				Amount
	Net Profit Total			211.20
	- Gross Profit	Gross Profit Total		70.40
		Revenue		35.20
		Cost of Goods		35.20
- Net Profit		Expenses Total		140.80
		Administrative		35.20
	- Expenses		Labor Total	105.60
		- Labor	Head Count	35.20
			Salary	35.20
			Benefits	35.20

Note   If neither the Member Key Column nor the Member Name Column of a dimension provides the correct sort order, you can use a third column to control the sort order. Simply add that column as a member property to the level you want to sort. Member properties for a level automatically appear in the Order By property's drop-down list.

The dimension members are now in the proper order. Even with sample data displayed, you can see that the values are not summarized properly because Expenses are added to Gross Profit rather than subtracted.

Use custom rollup operators

To properly aggregate the values along the Account dimension, each member of the dimension needs its own aggregation rule. The rule for Benefits should be "add me to my parent." The rule for Expenses Total should be "subtract me from my parent." The rule for Head Count should be "don't aggregate me at all." With a parent-child dimension, you can include a column in the dimension table that specifies a unique rule for each member.

The aggregation rule consists of a single-character code. The codes are simply the arithmetic operators: plus (+) for addition, minus (-) for subtraction, asterisk (*) for multiplication, and slash (/) for division. In addition, a tilde (~) is used to prevent the member from aggregating at all. These codes are called *unary operators* because each value gets its own operator.

The word unary *is related to the word* unit *and means "one."*

1. Click the Schema tab to see the dimension tables. Then right-click the heading of the Account table, and click Browse Data.

	Account_ID	Account	Parent_ID	Operator	
1	1000	Net Profit	1000	~	
2	2000	Gross Profit	1000	+	
3	2100	Revenue	2000	+	LookupCube("Sales","([Sales Dollars
4	2200	Cost of Goods	2000	-	
5	3000	Expenses	1000	-	
6	3100	Administrative	3000	+	
7	3200	Labor	3000	+	
8	3210	Head Count	3200	~	
9	3220	Salary	3200	+	
10	3230	Benefits	3200	+	

Browse Data: "Account" (First 1000 rows)

The Account table already contains a column named Operator that includes an appropriate unary code for each account.

2. Close the Browse Data window.

3. In the cube tree, select the Account Id level, and scroll to the bottom of the Advanced tab of the Properties pane. Select the Unary Operators property, and click the ellipsis button.

4. Select the Enable Unary Operators check box, click the Use An Existing Column option, select Operator from the Existing Column drop-down list, and click OK.

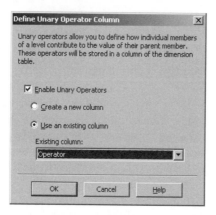

Before you can see the effect of the unary operators, you must process the cube.

5. Click the Process Cube button, accept the offer to save the cube, decline the offer to design storage, accept the default processing method, and close the Process log window. Click the Data tab to browse the cube.

- Level 01	- Level 02	- Level 03	Level 04	MeasuresLevel
				Amount
	Net Profit Total			-65,666.98
		Gross Profit Total		-30,694.67
	- Gross Profit	Revenue		
		Cost of Goods		30,694.67
- Net Profit		Expenses Total		34,972.31
		Administrative		6,562.31
	- Expenses		Labor Total	28,410.00
		- Labor	Head Count	54.00
			Salary	18,900.00
			Benefits	9,510.00

The operators appear to work correctly. The Head Count value is not included in Labor Total, and the Cost Of Goods and Expenses Total values are appropriately subtracted from the parent total. The only problem is that the Revenue line is empty, so the net profit picture appears bleaker than is probably true.

Use a custom member formula

The FinanceFact table does not include Revenue values. That's because Revenue values already exist in the Sales cube. You can't use a rollup operator to retrieve the Revenue value because a rollup operator tells how to aggregate the value of a member up to its parent but doesn't tell how to get a value for the member if it's not in the fact table.

A single member of a dimension (in this case, Revenue) needs special handling. All the other leaf-level members have values in the fact table. As with a rollup operator, however, you need a special rule for obtaining the value for just one member. Again, as with a rollup operator, the solution is to store the rule in the dimension table. This time, the rule must be stored as a multidimensional expressions (MDX) expression. The expression must retrieve a different Revenue value for each member of the Time.Calendar dimension. In Chapter 6, "MDX Values," you'll learn how to make an MDX expression vary with the current member of a dimension. For now, the formula is already stored in the Account dimension table, and you can learn how to apply the rule within a cube.

1. Click the Schema tab to display the dimension tables. Right-click the
   Account table, and click Browse Data.

Account_ID	Account	Parent_ID	Operator	
1	1000	Net Profit	1000	~
2	2000	Gross Profit	1000	+
3	2100	Revenue	2000	+	LookupCube("Sales","([Sales Dollars
4	2200	Cost of Goods	2000	-
5	3000	Expenses	1000	-
6	3100	Administrative	3000	+
7	3200	Labor	3000	+
8	3210	Head Count	3200	~
9	3220	Salary	3200	+
10	3230	Benefits	3200	+

Browse Data: "Account" (First 1000 rows)

The rightmost column is named Formula, even though you can't see
the name in the window. For the Revenue member, the Formula column
contains an MDX expression for looking up the value from another cube.
The Revenue member is the only one that has a custom member formula.
When the Formula column is blank, the cube will retrieve values from
the fact table.

In the sidebar "Using CurrentMember in a LookupCube Function" in Chapter 6, you'll learn how to create the LookupCube formula used for the Revenue member.

2. Close the Browse Data window.

3. In the cube tree, select the Account Id level. On the Advanced tab of the
   Properties pane, select the Custom Members property and click the
   ellipsis button.

4. Select the Enable Custom Members check box, click the Use An Existing
   Column option, and select Formula from the Existing Column drop-
   down list. Then click OK.

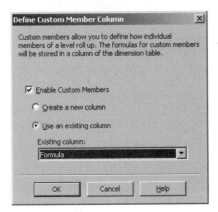

Before seeing the effect of the custom member formula, you must
process the cube.

5. Click the Process Cube button, accept the offer to save the cube and
   continue, close the Process log window, decline the offer to design
   storage, click the Full Process option, click OK, and close the Process
   log window.

6. Click the Data tab to browse the cube, and expand all the levels of the Account dimension.

- Level 01	- Level 02	- Level 03	Level 04	MeasuresLevel Amount
	Net Profit Total			11,074.30
		Gross Profit Total		46046.61
	- Gross Profit	Revenue		$76,741.28
		Cost of Goods		30,694.67
- Net Profit		Expenses Total		34,972.31
		Administrative		6,562.31
	- Expenses		Labor Total	28,410.00
		- Labor	Head Count	54.00
			Salary	18,900.00
			Benefits	9,510.00

The Revenue value is in place, and all the financial values calculate correctly. A financial style cube requires sophisticated rules, and a parent-child dimension allows you to create and apply those rules.

Creating an Internet Tracking Cube

Sometimes you might have information in a table that doesn't look like a standard star schema, with separate fact and dimension tables. For example, suppose that your company has a Web site and maintains a log of people who visit the site. In such a situation, the log file might contain nothing more than a Visitor ID and a date—certainly no discernible measure column. You need to be able to create a cube from a "fact" table that doesn't have a measure.

Also, the Analysis server has a limitation that there can be no more than approximately 64,000 children for any one parent in a hierarchy. A log of visitors could easily exceed that number of different visitors many times over, with no information available for building a hierarchy.

Create a cube from a measureless fact table

The Chapter4.mdb sample database contains a Visits table with only two columns: Visitor_ID and Day. Although the table is relatively small, it can give you an idea of how to deal with a large, flat fact table with no apparent measures.

1. From within the Cube Editor, select <New> from the Cube drop-down list on the toolbar to create a new cube. Select Visits as the fact table, and click OK. Click Yes when cautioned about counting the fact table rows.

2. Change the name of the new cube to **Visits**.

3. Drag the Visitor_ID column onto the Dimensions folder. Expand the Visitor Id dimension to show the Visitor Id level, and rename both the dimension and the level to **Visitor**.

So far, nothing is particularly unusual about this cube. You now need to create a measure. The only option for a measure when a fact table doesn't have a suitable measure column is to create a Count measure and count the entries. For a Visits cube, counting the visits, or the "hits," is an appropriate analytical task.

4. Drag the Visitor_ID column onto the Measures folder. Change the name of the new measure to **Total Visits**, and change the Aggregate Function property to *Count*.

5. Click the Process Cube button, accept the offer to save the cube, decline the offer to design storage, accept the default processing method, and close the Process log window. Then click the Data tab to browse the new cube.

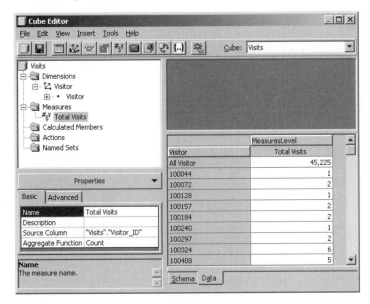

The number 45,225 corresponds to the number of rows in the Visits fact table. For each visitor, you can see the number of times that person visited the site. You cannot, however, see the specific days for the visits.

Enable drillthrough for a cube

Drillthrough is a feature that allows you to see the individual rows from the fact table that went into a specific value in the cube.

1. On the Tools menu, click Drillthrough Options.

2. In the Cube Drillthrough Options dialog box, select the Enable Drillthrough check box, click the Select All button, and click OK. Click OK when warned that the cube must be saved.

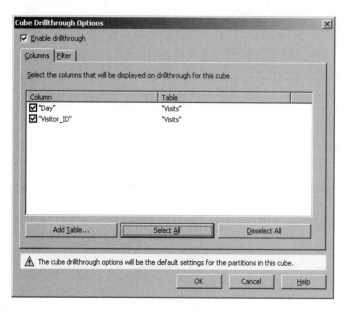

3. Click the Process Cube button, accept the offer to save the cube, decline the offer to design storage, click the Full Process processing option, click OK, and then close the Process log window.

4. Double-click the Visitor Id cell for Visitor 100324, the one with six visits.

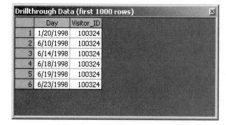

5. Close the Drillthrough Data window.

Drillthrough is a useful feature, but it might not go as far as you might like. If transaction tables in a database provided the data for the warehouse fact table, you might like to drill through to see the values from the original source tables. Enabling drillthrough for a cube does not provide access to original source data— only to the fact table. Even though drillthrough goes only to the fact table, it can be extremely useful in many situations. And it's very easy to implement.

Handle a very large, flat dimension

In "How the Analysis Server Processes a Dimension" in Chapter 9, "Processing Optimization," you'll learn why a parent can have only 64,000 children.

If the Visits table contained more than 64,000 unique Visitor_ID values, processing the dimension would have failed. That's because a parent in a hierarchy can have only 64,000 children. If a dimension is large and flat, it can easily exceed

64,000 members—with no suitable information available for grouping the members. A large log of visitors could easily have millions of different members in a dimension. Even though the Visits table has only a few thousand members, you can learn the tools for handling very large, flat dimensions.

1. Click the Schema tab to display the Visits table. Drag the Visitor_ID column onto the Visitor level of the Visitor dimension.

2. Change the name of the new level to **Visitor Group**.

3. With the Visitor Group level selected, on the Advanced tab of the Properties pane, change the Grouping property to *Automatic* and press Enter.

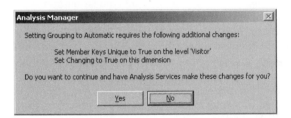

A message box warns you of additional changes this action will cause. The Member Keys Unique property for a level was discussed in Chapter 3.

4. Click Yes to accept the proposed changes.
   The new groups are not added to the dimension until you process the cube.

5. Click the Process Cube button, accept the offer to save the cube, decline the offer to design storage, accept the default processing method, and close the Process log window. Then click the Data tab to browse the cube.

6. If both the Visitor Group and the Visitor levels are visible, double-click the Visitor Group level heading to collapse it. You can see how the Visitor Group level automatically groups visitors.

+ Visitor Group	Total Visits
All Visitor	45,225
+ 100044 - 106339	336
+ 106361 - 111645	345
+ 111664 - 115828	361
+ 115843 - 119380	347
+ 119394 - 122883	288
+ 122895 - 125860	350
+ 125871 - 128340	325
+ 128350 - 130795	343
+ 130815 - 132981	307

7. Expand the first group of visitors. Each group contains individual visitors. Even if the groupings are not meaningful, they help manage an otherwise unwieldy list.

| - Visitor Group | Visitor | MeasuresLevel |
		Total Visits
All Visitor	All Visitor Total	45,225
- 100044 - 106339	100044 - 106339 Total	336
	100044	1
	100072	2
	100128	1
	100157	2
	100184	2
	100240	1
	100297	2
	100324	6
	100408	5

Note You have no direct control over the number of groups created by automatic grouping. Automatic grouping creates approximately the same number of groups as there are members in each group. It does that by using the square root of the number of members. (In the Visits table, there are 17,389 unique visitors. The square root of 17,389 is approximately 132, and there are 132 groups in the Visitor Group level.) This strategy enables grouping to automatically handle dimensions with over 4 billion members (64,000 groups with 64,000 members each). If you want to control the groups, create an expression for the Member Key Column and Member Name Column properties, as explained in Chapter 3. For example, the expression *Left("Visits"."Visitor_ID",3)* would group the visitors by the first three digits.

Link days to a Time dimension

Comparing values between cubes is explained in the section "Combine measures from multiple cubes," later in this chapter.

The Visits table contains a Day column. This is a Date/Time column that contains the actual date of the visit. A Date/Time column can be used to support a Date hierarchy. If you create a new, private dimension based on the Day field, you will not be able to compare the values in the Visits cube with those of other cubes in the database, such as the Sales cube. Whenever possible, you should use a shared dimension—particularly for the Time dimension—so that you can compare values between cubes. The Time.Calendar dimension, however, includes only Month, Quarter, and Year levels, while the Visits table contains only daily date values. By using an intermediate table, you can still use the shared dimension in conjunction with daily data.

1. Click the Schema tab to show the source table.

2. Click the Insert Dimension toolbar button. Double-click Time.Calendar, and click OK. Click OK when warned that an automatic join could not be found.

   The lowest level of the Time.Calendar dimension is Calendar Month, and its key is Month_ID. The Visits table has Day values. The TimeDay table in the Chapter4.mdb database contains Day values and their corresponding Month_ID values. This table can bridge the gap between the fact table and the dimension table, even though it's not part of the dimension.

3. Click the Insert Table toolbar button, double-click the TimeDay table, and click Close.

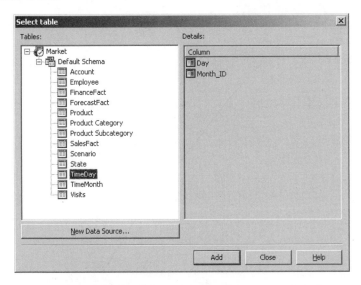

Adding the table should automatically create a join between the Day field of the Visits table and the Day field of the TimeDay table. You must manually create the join between the TimeDay table and the TimeMonth table.

4. Drag the Month_ID column from the TimeDay table onto the Month_ID column of the TimeMonth table.

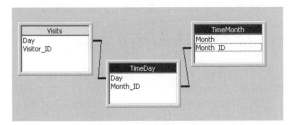

5. Click the Process Cube button, accept the offer to save the cube, decline the offer to design storage, accept the default processing method, and close the Process log window. Click the Data tab to browse the data.

6. Drag the Time.Calendar dimension down to the row axis replacing the Visitor dimension. Expand the 1998 and Qtr1 members. For the Visitor dimension, select the first Visitor Group.

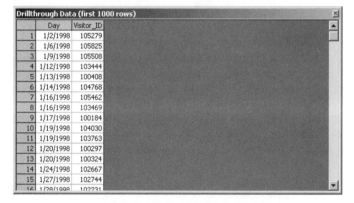

The dimension does not show daily values—it goes down to only the Calendar Month level. You can, however, see the specific days that go into a cell by using the drillthrough capability you added earlier.

7. Double-click the January cell—the one with the value *32*. After browsing the values, close the Drillthrough Data window.

Drillthrough Data (first 1000 rows)		
	Day	Visitor_ID
1	1/2/1998	105279
2	1/6/1998	105825
3	1/9/1998	105508
4	1/12/1998	103444
5	1/13/1998	100408
6	1/14/1998	104768
7	1/16/1998	105462
8	1/16/1998	103469
9	1/17/1998	100184
10	1/19/1998	104030
11	1/19/1998	103763
12	1/20/1998	100297
13	1/20/1998	100324
14	1/24/1998	102667
15	1/27/1998	102744
16	1/28/1998	102231

Sometimes you need to create a cube from a fact table that has more detail than a shared dimension you want to use. If you can create an intermediate table that allows the Analysis server to find the relationship between the fact table and the dimension, you can still use the shared dimension. In the section "Use only the top levels of a shared dimension," later in this chapter, you'll learn how to use a shared dimension when the fact table is more summarized than the lowest level of a shared dimension.

Calculate distinct counts for a dimension

The Total Visits measure is useful for determining how many visits your site received, but it doesn't tell you how many *different* visitors came. Perhaps three people accounted for 90 percent of the visits. To determine how many different visitors came to the site, you need to use the *Distinct Count* aggregation function. The *Distinct Count* function is extremely useful, but it has some important restrictions:

- Unlike the *Count* aggregation function, the fact table Source Column for the measure is critical; it determines what you're counting.

- Only one measure in a cube can use the *Distinct Count* function.

- You cannot use *Distinct Count* for a measure if any dimensions in the cube use custom rollup operators or formulas.

Using a *Distinct Count* aggregation function has restrictions because it's an extremely powerful analytical tool. Fortunately, the server does the difficult work behind the scenes. Adding a measure that uses *Distinct Count* to a cube is easy to do:

1. In the Cube Editor, click the Schema tab to display the source tables for the Visitors cube.

2. Drag the Visitor_ID column from the Visits table onto the Measures folder.
    Be sure to drag the correct column. Unlike the *Count* function, the column you use with a *Distinct Count* function completely determines the behavior of the measure.

3. Change the name of the new measure to **Unique Visitors**, and change the Aggregate Function property on the Basic tab to *Distinct Count*.

4. Click the Process Cube button, accept the offer to save the cube, decline the offer to design storage, accept the default processing method, and close the Process log window. Then click the Data tab to browse the cube.

5. Collapse the Calendar Quarter level in the grid.

See "Understand Analysis server aggregations" in Chapter 8 for performance implications of a measure using a Distinct Count function.

Custom rollup operators are explained in "Use custom rollup operators," earlier in this chapter.

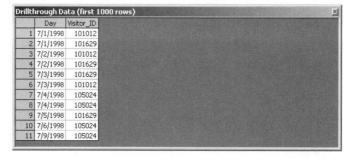

		MeasuresLevel	
- Calendar Year	+ Calendar Quarter	Total Visits	Unique Visitors
All Time	All Time Total	336	132
	1997 Total		
	+ Qtr1		
- 1997	+ Qtr2		
	+ Qtr3		
	+ Qtr4		
	1998 Total	336	132
	+ Qtr1	136	58
- 1998	+ Qtr2	189	102
	+ Qtr3	11	3
	+ Qtr4		

In 1998, Qtr2 had almost 40 percent more visits than Qtr1, but there were nearly twice as many unique visitors. Depending on whether you want to see new visitors or old visitors returning frequently, that trend could be either good or bad news. The important thing is that the Unique Visitors measure highlights important information. Qtr3 shows only a few visits, and they're predominantly by repeat visitors. You can drill through to see the detail values for Qtr3.

6. Double-click one of the Qtr3 values, and take a look at the drillthrough values. Then close the Drillthrough Data window.

Drillthrough Data (first 1000 rows)

	Day	Visitor_ID
1	7/1/1998	101012
2	7/1/1998	101629
3	7/2/1998	101012
4	7/2/1998	101629
5	7/3/1998	101629
6	7/3/1998	101012
7	7/4/1998	105024
8	7/4/1998	105024
9	7/5/1998	101629
10	7/6/1998	105024
11	7/9/1998	105024

When there are relatively few rows, drilling through to the fact table detail rows can help you see how the same visitor can be responsible for several different visits. The *Distinct Count* aggregation function highlights those patterns.

Creating a Forecast Cube

One important analytical activity is planning. Planning is an opportunity to anticipate the future and also to look back and see the truth of the parable that "life is what happens while you were making other plans." Planning has interesting challenges because it's an interactive process. Rather than simply looking at historical values generated by business systems, humans typically enter planning values. To effectively use the planning capabilities of Analysis Services, you need a client application that supports interactivity. In this section, you'll learn how to create and administer a forecast sales cube. The forecast sales cube will allow you to create a high-level forecast—at the quarter level, for product categories. You'll be able to create multiple scenarios of forecasts and even dynamically add new scenarios as needed. In the process, you'll get a taste of how a client application could make interactive changes to the cube, and you'll understand what to look for when acquiring or creating a client application to support planning activities.

Create a Scenario dimension

Typically, creating a forecast requires more than one iteration. You create a first-pass forecast and have meetings to discuss the ramifications. Then you create a second-pass forecast and have meetings to discuss that one. Often, it's important to keep track of each interim stage of the process. A Scenario dimension allows you to give a name to each pass of the forecast. You often need to add additional Scenario dimensions during the course of the planning cycle. Analysis Services allows you to create a dimension that you can modify dynamically—that is, you can write-enable a dimension—but only if it is a parent-child dimension. Before creating the sales forecast cube, first create a shared parent-child Scenario dimension.

1. Close the Cube Editor. Right-click the Chapter 4 database Shared Dimensions folder, point to New Dimension, and click Wizard. (You cannot create a parent-child dimension without using the Dimension Wizard.)

2. Click the parent-child option, and click Next. Then select the Scenario table, and click the Browse Data button.

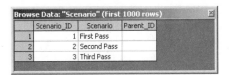

3. Close the Browse Data window, and click Next.

4. Select Scenario_ID as the member key, Parent_ID as the parent key, and Scenario as the member name. Then click Next twice.

5. Type **Scenario** as the name of the dimension, and click Finish. Click the Data tab, and expand the All Scenario member to browse the dimension.
    In a Scenario dimension, you do not want an All level. Summing the values of the scenarios is never appropriate.

6. In the Dimension Editor's dimension tree, select the Scenario dimension, and on the Advanced Tab of the Properties pane, change the All Level property to *No*.

7. Change the Write-Enabled property to *True*.

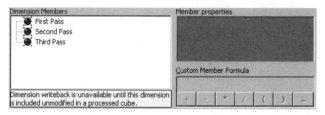

Level naming templates are discussed in "Manage levels within a parent-child dimension" in Chapter 3.

A parent-child dimension uses a level naming template to name dimension levels. The default template consists of the word "Level" followed by the level number. Even though the Scenario dimension is a parent-child dimension, it will have only one level, and you don't want the label *Level 01* appearing above the scenario names. Change the template to a more appropriate word.

8. In the dimension tree, select the Scenario Id level, and change the Level Naming Template property to **Scenario**.

9. Save the dimension, and close the Dimension Editor.

You now have a shared, single-level, write-enabled, parent-child Scenario dimension that you can use in creating a sales forecast cube.

Create a cube from an empty fact table

Logically, since all the values in the sales forecast cube will be hand-entered by you, the cube should not require a fact table. As you'll soon learn in "Enable write-back for a cube," that's because when you write values back to a cube, they're not stored in the fact table. Physically, however, you cannot create a cube without a fact table. If for no other reason, the columns of the fact table determine the potential dimensions and measures for the cube. The Chapter4.mdb sample database includes a fact table named ForecastFact. It has columns for three dimension keys: Category_ID, Quarter_ID, and Scenario_ID. It also has a column for a single measure: Sales_Units. The table is, however, completely empty. It does not, and never will, contain any rows. You must have a fact table to create a cube, but nobody said the fact table had to contain facts.

1. Right-click the Chapter 4 database Cubes folder, point to New Cube, and click Editor.

2. Select ForecastFact as the fact table, and click OK. Click Yes when cautioned about how long it will take to count the fact table rows. Click OK.

3. Right-click the heading of the ForecastFact table, and click Browse Data.

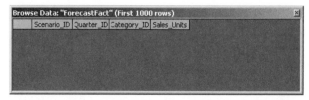

You can see the columns for the fact table, and confirm the fact that it is completely empty.

4. Close the window. Then change the name of the new dimension to **Sales Forecast**, and drag the Sales_Units column onto the Measures folder.

5. Right-click the Dimensions folder, and click Existing Dimensions. Double-click the Scenario dimension, and click OK.

6. If warned that an automatic join is not possible, click OK and drag the Scenario_ID column from the ForecastFact table onto the Scenario_ID column of the Scenario table.

    With one measure and one dimension, you should now have all you need to save and process the cube. If you were to try, however, you would see a message informing you that there are no rows in the fact table. Before processing a cube from a fact table with no rows, you must manually enter a nonzero value as the number of fact table rows. In other words, you must lie.

7. In the cube tree, select the cube, and on the Advanced tab of the Properties pane, type **1** as the value of the Fact Table Size property. (Any number greater than 0 will do.)

8. Click the Process Cube button, accept the offer to save the cube, decline the offer to design storage, accept the default processing method, and close the Process log window. Click the Data tab to browse the cube.

	MeasuresLevel
Scenario	Sales Units
First Pass	
Second Pass	
Third Pass	

Not surprisingly, the Sales Forecast cube is empty. The important points are that it exists and that it has placeholders where you can add forecast values.

Use only the top levels of a shared dimension

You'll forecast sales by product category and by quarter. Product categories are found in the Product dimension, but they're not at the lowest level of the dimension. Likewise, calendar quarters are found in the Time.Calendar dimension, but, again, they're not at the lowest level of the dimension. One possibility would be to create new, private dimensions just for this cube. You don't want to do that, however, because doing so would prevent you from comparing forecast values from the Sales Forecast cube with actual values from the Sales cube. Rather, you must figure out how to use only part of an existing shared dimension in the new cube.

1. Click the Schema tab to display the source tables. Right-click the Dimensions folder, and click Existing Dimensions. Double-click the

Product dimension, and click OK. Click OK when warned that no automatic join was found.

2. Drag the Category_ID column from the ForecastFact table onto the Category_ID column of the Product Category table. (You might want to rearrange the tables to make them easier to see.)

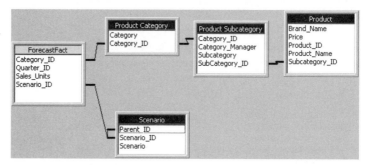

3. Expand the Product dimension, and select the Subcategory level. On the Advanced tab of the Properties pane, change the Disabled property to *Yes*. Disabling the Subcategory level automatically disables the Product Name level.

   The Disabled property is a property of a level, but it exists only within the Cube Editor. It wouldn't make sense to disable a level in the Dimension Editor because that would disable it for all cubes. Disabling a level does not merely hide the level from view; it completely removes that level and all levels below it from the dimension, as far as the current cube is concerned.

4. Right-click the Dimensions folder, and click Existing Dimensions. Double-click the Time.Calendar dimension, and click OK. Click OK when warned that no automatic join was found.

5. Drag the Quarter_ID column from the ForecastFact table onto the Month_ID column of the TimeMonth table.

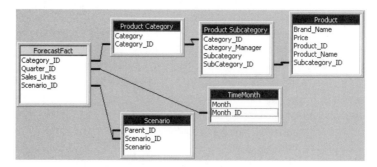

You can join the Quarter_ID of the fact table to the Month_ID of the TimeMonth table because Quarter_ID does refer to a month; it just refers to the first month in the quarter.

6. In the dimension tree, expand the Time.Calendar dimension and select the Calendar Month level. On the Advanced tab, change the Disabled property to *Yes*.

7. Click the Process Cube button, accept the offer to save the cube, decline the offer to design storage, select the Full Process processing method, and close the Process log window. Click the Data tab to browse the cube.

8. Drag the Product dimension to the Rows axis (exchanging places with Scenario). Drag the Time.Calendar dimension to the Columns axis (exchanging places with Measures). Expand the 1998 member. Scroll the grid until you can see the quarter columns.

	- Calendar Year	Calendar Quarter	
		- 1998	
Category	1998 Total	Qtr1	Qtr2
All Product			
Bread			
Dairy			
Meat			

9. Close the Cube Editor.

Shared dimensions can be, well, shared between multiple cubes. But cubes do not always have the same level of detail. The Disabled property of a dimension level allows you to customize a shared dimension to work with the cube at hand.

Enable write-back for a cube

In Analysis Services, you can write values only to the lowest level of a cube. In other words, you cannot change the value of an aggregation. If you could change the value of an aggregation, you would be able to make the cube internally inconsistent. Technically, Analysis Services writes incremental change values either to the client cache in the PivotTable service or to a special write-back table in a relational database. Analysis Services then dynamically combines the write-back values with any values from the fact table.

Note For application developers, Analysis Services includes a tool—the Update Cube MDX statement—that will allocate a given high-level input value to create the necessary lowest-level values. A client application can thus appear to write back at a high level. In reality, however, the values being written back to the cube are always at the lowest level of the cube.

To write values back to a cube, you must have a client application that includes write-back capabilities. None of the browsers included with Analysis Services or with Microsoft Office 2000 includes write-back capability. Included on the companion CD for this book is a Microsoft Excel 2000 workbook that includes macros that demonstrate how to write values back to the Sales Forecast cube of the Chapter 4 database.

Write values back to a cube temporarily

In addition to using Microsoft Excel 2000, you can use the Writeback workbook with Excel 97, provided that you run Excel on the computer on which Analysis Services is installed.

If clicking the Retrieve Values From Cube button causes an error message, process the entire Chapter 4 database and then click the Reset button in the Excel worksheet.

When performing a what-if analysis, you might want to write values back to a cube without making them permanent or visible to other users of the cube. Analysis Services allows you to write values back to the PivotTable services cache, which makes them temporary and private.

1. Start Excel. On the File menu, click Open, navigate to the folder containing the sample files for this book (the default is C:\Analysis), and then open the Writeback workbook. Agree to allow macros to run.

2. Click Retrieve Values From Cube.

The labels from the Sales Forecast cube of the Chapter 4 database appear. The Quarter values are at the detail level. The 1998 values are aggregations.

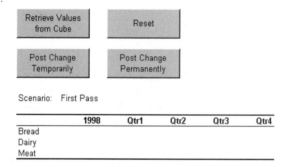

Scenario: First Pass

	1998	**Qtr1**	**Qtr2**	**Qtr3**	**Qtr4**
Bread					
Dairy					
Meat					

3. In the 1998 Bread cell (C13), type **2,000**. This is an aggregated value. In the Qtr1 Bread cell (D13), type **50,000**. This is a large enough number that you can easily watch its effect.

4. Click Post Change Temporarily.

This writes the current cell values back to the PivotTable service cache, which makes them appear as part of the cube until you reset the connection. No one else connected to the cube can see the changed values, and you will see the changed values only for the duration of the current connection.

5. Click Retrieve Values From Cube.

| Retrieve Values from Cube | Reset |
| Post Change Temporarily | Post Change Permanently |

Scenario: First Pass

	1998	Qtr1	Qtr2	Qtr3	Qtr4
Bread	50,000	50,000	0	0	0
Dairy	0	0	0	0	0
Meat	0	0	0	0	0

The Qtr1 Bread cell value remains as 50,000. The value you entered now appears to be in the cube. The 1998 Bread cell changes to 50,000. The value of 2,000 units you entered couldn't change the aggregated value in the cube. Rather, the new aggregation is calculated from the low level value you entered.

The changes disappear, however, when you close the connection. For example, closing the workbook and reopening it would close the connection.

6. Click Reset, which clears the data range and resets the connection to the server. Then click Retrieve Values From Cube.

   The cells are once again empty—as if you had never made any changes at all.

When a client application allows you to write back to a cube, that means you can write back to any cube, even a local cube. But, unless the cube is write-enabled, the write-back values are only stored within the PivotTable Service cache, which makes them invisible to any other users of the cube and makes them disappear when the current connection to the cube terminates.

Local cube files are explained in "Creating a Local Cube" in Chapter 5, "Office 2000 Analysis Components."

Write values back to a cube permanently

To write values back so that others can see them or so that they'll be retained for future use, the cube must be *write-enabled*. When you write-enable a cube, you specify the location of a relational table where the write-back values will be stored.

1. In Analysis Manager, expand the Cubes folder in the Chapter 4 database and right-click the Sales Forecast cube. When the Write-enable dialog box appears, accept the default data source and table name and click OK.

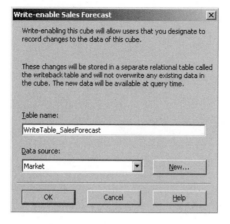

Note   You don't need to write the data back to the same data source as the one containing the fact table. For example, if the fact table for the cube is in a corporate data warehouse that you don't have permission to write to, you can create a Microsoft Access or Microsoft SQL Server database that you can use for the write-back table. The Write-enable dialog box even allows you to define a new data source dynamically.

2. Switch back to the Writeback workbook in Excel, and click Reset so that the PivotTable Service will create a new session that uses the write-back setting for the cube. Then click Retrieve Values From Cube.

The original empty cells and labels appear.

3. In the Bread row, type **3,000** for Qtr1 (D13), **4,000** for Qtr2 (E13), **5,000** for Qtr3 (F13), and **6,000** for Qtr4 (G13). Then click Post Change Permanently.

4. Click Reset, which clears the data range and resets the connection to the server, and then click Retrieve Values From Cube.

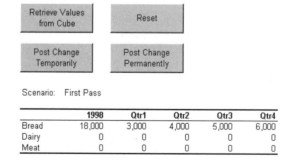

Scenario: First Pass

	1998	Qtr1	Qtr2	Qtr3	Qtr4
Bread	18,000	3,000	4,000	5,000	6,000
Dairy	0	0	0	0	0
Meat	0	0	0	0	0

The values reappear—along with the total for 1998. The values are stored in the write-back table and are now visible to anyone who accesses the cube. You can also write back values for a different scenario.

5. Change the scenario name in the worksheet (cell C10) from First Pass to **Second Pass**, and click the Retrieve Values From Cube button.

6. In the Bread row, type **3,500** for Qtr1 (D13), **4,500** for Qtr2 (E13), **5,500** for Qtr3 (F13), and **6,500** for Qtr4 (G13). Then click Post Change Permanently.

   You can write back to a cube in Analysis Services in either of two modes: you can write back only to the PivotTable Service cache, which would be useful for temporary what-if analysis, or you can write back to a relational table, which is useful for sharing changes with other users. To write back to a relational table, you must explicitly write-enable the cube.

You can find out more about how to use security to determine who can write values back to a cube in "Applying Cell-Level Security to a Cube" in Chapter 11, "Security."

Note If you know Microsoft Visual Basic and want to create your own application that can write values to a cube, look at the macros in the Writeback workbook for some useful sample code.

Because the values written back to a cube are stored in a relational table, you can browse them. You can use the native tool for the data source that contains the write-back table, or you can browse the values from within Analysis Manager.

7. In Analysis Manager, right-click the Sales Forecast cube. Point to Write-Back Options, and click Browse Writeback Data.

   The Browse Data window appears, showing the rows contained in the write-back table. You can resize the window as necessary to see all the columns.

	MS_AUDIT_USER	MS_AUDIT_TIME	ScenarioId_L1	Category_L3	CalendarYear_L7	CalendarQuarter_L8	SUM_SalesUnits
1	TOSHI\Administrator	5/19/2000 12:16:51 PM	1	Bread	1998	1	3000
2	TOSHI\Administrator	5/19/2000 12:16:51 PM	1	Bread	1998	2	4000
3	TOSHI\Administrator	5/19/2000 12:16:51 PM	1	Bread	1998	3	5000
4	TOSHI\Administrator	5/19/2000 12:16:51 PM	1	Bread	1998	4	6000
5	TOSHI\Administrator	5/19/2000 12:16:51 PM	1	Dairy	1998	1	0
6	TOSHI\Administrator	5/19/2000 12:16:51 PM	1	Dairy	1998	2	0
7	TOSHI\Administrator	5/19/2000 12:16:51 PM	1	Dairy	1998	3	0
8	TOSHI\Administrator	5/19/2000 12:16:51 PM	1	Dairy	1998	4	0
9	TOSHI\Administrator	5/19/2000 12:16:51 PM	1	Meat	1998	1	0
10	TOSHI\Administrator	5/19/2000 12:16:51 PM	1	Meat	1998	2	0
11	TOSHI\Administrator	5/19/2000 12:16:51 PM	1	Meat	1998	3	0
12	TOSHI\Administrator	5/19/2000 12:16:51 PM	1	Meat	1998	4	0
13	TOSHI\Administrator	5/19/2000 12:21:59 PM	2	Bread	1998	1	3500
14	TOSHI\Administrator	5/19/2000 12:21:59 PM	2	Bread	1998	2	4500
15	TOSHI\Administrator	5/19/2000 12:21:59 PM	2	Bread	1998	3	5500
16	TOSHI\Administrator	5/19/2000 12:21:59 PM	2	Bread	1998	4	6500

Browse Data: "WriteTable_SalesForecast" (First 1000 rows)

The MS_AUDIT_USER and MS_AUDIT_TIME columns on the left contain audit-trail information: the name of the user who made the changes, and the time the changes were made. The SUM_SalesUnits column on the right contains the measure for the cube. (The table includes one column for each measure in the cube.) The remaining columns contain the member keys for each level of each dimension in the cube.

The write-back table stores incremental values. If you were to change the value of First Pass value for Bread in Qtr1 of 1998 to *4,000* and write the value back to the cube again, you would get an additional row with new audit information and the value *1,000*.

8. Close the Browse Data window.

Note   Because the write-back values are stored in a relational table, you could use tools of your relational database system to append the values to the original fact table. Then, in Analysis Manager, process the cube and delete the write-back data.

Dynamically add members to a dimension

You can also write back to a shared dimension from the Dimension Editor.

In the course of a planning cycle, it's often necessary to add one more round than originally planned—preferably without disrupting the use of the data. Because you write-enabled the Scenario dimension, you can easily add a new scenario. Typically, writing new values into a dimension is something that a client application would help you do. Fortunately, the dimension browser in Analysis Manager will allow you to write new values to a dimension.

1. In Analysis Manager, right-click the Sales Forecast cube and click Edit.

2. In the Dimensions folder, right-click the Scenario dimension and click Browse.

3. Right-click the Third Pass scenario, point to New Member, and click Sibling.

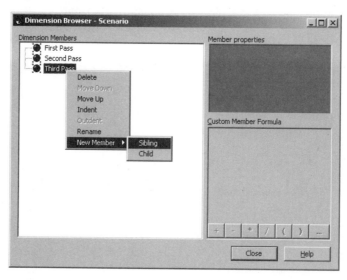

4. Type **Fourth Pass** as the name of the new member, and click OK.

You can see the new Scenario_ID that will be assigned to the scenario. Unlike writing back values to a cube—where values are stored in a special write-back table—when you add a new member to a dimension, the member is added directly to the original dimension table. You must have permission to add rows to the dimension table in order to use dimension write-back.

5. Close the Dimension Browser window, and click Yes to save the write-back changes.

6. Switch to Excel, and change the name of the Scenario (in cell C10) from Second Pass to **Fourth Pass**, the newly created Scenario name. Then click the Retrieve Values From Cube button.

   You don't need to process the cube or the dimension in order for new dimension members to take effect. The process is remarkably seamless.

7. In the Bread row, type **2,500** for Qtr1 (D13), **3,000** for Qtr2 (E13), **3,500** for Qtr3 (F13), and **4,000** for Qtr4 (G13). Then click Post Change Permanently, and close Excel. (It doesn't matter whether you save changes.)

8. In the Cube Editor, click the Data tab. Select Fourth Pass in the Scenario dimension and Qtr1 of 1998 in the Time Calendar dimension to see the new values in the Bread and All Product cells.

| Scenario | Fourth Pass |
| Time.Calendar | Qtr1 |

	MeasuresLevel
Category	Sales Units
All Product	2,500.00
Bread	2,500.00
Dairy	0.00
Meat	0.00

   It's even easy to write back data values that use the new dimension member. You do not need to stop the planning process. You do not need to process anything. The new member is instantly available and usable.

9. Close the Cube Editor.

   The ability to dynamically create new members—particularly for a Scenario dimension—is critical for a planning application. In this section, you've seen how the write-back process works, but only with limited tools. If planning will be a part of your work with Analysis Services, you'll need to obtain or create a client application that supports write-back—at least for cube data.

Creating Virtual Cubes

If you're familiar with a relational database system, you've encountered views (or queries, as views are known in Microsoft Access). In a relational database, a view is a mechanism for combining values from multiple tables into what appears to be a single table, or it's a mechanism for filtering the rows or columns of a table to see only a part of the table. In Analysis Services, a *virtual cube* provides some of the functions of a relational view.

A virtual cube, however, is much more restrictive than a relational view. In a relational view, you can combine essentially any two tables into a single view, and you can create extremely flexible filters to restrict the rows seen in the view. When you use a virtual cube to restrict the contents of a cube, you're limited to including or excluding measures and entire dimensions. You cannot include a portion of a dimension. For example, you could not create a virtual cube to display only 1998 values from the Sales cube. Likewise, you could not create a virtual cube to display years and quarters but omit the month level in the Time.Fiscal dimension of the Sales cube. If you include any member of a dimension, you must include all the members of the dimension.

Nonetheless, you can use a virtual cube to effectively remove dimensions or measures from a cube. And you can also use a virtual cube to combine measures from more than one cube.

Remove dimensions and measures from a cube

The Sales cube of the Chapter 4 database contains five dimensions, two of which are hierarchies of a single Time dimension. Five dimensions in a browser window can be confusing or intimidating to some people. Or perhaps you don't want certain people to be able to see sales by employee. The Sales cube also contains six visible measures (plus Count, which is set as not visible). Once again, this many measures might be too confusing or too revealing, so you might create a virtual cube that is a subset of the physical Sales cube:

1. In the Chapter 4 database, right-click the Cubes folder and click New Virtual Cube. Click Next to bypass the Virtual Cube Wizard's welcome screen. The wizard shows the existing cubes in the database.

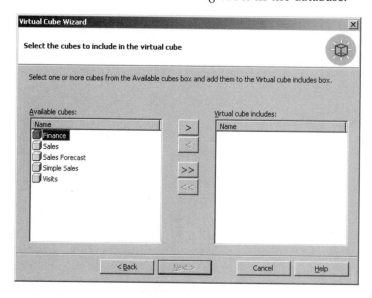

2. Double-click the Sales cube in the Available Cubes list, and click Next. The wizard shows the regular measures (not calculated measures) in the selected database.

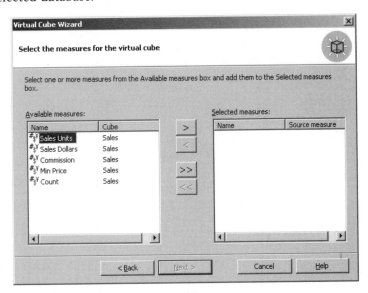

3. Double-click both Sales Units and Sales Dollars, and then click Next. The wizard shows the dimensions available in the selected cube.

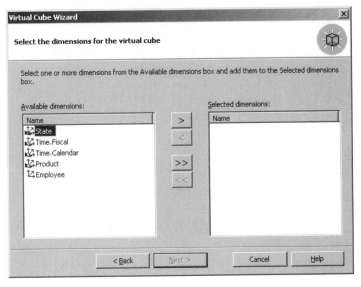

4. Double-click Time.Calendar, Product, and State, and then click Next.

5. Type **Basic Sales** as the name of the virtual cube, leave the Process Now option selected, and click Finish. Close the Process log window.

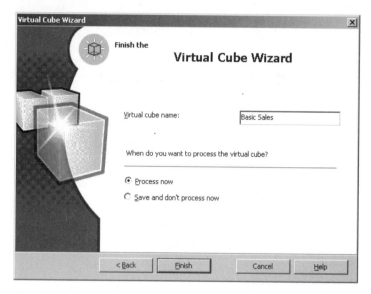

The Virtual Cube Wizard leaves you in the Virtual Cube Editor, which is a modified version of the Cube Editor. There is no Schema tab in the Virtual Cube Editor. If you want to make structural changes to the virtual cube, click the Edit Structure (Wizard) toolbar button to redisplay the Virtual Cube Wizard.

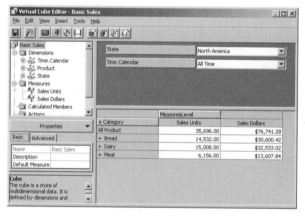

6. After reviewing the cube data, close the Virtual Cube Editor.

The Analysis server does need to process a virtual cube—processing creates enough files to identify the cube and indicate how to relate the virtual cube to the original cube—but unless it has to process the source cube, this processing is almost instantaneous.

Combine measures from multiple cubes

The Sales cube contains actual sales information. The Sales Forecast cube contains forecasted values that you added earlier in this chapter. Suppose that you want to compare forecast units with sales units. You can use a virtual cube to compare measures from two cubes:

1. Right-click the Cubes folder, and click New Virtual Cube. Click Next to bypass the welcome screen. In the list of available cubes, double-click both Sales and Sales Forecast.

2. Click Next. The Sales cube and the Sales Forecast cube both contain a measure named Sales Units. These are the two measures you want to compare. The virtual cube requires a unique name for each measure.

3. In the Available Measures list, double-click Sales Units from the Sales cube. Then double-click Sales Units from the Sales Forecast cube. The wizard gives the name Sales Units 1 to the newly added member.

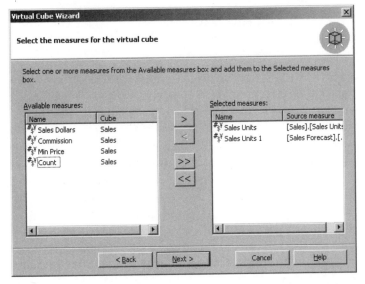

4. Select the Sales Units 1 member name, and press F2. When the name becomes selected, type **Forecast Units** as the new name for the measure and then click Next.

5. In the Available Dimensions list, double-click Product, Time.Calendar, and Scenario and then click Next.

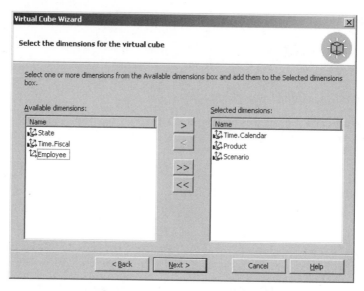

6. Type **Actual And Forecast** as the name of the virtual cube, leave the Process Now option selected, and click Finish. Then close the Process log window.

When you use a virtual cube to compare measures from multiple cubes, you must select a measure from each cube you want to include in the virtual cube. The wizard automatically removes any cubes that do not have a measure. It's technically possible to combine two cubes that do not have a common shared dimension, but none of the cells in the virtual cube will contain a value.

Create calculated members in a virtual cube

The Actual And Forecast virtual cube contains measures from the Sales cube and the Sales Forecast cube. Both cubes contain the Product dimension and the Time.Calendar dimension. In the Sales Forecast cube, however, the Subcategory and Product levels of the Product dimension were disabled, as was the Month level of the Time.Calendar dimension. In addition, only the Sales Forecast cube includes the Scenario dimension. You can see what happens when you combine cubes with dimensions that don't match.

1. Click the drop-down arrow next to the Time.Calendar dimension. Expand the All Time member, and select the 1998 member. Then double-click the Bread member.

Both Forecast Units and Sales Units are available for the 1998 member at the Product Category level. The Forecast Units values, however, do not extend to the Subcategory level. The All Product Total and Bread Total members shows values for both Forecast Units and Sales Units, but the children—Bagels, Muffins, and Sliced Bread—show only Sales Units; the Forecast Units cells are empty.

A virtual cube often includes members or dimensions for one cube that are not included in the other cube. In that case, the browser simply displays empty cells for the measures that don't have values in the underlying cube.

When you create a virtual cube that combines two or more cubes, you include at least one measure from each cube. It often makes sense to create a calculated measure to explicitly compare those measure values. Suppose, for example, that you want to create a Delta Units calculated measure that subtracts Sales Units from Forecast Units.

2. Click the Insert Calculated Member toolbar button. This displays the same Calculated Member Builder that appears when you create a calculated member in the Cube Editor. Type **Delta Units** in the Member Name box.

3. In the Data tree, expand Measures and MeasuresLevel. Double-click Forecast Units, click the minus sign (-) button, and then double-click Sales Units.

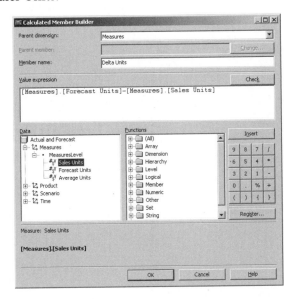

4. Click OK.

5. Click the drop-down button for the Scenario dimension, select Fourth Pass, and then collapse Category in the grid. The Sales Units column stays the same, but the Forecast Units and Delta Units columns change.

Scenario	Fourth Pass		
Time.Calendar	1998		

	MeasuresLevel		
+ Category	Sales Units	Forecast Units	Delta Units
All Product	30,137.00	13,000.00	-17,137.00
+ Bread	8,973.00	13,000.00	4,027.00
+ Dairy	15,008.00	0.00	-15,008.00
+ Meat	6,156.00	0.00	-6,156.00

The Virtual Cube Editor also allows you to import calculated members from a source cube into a virtual cube. The virtual cube must, naturally, include any members used by the calculated member. For example, the Sales cube contains a calculated member named Average Units, which uses both the Sales Units and the Count measures. If you attempt to import the Average Units calculated member into the Actual And Forecast cube without first adding the Count member to the virtual cube, you'll get an error, so first add the Count measure, and then import the Average Units calculated member.

6. Click the Edit Structure (Wizard) button, and agree to save the virtual cube. Click Next when asked to select the source cubes. In the Available Measures list, double-click Count. Then click Next twice, click Finish, and close the Process log window.

7. Click the Import Calculated Members button. Select the check box next to Average Units, and click OK. The Average Units column appears in the grid.

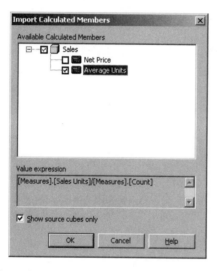

8. Close the Virtual Cube Editor, clicking Yes when asked if you want to save changes.

Virtual cubes can effectively remove dimensions or measures from a cube, combine measures from multiple cubes that share at least one common dimension, or both.

Chapter Summary

To	Do this
Use different aggregation methods for each member of a parent-child dimension	Add a column to the dimension table containing the codes + for addition, – for subtraction, and ~ for no aggregation. Then assign that column by using the dialog box for the Unary Operators property.
Add a custom formula to a specific member of a parent-child dimension	Add a column to the dimension table and store in it an MDX expression. Then assign that column to the level by using the dialog box for the Custom Members property.
Enable drillthrough for a cube	In the Cube Editor, click Drillthrough Options on the Tools menu to open the Cube Drillthrough Options dialog box. Select Enable Drillthrough.
Automatically divide members of a level into groups	Create a new level in the dimension, and change the Grouping property for the level to *Automatic*.
Disable levels of a shared dimension	In the Cube Editor, expand the dimension and select the highest level you want to disable. Then set the Disabled property to *Yes*.
Write enable a cube	In the Analysis Manager console tree, right-click the cube and click Write-Enable.
Write enable a parent-child dimension	In the Dimension Editor, change the Write-Enabled property for the dimension to *True*.
Create a cube from an empty fact table	In the Cube Editor, change the Fact Table Size property of the cube to *1*.
Add members to a write-enabled dimension	In the Cube Editor, right-click the write-enabled dimension and click Browse. Right-click an existing member, point to New Member, and click either Child or Sibling.
Create a virtual cube	In the console tree, right-click the Cubes folder and click New Virtual Cube. Using the wizard, select the cubes, dimensions, and measures for the virtual cube.
Make structural changes to a virtual cube	In the Virtual Cube Editor, click the Edit Structure (Wizard) toolbar button.
Add a calculated member to a virtual cube	In the Virtual Cube Editor, click the Insert Calculated Member toolbar button.

Chapter 5

Office 2000 Analysis Components

Chapter Objectives

In this chapter, you'll learn about the different components that share the PivotTable name and how to

- Create and manipulate a Microsoft Excel PivotTable report based on an OLAP cube.

- Create and use an Excel PivotChart report based on an OLAP cube.

- Create and manipulate a Microsoft Office PivotTable list for use in a Web page.

- Use Microsoft FrontPage to design an Office PivotTable list.

- Derive a local cube from an existing PivotTable report.

- Create a local cube directly from a relational data source.

Dr. Seuss once wrote a story about a mother who had 23 sons and named them all Dave. Even if you haven't read the story, you can imagine the chaos that ensued. Unfortunately, the Microsoft SQL Server 2000 Analysis Services designers didn't seem to have read their Dr. Seuss. Office 2000 includes three distinct components that have PivotTable as part of the component name, and all three components have some relationship to Analysis Services.

The first PivotTable is the PivotTable Service, which is included as part of Analysis Services but which is also installed as part of Office 2000. The PivotTable Service functions as the client liaison to the Analysis server, but it's also capable of creating and communicating with local cubes that don't require the Analysis server at all. The final section of this chapter will explain how to use the PivotTable Service to create and use local cubes.

The second PivotTable is the PivotTable report feature in Excel. The first known use of the name PivotTable was in the Excel PivotTable report feature. An Excel PivotTable report allows you to select and cross-tabulate numerical values in much the same way you do with an OLAP cube. In earlier versions of Excel, a PivotTable report could retrieve values only from a relational data source. In Excel 2000, a PivotTable report can also present data directly from an OLAP cube. The first section of this chapter will explain how to create and use an Excel PivotTable report.

The third PivotTable is the Office PivotTable list feature that is included as part of the Office Web Components. The Office PivotTable list performs many of the same functions as an Excel PivotTable report, but it includes capabilities that aren't available in the Excel component. Also, an Office PivotTable list is an ActiveX control, which means that you can use one in any application that can display an ActiveX control, not just as part of an Excel workbook. You can include an Office PivotTable list on a Web page, as part of a Microsoft Visual Basic application, in a Microsoft Word document, in a Microsoft PowerPoint presentation, or even in an Excel workbook. The second section of this chapter explains how to work with an Office PivotTable list.

Start the lesson

1. In Analysis Manager, right-click the server and click Restore Database. Navigate to the folder containing the sample files for this book (C:\Analysis), select Chapter 5, and click Open. Click Restore, and close the Restore Database Progress dialog box. Close Analysis Manager if you wish.

2. Launch Excel, and open the Chapter 5 workbook in the folder containing the sample files for this book. The Chapter 5 workbook is an empty Excel 2000 workbook.

Creating an Excel PivotTable Report

PivotTable reports have been a feature of Microsoft Excel since version 5. Traditionally, a PivotTable report has used a memory-cache method to provide values to the report. In this method, the PivotTable imports values from an Excel list or a database table and stores the values in memory. When a user manipulates the PivotTable report, the report retrieves necessary values from the memory cache. PivotTable reports have been an extremely popular and successful feature of Excel, but the memory-cache method for retrieving values can manipulate only a limited amount of data.

With Office 2000, Excel offers a second method for providing values to a PivotTable report: an OLAP cube. Using an OLAP cube, a PivotTable report can now communicate with the PivotTable Service to retrieve values from an Analysis server.

Establish a link from Excel

To create an Excel PivotTable report based on an OLAP cube, you use the Excel PivotTable Report Wizard, which uses the Microsoft Query application to define and create an OLAP query file. The OLAP query file provides all the information needed to connect to an OLAP cube. When Microsoft Query returns control to the PivotTable Report Wizard, the wizard uses the OLAP query file to connect to the cube. Once you've created the PivotTable report, neither Microsoft Query nor the query file is used again unless you want to create a new PivotTable report.

1. With the report worksheet of the Chapter 5 workbook active in Excel 2000, on the Data menu, click PivotTable And PivotChart Report. Step 1 of the PivotTable And PivotChart Wizard appears.

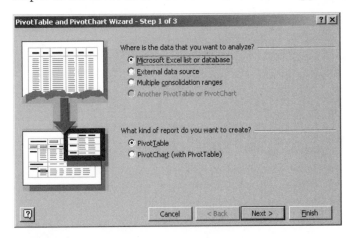

2. Click External Data Source, and then click Next. Step 2 of the wizard allows you to specify the external data source.

3. Click Get Data. Clicking the button starts Microsoft Query. In the Choose Data Source dialog box, click the OLAP Cubes tab.

If you haven't previously accessed Microsoft Query, you'll need your Office 2000 installation media to install it.

4. Select <New Data Source> and click OK.

5. Type **Market Sales** as the name of the data source, and select Microsoft OLE DB Provider For OLAP Services 8.0 as the OLAP provider. Then click Connect.

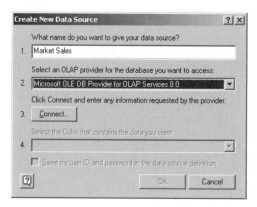

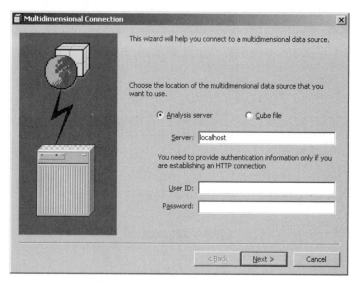

The server name localhost always refers to the current computer.

6. In the Multidimensional Connection dialog box, leave Analysis Server selected as the data source type, type the server computer name—or **localhost** if you're running Excel on the server machine—in the Server box, and click Next.

7. Select Chapter 5 as the database, and click Finish.

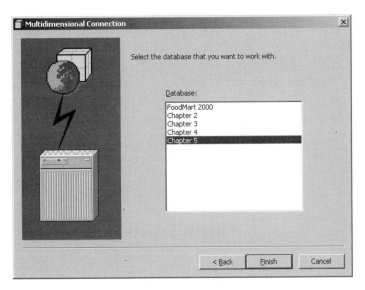

You've now defined a connection to a server database. If there's more than one cube in the database, you'll need to select the cube you want. In the Chapter 5 database, the Sales cube is the only cube, so it's preselected in the list.

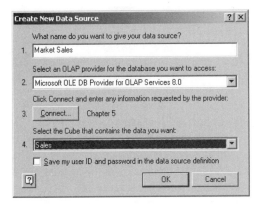

8. Click OK to continue.

The Market Sales data source now appears in the list of OLAP cubes.

Note Creating an OLAP cube data source creates a file in the Application Data\ Microsoft\Queries folder for the current user. (The location of the Application Data folder varies depending on the version of Microsoft Windows you're using and whether you have set up Windows to allow multiple users.) The file has the name you gave to the data source, with .oqy (for OLAP query) as the extension, and is registered with the Microsoft Excel OLAP Query File type. Double-clicking the OLAP Query data source file starts Excel and creates a new PivotTable report based on that data source.

---

9. With the Market Sales data source selected, click OK.

Microsoft Query returns the OLAP Query data source definition to Excel and closes. At this point, you're back to step 2 of the PivotTable And PivotChart Wizard.

If the PivotTable toolbar does not appear, right-click any visible toolbar and click PivotTable.

10. Click Finish to create a skeleton PivotTable report, along with a PivotTable toolbar that displays all the dimensions and measures in the cube.

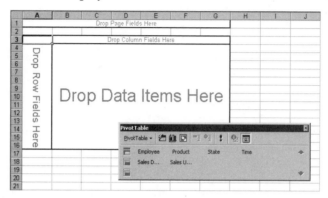

The PivotTable toolbar—with its buttons for the dimensions and measures—is the key to creating an Excel PivotTable report. Once the buttons appear on the toolbar, you know you have a connection to the Analysis server.

Browse a cube by using a PivotTable report

An Excel PivotTable report is similar in some ways to the Cube Browser included with Analysis Manager. A PivotTable report consists of four areas: the first three areas—the page area, the column area, and the row area—contain member names and are called *axes*. The fourth area, the data area, contains the values, or the measures.

The PivotTable toolbar contains one button for each measure, plus one button for each nonmeasure dimension. A single row of buttons in the toolbar contains either measures or dimensions, but not both. An icon at the left of the row of buttons indicates whether the buttons in the row are measures or dimensions. You can drag measures—and only measures—to the data area. You can drag buttons for other dimensions—but not measures—to any of the axes: page, column, or row.

Note   There are a few terminology differences between the simple browser in Analysis Manager, an Excel PivotTable report, and an Office PivotTable list. A cube contains measures. In the Analysis Manager Cube Browser, measures are called *measures* and are treated like any other dimension. In an Office PivotTable list, measures are called *totals*; they can be used only in the data area, and they appear grouped under the Totals heading in the PivotTable Field List window. In an Excel PivotTable report, measures are never referred to by name; they are identified by a special icon and can be used only in the PivotTable data area. In a browser, some dimensions typically appear above the grid and are used to filter the data. In the Analysis Manager data browser, these dimensions are called *slicer dimensions*. In the Office PivotTable list, they're called *filter fields*, and in the Excel PivotTable report, they're called *page fields*. The concepts are the same between the different browsers; only the terminology varies.

If a dimension or measure has a long name, the toolbar button doesn't show the entire name. If you hover the mouse over a button, Excel displays a ScreenTip showing the full name and an additional indicator of whether the button is a dimension or a measure.

1. Hover the mouse pointer over the button labeled Sales U....

The ScreenTip gives the full name of the measure, Sales Units, and informs you that you can drag the button to the PivotTable data area. This message confirms that the button is a measure.

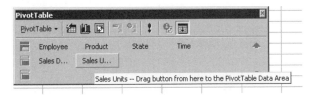

2. Drag the Sales Units button from the PivotTable toolbar onto the data area, which is labeled Drop Data Items Here.

The PivotTable report changes from a skeletal framework to an actual report, showing a single cell, the total of sales units.

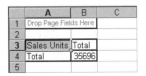

3. Hover the mouse pointer over the button labeled Product.

The ScreenTip repeats the name of the dimension and informs you that you can drag the button to the PivotTable. This message confirms that the button is a dimension. You can drag this button to any axis in the PivotTable report.

4. Drag the Product dimension button to the row axis of the PivotTable report, which is cell A4 on the worksheet. The category names appear as row headings.

	A	B	C
1	Drop Page Fields Here		
2			
3	Sales Units		
4	Category ▼	Total	
5	Bread	14532	
6	Dairy	15008	
7	Meat	6156	
8	Grand Total *	35696	
9			

5. Drag the Time dimension button to the column axis of the PivotTable report, which is cell B3 on the worksheet.

The year labels appear as column headings.

	A	B	C	D	E
1		Drop Page Fields Here			
2					
3	Sales Units	Year ▾			
4	Category ▾	1997	1998	Grand Total *	
5	Bread	5559	8973	14532	
6	Dairy		15008	15008	
7	Meat		6156	6156	
8	Grand Total *	5559	30137	35696	
9					

The section "Specify a default member" in Chapter 3, "Dimension and Cube Editors," explains how to set a default member.

6. Drag the State dimension button to the page axis of the PivotTable report, which is cell A1 of the worksheet.

You can choose whether to display a dimension button on the page axis. If you do not include a dimension on the PivotTable report, it behaves as if it were on the page axis with the default member selected.

	A	B	C	D	E
1	State	All State ▾			
2					
3	Sales Units	Year ▾			
4	Category ▾	1997	1998	Grand Total *	
5	Bread	5559	8973	14532	
6	Dairy		15008	15008	
7	Meat		6156	6156	
8	Grand Total *	5559	30137	35696	
9					

When a PivotTable report is connected to an OLAP cube, the PivotTable toolbar gives clues indicating which buttons are dimensions and which are measures. You can move dimensions only to the axes and move measures only to the data area.

Drill down to member children in a PivotTable report

You can also drill down to the children of a member by selecting the member label and clicking the Show Detail button on the PivotTable toolbar. Click the Hide Detail button to drill up.

Much of the benefit of working with an OLAP cube is the ability to drill down to view member details and zoom back up to see the big picture. The Excel PivotTable report allows you to navigate members, either one at a time or all together.

1. Double-click the Bread category label in cell A5. The subcategories that are children of Bread appear. Double-click Bread again to hide the children.

	A	B	C	D	E	F
1	State	All State ▾				
2						
3	Sales Units		Year ▾			
4	Category ▾	Subcategory	1997	1998	Grand Total *	
5	Bread	Bagels	557	984	1541	
6		Muffins	2479	3966	6445	
7		Sliced Bread	2523	4023	6546	
8	Bread Total *		5559	8973	14532	
9	Dairy			15008	15008	
10	Meat			6156	6156	
11	Grand Total *		5559	30137	35696	
12						

2. Click the Category level button in cell A4. Then click the Show Detail button on the PivotTable toolbar to drill down to the children of all the members at the Category level.

	A	B	C	D	E	F
1	State	All State ▾				
2						
3	Sales Units		Year ▾			
4	Category ▾	Subcategory	1997	1998	Grand Total *	
5	Bread	Bagels	557	984	1541	
6		Muffins	2479	3966	6445	
7		Sliced Bread	2523	4023	6546	
8	Bread Total *		5559	8973	14532	
9	Dairy	Cheese		7493	7493	
10		Milk		4151	4151	
11		Sour Cream		1607	1607	
12		Yogurt		1757	1757	
13	Dairy Total *			15008	15008	
14	Meat	Deli Meats		1977	1977	
15		Fresh Chicken		485	485	
16		Frozen Chicken		1338	1338	
17		Hamburger		1015	1015	
18		Hot Dogs		1341	1341	
19	Meat Total *			6156	6156	
20	Grand Total *		5559	30137	35696	
21						

3. Click the Subcategory level button in cell B4. Then click the Show Detail button to drill down to the children of all the members at the Subcategory level.

To hide the Category level while leaving the lower levels visible, right-click the Category heading and click Hide Levels.

	A	B	C	D	E	F	G
1	State	All State ▾					
2							
3	Sales Units			Year ▾			
4	Category ▾	Subcategory	Product Name	1997	1998	Grand Total *	
5	Bread	Bagels	Bagels	557	984	1541	
6		Bagels Total *		557	984	1541	
7		Muffins	Blueberry Muffins	616	884	1500	
8			Cranberry Muffins	644	956	1600	
9			English Muffins	602	1099	1701	
10			Muffins	617	1027	1644	
11		Muffins Total *		2479	3966	6445	
12		Sliced Bread	Pumpernickel Bread	624	1009	1633	

4. Click the dimension drop-down arrow on the button for the highest level of the Product dimension, in cell A4.

The members of the Category level appear, each with a check box that contains a double check mark. The double check mark indicates that the member is visible, along with at least some of its children.

5. Expand the Bread node, and then click the check box next to Bread once to clear it. This hides the Bread member along with all of its children. Click the check box a second time to put a single check in the box, and click OK. All the descendants of Bread disappear. A single check mark indicates that the member is visible but all of its children are hidden.

6. Click the Category level button in cell A4, and click the Hide Detail toolbar button. Then click the Show Detail button.

All the Categories and Subcategories appear.

7. Click the drop-down arrow next to the State dimension, in cell B1. Expand All State, USA, and North West. Select Washington, and click OK.

The drop-down list for a dimension on the page axis contains a hierarchy of members, and each member has a plus sign but not a check box. On the page axis, you can select only a single member from a dimension. The drop-down list for a dimension on the row or column axis also contains a hierarchy of members, but each member has a check box. On the row or column axes, you can select multiple members from a dimension.

Add multiple dimensions to a single axis

Aside from the page axis, a PivotTable report has at most two axes: one for rows and one for columns. Even a simple OLAP cube typically has three or more dimensions that you could include in a report. To display information from more than two dimensions, a PivotTable report must combine multiple dimensions on a single axis.

1. Drag the Year level button from the column axis to the left edge of the row axis, to the left of column A.

You can drop the new dimension at the left of column A, or at the right of column B, but not at the right of column A because that would split the levels of an existing dimension.

	A	B	C	D	E
1	State	Washington ▾			
2					
3	Sales Units				
4	Year ▾	Category ▾	Subcategory	Total	
5	1997	Bread	Bagels	404	
6			Muffins	1645	
7			Sliced Bread	1658	
8		Bread Total *		3707	
9	1997 Total *			3707	
10	1998	Bread	Bagels	345	

The row axis now has three columns of labels: one for the Year level of the Time dimension, one for the Category level of the Product dimension, and one for the Subcategory level of the Product dimension. The drop-down arrow that appears only on the top level of each dimension is the only visible indicator of which label starts a new dimension.

2. Drag the Employee dimension button from the toolbar to the row axis, to the left of the Year level.

   Multiple dimensions—and multiple levels for a single dimension—can exist on a single axis.

	A	B	C	D	E
1	State	Washington ▾			
2					
3	Sales Units				
4	Level 02 ▾	Year ▾	Category ▾	Subcategory	Total
5	Sheri Nowmer	1997	Bread	Bagels	404
6				Muffins	1645
7				Sliced Bread	1658
8			Bread Total *		3707
9		1997 Total *			3707
10		1998	Bread	Bagels	345

3. Drag the Sales Dollars measure button from the toolbar to the data area.

	A	B	C	D	E	F	G
1	State	Washington ▾					
2							
3	Level 02 ▾	Year ▾	Category ▾	Subcategory	Data ▾	Total	
4	Sheri Nowmer	1997	Bread	Bagels	Sales Units	404	
5					Sales Dollars	936.61	
6				Muffins	Sales Units	1645	
7					Sales Dollars	3346.32	

As soon as you add a second measure to the PivotTable report, the measures act as if they form a new Data dimension. The default location for the Data dimension is the row axis, but you can move the dimension to the column axis.

4. Drag the Data dimension button to the column axis, in cell F3.

	A	B	C	D	E	F	G
1	State	Washington ▾					
2							
3					Data ▾		
4	Level 02 ▾	Year ▾	Category ▾	Subcategory	Sales Units	Sales Dollars	
5	Sheri Nowmer	1997	Bread	Bagels	404	936.61	
6				Muffins	1645	3346.32	
7				Sliced Bread	1658	3463.74	
8			Bread Total *		3707	7746.67	

You cannot drag the Data dimension to the page axis; it can go on either the column axis or the row axis. To remove a measure from the Data dimension, follow the same procedure you would to hide a member from an ordinary dimension.

5. Click the drop-down arrow next to the Data dimension button. Clear the check box next to the Sales Dollars measure, and click OK.

Hiding a measure from the Data dimension deletes the measure from the report. If only one measure remains on the report, the Data dimension goes away.

Format a PivotTable report

A PivotTable report has many formatting options. This section will touch upon a few of the most useful. As a default, a PivotTable report displays each label in only the top cell of a group. You use the PivotTable Options dialog box to center the label within the available space.

1. Click the PivotTable menu on the PivotTable toolbar, and click Table Options.

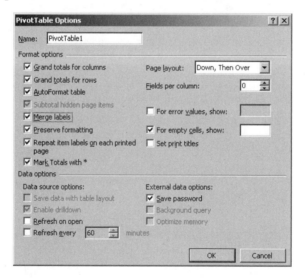

2. Select the Merge Labels check box. Look over some of the other formatting options available in the PivotTable Options dialog box, and then click OK.

	A	B	C	D	E
1	State	Washington ▾			
2					
3	Sales Units				
4	Level 02 ▾	Year ▾	Category ▾	Subcategory	Total
5				Bagels	404
6		1997	Bread	Muffins	1645
7				Sliced Bread	1658
8			Bread Total *		3707
9			1997 Total *		3707
10				Bagels	345
11			Bread	Muffins	1451
12				Sliced Bread	1367
13			Bread Total *		3163

Each member's label is now centered in a single, merged cell next to its children.

3. Click the Undo button on the toolbar to change the labels back to the unmerged form.

You might want to show the Category and Subcategory labels for the Product dimension in a single column, with the Subcategory indented. You can't do that directly in a PivotTable report, but you can get the same effect.

4. Double-click the Category level button. In the PivotTable Field dialog box, click the Layout button.

5. In the PivotTable Field Layout dialog box, click the Show Items In Outline Form option. Leave all the check boxes cleared, and click OK. Then click OK to close the PivotTable Field dialog box.

	A	B	C	D	E	F
1	State	Washington ▾				
2						
3	Sales Units					
4	Level 02 ▾	Year ▾	Category ▾	Subcategory	Total	
5	Sheri Nowmer	1997	Bread			
6				Bagels	404	
7				Muffins	1645	
8				Sliced Bread	1658	
9			Bread Total *		3707	
10		1997 Total *			3707	
11		1998	Bread			
12				Bagels	345	
13				Muffins	1451	

Each Category label now has a blank cell to its right in the Subcategory column. You can adjust the width of the Category column to make the two columns appear as one.

6. With the Category label (in cell C4) selected, click the Format menu, point to Column, and click Width. Type **1.5** and click OK.

The Category and Subcategory labels now appear to be part of a single, indented list.

	A	B	C	D	E	F
1	State	Washington ▼				
2						
3	Sales Units					
4	Level 02 ▼	Year ▼	▼	Subcategory	Total	
5	Sheri Nowmer	1997		Bread		
6				Bagels	404	
7				Muffins	1645	
8				Sliced Bread	1658	
9				Bread Total *	3707	
10		1997 Total *			3707	
11		1998		Bread		
12				Bagels	345	
13				Muffins	1451	

The default layout for a PivotTable report is often sufficient, but a PivotTable report also allows more flexibility when your report needs to have a specific format.

Note   You can use the AutoFormat command on the Format menu to assign any of several predefined columnar or tabular formats to a PivotTable report.

Create a PivotChart report

Excel 2000 can create interactive PivotChart reports as well as PivotTable reports. In fact, a PivotChart is linked directly to a PivotTable report, and it has buttons to allow you to interact directly with the chart.

1. Press the Ctrl key as you click the Report worksheet tab, and drag the tab to the right. Release the mouse button before releasing the Ctrl key. Double-click the sheet tab, type **Chart Report** as the name for the copied worksheet, and press Enter.

2. Drag the Year level button up to the page axis. Drag the State button to the column axis. Drag the Level 02 button away from the PivotTable. Click the Category level button, and click the Hide Detail toolbar button.

	A	B	C	D	E	F
1						
2	Time	All Time ▼				
3						
4	Sales Units	Country ▼				
5	Category ▼	Canada	Mexico	USA	Grand Total *	
6	Bread	1046	1289	12197	14532	
7	Dairy	1884	2407	10717	15008	
8	Meat	785	1470	3901	6156	
9	Grand Total *	3715	5166	26815	35696	
10						

3. Click the Chart Wizard button on the PivotTable toolbar.

A new worksheet appears, containing a chart with category labels across the bottom, countries listed in the legend, and a Time field button above the chart. These are interactive PivotChart controls.

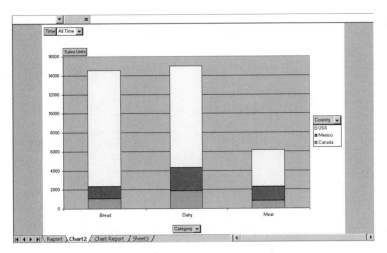

4. Click the drop-down arrow adjacent to the Time button. Expand the tree, select Quarter 1 of 1998, and click OK.

You use the PivotChart buttons just as you use the PivotTable report buttons.

5. Click the Category button, and then click the Show Detail button on the PivotTable toolbar.

The chart changes to show columns for only the subcategories. The PivotChart is intelligent enough not to show totals from the report; it displays the Category labels under the appropriate Subcategory labels.

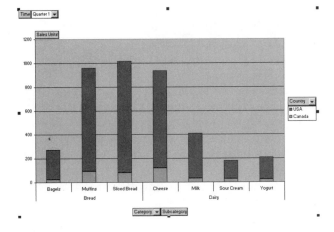

6. Click the Country button, and then click the Show Detail button. Then select the Region button, and click the Show Detail button again.

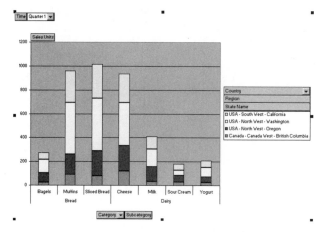

Once again, the PivotChart shows the appropriate detail, using the parent levels of the hierarchy only as part of the labels.

7. On the PivotTable toolbar, click the PivotChart menu and click Hide PivotChart Field Buttons.

This removes the buttons, making the chart suitable for printing or displaying in a meeting.

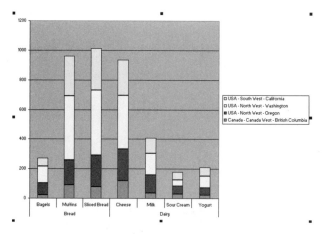

A PivotChart report is always linked to a PivotTable report. Manipulating the buttons on a PivotChart report changes the layout of the PivotTable report. There's no way, for example, to create a chart that shows dates as the *category* (x-axis) labels, when that chart is based on a PivotTable that shows dates as column headings. Moving the dates to the category axis of the chart will move dates to the row axis of the PivotTable report. If you want the layout of a PivotTable report to be independent of a PivotChart report, you must copy the PivotTable report before creating the chart.

Creating an Office PivotTable List

An Office PivotTable list is superficially similar to an Excel PivotTable report. Both tools can link to an Analysis Services cube. Both tools can use a member to filter, and both tools allow you to show and hide levels of a dimension on an axis. But the tools behave differently in many ways. With an Excel PivotTable report, the ability to communicate with an OLAP cube was added to an existing feature, and the user interface sometimes seems more closely adapted to the old features than to the new ones. The interface for an Office PivotTable list was created with OLAP cubes in mind, so the PivotTable list is often a more flexible tool for working with an OLAP cube.

Create a PivotTable list from a PivotTable report

The easiest way to add a PivotTable list to a Web page is to first create a PivotTable report in Excel and then publish the PivotTable report as an interactive Web page.

1. Activate the Chart Report sheet of the Chapter 5 workbook. On the File menu, click Save As Web Page.

2. In the Save As dialog box, click the Publish button.

3. Under Item To Publish, select PivotTable in the list. Under Viewing Options, select the Add Interactivity With check box and select PivotTable Functionality from the drop-down list. Select the Open Published Web Page In Browser check box, and click Publish.

Your browser must be able to use ActiveX controls for you to browse the PivotTable list.

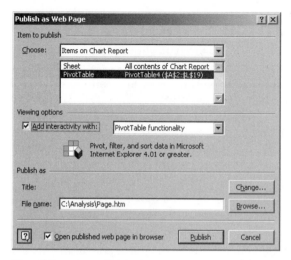

The Office PivotTable list appears in the browser window. An Excel PivotTable report toolbar automatically shows each dimension and measure as a button when part of the report is selected. The Office PivotTable list toolbar contains a single button that displays a list of dimensions, levels, and measures.

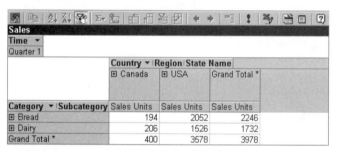

4. On the toolbar, click the Field List button.

The PivotTable Field List window appears. This field list is roughly equivalent to the list of buttons on an Excel PivotTable toolbar.

Tip   The PivotTable list report created from an Excel workbook is always centered within the browser window, making it difficult to position the PivotTable field list in the margin. If you resize the browser window to take up only a portion of the screen, the PivotTable list will center itself within the smaller browser window and you can position the field list outside the browser window.

5. Click the PivotTable list heading. Then, on the toolbar, click the Property Toolbox button.

The PivotTable Property Toolbox appears. This toolbox includes properties appropriate to the currently selected portion of the PivotTable list.

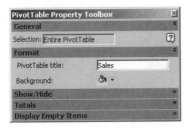

6. Click various places on the PivotTable list to watch the contents of the PivotTable Property Toolbox change. An Excel PivotTable has no direct equivalent to the property toolbox.

Manipulate levels in a PivotTable list

In an Excel PivotTable report, you interact frequently with dimensions and members but not with levels. Dimension levels appear and disappear as you show or hide detail for members on the report, and the button for the top level is the only one that ever displays a drop-down list. In an Office PivotTable list, you can deal much more directly with levels within a dimension.

1. In the PivotTable list, expand the Bread member.

The children of Bread appear under the Subcategory level heading. None of the subcategory labels shows a plus sign, however, even though the Product dimension contains one more level of detail below Subcategory. If you try to double-click the Bagels member, nothing happens.

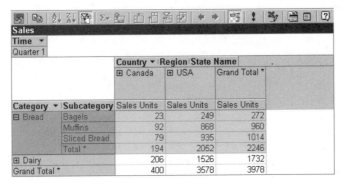

You can also drag the Product level to the row area of the PivotTable list.

2. In the PivotTable Field List window, expand the Product dimension. Select the Product Name level. Then, at the bottom of the field list window, in the Add To drop-down list, select Row Area and click Add To. The Product field appears in the PivotTable list.

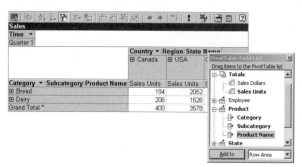

3. Expand the Bread member, and then expand the Bagels member.

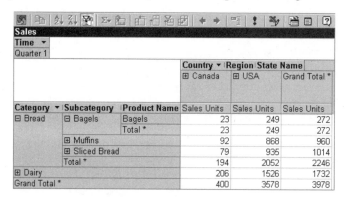

Category ▼	Subcategory	Product Name	Sales Units	Sales Units	Sales Units
⊟ Bread	⊟ Bagels	Bagels	23	249	272
		Total *	23	249	272
	⊞ Muffins		92	868	960
	⊞ Sliced Bread		79	935	1014
	Total *		194	2052	2246
⊞ Dairy			206	1526	1732
Grand Total *			400	3578	3978

In an Excel PivotTable report, a level appears on an axis only if members from that level are visible. Showing the children for a member adds the next level if it's available. In an Office PivotTable list, levels can be added to or removed from an axis, even if no members are visible. You can see only members from levels that are explicitly on an axis.

Note   The use of levels in a PivotTable list also affects what you see in the dimension tree. In an Excel PivotTable report, selecting or deselecting items in the dimension tree determines whether that item will appear on the axis, and levels are added if necessary. In an Office PivotTable list, selecting or deselecting items in the dimension tree merely *filters* those items. In other words, deselecting an item hides it in the dimension tree, but only if that item would otherwise be displayed.

---

4. Drag the Subcategory level label past the edge of the PivotTable list. (A red X appears on the mouse pointer.)
This removes the Subcategory level, leaving only the Category level and the Product Name level on the row axis.

Sales				
Time ▾				
Quarter 1				
		Country ▾	**Region**	**State Name**
		⊞ Canada	⊞ USA	Grand Total *
Category ▾	**Product Name**	Sales Units	Sales Units	Sales Units
⊞ Bread		194	2052	2246
⊞ Dairy		206	1526	1732
Grand Total *		400	3578	3978

5. Expand the Bread and Dairy members.

All the Products in the Bread category appear; they just aren't grouped by the Subcategory level members.

Sales				
Time ▾				
Quarter 1				
		Country ▾	**Region**	**State Name**
		⊞ Canada	⊞ USA	Grand Total *
Category ▾	**Product Name**	Sales Units	Sales Units	Sales Units
⊟ Bread	Bagels	23	249	272
	Blueberry Muffins	23	142	165
	Cranberry Muffins	21	215	236
	English Muffins	29	288	317
	Muffins	19	223	242
	Pumpernickel Bread	11	208	219
	Rye Bread	28	252	280
	Wheat Bread	16	208	224
	White Bread	24	267	291
	Total *	194	2052	2246
⊟ Dairy	Cheese Spread	20	84	104
	Havarti Cheese	16	74	90

6. Drag the Category label off the PivotTable list.

The report shows the complete list of products, still arranged in the order of the category and subcategory groups. This is the hierarchy order for the members, and it's the default order for members of a level even if the parent members aren't visible. You can override the default sort order.

Sales				
Time ▾				
Quarter 1				
	Country ▾	**Region**	**State Name**	
	⊞ Canada	⊞ USA	Grand Total *	
Product Name ▾	Sales Units	Sales Units	Sales Units	
Bagels	23	249	272	
Blueberry Muffins	23	142	165	
Cranberry Muffins	21	215	236	
English Muffins	29	288	317	
Muffins	19	223	242	
Pumpernickel Bread	11	208	219	
Rye Bread	28	252	280	
Wheat Bread	16	208	224	
White Bread	24	267	291	

7. Click the Product Name level label, and activate the PivotTable Property Toolbox. Expand the Sort section of the toolbox, and select Ascending from the Sort Direction drop-down list.

You can also sort the list of products in descending order of total sales. Unfortunately, you cannot use the PivotTable Property Toolbox to do this.

Sorting by a measure column removes the sort direction from the row members or from any other measure column.

8. Right-click any cell in the Grand Total column, and click Sort Descending from the shortcut menu.

The list of products sorts in descending order.

9. Select the Sort Descending command a second time to remove the Sort Descending flag for the measure.

This sets the sort for the Products back to the default, not to the sort direction set previously.

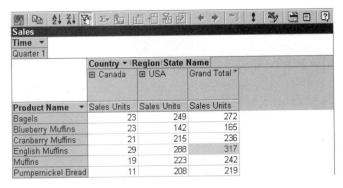

In an Excel PivotTable report, you can not have a report that shows all products at only the Product level—sorted or not. An Office PivotTable list gives you more control over how to use levels within a report.

Note   You can export an Office PivotTable list back to an Excel PivotTable report. To do so, click the Export To Excel toolbar button. Interestingly, if you show only selected levels in a PivotTable list and then export that list to Excel, the resulting PivotTable report will include only the selected levels.

Manipulate subtotals in a PivotTable list

An Excel PivotTable report always shows the complete subtotal for a group, even if some of the items are hidden. An Office PivotTable report allows you more control over how to display subtotals.

1. Click the Time dimension drop-down arrow, select the 1998 check box, and click OK.

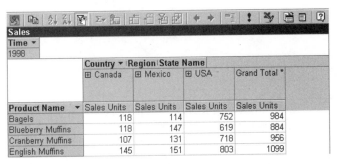

The total in the Sales Units column for Bagels in 1998 was 984. This is equal to the sum of sales units for the three countries. Hiding the USA column demonstrates how the PivotTable list manages totals.

2. Click the Country drop-down arrow, clear the USA check box, and click OK.

The total for Bagels is still 984, even though that total doesn't equal the sum of the two visible countries. An asterisk follows the Grand Total label. The asterisk indicates that the total might include hidden items.

Product Name ▾	Canada Sales Units	Mexico Sales Units	Grand Total * Sales Units
Bagels	118	114	984
Blueberry Muffins	118	147	884
Cranberry Muffins	107	131	956
English Muffins	145	151	1099
Muffins	114	169	1027

3. Click the PivotTable list caption bar (to select the entire PivotTable list). Activate the PivotTable Property Toolbox, and expand the Totals section. Clear the Total All Items check box.

The value in the Grand Total column changes to 232, which is the sum of the two visible countries. The asterisk also disappears from the Grand Total label.

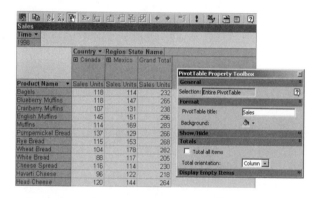

Note   In an Excel PivotTable report, subtotal labels include a trailing asterisk as a default. In the PivotTable Options dialog box, you can turn off the trailing asterisk. In an Excel PivotTable report, however, you can't make the subtotals match the total of only the visible cells.

---

4. Click the Country label drop-down arrow, select the Show All check box, and click OK to redisplay USA. The total changes to match the sum of the visible cells.

Your hypothetical company didn't start selling products in Mexico until the third quarter of 1998. You can choose how Mexico totals are displayed when no data is available.

5. Click the Time drop-down arrow, expand 1998, select the Quarter 1 check box, and click OK. Mexico disappears from the list of countries.

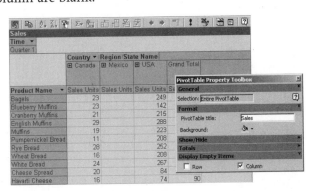

Sales				
Time ▾				
Quarter 1				

	Country ▾	Region State Name	
	⊞ Canada	⊞ USA	Grand Total
Product Name ▾	Sales Units	Sales Units	Sales Units
Bagels	23	249	272
Blueberry Muffins	23	142	165
Cranberry Muffins	21	215	236
English Muffins	29	288	317
Muffins	19	223	242

6. With the entire PivotTable list selected, activate the PivotTable Property Toolbox and expand the Display Empty Items section. Select the Column check box.

The Mexico member reappears, even though all the cells for the column are blank.

Sales					
Time ▾					
Quarter 1					

	Country ▾	Region State Name		
	⊞ Canada	⊞ Mexico	⊞ USA	Grand Total
Product Name ▾	Sales Units	Sales Units	Sales Units	S
Bagels	23		249	
Blueberry Muffins	23		142	
Cranberry Muffins	21		215	
English Muffins	29		288	
Muffins	19		223	
Pumpernickel Bread	11		208	
Rye Bread	28		252	
Wheat Bread	16		208	
White Bread	24		267	
Cheese Spread	20		84	
Havarti Cheese	16		74	90

PivotTable Property Toolbox
General
Selection: Entire PivotTable
Format
PivotTable title: Sales
Background:
Show/Hide
Totals
Display Empty Items
☐ Row   ☑ Column

7. Clear the Column check box for Display Empty Items. Then Drag the Sales Dollars measure from the Field List window to the data area, to the right of any Sales Units column.

The new measure appears in the Columns area. Unlike an Excel PivotTable report, where multiple measures create a new Data dimension, an Office PivotTable list has a property for controlling the orientation of the measures.

Sales						
Time ▾						
Quarter 1						

	Country ▾	Region State Name				
	⊞ Canada		⊞ USA		Grand Total	
Product Name ▾	Sales Units	Sales Dollars	Sales Units	Sales Dollars	Sales Units	Sales Dollars
Bagels	23	57.65	249	574	272	631.65
Blueberry Muffins	23	43.59	142	267.26	165	310.85
Cranberry Muffins	21	61.79	215	596.12	236	657.91
English Muffins	29	49.69	288	507.16	317	556.85
Muffins	19	34.33	223	414.5	242	448.83

8. With the entire PivotTable list selected, activate the PivotTable Property Toolbox and expand the Totals section. In the Total Orientation drop-down list, select Row.

The two measures switch to the row axis.

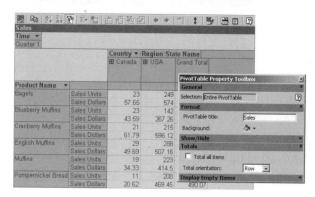

9. Close the browser.

A PivotTable list gives you a great deal of flexibility in how to deal with measures—or *totals*, as they're called in the PivotTable list.

Note An Excel PivotTable report offers you a greater degree of control over label and measure formatting than an Office PivotTable list. In an Excel PivotTable report, you can apply any cell formatting—including fonts, backgrounds, and custom number formats—to any relevant portion of the report. In an Office PivotTable list, you can apply different fonts or backgrounds to only three groups of items. Changing a single dimension or level label changes all dimension and level labels. Changing a single item label changes all item labels. Changing the font or background for a single measure changes the format of all measures. You can apply a unique number format to each measure, but you must select the format from a predefined list; you cannot apply custom number formats or even change the number of displayed decimal places.

Design a PivotTable list in FrontPage

You use a browser such as Microsoft Internet Explorer to display a PivotTable list. Within the browser, you can rearrange dimensions and change formatting. When you close the browser, however, all changes you made are lost. The next time you open the page containing the PivotTable list, the list returns to its original state. To create or define a PivotTable list, you must use an application capable of entering *design mode*. FrontPage, included in the Premium edition of Office 2000, is capable of designing a PivotTable list.

1. Start FrontPage. With a blank, new page active, on the Insert menu, point to Component and click Office PivotTable.

An empty PivotTable list, showing the text No Data Source Specified, appears. Your first task is to define a data source.

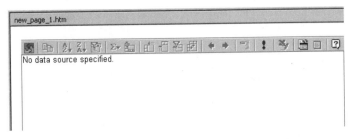

2. On the PivotTable list toolbar, click the Property Toolbox button (one of the few buttons that's not disabled). In the PivotTable Property Toolbox, expand the Data Source section.

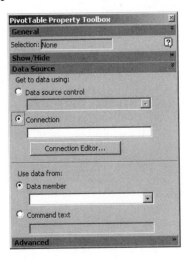

3. Under Get To Data Using, click the Connection option and click the Connection Editor button. This dialog box is similar to the Data Link Properties dialog box used in Analysis Manager, except this one defaults to use Microsoft SQL Server as a provider.

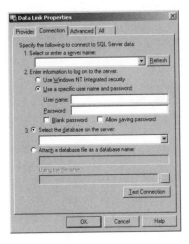

4. Click the Provider tab, and select Microsoft OLE DB Provider For OLAP Services 8.0.

5. Click Next, and type **localhost** or the name of the computer running the Analysis server in the Data Source box. In the Enter The Initial Catalog To Use drop-down list, select the Chapter 5 database. Then click OK. You still need to specify a cube from the database.

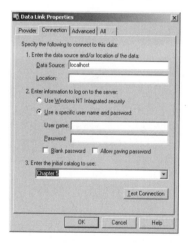

6. Under Use Data From in the PivotTable Property Toolbox, click the Data Member option and then select Sales from the drop-down list.
    The PivotTable list immediately changes to show the drop areas.

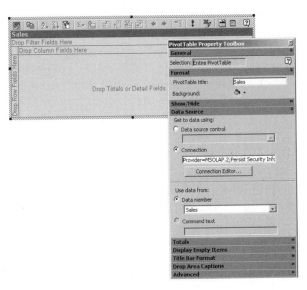

7. Click the Field List toolbar button. Drag Sales Units to the Totals area, drag Product to the Filter area, drag Time to the Column area, and drag State to the row area.

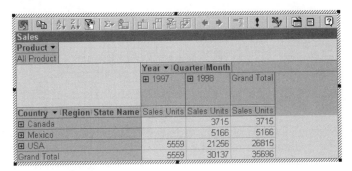

8. Click the Preview tab to see how the control will appear in a browser. Click the Save button, type **Market Test** as the name of the HTML file, and click Save.

Any changes you make to the document while in FrontPage—whether on the Normal tab, the HTML tab, or the Preview tab—will be retained in the HTML file.

When you want control over the initial layout of a PivotTable list, you need to use a design program to make the changes. An HTML editor such as FrontPage can serve as a design program for the Office PivotTable list.

Create a restricted PivotTable list

You might want to create a PivotTable list for others to use. Often, you want to provide some of the functionality of the PivotTable list but not all. For example, you might want to allow users of the list to drill down from a member to its children on the row axis but not move dimensions from one axis to another, change filters, or change formatting. With an Excel PivotTable report, you can write Visual Basic macros to restrict the capabilities of the report, but by using an Office PivotTable list, you can restrict the capabilities without any programming.

1. In FrontPage, click the Normal tab to change to design mode for the PivotTable list. Customize certain settings before restricting the capabilities of the PivotTable list.

2. In the Product drop-down list, select the Bread check box, and click OK. In the Country drop-down list, clear the check boxes for Mexico and Canada, leaving only USA selected, and then click OK. Select the Country caption, and click the Subtotal button in the toolbar to remove the redundant Grand Total row. Drag the Quarter level label from the report, leaving only Year and Month. This is the general structure of the report you'll allow users to see.

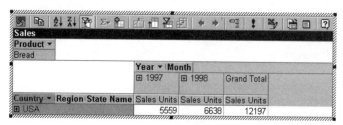

3. Click the caption bar of the list (to select the entire list), and click the Property Toolbox toolbar button. Expand the Advanced section.

   The PivotTable Property Toolbox contains sections in design mode that aren't available when viewing the list in a browser.

4. Clear the Allow Property Toolbox check box. This prevents a user from changing the formatting of the PivotTable list. Select the Lock Filters check box and the Lock Row/Column Fields check box. This prevents a user from moving dimensions from one area to another or displaying items you have filtered.

5. In the Maximum Height box, type **480**. In the Maximum Width box, type **640**.

   This keeps the PivotTable list from expanding beyond the specified size. If the PivotTable list becomes larger than these dimensions, it will display scroll bars.

6. Collapse the Advanced section of the toolbox, and expand the Show/Hide section. Click the Toolbar button to hide the toolbar from the PivotTable list.

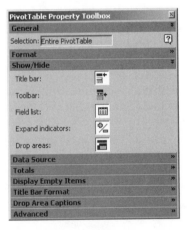

7. Save the HTML page, and click the Preview tab to see how the PivotTable list will appear to a user. Try expanding and collapsing members. Notice the horizontal scroll bar that appears when you expand years. Try dragging level labels off the list or to a different area. Try displaying values for Meat, Dairy, Mexico, or Canada.

8. Close FrontPage.

As a PivotTable list designer, you can limit the capabilities you allow a user. By using an Office PivotTable list, you can generate a list that provides considerable flexibility—particularly for drilling down to detail levels—without writing any customization code.

Note If you write Visual Basic code and are familiar with creating event handlers to react to the behavior of users, you might be interested to know that an Office PivotTable list supports events for several user actions. In contrast, an Excel PivotTable report doesn't have any events.

Creating a Local Cube

Office 2000 includes all the necessary pieces to create and use local cubes. A local cube functions much the same as a server-based cube. It has dimensions (complete with hierarchies) and measures. You typically store much less data in a local cube than in a server-based cube, and a local cube doesn't include many of the capabilities of a server-based cube. For example, a local cube doesn't include aggregations, member properties, shared dimensions, virtual dimensions, virtual cubes, partitions, or write-back tables.

Any client application that can interact with a server-based cube can also use a local cube because the client application communicates with the PivotTable Service and the PivotTable Service can communicate with either the Analysis server or with a local cube. The PivotTable Service is also the component that creates local cubes.

Office 2000 offers two different approaches for creating a local cube. With either approach it's actually the PivotTable Service that creates the local cube, but the steps you go through are different in each case. One option is to connect to an Analysis server by using an Excel PivotTable report and then use the PivotTable report to create a local cube that is a subset of the server-based cube. The other option is to use Microsoft Query to define a local cube based on a relational data source.

Create a local cube from a PivotTable report

Using a PivotTable report to create the local cube is simple, but you must have an existing server-based cube.

1. In Excel, open the Chapter 5 workbook. Press the Ctrl key as you drag the Chart Report sheet tab to the right. Double-click the sheet tab, type **Cube Report** as the name for the new sheet, and press Enter.

   The PivotTable report has the Time dimension on the page axis, the State dimension on the column axis, the Product dimension on the row axis, and the Sales Units measure in the data area.

2. Drag the State Name caption away from the report, leaving no dimension on the column axis. This is one possible starting point for creating a local cube from a PivotTable report.

	A	B	C
1			
2	Time	Quarter 1 ▼	
3			
4	Sales Units		
5	Category ▼	Subcategory	Total
6	Bread		
7		Bagels	272
8		Muffins	960
9		Sliced Bread	1014
10	Bread Total *		2246
11	Dairy		
12		Cheese	934
13		Milk	409
14		Sour Cream	179
15		Yogurt	210
16	Dairy Total *		1732
17	Grand Total *		3978
18			

3. On the PivotTable toolbar, click the PivotTable menu and click Client-Server Settings. Click the Create Local Data File button, and click Next to pass step 1 of the Create Cube File wizard.

   Step 2 of the wizard appears, showing the Employee, Product, State, and Time dimensions, with a check mark in the box next to the Product and Time dimensions.

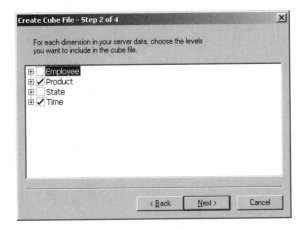

   The Create Cube File wizard displays the name of each dimension in the server-based cube. Any dimension that appears in the PivotTable report has the check box preselected.

Note   Dimensions containing multiple hierarchies (as described in Chapter 3) and virtual dimensions (as described in Chapter 10, "Dimension Optimization") do not appear in the Create Cube File wizard.

---

4. Expand the Product dimension.

   The three levels appear, with Category and Subcategory already selected. The wizard defaults to select levels that are currently displayed on the report.

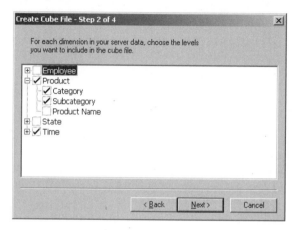

5. Expand the State dimension.

   The three levels for the State dimension appear, but none of the check boxes are selected.

6. Select the State dimension check box. All the levels are automatically selected when you select the dimension. Clear the Region check box. When you remove a level, all levels below that level in the dimension are automatically removed.

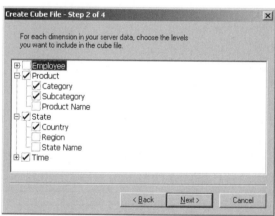

You can choose one or more items from the top level of each dimension. If you fail to include at least one item from a dimension, the wizard displays a warning when you click Next.

7. Click Next to continue to step 3 of the wizard, and expand all four items. This step displays the name of the top level for each selected dimension, including the measures dimension. Each level name expands to show the members of that level. In addition to the preselected items, select Sales Dollars from the Measures level and USA from the Country level. Then click Next.

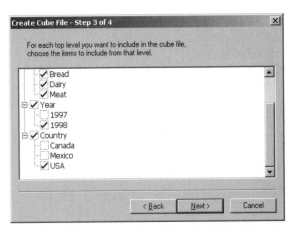

8. The final step of the wizard allows you to name the local cube file, suggesting the name of the server-based cube. Type **Sales.cub** as the name of the cube, and click Finish to create it. Then click OK to use the local cube as the source of the Office PivotTable report.

Once the cube file exists, you can switch the Excel PivotTable report between the cube file and the server-based cube by using the Client-Server Settings dialog box which you access from the PivotTable menu. Also, within the Client-Server Settings dialog box, the caption of the Create Local Data File button changes to Edit Local Data File to allow you to redefine the local cube. Once the cube file exists, you can also access it by using other client applications, such as the MDX Sample application that will be explained in Chapter 7, "MDX Sets."

Create a local cube from a relational data source

Even if you don't have an Analysis server available to you, you can create and use a local cube by creating one directly from a relational data source. The PivotTable Service, which is included with Office 2000, can create and access a local cube. To create a local cube directly from a relational data source, you use the Microsoft Query application. Microsoft Query includes a wizard for turning a relational data set into a cube.

When you create a local cube, you first create a relational rowset by using standard SQL. In that rowset, you can join dimension tables with the fact table and create calculated columns. Once you have the relational rowset, you then use the OLAP Cube Wizard to design dimensions, hierarchies, and measures for the cube. To simplify the process of creating a rowset, the Chapter 5 database included on this book's companion CD contains a query named CubeSource that already includes the joins needed to create a Sales cube.

Note You cannot create a local cube that contains a parent-child dimension, so the local Sales cube will not contain the Employee dimension.

1. In Excel, activate a blank worksheet. Double-click the sheet tab, type **Relational Cube** as the name of the sheet, and press Enter. On the Data menu, point to Get External Data and click New Database Query. Don't click the OLAP Cubes tab. On the Databases tab, select MS Access Database and click OK.

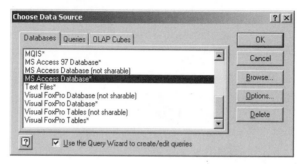

2. In the Select Database dialog box, navigate to the folder containing the sample files for this book, select the Chapter5.mdb database file, and click OK.

3. On the Choose Columns screen of the Query Wizard, select the CubeSource table and click the add columns (>) button, adding all the columns from the table to the query.

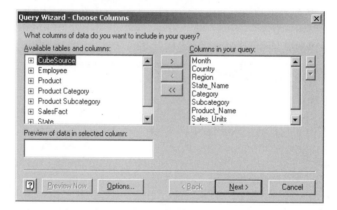

In the list of columns, you can see the columns that will be used in the cube. The Month column will create a Time dimension. The Country, Region, and State_Name columns will create a State dimension. The Category, Subcategory, and Product_Name columns will create a Product dimension. The Sales_Units column and the Sales_Dollars column (almost visible at the bottom of the list) will become the measure of the local cube.

4. Click Next three times to get to the final screen of the Query Wizard.

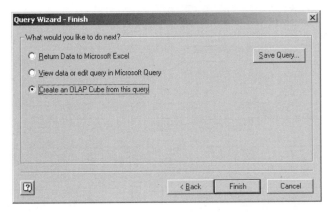

5. Click the Create An OLAP Cube From This Query option, and click Finish. This launches the OLAP Cube Wizard, which will be covered in the following section.

When you create a server cube by using Analysis Manager, you can create SQL expressions as part of a dimension level or measure definition. When you create a local cube, however, all SQL expressions must occur in the relational view, whether you create that view in Microsoft Query or in the relational data source.

Use the OLAP Cube Wizard to create a cube file

Once you have created a rowset in Microsoft Query, you can use the OLAP Cube Wizard to define the dimensions and measures for the cube. The OLAP Cube Wizard is like a miniature version of the Analysis Manager application.

1. Click Next to skip the welcome screen of the OLAP Cube Wizard. In step 1 of the wizard, make the measure names more readable: Select the Sum Of Sales_Units data field name, and type **Sales Units** as the new name. Then select the Sum Of Sales_Dollars data field name, and type **Sales Dollars** as the new name. Click Next.

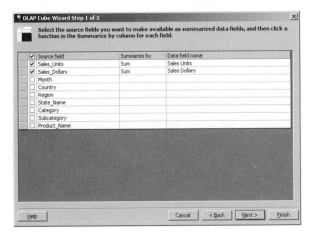

2. In the Source Fields list, double-click Country, Category, and Month. This creates three new dimensions. The Month dimension has a proposed hierarchy automatically created.

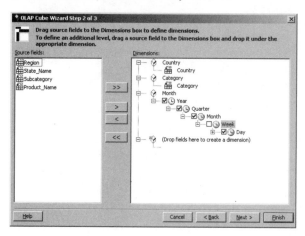

3. Clear the check box next to the Day level for the Month dimension. From the Source Fields list, drag Region to the Country level, and drag State_Name to the Region level. Then drag Subcategory to the Category level, and drag Product_Name to the Subcategory level.

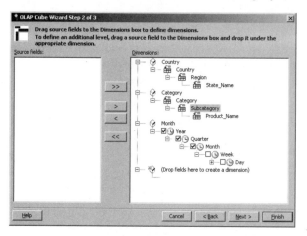

You can rename a dimension or a level by right-clicking the name and clicking Rename. You can rename dimensions and levels to match the Sales cube in the Chapter 5 database on the Analysis server.

You can also rename a dimension or level name by selecting it and pressing F2.

4. Type **Product** as the new name for the Category dimension, remove the underscore from the Product_Name and State_Name levels, type **State** as the new name for the Country dimension, and type **Time** as the new name for the Month dimension. Click Next.

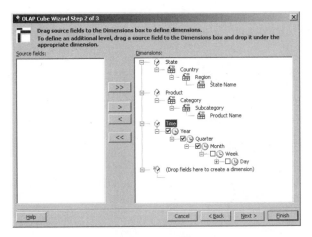

5. On the final page of the OLAP Cube Wizard, click the Save A Cube File Containing All Data For The Cube option, type **C:\Analysis\NewSales.cub** as the name of the cube file, and click Finish.

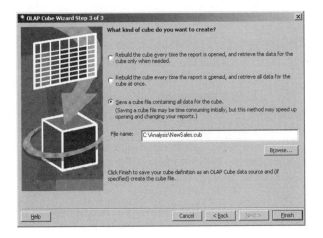

Note   The first two options on the final page of the OLAP Cube Wizard allow you to create a cube that exists only in the PivotTable Service cache. The first option creates the equivalent of a relational OLAP (ROLAP) cube, retrieving values into the PivotTable Service cache directly from the relational data source only as they are needed. The second option creates the equivalent of a multidimensional OLAP (MOLAP) cube (with no aggregations) completely in the PivotTable Service cache. With either of the first two options, the cube exists only as long as the client application remains connected to the cube. For information about aggregations and ROLAP and MOLAP cubes, see Chapter 8, "Storage Optimization."

The Save As dialog box asks you to save the definition of the OLAP query. This information is then used to create the cube, either permanently as a cube file, or temporarily, in memory, each time you access the OLAP query.

6. Type **NewSales.oqy** for the query, and click Save.

After Microsoft Query creates the OLAP query file, it directs the PivotTable Service to use the definition in the query file to create the local cube.

7. When the OLAP Cube Wizard returns you to Excel, it puts you into step 3 of the PivotTable And PivotChart Wizard. Click Finish to create the PivotTable on the active sheet.

8. In Excel, a new PivotTable report connects to the cube file you just created.

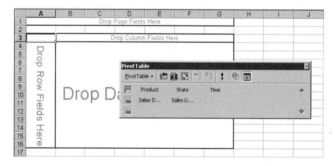

Once you've created a local cube, it's almost indistinguishable to a client application from a server-based cube. As explained in "Enable write-back for a cube" in Chapter 4, "Advanced Dimensions and Cubes," you can even write back to a local cube; the cube simply won't retain the write-back values once you close the connection to the cube.

Chapter Summary

To	Do this
Create an Excel PivotTable report from an OLAP cube	On the Data menu in Excel, click PivotTable And PivotChart Report. Click the External Data Source option and the Get Data button. In Microsoft Query, click the OLAP Cubes tab.
Hide selected members on an axis	Click the drop-down arrow next to the dimension name (on the filter axis) or level name (row and column axis). Select or clear check boxes, and click OK.
Move multiple measures from the row axis to the column axis in an Excel PivotTable report	Drag the row axis button to the column area.
Move measures from the column axis to the rows axis in an Office PivotTable list	Select the caption bar, and in the property toolbox, expand the Totals section. In the Total Orientation drop-down list, select row.
Remove the interactive buttons from an Excel PivotChart report	On the PivotChart toolbar, click the PivotChart menu and click Hide PivotChart Field Buttons.
Publish an Excel PivotTable report as an Office PivotTable list	On the File menu in Excel, click Save As Web Page. Click Publish. Select PivotTable, select the Add Interactivity With check box, and select PivotTable Functionality.
Show only a single level on an axis in an Office PivotTable list	Drag the dimension to the axis, and then drag away the unwanted levels.
Add an Office PivotTable list to an HTML document	In FrontPage, point to Component on the Insert menu and click Office PivotTable. In the property toolbox, expand the Data Source section, select the Connection option, and click Connection Editor. Switch to the Provider tab, and select OLE DB Provider For OLAP Services 8.0. Then switch to the Connection tab, type the name of the server, and select the initial database.
Restrict capabilities of the Office PivotTable list control	In FrontPage, select the control, and in the property toolbox, set values in the Advanced section.

(continued)

(continued)

To	Do this
Create a local cube file based on an existing server cube	With an Excel PivotTable report selected, on the PivotTable toolbar, click the PivotTable menu, click Client Server Settings, and follow the instructions in the wizard.
Create a local cube directly from a relational data source	In Excel, on the Data menu, point at Get External Data and click New Database Query. Use Microsoft Query to define the relational data source, and then—either in the last page of the Query Wizard or from the File menu in Microsoft Query—select Create An OLAP Cube From This Query and follow the instructions in the wizard.

Multidimensional Expressions

MDX Values

Estimated time: 2 hours

Chapter Objectives

In this chapter, you'll learn how an MDX expression works and how to

- Use MDX to navigate a dimension hierarchy.

- Display the name or member property of a member.

- Create conditional expressions using MDX.

- Use MDX to retrieve values from a cube.

- Use MDX to calculate contribution.

- Use MDX to calculate growth over time.

Start the lesson

1. Start Analysis Manager. Right-click the server, and click Restore Database.

2. Navigate to the folder containing the sample files for this book, select Chapter 6, and click Open. Click Restore, and then close the Restore Database Progress dialog box. The archived Chapter 6 OLAP database contains a Sales cube identical to the one you created in Chapter 3, "Dimension and Cube Editors," but without calculated and derived measures.

A spreadsheet is an effective tool for analyzing numbers, allowing you to create extremely flexible formulas. A spreadsheet gets very cumbersome, however, when you're dealing with large masses of data or when you need to organize the values differently.

A database is an effective tool for storing and retrieving numbers, allowing you to use the same values in multiple reports or views. A database gets very frustrating, however, when you need to create complex formulas—particularly formulas that need to know about the relationships between different members of a dimension.

Imagine a database that allows you to store and retrieve massive quantities of data, with whatever degree of flexibility you want, but that also allows you to create formulas as complex and sophisticated as those in any spreadsheet. Imagine a spreadsheet with formulas and functions specifically designed for business analysis but that also automatically fills formulas into the necessary ranges. In this chapter, you'll learn about MDX—a tool that enables you to turn a large OLAP database into a sophisticated calculation engine.

Creating Simple MDX Expressions

MDX is a pseudoacronym for *multidimensional expressions*. MDX was created expressly for use with multidimensional OLAP data sources. MDX is used in two different ways within Microsoft SQL Server 2000 Analysis Services. First, it is a query language—the tool for retrieving reports from an OLAP cube. In other words, MDX is the tool used by client applications (such as the Microsoft Excel 2000 PivotTable report) to retrieve values. Second, MDX is an expression language—the tool used to calculate single values. For example, MDX is what you use to create calculated members in a cube or to create a dynamic default member. In this chapter, you'll learn how to create MDX expressions based on single values. In Chapter 7, "MDX Sets," you'll learn how to create MDX queries and also how to create expressions based on multiple values. In Chapter 8, "Storage Optimization," you'll learn how to apply MDX expressions in a variety of contexts within a cube, including calculating default members, calculating custom rollup formulas, and creating custom actions. If you understand MDX, you can create sophisticated expressions that put the A (for *analytical*) into OLAP.

Chapter 7 will show you how to create MDX queries and how to create expressions based on multiple values.

MDX is not exclusive to Analysis Services. It's part of a specification called OLE DB for OLAP, which Microsoft has sponsored to industry standards boards as a tool for querying a multidimensional data source. MDX is a standardized language that will soon be supported by several OLAP providers, just as structured query language (SQL) is a standardized language that is supported by many relational database providers. Of course, just as relational database providers make modifications to the SQL standard, so OLAP providers will make minor customizations to the MDX standard. In fact, the MDX implemented in Analysis Services does vary somewhat from the OLE DB for OLAP specification. This book will refer only to the Analysis Services flavor of MDX.

Create a calculated member using constant values

One important use of MDX expressions is in creating calculated members. Calculated members add the calculating ability of a spreadsheet to an OLAP database. In a spreadsheet, each cell gets its own value. That value can be a constant that you type into a cell or it can be calculated as a formula. To understand how calculated members work, start by creating calculated members that use constant values.

1. In the Chapter 6 database, expand the Cubes folder, right-click the Sales cube, and click Edit. Click the Data tab to activate the Preview pane, and drag the Product dimension to the rows area, replacing the Employee dimension.

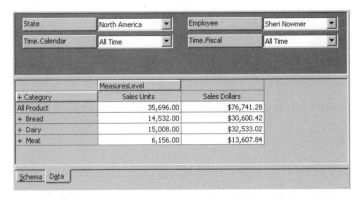

2. Click the Insert Calculated Member toolbar button. In the Calculated Member Builder dialog box, type **Sample** as the name of the new member. In the Value Expression box, type **500**.

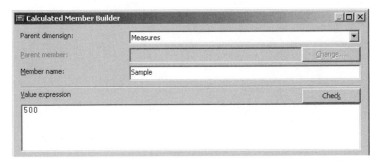

3. Click OK to create the member.

	MeasuresLevel		
+ Category	Sales Units	Sales Dollars	Sample
All Product	35,696.00	$76,741.28	500
+ Bread	14,532.00	$30,600.42	500
+ Dairy	15,008.00	$32,533.02	500
+ Meat	6,156.00	$13,607.84	500

A new column labeled Sample appears, filled with the value *500*. If you think of the grid as a spreadsheet, you can think of a calculated member as a value or formula that automatically fills all the cells of the column. You can change the expression for a calculated member simply by changing the Value property in the Properties pane.

4. In the cube tree, select Sample in the Calculated Members folder. Select the Value property, type **"Hello"**, and press Enter.

	MeasuresLevel		
+ Category	Sales Units	Sales Dollars	Sample
All Product	35,696.00	$76,741.28	Hello
+ Bread	14,532.00	$30,600.42	Hello
+ Dairy	15,008.00	$32,533.02	Hello
+ Meat	6,156.00	$13,607.84	Hello

The values in the Sample column change to the word *Hello*. You can use a text string as a constant value in a calculated member as long as you enclose the string in double quotation marks.

5. Select the Value property of the Sample member, type **Null**, and press Enter.

+ Category	MeasuresLevel		
	Sales Units	Sales Dollars	Sample
All Product	35,696.00	$76,741.28	
+ Bread	14,532.00	$30,600.42	
+ Dairy	15,008.00	$32,533.02	
+ Meat	6,156.00	$13,607.84	

The cells in the Sample column appear empty. You can't leave the Value property empty; to create an empty cell, use the keyword *Null*.

6. Select the Value property of the Sample member, type **50+17**, and press Enter.

+ Category	MeasuresLevel		
	Sales Units	Sales Dollars	Sample
All Product	35,696.00	$76,741.28	67
+ Bread	14,532.00	$30,600.42	67
+ Dairy	15,008.00	$32,533.02	67
+ Meat	6,156.00	$13,607.84	67

The number 67—the result of the expression—appears in all the cells of the Sample column. Again, think of the grid as a spreadsheet where the value or formula you type is automatically copied into all the relevant cells. It's as if there were four different copies of the formula, each one calculating a value. In an MDX expression, you can use any standard arithmetic operator: plus (+) for addition, minus (–) for subtraction, asterisk (*) for multiplication, slash (/) for division, and caret (^) for exponentiation.

7. Select the Value property of the Sample member, type **"Hello" + " , " + "World"**, and press Enter.

+ Category	MeasuresLevel		
	Sales Units	Sales Dollars	Sample
All Product	35,696.00	$76,741.28	Hello, World
+ Bread	14,532.00	$30,600.42	Hello, World
+ Dairy	15,008.00	$32,533.02	Hello, World
+ Meat	6,156.00	$13,607.84	Hello, World

See "Use an external function to convert a string to a number" later in this chapter to learn how to combine text with a number.

The string *Hello, World* appears. An MDX expression can combine text strings. Unlike an Excel formula, in which you use an ampersand (&) to combine text strings, in an MDX expression, you must use a plus sign (+). Also unlike an Excel formula, an MDX expression does not automatically convert a number into a text string, so you cannot use an expression such as *"The value is " + 45*. (Later in this chapter, you'll learn how to combine text with a number.)

Display the name of the current member

An MDX expression can return either a number or a text string. You can use MDX expressions to display member names. Doing so can help you see how MDX expressions and dimension members interact.

1. Select the Value property of the Sample member, and click the ellipsis (...) button. Clear the contents of the Value Expression box.

   MDX includes a large number of functions. MDX functions are all listed in the Functions tree of the Calculated Member Builder, grouped based on what the function returns. There is a *Name* function that returns a name. A name is a text string, so the *Name* function appears in the String group.

2. In the Functions tree, expand String and double-click the *Name - Dimension* function.

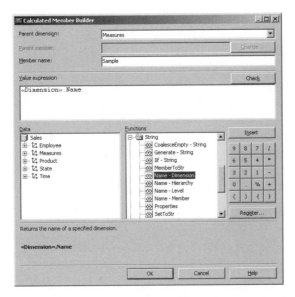

   The function appears in the Value Expression box, preceded by the token «Dimension». When you insert a function from the Functions tree, it shows you the syntax for the function, using placeholder tokens enclosed in double pointed brackets. Tokens are easy to replace: simply click anywhere within the token to select it, and then double-click an appropriate item from the Data or Functions tree.

3. Click the «Dimension» token, and then double-click the Product dimension in the Data tree to change the expression to *[Product].Name*. Then click OK.

+ Category	MeasuresLevel		
	Sales Units	Sales Dollars	Sample
All Product	35,696.00	$76,741.28	Product
+ Bread	14,532.00	$30,600.42	Product
+ Dairy	15,008.00	$32,533.02	Product
+ Meat	6,156.00	$13,607.84	Product

The Sample column shows the word *Product* in all the rows. The expression is displaying the name of the dimension, which doesn't change from member to member. To display the name of a specific member, you must use a different version of the *Name* function.

4. Select the Value property, and click the ellipsis button. Clear the Value Expression box, expand String in the Functions tree, double-click *Name - Member*, and click the «Member» token.

You need a function that will return a member, so look in the Member group of the Functions tree.

5. Expand the Member group, and double-click the *CurrentMember* function.

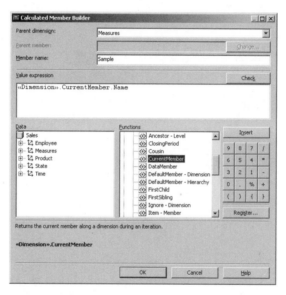

6. Click the «Dimension» token that precedes the function. Double-click *Product* in the Data tree to change the expression to *[Product]. CurrentMember.Name*. Then click OK.

	MeasuresLevel		
+ Category	Sales Units	Sales Dollars	Sample
All Product	35,696.00	$76,741.28	All Product
+ Bread	14,532.00	$30,600.42	Bread
+ Dairy	15,008.00	$32,533.02	Dairy
+ Meat	6,156.00	$13,607.84	Meat

The Sample column displays the name of each member.

7. Drag the State dimension down to the rows axis, replacing the Product dimension (that is, the Category heading).

| Time.Calendar | All Time ▼ | Product | All Product ▼ |
| Employee | Sheri Nowmer ▼ | Time.Fiscal | All Time ▼ |

	MeasuresLevel		
	Sales Units	Sales Dollars	Sample
+ Country			
North America	35,696.00	$76,741.28	All Product
+ Canada	3,715.00	$7,874.22	All Product
+ Mexico	5,166.00	$11,138.41	All Product
+ USA	26,815.00	$57,728.65	All Product

The value in the Sample column changes to All Product for all the rows. That's because the All Product member is selected in the filter list above the grid. The value in the filter list is the current member for that dimension.

8. In the Product filter list, select Bread.

| Time.Calendar | All Time ▼ | Product | Bread ▼ |
| Employee | Sheri Nowmer ▼ | Time.Fiscal | All Time ▼ |

	MeasuresLevel		
	Sales Units	Sales Dollars	Sample
+ Country			
North America	14,532.00	$30,600.42	Bread
+ Canada	1,046.00	$2,180.74	Bread
+ Mexico	1,289.00	$2,697.92	Bread
+ USA	12,197.00	$25,721.76	Bread

The value in the Sample column changes to *Bread* because Bread is now the current member of the Product dimension. Each cell in the grid has a current member for each dimension. If a dimension is represented on the row or column axis, the current member is the member that appears on the current row or column. If a dimension appears in the filter area, the current member is the member that appears in the filter box.

9. Drag the Product dimension back to the row axis, replacing the State dimension, and double-click the Category heading so that both Category and Subcategory levels are visible. Scroll as needed to see the Sample member.

		MeasuresLevel
- Category	+ Subcategory	Sample
All Product	All Product Total	All Product
	Bread Total	Bread
	+ Bagels	Bagels
- Bread	+ Muffins	Muffins
	+ Sliced Bread	Sliced Bread
	Dairy Total	Dairy
	+ Cheese	Cheese
- Dairy	+ Milk	Milk
	+ Sour Cream	Sour Cream
	+ Yogurt	Yogurt
	Meat Total	Meat
- Meat	+ Deli Meats	Deli Meats
	+ Fresh Chicken	Fresh Chicken

The current member of a dimension can be at any level of the hierarchy.

Note   MDX has other string functions that behave very similarly to the *Name* function. The *UniqueName* function returns a string that includes the entire hierarchy for the member. The *UserName* function returns the name of the current user, including both the domain name and the user ID. The name of the current user is independent of the current cube, so the *UserName* function stands completely alone—as if it were a string constant.

Display the ancestor of a current member

CurrentMember is an MDX function. It is a function that returns a member. Once you have a member, you can display that member's name. There are other functions that return a member, often using the current member of a dimension as a starting point. For example, you can find the ancestor of the current member at any level of the hierarchy.

1. Click the Value property of the Sample member, click the ellipsis button to display the Calculated Member Builder dialog box, and clear the contents of the Value Expression box.

2. In the Functions tree, expand String and double-click the *Name - Member* function.

3. Click the «Member» token, and expand Member in the Functions tree.

Like *CurrentMember*, *Ancestor* is a function in the Member group. There are two versions of the *Ancestor* function.

4. Double-click *Ancestor - Level* in the Functions tree, and look at the description at the bottom of the dialog box.

This function returns the ancestor of a member at a given level. The *CurrentMember* function returns a member, so you can use it to replace the «Member» token.

5. Click the «Member» token. Then double-click *CurrentMember* in the Functions tree. Click the «Dimension» token. Then double-click Product in the Data tree.

6. Click the «Level» token. Then expand the Product dimension, and double-click the Category level. Click OK to accept the new expression.

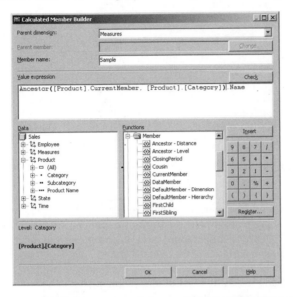

Note   Putting the insertion point after one item in a pair of punctuation marks (such as parentheses, brackets, or quotation marks) turns both items bold. Omitting one of a pair of punctuation marks turns the remaining item red. These signals help you properly match punctuation that must come in pairs.

---

7. Double-click the Subcategory level, and browse the Sample column to see how it always displays the appropriate category ancestor of the current product.

- Category	- Subcategory	Product Name	MeasuresLevel Sample
			Sample
		Sphinx Pumpernickel Bread	Bread
- Bread	- Sliced Bread	Sphinx Rye Bread	Bread
		Sphinx Wheat Bread	Bread
		Sphinx White Bread	Bread
	Dairy Total		Dairy
		Cheese Total	Dairy
		Booker Cheese Spread	Dairy
		Booker Havarti Cheese	Dairy
		Booker Head Cheese	Dairy
- Dairy	- Cheese	Booker Jack Cheese	Dairy
		Booker Low Fat String Che	Dairy

The parent of a member is just a special kind of ancestor—the ancestor that is only one level away. A second variation of the *Ancestor* function allows you to specify the distance from the original member to the desired member. For a parent, the distance is 1 level.

8. Select the Value property of the Sample member, and change the expression to **Ancestor([Product].CurrentMember,1).Name**. Then press Enter to display the name of the parent for each member.

- Category	- Subcategory	Product Name	MeasuresLevel
			Sample
All Product	All Product Total		
	Bread Total		All Product
		Bagels Total	Bread
		Colony Bagels	Bagels
		Fantastic Bagels	Bagels
	- Bagels	Great Bagels	Bagels
		Modell Bagels	Bagels
- Bread		Sphinx Bagels	Bagels
		Muffins Total	Bread
		Colony Blueberry Muffins	Muffins
		Colony Cranberry Muffins	Muffins
	- Muffins	Colony English Muffins	Muffins

By using the *Ancestor* function—coupled with the *CurrentMember* function—you can display the ancestor of the current member, either at a relative position in the hierarchy or at a specific level of the hierarchy.

Note   MDX has other member functions that are very similar to the *Ancestor* function. The *Parent* function returns the parent of a member. Therefore, the expression *[Product].CurrentMember.Parent* is functionally equivalent to *Ancestor([Product].CurrentMember,1)*. The *FirstChild* and *LastChild* functions return the first or last member that is a child of the given member. The *FirstSibling* and *LastSibling* functions return the first or last member that is a child of the given member's parent. The expression *[Product].CurrentMember.FirstSibling* is functionally equivalent to *[Product].CurrentMember.Parent.FirstChild*.

Test a member name against a string

MDX allows you to make comparison tests in an expression. For example, you can test whether a product belongs in a specific category by testing the name of the product's ancestor.

1. Select the Value property of the Sample calculated member, and click the ellipsis button. Change the value expression to **Ancestor([Product]. CurrentMember, [Product].[Category]).Name = "Bread"**.

The value of True as 1 and False as 0 is similar to the usage in Excel but differs from Microsoft Visual Basic in which True is –1 and False is 0.

2. Click OK to accept the revised expression. In the browser, display the Product Category and Subcategory levels and look at the value in the Sample column.

- Category	+ Subcategory	MeasuresLevel Sales Units	Sales Dollars	Sample
All Product	All Product Total	35,696.00	$76,741.28	0
	Bread Total	14,532.00	$30,600.42	1
- Bread	+ Bagels	1,541.00	$3,552.28	1
	+ Muffins	6,445.00	$13,081.28	1
	+ Sliced Bread	6,546.00	$13,966.86	1
	Dairy Total	15,008.00	$32,533.02	0
	+ Cheese	7,493.00	$17,709.11	0
- Dairy	+ Milk	4,151.00	$7,259.42	0

The Sample column shows the value *1* for all products that are within the Bread category and *0* for all products that are not in the Bread category. The value *1* is equivalent to *True*, and *0* is equivalent to *False*.

Note   MDX uses standard comparison operators: = (equals), <> (not equal), > (greater than), < (less than), >= (greater than or equal), and <= (less than or equal).

You might want to display something other than *1* or *0* in the cells. Suppose, for example, that you wanted to flag all the products that would be OK to bring to a bread-tasting social. The *IIF* function allows you to return different values depending on the result of a conditional test. The MDX *IIF* function is similar to the *IF* function in Excel or the *IIF* function in Visual Basic.

3. Click the Value property ellipsis button to redisplay the Calculated Member Builder dialog box. In the Functions tree, expand String and select the *IIF - String* function. Look at the description of the function at the bottom of the dialog box.

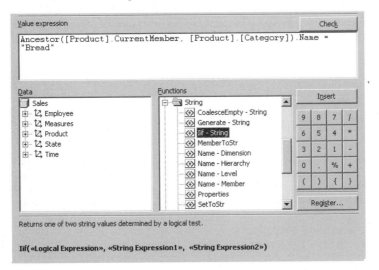

The first argument of the *IIF* function is a conditional test—an expression that returns *True* or *False*. The second argument is the value that will be returned if the conditional test is *True*; it can be either a string or a number. The third argument is the value that will be returned if the conditional test returns *False*; it must be the same type of value as that of the second argument. If the second argument is a string, the third argument must also be a string. Likewise, if the second argument is a number, the third argument must also be a number. This is different from the *IF* function in Excel or the *IIF* function in Microsoft Visual Basic for Applications (VBA), where the arguments can have different data types.

4. Change the contents of the Value Expression box to **IIF(Ancestor ([Product].CurrentMember, [Product].Category).Name = "Bread" , "Bring" , "Don't Bring")**. (Specifically, enter **IIF** and an opening parenthesis at the beginning of the expression. Type a comma, **"Bring"**, another comma, **"Don't Bring"**, and a closing parenthesis at the end of the expression.)

5. Click OK to accept the definition, and browse the values in the Sample column.

		MeasuresLevel		
- Category	+ Subcategory	Sales Units	Sales Dollars	Sample
All Product	All Product Total	35,696.00	$76,741.28	Don't Bring
	Bread Total	14,532.00	$30,600.42	Bring
- Bread	+ Bagels	1,541.00	$3,552.28	Bring
	+ Muffins	6,445.00	$13,081.28	Bring
	+ Sliced Bread	6,546.00	$13,966.86	Bring
	Dairy Total	15,008.00	$32,533.02	Don't Bring
	+ Cheese	7,493.00	$17,709.11	Don't Bring
- Dairy	+ Milk	4,151.00	$7,259.42	Don't Bring

A conditional test, such as the one used in the *IIF* function, can be composed of more than one sub test. For example, if your bread party changes to a bread and cheese party, you could expand the conditional test.

6. Select the Value property, and click the ellipsis button. Change the expression to **IIF(Ancestor([Product].CurrentMember, [Product]. Category).Name = "Bread" OR Ancestor([Product]. CurrentMember, [Product].Subcategory).Name = "Cheese" , "Bring" , "Don't Bring").**

7. Click OK, and browse the results in the Sample column

		MeasuresLevel		
- Category	+ Subcategory	Sales Units	Sales Dollars	Sample
All Product	All Product Total	35,696.00	$76,741.28	Don't Bring
	Bread Total	14,532.00	$30,600.42	Bring
- Bread	+ Bagels	1,541.00	$3,552.28	Bring
	+ Muffins	6,445.00	$13,081.28	Bring
	+ Sliced Bread	6,546.00	$13,966.86	Bring
	Dairy Total	15,008.00	$32,533.02	Don't Bring
	+ Cheese	7,493.00	$17,709.11	Bring
- Dairy	+ Milk	4,151.00	$7,259.42	Don't Bring

Note   In addition to *OR* (which returns *True* if either of two conditional tests returns *True*), MDX also allows you to combine two conditional tests using *AND* (which returns *True* only if both values are *True*) and *XOR* (which returns *True* if one and only one value is *True*). You can also precede a conditional test with *NOT* (which reverses the *True* and *False* results of the test).

Display a member property for a member

In addition to names, members can have member properties as well. For example, in the Product Dimension, the Subcategory level has a Category Manager member property assigned. You can display the name of that manager.

1. Select the Value property of the Sample calculated member, and click the ellipsis button. Change the expression to **Ancestor([Product]. CurrentMember, [Product].[SubCategory]).Name**.

This expression would display the name of the current product's subcategory.

2. Delete the *Name* function from the end of the expression, and add **Properties("Category Manager")**.

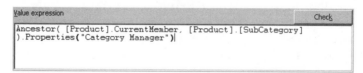

```
Value expression                                              Check

Ancestor( [Product].CurrentMember, [Product].[SubCategory]
).Properties("Category Manager")|
```

The name of the member property must be enclosed in double quotation marks. If the member property name does not exist, the expression will return an error.

3. Click OK, and then expand the levels to show the Product Name level and see the manager change with the subcategory.

			MeasuresLevel
- Category	- Subcategory	Product Name	Sample
	- Frozen Chicken	Imagine Frozen Chicken W	Maya Gutierrez
		PigTail Frozen Chicken Brea	Maya Gutierrez
		PigTail Frozen Chicken Thig	Maya Gutierrez
		PigTail Frozen Chicken Win	Maya Gutierrez
- Meat		Hamburger Total	Derrick Whelply
		Footnote Extra Lean Hamk	Derrick Whelply
		Footnote Seasoned Hambu	Derrick Whelply
		Genteel Extra Lean Hambu	Derrick Whelply

Use an external function to convert a string to a number

A member property is always returned as a string, even if the member property stores a number. If you want to use the member property as a number in an expression, you will have to use an external function to convert it.

For example, the Product Name level of the Product dimension includes a Price member property that contains the list price for each product. If you try to use the Price member property in a numeric expression, you'll get a syntax error. To use the member property in an expression, you must convert it to a number. MDX does not have any functions that will convert a string to a number, but MDX does allow you to access functions from other sources. In fact, MDX automatically includes functions from VBA and from Excel. VBA includes a function named *CDbl* (for "convert to double") that will convert a string into a number.

As a simple example, try to display what the list price would be after a 10 percent across-the-board price hike. The first step is to display the Price member property.

For a more sophisticated example of using a member property as a numeric value in an expression, see the section "Calculate discount dollars by using a member function" in Chapter 7.

1. Replace the Value property of the Sample member with **[Product]. CurrentMember.Properties("Price")**, and press Enter.

			MeasuresLevel	
- Category	- Subcategory	Product Name	Sales Dollars	Sample
All Product	All Product Total		$76,741.28	#ERR
	Bread Total		$30,600.42	#ERR
		Bagels Total	$3,552.28	#ERR
	- Bagels	Colony Bagels	$308.88	1.22
		Fantastic Bagels	$1,022.58	3.69
		Great Bagels	$604.54	1.86
- Bread		Modell Bagels	$994.08	3.4
		Sphinx Bagels	$622.20	1.85
		Muffins Total	$13,081.28	#ERR
		Colony Blueberry Muffins	$739.04	2.65

The prices appear for the individual products, but an error value occurs for each higher-level member. You can use an *IIF* function to display a value only for the lowest level.

You might want to open the Calculated Member Builder dialog box to edit the expression.

2. Change the Value property of the Sample member to **IIF(Product. CurrentMember.Level.Name = "Product Name",Product. CurrentMember.Properties("Price"),"")**, and press Enter.

			MeasuresLevel	
- Category	- Subcategory	Product Name	Sales Dollars	Sample
All Product	All Product Total		$76,741.28	
	Bread Total		$30,600.42	
		Bagels Total	$3,552.28	
		Colony Bagels	$308.88	1.22
	- Bagels	Fantastic Bagels	$1,022.58	3.69
		Great Bagels	$604.54	1.86
		Modell Bagels	$994.08	3.4
- Bread		Sphinx Bagels	$622.20	1.85
		Muffins Total	$13,081.28	
		Colony Blueberry Muffins	$739.04	2.65

The error values are now gone. With the *IIF* function, if the second argument is a string, the third argument must also be a string. Even though the Price member property is really a number, member properties are always returned as a string. The third argument must, therefore, be an empty string. To multiply the Price by a value, you must convert it to a number.

3. Change the Value property of the Sample member to **IIF(Product. CurrentMember.Level.Name = "Product Name",CDbl(Product. CurrentMember.Properties("Price")),Null)**, and press Enter.

To convert a number to a string, use the CStr function or the Format function from VBA.

The values in the browser look the same, but now the prices are numbers, not strings. The revised expression required two changes: adding the *CDbl* function and its parentheses around the member property value, and replacing the empty string with *Null*. The *CDbl* function is not an MDX function. It does not appear in the Number group of the Functions tree—in fact, it doesn't appear anywhere in the Functions tree. The function is a VBA function. You don't have to do anything special to include it in an MDX expression. All that remains is to multiply the value by 1.1 to get a 10 percent increase in price.

4. Append *** 1.1** to the end of the Value expression for the Sample member. The resulting expression will be *IIF(Product.CurrentMember.Level.Name = "Product Name",CDbl(Product.CurrentMember.Properties("Price")),Null)*1.1*. Then press Enter to see the updated values.

			MeasuresLevel	
- Category	- Subcategory	Product Name	Sales Dollars	Sample
All Product	All Product Total		$76,741.28	
	Bread Total		$30,600.42	
		Bagels Total	$3,552.28	
		Colony Bagels	$308.88	1.342
	- Bagels	Fantastic Bagels	$1,022.58	4.059
		Great Bagels	$604.54	2.046
		Modell Bagels	$994.08	3.74
- Bread		Sphinx Bagels	$622.20	2.035
		Muffins Total	$13,081.28	
		Colony Blueberry Muffins	$739.04	2.915

If you attempt to use a member property value in an arithmetic expression, the result is an error unless you first convert the value to a number.

Note   To find the list of available functions from VBA and Excel, go to SQL Server Books Online by clicking Contents And Index on the Help menu. In the Keyword box on the Index tab, type **Registered Function Libraries, Visual Basic for Applications** or **Registered Function Libraries, Excel**.

Specifying a Member Name in MDX

Each dimension of an OLAP cube contains many members. In an MDX query, you often specify a member from a dimension. Here are the rules for creating a legal member name, using the Colony Bagels member of the Product dimension as an example.

1. Begin with the member name or the member key, enclosed in brackets. If the member name or key does not include spaces or special characters, begins with a letter, and is not an MDX keyword, you can omit the brackets. If you use the member key, precede it with an ampersand (&) For example, *[Colony Bagels]* and *&[591]* are valid member names.

2. Optionally, precede the member name or key with its parent member, its level name, or its dimension name. For example, *[Bagels].[Colony Bagels]*, *[Product Name].[Colony Bagels]*, and *[Product].&[591]* are all valid member names.

3. If you used a parent member name or key, optionally repeat step 2. For example, *[All Product].[Bread].[Bagels].[Colony Bagels]* is a valid member name. *[Bread].[Colony Bagels]* is not a valid member name because *[Bread]* is not the parent of *[Colony Bagels]*.

4. If you used a level name, optionally precede the level name with the dimension name.

5. Technically, you can precede the dimension name with the cube name, but this is rarely useful.

The full name of a member consists of the dimension name, the hierarchy name (if one exists), the name of each ancestor, and the lowest-level member name, with each component enclosed in brackets and separated by periods. Using members from the Sales cube of the Chapter 6 database, *[Time].[All Time].[1998].[Quarter 3].[October]* and *[State].[All State].[USA].[North West].[Oregon]* are two examples of the full name for a member. The full name for a member is always unambiguous and unique. The full name for a member is also long and can sometimes be hard to read. MDX allows you to simplify a member name.

When a dimension includes an explicit hierarchy, you can bracket the dimension and hierarchy names separately or treat the combination as a single name. For example, both *[Time.Fiscal]* and *[Time].[Fiscal]* are acceptable to MDX. You must, however, always include both the dimension and the hierarchy as if the combination were the dimension name. If Time.Fiscal is a dimension in a cube, *[Time].[Fiscal].[1998]* is a valid member name but *[Fiscal].[1998]* and *[Time].[1998]* are not.

(continued)

Specifying a Member Name in MDX *(continued)*

It's possible to create an ambiguous member name, but MDX will accept a name even if it is ambiguous. It simply uses the first member within the cube that matches the partial name. For example, MDX interprets the partial name *[Time].[Fiscal].[October]* as *[Time].[Fiscal].[1997].[Quarter 3].[October]* because 1997 is the first year in the Time.Fiscal dimension that has an October member. Likewise, MDX interprets the partial name *[1998]* as *[Time].[Calendar].[1998]* if the Time.Calendar dimension comes before the Time.Fiscal dimension in the Sales cube. You should, of course, avoid using ambiguous names, however, because MDX might interpret the name differently than you intended.

Retrieving Values from Cells

You can create many useful MDX expressions that look only at the names of members, but expressions get even more interesting when you refer to values from cells in the cube. To see how MDX refers to values in cells, consider first how an Excel formula refers to values in other cells.

Retrieve a value by specifying a single dimension

Imagine that you are creating a spreadsheet that calculates the margin (that is, sales minus cost) for three product categories. Traditionally, spreadsheet formulas have used addresses to refer to cells.

	A	B	C	D	E
1	Category	Sales	Cost	Margin	
2	Bread	$33,886	$13,506	$20,380	
3	Dairy	$38,932	$15,593	=B3-C3	
4	Meat	$18,362	$7,345	$11,017	
5					

The formula in cell D3 uses the address B3 to refer to dairy sales. The address B3 refers to the *position* of the cell, not to its *meaning*. When you copy the formula from cell D3 to cell D4, the address B3 must change to B4. Each copy of the formula appears slightly different. Recent versions of Excel allow you to create formulas that use cell labels. The same worksheet could have formulas that look like these:

	A	B	C	D	E
1	Category	Sales	Cost	Margin	
2	Bread	$33,886	$13,506	$20,380	
3	Dairy	$38,932	$15,593	=Sales-Cost	
4	Meat	$18,362	$7,345	$11,017	
5					

The new formula in cell D3 uses the label Sales to refer to dairy sales. This time, the word *Sales* refers to the *meaning* of the cell (as defined by its column label), not to its position. The formula assumes that you want the Sales value for the product category that is on the *same row* as the formula. When you copy the formula from cell D3 to cell D4, the formula doesn't change. In MDX terminology, the formula implicitly uses the current member of the row axis.

Excel formulas that use labels are easy to understand. MDX expressions work in a very similar way. You can create a new calculated measure that automatically refers to the current state, or you can create a new calculated member of the Product dimension that automatically refers to the current measure.

1. In the Cube Editor, select the Value property of the Sample member. Type **[Sales Units]*2** and press Enter. Then collapse the Category level.

	MeasuresLevel		
+ Category	Sales Units	Sales Dollars	Sample
All Product	35,696.00	$76,741.28	71,392.00
+ Bread	14,532.00	$30,600.42	29,064.00
+ Dairy	15,008.00	$32,533.02	30,016.00
+ Meat	6,156.00	$13,607.84	12,312.00

The values in the Sample column change to double the value of the current row's Sales Units. This behaves precisely the same as Excel formulas using labels. The formula is calculated independently in each cell and uses the Sales Units value for current member of the Product dimension.

2. Select the Parent Dimension property of the Sample calculated member. Click the drop-down arrow, select the Product dimension, and press Enter.

	MeasuresLevel	
+ Category	Sales Units	Sales Dollars
All Product	35,696.00	$76,741.28
+ Bread	14,532.00	$30,600.42
+ Dairy	15,008.00	$32,533.02
+ Meat	6,156.00	$13,607.84
Sample	#ERR	#ERR

The Sample member moves to the Product dimension. The values for the member show an error (temporarily) because the Sales Units member for the current row (Sample) does not have a value.

3. Change the Value property of the Sample member to **[Bread]*2**, and press Enter.

	MeasuresLevel	
+ Category	Sales Units	Sales Dollars
All Product	35,696.00	$76,741.28
+ Bread	14,532.00	$30,600.42
+ Dairy	15,008.00	$32,533.02
+ Meat	6,156.00	$13,607.84
Sample	29,064.00	$61,200.84

The values in the Sample row change to twice those of the Bread row. The formulas work the same as if the grid were a spreadsheet and you entered the formulas directly into the cells. Of course, the power of a calculated member comes from the fact that you don't have to enter the formula into each cell: a single formula automatically propagates to all the necessary cells. This works even when you change the dimensions on the axes.

4. Drag the State dimension to the Columns axis, replacing the Measures dimension.

	+ Country		
+ Category	North America	+ Canada	+ Mexico
All Product	35,696.00	3,715.00	5,166.00
+ Bread	14,532.00	1,046.00	1,289.00
+ Dairy	15,008.00	1,884.00	2,407.00
+ Meat	6,156.00	785.00	1,470.00
Sample	29,064.00	2,092.00	2,578.00

The expression for the Sample member automatically fills all the necessary cells. In each cell, it simply retrieves the value of the Bread member for the current country. An MDX expression can even refer to a value that does not currently appear in the grid—something you cannot do with an Excel formula.

5. Drag the Measures dimension to the Rows axis, replacing the Product dimension. Then click the Product dimension drop-down arrow, and select Sample.

Product	Sample ▼	Employee	Sheri Nowmer ▼
Time.Calendar	All Time ▼	Time.Fiscal	All Time ▼

	+ Country		
MeasuresLevel	North America	+ Canada	+ Mexico
Sales Units	29,064.00	2,092.00	2,578.00
Sales Dollars	$61,200.84	$4,361.48	$5,395.84

This time, all the cells in the grid are filled with the calculated member formula. In each case, the formula retrieves the value of the Bread member for the current row or column.

An MDX expression always calculates using the context of the cell in which it's actually calculated. Each cell has a current member for each dimension. Take, for example, the Canada Sales Dollars cell (with the value $4,361.48). For that one cell, the current member of the Measures dimension (*[Sales Units]*) comes from the row label. The current member of the State dimension (*[Canada]*) comes from the column label. The current member of the Employee dimension (*[Sheri Nowmer]*), the Time.Calendar dimension (*[All Time]*), and the Time.Fiscal dimension (*[All Time]*) come from the filter fields. The current member of the Product dimension is *[Sample]*, but it is a formula that redirects the Product dimension to the [Bread] member. Retrieving a value from a cube requires a member from each dimension of the cube; you can use the current member for most dimensions.

Retrieve a value by specifying two or more dimensions

A spreadsheet formula often must refer to a cell that is not on the same row or column as the cell containing the formula. For example, suppose you want to calculate the percent a specific product category contributed to total sales. Using traditional spreadsheet references, you would need to create a formula similar to the following:

	A	B	C	D
1	Category	Sales	Contrib	
2	Bread	$33,886	37%	
3	Dairy	$38,932	=B3/B$5	
4	Meat	$18,362	20%	
5	Total	$91,180	100%	
6				

The formula in cell C3 refers to cell B5. To be able to copy the formula to the other cells in column C, it's necessary to add a dollar sign to "anchor" the row. This notation technique works, but it's clumsy and hard to understand, and it would not translate well to the multidimensional world. If you create the formula by using labels, it looks like this:

	A	B	C	D	E
1	Category	Sales	Contrib		
2	Bread	$33,886	37%		
3	Dairy	$38,932	=Sales/$Total Sales		
4	Meat	$18,362	20%		
5	Total	$91,180	100%		
6					

The reference *Total Sales* refers to cell B5. (The new formula still needs a dollar sign if you want to copy it, but that's not the important part.) When using labels to refer to a cell that is not on the current row or column, you must include *both* the row and column labels, separated by a space. The result is remarkably readable. MDX, however, cannot simply use member names separated by spaces because an OLAP cube typically contains many more than two dimensions. MDX uses a notation and terminology for referring to an explicit cell that can be best understood by seeing how to specify a point on a chart.

Imagine a mathematical line. A line has one dimension. In basic charting, if you want to specify a point on the line, you specify a single number or a single coordinate. On the following line, the coordinate for the marked point is 3.

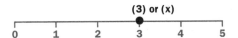

Now imagine a cube with one dimension. If you want to specify a value from the cube, you specify a single member from the dimension. This single value is the coordinate for the cell. In the following hypothetical cube, the coordinate for the marked cell is [February].

January	February	March	April
14	41	33	25

Imagine a mathematical grid. A grid has two dimensions. In basic charting, if you want to specify a point on the grid, you specify a pair of numbers or a double coordinate, typically enclosed in parentheses. On the following grid, the coordinate for the marked point is (3,4).

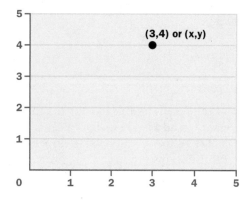

Now imagine a cube with two dimensions. If you want to specify a value from the cube, you specify a single member from each dimension. This double value is the coordinate for the cell. In the following hypothetical cube, the coordinate for the marked cell is (*[January],[Sphinx Bagels]*).

	January	February	March	April
Colony Blueberry Muffins			6	17
Colony Cranberry Muffins	6	16	6	8
Sphinx Bagels	8	25	21	

Imagine a three-dimensional mathematical space. In charting, to specify a point in the space, you specify three numbers, or a triple coordinate. In the following space, the coordinate for the marked point is (4,2,2).

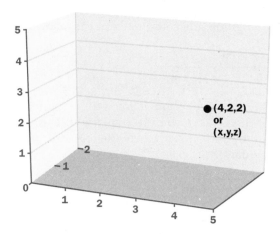

Now imagine a cube with three dimensions. Rather than format the cube as a cube or a rectangle, imagine the three dimensions of the cube as key columns, as described in Chapter 1, "A Data Analysis Foundation." To specify a member from the cube, you specify a single member from each dimension. In the following hypothetical cube, the coordinate for the marked cell is (*[WA],[Colony Blueberry Muffins],[Month].[All]*).

State	Product	Month	Units
All	All	All	113
WA	All	All	64
WA	Muffins	All	38
WA	Colony Blueberry Muffins	All	13
WA	Colony Blueberry Muffins	Qtr1	3
WA	Colony Blueberry Muffins	Mar	3

With more than two or three dimensions, it's usually easier to visualize a cube as a table with dimensions represented by key columns. To retrieve a single value from the cube—that is, to specify a single cell in the cube—you must specify one member from each dimension.

Watch for a pattern in the terminology for a coordinate as it includes more dimensions: A coordinate containing one dimension is a *single* coordinate. A coordinate containing two dimensions is a *double* coordinate. With three dimensions, it is a *triple* coordinate. With four dimensions, it is a *quadruple* coordinate; with five, a quin*tuple*; with six, a sex*tuple*, with seven, a sep*tuple*; and with eight, an oc*tuple*. Once you get past four dimensions in a coordinate, each of the coordinate numbers ends in the suffix *tuple*. The generic term for a coordinate that includes one or more dimensions is a *tuple*.

Note Some people pronounce the first syllable of *tuple* to rhyme with *cup* (as in the word *quintuple*). Others pronounce it to rhyme with *coop* (as in the word *quadruple*). Each group considers the other to be uncivilized. Since this is a book, you don't have to know how I pronounce it.

As is the case with a mathematical coordinate, a tuple that contains more than a single dimension must be enclosed in parentheses. A tuple that contains one member from each dimension of a cube identifies a unique value in the cube. When you extract a value from a cube, the measures are considered to be a dimension, and you must include a measure within a tuple to uniquely identify a value. When you need to refer to a value from a cube, you use a tuple. Include in the tuple members for only the dimensions where you don't just want the current member. Most of the time, you'll be able to use the current member for all but one or two dimensions. You can use a calculated member to practice referring to specific cell values.

1. In the Cube Editor, make sure the Product dimension is on the row axis and the State dimension is on the column axis.

2. Select the Value property of the Sample calculated member. Type the tuple **([Canada] , [Dairy])**, and press Enter.

+ Category	+ Country North America	+ Canada	+ Mexico
All Product	35,696.00	3,715.00	5,166.00
+ Bread	14,532.00	1,046.00	1,289.00
+ Dairy	15,008.00	1,884.00	2,407.00
+ Meat	6,156.00	785.00	1,470.00
Sample	1,884.00	1,884.00	1,884.00

The value 1,884.00 appears across the entire Sample row. Within the context of this grid view, the value of Canada Dairy is a constant, much as if you had simply entered the number *1,884* for the Value property. The tuple, however, still uses the current member for all the other dimensions.

3. Drag the Measures dimension to the column axis, replacing the State dimension.

| State | North America ▼ | Employee | Sheri Nowmer ▼ |
| Time.Calendar | All Time ▼ | Time.Fiscal | All Time ▼ |

	MeasuresLevel	
+ Category	Sales Units	Sales Dollars
All Product	35,696.00	$76,741.28
+ Bread	14,532.00	$30,600.42
+ Dairy	15,008.00	$32,533.02
+ Meat	6,156.00	$13,607.84
Sample	1,884.00	$4,014.91

The Sample row shows the Canada Dairy sales for each measure, even though Canada is not visible. The current member of the State dimension is *[North America]*, but the Canada member in the tuple overrides the current member of the dimension. Any dimension not included in a tuple uses the current member.

4. Change the Value property of the Sample member to the expression **([Dairy] , [Sales Units]) – ([Meat] , [Sales Dollars])**.

	MeasuresLevel	
+ Category	Sales Units	Sales Dollars
All Product	35,696.00	$76,741.28
+ Bread	14,532.00	$30,600.42
+ Dairy	15,008.00	$32,533.02
+ Meat	6,156.00	$13,607.84
Sample	1400.16	1400.16

The expression does not have any meaningful business use, but it does illustrate how to specify multiple tuples in an expression. You can check the value by finding the Dairy Sales Units value and the Meat Sales Dollars values in the grid and performing the calculation.

The general form for many MDX expressions consists of two or more discrete values combined by an operator. Each of the original values can be a constant, a value from a cube (that is, a tuple), or the result of another MDX expression.

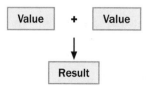

Calculating Relative Contribution

A tuple such as *[Sales Units]*—which uses an explicit member name from one dimension—are very common in MDX expressions. A tuple such as *([Dairy] , [Sales Units])*—which uses explicit member names from two or more dimensions—are quite rare. Usually, when you explicitly include members from more than one dimension in a tuple, you use functions to calculate a member based on the current member.

Using *CurrentMember* in a *LookupCube* Function

In "Use a custom member formula" in Chapter 4, "Advanced Dimensions and Cubes," you associated a custom formula with the Revenue member of the Finance cube. The formula was already stored in the database. You can now understand the formula needed to look up a value from a different cube. The formula uses the *LookupCube* function, with two arguments, both of which are text strings. The first argument is the name of the cube you want to retrieve a value from. The second argument is a tuple that specifies the value you want to retrieve. Typically, when retrieving a value from a cube, you want to retrieve the value that corresponds to the current member of one or more dimensions in the target cube. Since the tuple is a string, to insert the current member of a dimension, you must close the string, append the name—the unique name—of the current member by using the plus (+) operator, and then append the rest of the string. The final expression looks like this:

```
LookupCube("Sales","([Sales Dollars],[All Product],"
+[Time].[Calendar].CurrentMember.UniqueName + ")")
```

In a *LookupCube* function, any dimension not explicitly included in the tuple uses the default member of the dimension.

Calculate contribution as a percent of the total

Suppose that you want to calculate what percent each product or product category contributes to the total sales for all products. This expression would have two component values: a numerator value (Sales for the current product) divided by a denominator value (Sales for All Products). The numerator value will change from product to product, but the denominator value always retrieves the member from the All level of the Product dimension. Start by creating a calculated member that displays the Sales for All Products.

1. In the Cube Editor, change the Parent Dimension property of the Sample calculated member to *Measures*. Select the Value property, click the ellipsis button, and clear the current contents of the Value Expression box.

2. Type **([Sales Units], Ancestor([Product].CurrentMember, [Product].[(All)]))** in the Value Expression box.

The name of the All level in the *Ancestor* function includes parentheses. The brackets are then required because parentheses are special characters. The complete expression consists of a tuple that retrieves the value from the *[Sales Units]* member of the Measures dimension and from the All level member of the Product dimension (using the current member of all remaining dimensions). You could, of course, just enter *[All Product]* as the second part of the tuple, but then the expression would become invalid if you were to change the name of the Product dimension All level member.

Note   MDX has a *DefaultMember* function for a dimension. You should avoid using the *DefaultMember* function to refer to the All level member of a dimension because you can change the default member of a dimension, as described in "Specify a default member" in Chapter 3.

---

3. Click the OK button to save the changes to the Sample member.

	MeasuresLevel		
+ Category	Sales Units	Sales Dollars	Sample
All Product	35,696.00	$76,741.28	35,696.00
+ Bread	14,532.00	$30,600.42	35,696.00
+ Dairy	15,008.00	$32,533.02	35,696.00
+ Meat	6,156.00	$13,607.84	35,696.00

4. Click the Value property ellipsis button, and change the contents of the Value Expression box to **[Sales Units] / ([Sales Units], Ancestor([Product].CurrentMember, [Product].[(All)]))**.

This adds the numerator to the relative contribution expression. The numerator includes only the Measures dimension because it should "float" with the current member of the Product dimension. Since the numerator contains only a single member, parentheses are not required. This tuple returns the value of the Sales Units measure for the current product, the current state, the current time period, and so forth. The numerator tuple varies from product to product. The denominator tuple always returns the same product—the default member.

5. Click OK to accept the revised definition.

	MeasuresLevel		
+ Category	Sales Units	Sales Dollars	Sample
All Product	35,696.00	$76,741.28	1.00
+ Bread	14,532.00	$30,600.42	0.41
+ Dairy	15,008.00	$32,533.02	0.42
+ Meat	6,156.00	$13,607.84	0.17

6. Drag the State dimension to the row area of the grid, replacing the Product dimension.

	MeasuresLevel		
+ Country	Sales Units	Sales Dollars	Sample
North America	35,696.00	$76,741.28	1.00
+ Canada	3,715.00	$7,874.22	1.00
+ Mexico	5,166.00	$11,138.41	1.00
+ USA	26,815.00	$57,728.65	1.00

The values for the Sample member all become *1.00*. The numerator calculates the value of Sales Units for the current state and current product. The denominator calculates the value of Sales Units for the current state and default product. But each row of the grid shows the same product—the default product. When you create a calculated member, you must take into consideration any dimension that might appear in a grid browser. To make the Sample measure calculate the percent of total for both the State dimension and the Product dimension, you must add the State dimension to the denominator tuple.

7. Select the Value property, and click the ellipsis button. Click between the final two closing parentheses, type a comma, and type the expresstion **Ancestor([State].CurrentMember, [State].[(All)])**. The final full expression should be *[Sales Units] / ([Sales Units], Ancestor([Product].CurrentMember, [Product].[(All)]), Ancestor([State].CurrentMember, [State].[(All)]))*. Click OK to accept the expression.

	MeasuresLevel		
+ Country	Sales Units	Sales Dollars	Sample
North America	35,696.00	$76,741.28	1.00
+ Canada	3,715.00	$7,874.22	0.10
+ Mexico	5,166.00	$11,138.41	0.14
+ USA	26,815.00	$57,728.65	0.75

The denominator tuple now includes members from three dimensions. The Sample member now shows the relative contribution of each member of the State dimension (while still retaining the ability to show the relative contribution of members of the Product dimension). If you want to expand the member to be able to show relative contribution for the Time.Fiscal, Time.Calendar, and Employee dimensions as well, you simply add an appropriate *Ancestor* function for each of those dimensions to the denominator tuple.

8. Double-click the Country level to show the relative contribution of each region.

		MeasuresLevel		
- Country	+ Region	Sales Units	Sales Dollars	Sample
North America	North America Total	35,696.00	$76,741.28	1.00
+ Canada	Canada Total	3,715.00	$7,874.22	0.10
+ Mexico	Mexico Total	5,166.00	$11,138.41	0.14
	USA Total	26,815.00	$57,728.65	0.75
- USA	+ North West	20,484.00	$44,133.68	0.57
	+ South West	6,331.00	$13,594.97	0.18

Calculate contribution as a percent of a parent

Calculating the relative contribution to the total is a relatively easy calculation to create in a spreadsheet. A spreadsheet, however, has no conception of a hierarchy. In a spreadsheet, it's extremely difficult to create a formula that will calculate the relative contribution of each region to its country or of each state to its region. One of the remarkable strengths of OLAP is the ability of expressions to understand the hierarchical relationships in dimensions.

1. Select the Value property of the Sample calculated member, and click the ellipsis button. Change the Value Expression to **[Sales Units] / ([Sales Units], Ancestor([State].CurrentMember, 1))**. In the revised expression, the denominator tuple uses the distance version of the *Ancestor* function to find the parent of the current product.

2. Click OK to accept the revised definition.

- Country	+ Region	MeasuresLevel Sales Units	Sales Dollars	Sample
North America	North America Total	35,696.00	$76,741.28	1.#J
+ Canada	Canada Total	3,715.00	$7,874.22	0.10
+ Mexico	Mexico Total	5,166.00	$11,138.41	0.14
	USA Total	26,815.00	$57,728.65	0.75
- USA	+ North West	20,484.00	$44,133.68	0.76
	+ South West	6,331.00	$13,594.97	0.24

The totals for Bread, Dairy, and Meat sum to 1 (100 percent). Likewise, the totals for the Bread subcategories sum to 1. The value for the All Product member, however, appears strange. This is a divide-by-zero error that the browser is attempting to format with two decimal places. The All Product member does not have a parent, so the value of for that parent is "empty," which is treated as 0.

Check for an empty member

The expression to calculate the percent of parent must behave differently for the top member of a dimension than it does for all the other members. To do that, you use the *IIF* function described earlier in this chapter. As the conditional test, you can check whether the value of the denominator tuple is empty.

1. Select the Value property of the Sample calculated member, and click the ellipsis button. In the Functions tree, expand the Logical folder and select the *IsEmpty* function. Look at the description of the function at the bottom of the dialog box.

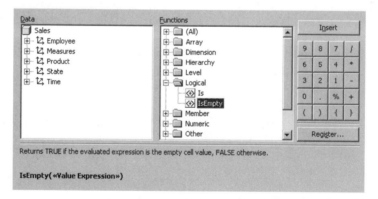

2. Select the current contents of the Value Expression box, and press Ctrl+C to copy it to the clipboard.

3. Change the contents of the Value Expression box to **IsEmpty(([Sales Units], Ancestor([State].CurrentMember, 1)))**. (Specifically, delete the numerator and the slash. Add **IsEmpty** at the beginning of the expression, and add a third set of parentheses after the tuple.)

You need three sets of parentheses: the outer set of parentheses is required by the *IsEmpty* function. The inner set of parentheses is required by the tuple. The middle set of parentheses is required by the *Ancestor* function.

4. Click OK to accept the definition.

| - Country | + Region | MeasuresLevel | | Sample |
		Sales Units	Sales Dollars	
North America	North America Total	35,696.00	$76,741.28	1
+ Canada	Canada Total	3,715.00	$7,874.22	0
+ Mexico	Mexico Total	5,166.00	$11,138.41	0
	USA Total	26,815.00	$57,728.65	0
- USA	+ North West	20,484.00	$44,133.68	0
	+ South West	6,331.00	$13,594.97	0

5. Click the Value property ellipsis button to redisplay the Calculated Member Builder. Change the contents of the Value Expression box to **IIF(IsEmpty(([Sales Units], Ancestor([State].CurrentMember, 1))) , 1 , [Sales Units] / ([Sales Units], Ancestor([State].CurrentMember, 1)))**. (Specifically, enter **IIF** and an opening parenthesis at the beginning of the expression. Type a comma, a **1**, another comma, and then press Ctrl+P to paste the previous expression. Finally, type a closing parenthesis at the end of the expression.)

6. Click OK to accept the definition.

| - Country | + Region | MeasuresLevel | | Sample |
		Sales Units	Sales Dollars	
North America	North America Total	35,696.00	$76,741.28	1
+ Canada	Canada Total	3,715.00	$7,874.22	0.10
+ Mexico	Mexico Total	5,166.00	$11,138.41	0.14
	USA Total	26,815.00	$57,728.65	0.75
- USA	+ North West	20,484.00	$44,133.68	0.76
	+ South West	6,331.00	$13,594.97	0.24

Note   Rather than test for an empty value, you may prefer to test for when the current member is at the All level of the hierarchy. The expression *[Product].CurrentMember.Level.Name* returns the level name of the current product. For the All level, it will be equal to *"(All)"*. Alternatively, the expression *[Product].CurrentMember.Level.Ordinal* returns the level number of the current product. For the All level, it will be equal to 0.

Comparing Values over Time

Almost all OLAP cubes contain a time dimension. That's because almost all business activities take place over time, and it's always useful to compare where one *is* with where one *was*. Not surprisingly, many business reporting requirements involve the use of time, and consequently, MDX supports a large number of functions that facilitate analyzing values with time. In this section, you'll learn how to use member functions that help you compare values over time. In Chapter 7, you'll learn how to summarize values over time, such as calculating year-to-date totals.

Calculate growth from the previous period

Calculating growth from one period to another is an extremely common business task. In the context of a hierarchy, the calculations can seem somewhat complicated: for June, you must find the previous month, and for Qtr2, you must find the previous quarter. Fortunately, MDX was designed with an understanding of hierarchies already built in, and calculating growth from the previous period is a simple task.

1. Drag the Time.Calendar dimension to the row axis of the browser, replacing the State dimension.

2. Select the Value property of the Sample member, click the ellipsis button, and clear the current contents of the Value Expression box.

3. In the Functions tree, expand the Member group and double-click the *PrevMember* function. Click the «Member» token, and double-click the *CurrentMember* function in the Member group of the Functions tree.

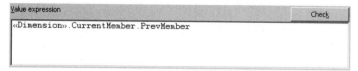

The *PrevMember* function starts with one member—typically the current member of a dimension—and returns the member that immediately precedes it on the same level. The *PrevMember* function ignores the parents of the members. For example, the previous member of January 1998 is December 1997, even though that crosses both quarter and year boundaries. For the first member of a level (such as January 1997), the *PrevMember* function simply returns an "empty" member.

4. Click the «Dimension» token, expand the Time dimension in the Data tree, and double-click the Calendar hierarchy.

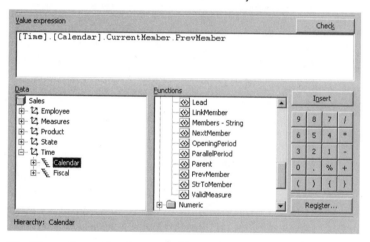

The Time dimension has two hierarchies, so the Data tree shows the two hierarchies. Double-clicking the hierarchy automatically includes the dimension name. Think of a dimension and hierarchy together as if they were a single dimension.

5. Type a comma and then **[Sales Dollars]**, and then put parentheses around the entire expression. The resulting expression should be *([Time].[Calendar].CurrentMember.PrevMember, [Sales Dollars])*. Click OK.

6. Expand the Calendar Year and Calendar Quarter levels, and browse the values in the Sample column.

			MeasuresLevel	
			Sales Dollars	Sample
- Calendar Year	- Calendar Quarter	Calendar Month		
All Time	All Time Total		$76,741.28	
	1997 Total		$11,523.31	
		Qtr1 Total	$1,703.08	
		Jan	$486.58	
	- Qtr1	Feb	$675.53	$486.58
		Mar	$540.97	$675.53
		Qtr2 Total	$2,430.41	$1,703.08
- 1997		Apr	$587.31	$540.97
	- Qtr2	May	$964.60	$587.31
		Jun	$878.50	$964.60

The Sample value for Feb 1997 matches the Sales Dollars value for Jan 1997. Likewise, the Sample value for Qtr2 1997 matches the Sales Dollars value for Qtr1 1997. The *PrevMember* function returns the previous member on the same level as the current member, so the same expression works properly on any level of the hierarchy.

7. In the Value property of the Sample member, insert **[Sales Dollars]**, followed by a minus sign, at the beginning of the expression, and press Enter. (You can also use the Calculated Member Builder to make the change to the expression.) The resulting expression should be *[Sales Dollars] - ([Time].[Calendar].CurrentMember.PrevMember, [Sales Dollars])*.

			MeasuresLevel	
			Sales Dollars	Sample
- Calendar Year	- Calendar Quarter	Calendar Month		
All Time	All Time Total		$76,741.28	$76,741.28
	1997 Total		$11,523.31	$11,523.31
		Qtr1 Total	$1,703.08	$1,703.08
		Jan	$486.58	$486.58
	- Qtr1	Feb	$675.53	$188.95
		Mar	$540.97	($134.56)
		Qtr2 Total	$2,430.41	$727.33
- 1997		Apr	$587.31	$46.34
	- Qtr2	May	$964.60	$377.29

The expression now calculates the growth from the previous period. The 1997 Total value equals that of the Sales Dollars because there was no previous period to 1997, so the previous value is Empty, which is treated like 0. You could use the *IIF* and *IsEmpty* functions to enhance this expression so that it would show blank cells if the previous member cells were empty.

Note   MDX includes other member functions that are very similar to *PrevMember*. The *NextMember* function is equivalent to *PrevMember* except that it gets the member following the starting member. The *Lag* function is a generalized version of the *NextMember* and *PrevMember* functions. You give it an argument telling how many periods back or forward it should go. For example, *Lag(-1)* is the same as *PrevMember*, and *Lag(1)* is the same as *NextMember*. The *Lead* function is identical to the *Lag* function but with the sign of the argument reversed: *Lead(1)* is the same as *PrevMember*, and *Lead(-1)* is the same as *NextMember*.

Calculate growth from a parallel period

Often, activities vary from month to month in a somewhat predictable way. For example, retail sales are much higher during November and December than in other parts of the year. Comparing November to October might show a misleadingly high growth rate, while comparing January to December might paint an inaccurately bleak picture. In some industries, the final month of a quarter typically has higher sales than other months. To avoid the misrepresentation caused by these seasonal factors, you might want to compare the months of the current quarter with the corresponding months of the previous quarter. Or you might want to compare November sales of this year to November sales of the previous year. MDX has functions to make that kind of comparison easy.

1. Select the Value property of the Sample member, click the ellipsis button, and clear the Value Expression box.

2. In the Functions tree, expand the Member group and double-click the *ParallelPeriod* function.

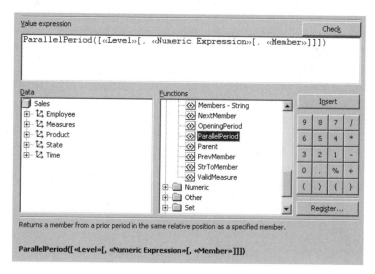

The brackets show that the arguments are optional but that if you include the second argument, you must include the first. The simplest use of the *ParallelPeriod* function simply omits all the arguments.

3. Clear all the arguments of the *ParallelPeriod* function, leaving only the empty parentheses.

4. Create a tuple using *[Sales Dollars]* as the member from the Measures dimension. The final expression should be (*ParallelPeriod(), [Sales Dollars]*). Click OK.

5. If necessary, expand the Calendar Year and Calendar Quarter levels, and browse the Sample member. Scroll down as needed to see values.

Calendar Year	Calendar Quarter	Calendar Month	MeasuresLevel Sales Dollars	Sample
		Mar	$540.97	
	Qtr1	Qtr2 Total	$2,430.41	
		Apr	$587.31	$486.58
	Qtr2	May	$964.60	$675.53
		Jun	$878.50	$540.97
		Qtr3 Total	$3,052.62	
1997		Jul	$1,228.89	$587.31
	Qtr3	Aug	$905.87	$964.60
		Sep	$917.86	$878.50
		Qtr4 Total	$4,337.20	
	Qtr4	Oct	$872.01	$1,228.89
		Nov	$1,660.16	$905.87
		Dec	$1,805.03	$917.86
	1998 Total		$65,217.97	
		Qtr1 Total	$8,574.38	$1,703.08
	Qtr1	Jan	$1,463.49	$872.01
1998		Feb	$1,555.51	$1,660.16
		Mar	$5,555.38	$1,805.03
	Qtr2	Qtr2 Total	$16,918.45	$2,430.41
		Apr	$5,062.12	$1,463.49

The Sample value for Qtr2 of 1998 is the same as the Sales Dollars value for Qtr2 of 1997. Likewise, the Sample value for May 1998 (the second month of the second quarter) is the same as the Sales Dollars value for February 1998 (the second month of the first quarter). With no arguments, the *ParallelPeriod* function returns the corresponding month of the previous quarter and the corresponding quarter of the previous year. If you want to see the corresponding period of the previous year, you must include the name of the level as the first argument.

6. In the Value property, insert **[Calendar Year]** as an argument within the *ParallelPeriod* parentheses, and press Enter. The revised expression should be (*ParallelPeriod([Calendar Year]), [Sales Dollars]*).

Calendar Year	Calendar Quarter	Calendar Month	Sales Dollars	Sample
			MeasuresLevel	
1997	Qtr1	Mar	$540.97	
	Qtr2	Qtr2 Total	$2,430.41	
		Apr	$587.31	
		May	$964.60	
		Jun	$878.50	
	Qtr3	Qtr3 Total	$3,052.62	
		Jul	$1,228.89	
		Aug	$905.87	
		Sep	$917.86	
	Qtr4	Qtr4 Total	$4,337.20	
		Oct	$872.01	
		Nov	$1,660.16	
		Dec	$1,805.03	
	1998 Total		$65,217.97	$11,523.31
1998	Qtr1	Qtr1 Total	$8,574.38	$1,703.08
		Jan	$1,463.49	$486.58
		Feb	$1,555.51	$675.53
		Mar	$5,555.38	$540.97
	Qtr2	Qtr2 Total	$16,918.45	$2,430.41
		Apr	$5,062.12	$587.31

Now each Sample value corresponds to parallel periods within the previous calendar year. The Sample values for the quarters don't change, but the Sample value for May 1998 is now the same as the Sales Dollars value for May 1997.

7. At the beginning of the Value expression, insert **[Sales Dollars]**, followed by a minus sign. Then press Enter to see the change from period to period.

Calendar Year	Calendar Quarter	Calendar Month	Sales Dollars	Sample
			MeasuresLevel	
1997	Qtr1	Mar	$540.97	$540.97
	Qtr2	Qtr2 Total	$2,430.41	$2,430.41
		Apr	$587.31	$587.31
		May	$964.60	$964.60
		Jun	$878.50	$878.50
	Qtr3	Qtr3 Total	$3,052.62	$3,052.62
		Jul	$1,228.89	$1,228.89
		Aug	$905.87	$905.87
		Sep	$917.86	$917.86
	Qtr4	Qtr4 Total	$4,337.20	$4,337.20
		Oct	$872.01	$872.01
		Nov	$1,660.16	$1,660.16
		Dec	$1,805.03	$1,805.03
	1998 Total		$65,217.97	$53,694.66
1998	Qtr1	Qtr1 Total	$8,574.38	$6,871.30
		Jan	$1,463.49	$976.91
		Feb	$1,555.51	$879.98
		Mar	$5,555.38	$5,014.41
	Qtr2	Qtr2 Total	$16,918.45	$14,488.04
		Apr	$5,062.12	$4,474.81

Once again, when there is no preceding parallel period, 0 is subtracted, leaving unduly large growth values. You can use *IIF* with *IsEmpty* to enhance the expression to display a value only when there is an earlier value.

For information about flagging a dimension as type Time, see "Working with Time Dimensions" in Chapter 3.

8. Save the cube, and close the Cube Editor.

Most member functions are used in conjunction with the current member of a dimension. The *ParallelPeriod* function appears to use the current member of the Time.Calendar dimension, but the base member is never explicitly mentioned. The third (optional) argument of the *ParallelPeriod* function allows you to specify a starting member. In almost every case, the appropriate value for that argument would be the current member of the time dimension, and that's what the function uses if you omit the third argument. If you have two dimensions flagged with type Time, the function uses the one that comes first in the cube definition.

Note MDX has member functions that are similar to the *ParallelPeriod* function. The *Cousin* function allows you to define the specific member you want the parallel period to be relative to. The *OpeningPeriod* and *ClosingPeriod* functions return the first and last members that share the same parent with the current member of the time dimension at a given level.

Chapter Summary

To	Do this
Return an empty value from an MDX expression	Use the keyword *Null*.
Calculate the ancestor of the current product at the Category level	Use the expression *Ancestor(Product. CurrentMember, Category)*.
Test for an empty cell	Use the *IsEmpty* function.
Make a choice based on a conditional expression	Use the *IIF* function.
Display the value of a member property named Test for the current member of the Product dimension	Use the expression *Product. CurrentMember.Properties("Test")*.
Convert an expression from a string to a number	Use the *CDbl* function from VBA.
Retrieve the value from a specific cell in a cube	Create a tuple, with one member from each dimension separated by commas and enclosed in parentheses.
Reference the Sales Units value for the top member of the Product dimension	Use the expression *([Sales Units], Ancestor(Product.CurrentMember, Product.[(All)]))*.
Reference the Sales Units value for the previous time period	Use the expression *([Sales Units], Time.CurrentMember.PrevMember)*.

MDX Sets

Estimated time: 2 hours

Chapter Objectives

In this chapter, you'll learn MDX query terminology and how to

- Use the MDX Sample application to enter queries.

- Use set functions.

- Create sets by using member constants.

- Create calculated members that aggregate sets of values.

Start the lesson

1. Start Analysis Manager. Right-click the server, and click Restore Database.

2. Navigate to the folder containing the sample files for this book, select Chapter 7, and click Open. The archived Chapter 7 OLAP database is identical to the one used in Chapter 6, "MDX Values." Click Restore, and then close the Restore Database Progress dialog box.

3. Open the Chapter 7 HTML file included with the sample files for this book. This HTML file contains a Microsoft Office PivotTable list that retrieves values from the Sales cube of the Chapter 7 OLAP database.

Have you ever noticed that no matter how many times you travel to a location as a passenger, the route seems entirely different the first time you have to navigate—especially if you're alone. The Microsoft Excel PivotTable report and the Office PivotTable list features create multidimensional expressions (MDX) statements to retrieve values from a cube, but creating a report yourself can give you a tremendous appreciation for how Microsoft SQL Server 2000 Analysis Services works.

An MDX query statement is different from an MDX expression. An expression is a formula that calculates a single value. A query is a command that populates a report with many values from a cube. The Office PivotTable list, the Excel PivotTable report, and the browser included in Analysis Manager all generate MDX queries to retrieve values from a cube. You can use tools like these to create reports without writing any MDX statements of your own. Unless you're a developer creating a custom report generator, you'll probably have little occasion to write MDX query statements. So, why should you learn how to create an MDX query statement? Because the most interesting MDX expressions involve creating a single result based on a large set of values from a cube. Those expressions, in effect, create a subquery behind the scenes. Learning how to create an MDX query will enable you to understand clearly what the subquery is doing when you create complex MDX expressions. In the first part of this chapter, you'll learn how to create explicit queries. In the latter part of the chapter, you'll use the concepts learned in creating the reports to create calculated members based on large sets of values.

Preparing to Create MDX Queries

The purpose of an MDX query is to extract values from an OLAP cube into a report. As explained in Chapter 1, "A Data Analysis Foundation," a cube has dimensions (up to 64, if you count Measures as a dimension). A report does not have dimensions; it has axes (typically, a row axis, a column axis, and a filter axis). An axis can include labels from more than one dimension. A cube contains all possible values for all members of all levels of all dimensions. A report contains only selected values from selected levels of selected dimensions. An MDX query statement consists of the instructions for extracting a report from a cube.

Use a PivotTable list to understand MDX terms

An MDX query statement uses several new terms. Seeing the terms in a familiar context will make them easier to learn and understand. Browsers such as the Office PivotTable list use MDX query statements to populate a report. You can use the Office PivotTable list to learn MDX terminology. The initial report in the Chapter 7 HTML file shows only a single cell showing the total value for the Sales Dollars measure. The grand total is a single value from the cube. To retrieve this value, Analysis Services used the default member for each dimension.

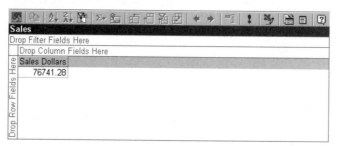

1. In the Web browser, click the Field List toolbar button. Drag the Product, State, Employee, and Time Calendar dimensions from the PivotTable Field List window to the filter area of the report. Each dimension displays the default member in the filter area, and the total value never changes as you add the dimensions. (Since the Time Fiscal and Time Calendar dimensions are really hierarchies of the same dimension, you can include only one in the report at a time. The report still uses the default member of the unused dimension.)

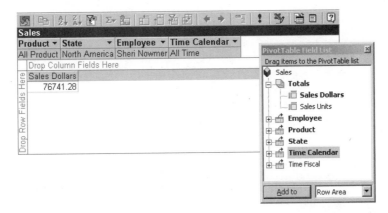

The default member allows a query to ignore some of the dimensions in a cube. If a dimension does not appear on the filter axis, it always uses the default member. If a dimension does appear on the filter axis, it can either use the default member or a different member. Putting a dimension on the filter area of a report overrides the default member for that dimension.

2. Click the arrow next to the Product dimension list, select the Meat check box, and click OK to show only the total for meat.

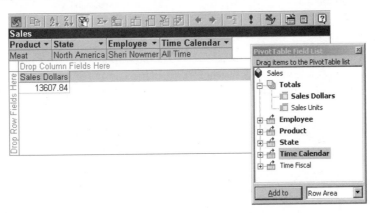

If you use nothing but the filter area, you create a report that displays only a single value, which is rarely useful. The row and column axes of a report allow you to display more than one member from a dimension. More than one member from a single dimension is called a *set*.

3. Drag the State dimension to the row axis. The three countries—plus the total—appear. The row axis now displays a set that contains four *positions*. Each position in the set corresponds to a member from the State dimension.

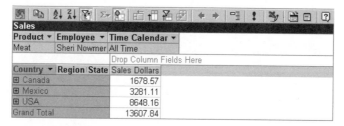

4. Click the Country level label, and click the Expand toolbar button.

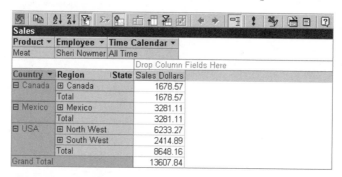

The regions appear. The row axis now displays a set that contains eight positions. Even though the labels are split into two columns—to show the levels of the dimension—each position in the set still contains only a single member from the State dimension.

5. Drag the Sales Units measure to the data area. The column axis now displays a set that contains two positions, each of which corresponds to a single member from the Measures dimension.

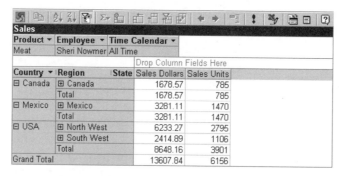

6. For each cell value you see in the report, you can determine a complete tuple that includes one member from each dimension in the cube. For the cell in the Sales Dollars column with the value 6233.27, the Product dimension contributes Meat, the Employee Dimension contributes Sheri Nowmer, the Time Calendar dimension contributes All Time, and the State dimension contributes North West.

Every value in an MDX report requires a single member from each dimension. The filter axis can include only a single member for any one dimension. The row and column axes can include only sets, which include multiple values from a single dimension.

It's not unusual for a cube to contain at least six or seven dimensions. Not counting the filter axis, a report based on an OLAP cube typically contains only two axes—columns and rows. Often, it's useful to combine multiple dimensions from the cube onto a single axis of the report.

7. In the PivotTable List document, drag the Region and State level headings away from the row area, leaving only the countries and Grand Total on the axis.

Sales			
Product ▾	**Employee** ▾	**Time Calendar** ▾	
Meat	Sheri Nowmer	All Time	
	Drop Column Fields Here		
Country ▾	Sales Dollars	Sales Units	
Canada	1678.57	785	
Mexico	3281.11	1470	
USA	8648.16	3901	
Grand Total	13607.84	6156	

8. Drag the Product level from the filter area to the row area, to the left of the State level. Drag the Subcategory and Product Name labels away from the report. Select the Category label, and click the Expand toolbar button. The report now shows both categories and countries on the row axis. The row axis still contains a set—a set with 13 positions. But each position within the set now contains a two-member tuple—a coordinate from more than one dimension.

Sales			
Employee ▾	**Time Calendar** ▾		
Sheri Nowmer	All Time		
	Drop Column Fields Here		
Category ▾	**Country** ▾	Sales Dollars	Sales Units
⊟ Bread	Canada	2180.74	1046
	Mexico	2697.92	1289
	USA	25721.76	12197
	Total	30600.42	14532
⊟ Dairy	Canada	4014.91	1884
	Mexico	5159.38	2407
	USA	23358.73	10717
	Total	32533.02	15008
⊟ Meat	Canada	1678.57	785

Note   Technically, a set always contains tuples. Even when there is only one dimension on an axis, the set consists of single-member tuples.

9. Drag the Time Calendar dimension from the filter area to the row area, to the left of the Category label. Drag the Calendar Quarter and Calendar Month labels away from the report. Then select the Calendar Year label, and click Expand. The report now shows years, categories, and countries on the row axis. The row axis still contains a set—now a set with 17 positions. But each position in the set now contains a three-member tuple.

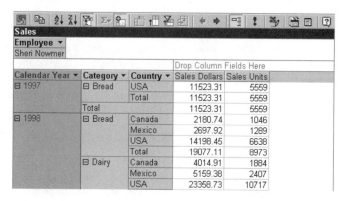

A tuple is a way to specify coordinates from more than one dimension on a single axis. The filter axis can contain only a single tuple. Row and column axes can each contain a set of tuples. The bottom line remains: for each value in the report, there's a single member from each dimension that contributed to the complete coordinate for that cell in the cube. The member for a dimension can come from any of the axes—and more than one dimension can be represented on a single axis. Any dimension not found on the column, row, or filter axis uses the default member.

Use the MDX Sample application

Analysis Services comes with the MDX Sample application. The application allows you to type an MDX statement, run it, and see the results in a grid. The MDX Sample application includes a *metadata pane,* which allows you to browse the hierarchies and members of a cube, inserting dimension, level, and member names into the MDX expression. The application also comes with complete source files for the Microsoft Visual Basic project used to create it. If you're a programmer of Visual Basic, you can customize or add enhancements to the application. Some of the controls in the MDX Sample application are similar to those in the Calculated Member Builder. In this section, you'll take a few minutes to explore the interface.

1. Launch the MDX Sample application, which is on the Analysis Services menu along with Analysis Manager. Click OK to connect to the server. Click the New Query File toolbar button to create a new query file. A query file can contain multiple queries.

2. In the toolbar, select Chapter 7 as the database name. Then, in the Cube drop-down list box, select Sales as the cube name.

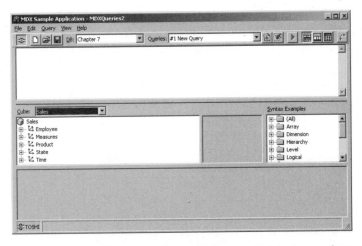

The MDX Sample application window is divided into three vertical panes. The top pane is the *query pane,* where you build an MDX query statement. The middle pane is the *metadata pane,* where you inspect information in a selected cube. The bottom pane is the *results pane,* which shows the output of an MDX query. Across the top of the application are a menu bar and a toolbar.

Once you select a cube, the Metadata tree—the leftmost section of the metadata pane—displays the cube name as the top-level parent, plus the names of all the dimensions in the cube. The Metadata tree is equivalent to the Data tree in the Calculated Member Builder. The cube name has a cube icon to its left, and each dimension name has a triple-arrow icon to its left. Unlike the icons in Analysis Manager, the icons in the metadata view do not vary between different types of dimensions. The Metadata tree also displays members, but members often appear multiple times in the tree. Taking a close look at the metadata window can help you avoid confusion and get the most benefit from the MDX Sample application.

3. Expand the State dimension. You see one entry for each level in the dimension, including the All level. The All level has a small rectangular icon to the left of the level name. Every other level has a dot-cluster icon. The number of dots represents the level's depth in the hierarchy.

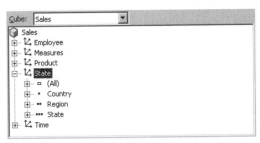

4. Expand the State level. You see one entry for each member in the level. Each member name has a lollipop icon to its left. (It's probably supposed to be a magnifying glass, but thinking of it as a lollipop is more vivid.)

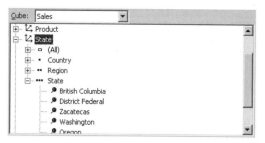

5. Collapse the State dimension, and then expand the Time dimension. You see two stair-step icons, one for the Calendar hierarchy and one for the Fiscal hierarchy. Then expand the Calendar hierarchy to see the level names.

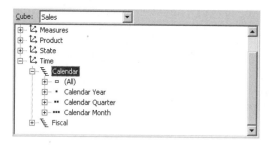

Note   Each item in the Metadata tree is a cube, a dimension, a hierarchy, a level, or a member. These are all entities that exist within an OLAP database. That contrasts with sets and tuples, which exist only in an MDX expression. In other words, there are no sets or tuples in an OLAP database, just cubes, dimensions, hierarchies, levels, and members.

For your convenience, the Metadata tree usually adds each member node to multiple locations in the tree. Specifically, in addition to adding a member node below the level at which it belongs—as with the State level—the Metadata tree also adds the same member as a child of its parent member. Some people find this redundancy confusing at first, but once you understand how the Metadata tree works, it really is convenient.

6. In the State dimension, expand the Region level and the South West member. The California member appears below South West. California is the child—the only child—of the South West member. The California member appears both in the State level and also as a child of the South West member.

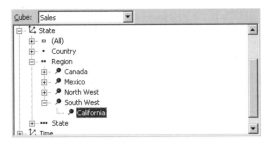

7. Expand the Country level, the USA member, and the South West member. You see the California member once again—this time as a "grandchild" of USA. The California member is still on the State level.

The highest member in an ancestry tree belongs to the level name just above it. For example, USA belongs to the Country level. For each degree of indentation, the members belong to a level one lower in the cube. For example, South West belongs to the Region level—even though the member node can appear under the Country level. Likewise, California belongs to the State level—even though the member node can appear under the Country or Region levels as well as the State level.

You can double-click any node to have the fully qualified name of the item appear in the query pane. You can also drag a node to the query pane, in case you didn't put the insertion point in the proper place.

8. Double-click the California member. The full name of the member appears in the query pane.

[State].[North America].[USA].[South West].[California]

In the Metadata tree, when you select either a level or a member that has children, the members appear in the list to the right of the metadata pane. You can double-click or drag members from the member list to add them to the query pane.

Double-clicking a leaf-level member in the tree view does not move the member into the query pane. You can, however, drag a leaf-level member into the query pane or select the level name and double-click a member from the member list.

Creating Basic MDX Queries

You can create MDX queries to replicate the reports you create by using a browser such as the Office PivotTable list control.

Create a minimal MDX query

Start by creating the simplest possible query from the Sales cube.

1. Replace the contents of the query pane with **SELECT FROM Sales**. This is the simplest possible MDX query. You can now run this query.

You can also press F5 to run a query.

2. Click the Run Query button on the toolbar. (If you don't see the results pane, click the Split View button to the right of the Run Query button; the Split View button displays the results pane below the metadata pane.) A single number appears in the report. The number in the report—35,696.00—is the total Sales Dollars for the entire cube. Because the query does not specify a member from any dimension, the query uses the default member from each dimension.

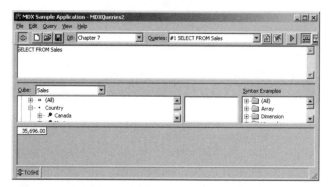

To add a comment to an MDX statement, you simply enter two adjacent slash characters (//), and MDX will ignore everything from that point to the end of the line.

3. Move the insertion point before the word *SELECT*. Type **//Simple Query**, and press Enter. Then click the Run Query button to run the query again. You don't see any difference—or an error message.

4. Click the Save Query File button on the toolbar, type **Queries** as the name of the file, and click Save. You can add multiple queries to this single file, but you can't save a file until you've entered something in the query pane.

This simple query retrieves a single value from the cube. You can create more interesting reports by adding sets of members to the column or row axis.

Note   In addition to using two sequential slash characters (//) to comment the remainder of the line, you can also use two sequential hyphen characters (--) for the same purpose. If you want to create a comment that either is a partial line or spans multiple lines, you begin the comment with a slash followed by an asterisk (/*) and end it with an asterisk followed by a slash (*/).

Add a set to the column axis

To display more than one cell in the result grid, you must put a set of members on an axis. Before creating the new query, add a new query to the query file so that you can keep both queries intact.

1. Select the contents of the query pane, and press Ctrl+C to copy it. Click the New Query button, and press Ctrl+V. Change the comment to **//Set on Axis**.

   To display more than one member on an axis, you use a *set* of members, precisely as in the browser. MDX has a number of functions that return sets. To the right of the member list, in the metadata pane, there's a tree labeled Syntax Examples. This list is the same as the Functions tree in the Calculated Member Builder. To get a set of members that you can put on an axis, select a function from the Set group.

2. Click immediately after the word *SELECT*, and type a space. In the Syntax Examples list, expand the Set group and double-click the *Members - Level* function. Then click after the *Members* function, and type a space and **ON COLUMNS**.

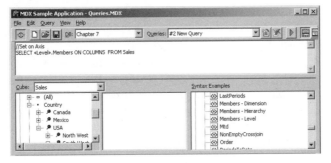

3. Click the word *«Level»*. In the Metadata tree, double-click the Category level node in the Product dimension. The level name appears in the query.

4. Click the Run Query button to see the results of the query. The labels from the Category level appear as column headings in the report. The client application, however, can choose to put the "column" axis on either the columns or the rows.

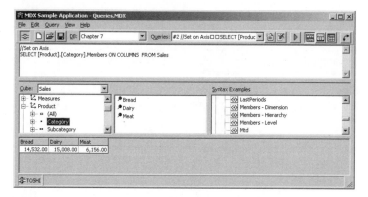

5. Click the Pivot Results button on the toolbar. The Category labels now appear as row headings, even though the query still says ON COLUMNS.

Bread	14,532.00
Dairy	15,008.00
Meat	6,156.00

6. Click the Pivot Results button again to return the labels to the column headings, and save the query file.

> **Note** The terms *COLUMNS* and *ROWS* are simply aliases for the true names of the axes, Axis(0), and Axis(1), respectively. The underlying names make it clearer to understand why a single-axis report must include a COLUMNS axis but not a ROWS axis. Technically, an MDX query can have up to 63 axes, with alias names for the first few. There are, however, essentially no situations in which it's necessary to use more than two heading axes for a report.

The tokens in the function templates help you know what kind of item to add to a specific location of the query. You must replace the *«Level»* token with the name of a level. In various contexts, you might also see tokens *«Member»*, *«Set»*, *«Tuple»*, *«Dimension»*, and *«Hierarchy»*. *«Set»* and *«Tuple»* are MDX constructs that do not exist in the OLAP database, so you typically replace them with functions from the appropriate groups. *«Cube»*, *«Dimension»*, *«Hierarchy»*, and *«Level»* all are OLAP objects, so you typically replace these tokens with items from the Metadata tree. A *«Member»* is the place where MDX and the cube meet. You can replace the *«Member»* token either with a constant member from the Metadata tree or with a function from the Member group.

Add a set to a second axis

You can also add a set to the row axis. In MDX, if you create a query that has only one axis, it must be the column axis. If you create two axes, one must be the column axis and one must be the row axis, although it doesn't matter in which order they appear within the query.

1. Copy the current contents of the query pane, click the New Query button to add a new query to the current file, and paste the previous query. Change the comment to //**Two axes**.

2. Click after the word *COLUMNS*, and type a comma and a space. You can now add another set.

3. In the Syntax Examples list, look in the Set group and double-click the *Children* function. Then click after the Children function, and type **ON ROWS**.

//Two axes
SELECT [Product].[Category].Members ON COLUMNS, «Member».Children ON ROWS |FROM Sales

The token that precedes the *Children* function name is *«Member»*. A member has children.

4. Select the *«Member»* token, and in the Metadata tree, find and double-click the 1998 member. The formatted statement will look like this:

```
//Two axes
SELECT
    [Product].[Category].Members ON COLUMNS,
    [Time].[Calendar].[All Time].[1998].Children ON ROWS
FROM Sales
```

This function will now add a set of all the quarters of the year 1998 to the row axis.

5. Click the Run Query button to run the query.

	Bread	Dairy	Meat
Qtr1	2,246.00	1,732.00	
Qtr2	2,522.00	5,240.00	
Qtr3	3,150.00	6,056.00	4,646.00
Qtr4	1,055.00	1,980.00	1,510.00

On the column axis, the *Members* function displays only the members from the Category level. There are actually three versions of the *Members* function—one that returns the members of a level, one that returns the members from a dimension, and one that returns the members from a hierarchy. You can change the query to retrieve all the members of the Product dimension.

6. Delete the Category level name and the period following it, but leave the dimension name. The function will now return all the members of the Product dimension.

7. Click the Run Query button to see the results of the query. Click the Pivot Results button to move the products to the row axis.

	Qtr1	Qtr2	Qtr3	Qtr4
All Product	3,978.00	7,762.00	13,852.00	4,545.00
Bread	2,246.00	2,522.00	3,150.00	1,055.00
Bagels	272.00	275.00	327.00	110.00
Colony Bage	32.00	50.00	36.00	20.00
Fantastic Ba	73.00	53.00	60.00	13.00
Great Bagels	69.00	53.00	60.00	51.00
Modell Bagel	28.00	67.00	76.00	13.00
Sphinx Bage	70.00	52.00	95.00	13.00
Muffins	960.00	1,131.00	1,378.00	497.00
Colony Blueb	20.00	51.00	65.00	16.00
Colony Cran	45.00	52.00	76.00	32.00
Colony Engli	70.00	30.00	67.00	27.00

8. Save the query file, and click the Pivot Results button to return the orientation to normal.

Both axes contain sets. Even though the products are not indented, all the members of the Product hierarchy are in the set.

Note   One important rule for working with axes in an MDX query is that a dimension can be represented on only one of the three axes—column, row, and filter—because each axis contributes a member towards the complete tuple required to retrieve a value from the cube. If a single dimension is represented on more than one axis, the tuple will contain two members for a single dimension, which is invalid.

The Syntax Examples list shows three functions named *members*—one for levels, one for hierarchies, and one for dimensions. When a dimension has a dual hierarchy—as with the Time.Fiscal dimension—you must use the hierarchy version, not the dimension version, even if only one of the hierarchies exists in the current cube (as in the Basic Sales virtual cube created in Chapter 4, "Advanced Dimensions and Cubes").

Create a set by using explicit member names

The only thing you can put on an axis is a set. A set function is one way to get a set to put on the axis. But sometimes, particularly with the Measures dimension, you want to be able to pick one or more individual members to put on an axis. You must be able to put the members into a set. To include members in a set, you must enclose the set in braces ({}). The braces aren't necessary when you use set functions but are necessary when entering specific member names.

1. Click the New Query button. Type **Select {[Sales Dollars]} On Columns From Sales**. Then run the query.

When you create a set without using a set function, you need to enclose the set in braces, even if it contains only a single member.

2. After the *[Sales Dollars]* measure, type a comma, a space to enhance legibility, and then **[Sales Units]**. Then run the query.

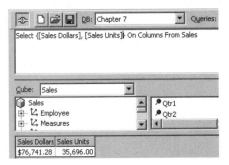

The set on the column axis consists of two positions. Each position corresponds to a tuple, and each tuple contains a single member. If you want, you can add parentheses around each tuple, writing the set as *{([Sales Dollars]), ([Sales Units])}*, to show that each member is a separate tuple within the set. When you create a set by using a set function, you don't need to enclose the set in braces (but braces around a set are always acceptable). When you create a set by using explicit members, you do need to enclose the set in braces. If the first tuple in a set consists of a single member, each subsequent tuple in that set must be a member of the same dimension.

Note   You can also manually create a set that includes tuples with multiple members. For example, the following is a legitimate set and could be placed on an axis in an MDX query: *{([Bread],[California]),([Meat],[Oregon])}*. It's unusual, however, to create a set with constant member names in multimember tuples. You're much more likely to use the *CrossJoin* function described in the following section to create a set with multiple members in each tuple.

---

3. Add a comment to the query, and save the query file.

The terminology of an MDX query centers on sets, tuples, and members. A set includes one or more tuples, and a tuple includes one or more members. Sets appear on the axes. Tuples appear either in a set (on a column or row axis), or in the *WHERE* clause to create the filter axis. Aside from the cube name in the *FROM* clause, a member is the only object from a cube that appears directly in an MDX query.

Put two dimensions on one axis

In "Use a PivotTable list to understand MDX terms" earlier in this chapter, you saw how the Office PivotTable list can put two dimensions onto the same axis, creating a set where each position in the set includes a tuple with more than one member. In an MDX query, to combine two sets from two dimensions into a single set that you can put onto a single axis, use the *CrossJoin* function.

1. Click the New Query button. Type **Select Country.Members on Columns, Category.Members On Rows From Sales**. Click the Run Query button.

	Canada	Mexico	USA
Bread	1,046.00	1,289.00	12,197.00
Dairy	1,884.00	2,407.00	10,717.00
Meat	785.00	1,470.00	3,901.00

This query puts the members of the country level (of the State dimension) on one axis, and the members of the category level (of the Product dimension) on the second axis. Each axis contains a set, and each set has a single member in each tuple. You can use the *CrossJoin* function to combine the two sets into one set, with two members in each tuple.

2. Change the query definition to **Select CrossJoin(Country.Members, Category.Members) On Columns From Sales**. Click Run Query to see the results.

Canada			Mexico			USA		
Bread	Dairy	Meat	Bread	Dairy	Meat	Bread	Dairy	Meat
1,046.00	1,884.00	785.00	1,289.00	2,407.00	1,470.00	12,197.00	10,717.00	3,901.00

The column axis contains a set with nine positions. Each position is a tuple that includes one member from each of two dimensions. The nine positions correspond to all the possible combinations of the three categories and the three countries.

3. After the Columns keyword, type a comma, and press Enter. Then type **CrossJoin([Calendar Year].Members, [Measures].Members) ON ROWS**, and click Run Query to run the query.

		Canada			Mexico			USA		
		Bread	Dairy	Meat	Bread	Dairy	Meat	Bread	Dairy	Meat
1997	Sales Units							5,559.00		
	Sales Dollars							$11,523.31		
1998	Sales Units	1,046.00	1,884.00	785.00	1,289.00	2,407.00	1,470.00	6,638.00	10,717.00	3,901.00
	Sales Dollars	$2,180.74	$4,014.91	$1,678.57	$2,697.92	$5,159.38	$3,281.11	$14,198.45	$23,358.73	$8,648.16

This query contains four dimensions from the Sales cube—two on each axis. Remember that you can put a dimension onto only one axis in a single query.

4. Add a comment, and save the query file.

The *CrossJoin* function is a powerful way to create reports that compare multiple dimensions. Because the function is so powerful, it's easy to create sets that are extremely large, particularly when combined with the *Members* function of multiple dimensions.

Creating Calculations by Using Aggregation Functions

In Chapter 6, you created calculated members in a cube by using arithmetic operators and discrete values. Now that you know how to use sets, you can create calculated members that use aggregation functions. First, however, create a simple calculated member within an MDX query statement. The calculated member created as part of an MDX statement works the same as one created in a cube, except that when stored in the cube the member is permanent and is available to all users of a cube. Sometimes it can be effective to create calculated members in a query statement as you develop them and then copy the expressions to a cube when you're satisfied with them.

Create a calculated member as part of a query

To see how to create a dynamic calculated member in an MDX query, create an Average Price member.

1. In the MDX Sample application, add a new query that looks like the following:

```
SELECT
   [Measures].Members ON COLUMNS,
   [Product].[Subcategory].Members ON ROWS
FROM [Sales]
```

2. Click the Run Query button to see the results of the query, and save the query file. The query shows the two measures from the cube—Sales Units and Sales Dollars—as column headings.

	Sales Units	Sales Dollars
Bagels	1,541.00	$3,552.28
Muffins	6,445.00	$13,081.28
Sliced Bread	6,546.00	$13,966.86
Cheese	7,493.00	$17,709.11
Milk	4,151.00	$7,259.42
Sour Cream	1,607.00	$2,746.58
Yogurt	1,757.00	$4,817.91
Deli Meats	1,977.00	$4,337.12
Fresh Chicke	485.00	$1,143.56
Frozen Chick	1,338.00	$3,214.98
Hamburger	1,015.00	$2,175.56
Hot Dogs	1,341.00	$2,736.62

For a calculated member, you must specify a parent. For the Measures dimension—which has only one level—use the dimension name as the parent. You can enter almost anything as the name of the member, but it must be enclosed in brackets following the same guidelines as any member name. The expression for a calculated member consists of instructions to generate a new value.

3. Before the Select keyword, insert the following:

```
WITH MEMBER [Measures].[Average Price] AS '[Sales Dollars]/
[Sales Units]'
```

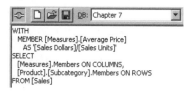

In the main query, the set for the column axis is *[Measures].Members*, which would seem to include all measures, but see what happens when you run the query after defining a new calculated measure.

4. Click the Run Query button. Nothing changes. Calculated members are not retrieved by the *Members* function of a dimension or level.

5. Change the expression *[Measures].Members* to **[Measures].AllMembers**. The *AllMembers* function is like *Members*, except that it also includes calculated members. Click the Run Query button to see the calculated member.

	Sales Units	Sales Dollars	Average Pri
Bagels	1,541.00	$3,552.28	2.3051
Muffins	6,445.00	$13,081.28	2.0296
Sliced Bread	6,546.00	$13,966.86	2.1336
Cheese	7,493.00	$17,709.11	2.3634
Milk	4,151.00	$7,259.42	1.7488
Sour Cream	1,607.00	$2,746.58	1.7091
Yogurt	1,757.00	$4,817.91	2.7421
Deli Meats	1,977.00	$4,337.12	2.1937
Fresh Chicke	485.00	$1,143.56	2.3578
Frozen Chick	1,338.00	$3,214.98	2.4028
Hamburger	1,015.00	$2,175.56	2.1434
Hot Dogs	1,341.00	$2,736.62	2.0407

6. Add a comment to the query, and save the query file.

To dynamically create a calculated member, add a *MEMBER* clause at the beginning of the MDX query. You can add more than one *MEMBER* clause to a query. The word *WITH* must precede the first *MEMBER* clause. You do *not* put commas between successive *MEMBER* clauses.

Create a calculated member of a nonmeasure dimension

The most frequent calculated member you'll create is a calculated measure—a member of the Measures dimension—but you can also create a calculated member of any dimension. When you create a calculated member of a nonmeasure dimension, you must specify where in the dimension hierarchy you want the new member to go. Suppose, for example, that you want to create a new member that shows the total Sales Units and Sales Dollars for all countries other than the United States—that is, for the total of Canada and Mexico.

1. Create a new query, insert the following MDX query statement, and then run the query:

```
SELECT
   [Measures].Members ON COLUMNS,
   [State].[Country].Members ON ROWS
FROM Sales
```

	Sales Units	Sales Dollars
Canada	3,715.00	$7,874.22
Mexico	5,166.00	$11,138.41
USA	26,815.00	$57,728.65

The query shows three countries on the row axis.

2. Before the SELECT keyword, insert the following clause:

```
WITH
   MEMBER [State].[North America].[Non-US] AS
     '[Canada]+[Mexico]'
```

Specifying *[State].[North America]* as the parent of the new member puts the new member at the Country level—the same level as Canada, Mexico, and USA. This is the level already specified in the query.

3. Run the query to see the results. The new member does not appear. As with the Measures dimension, the *Members* function does not retrieve calculated members of nonmeasure dimensions.

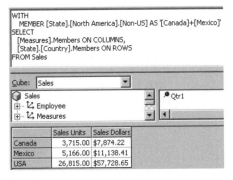

4. On the row axis, change the expression *[State].[Country].Members* to **[State].[Country].AllMembers**. Then run the query again.

   The new member is now included on the row axis.

	Sales Units	Sales Dollars
Canada	3,715.00	$7,874.22
Mexico	5,166.00	$11,138.41
USA	26,815.00	$57,728.65
Non-US	8,881.00	$19,012.63

Think through the tuple that generates the 8,881.00 value in the result grid. The Product, Employee, and Time dimensions do not appear in the MDX statement and thus use the default members. The column axis supplies the member from the Measures dimension (Sales Units), and the row axis supplies the member from the State dimension (Non-US). The Non-US member is a calculated member. That calculated member's expression requires two values. The expression overrides the State dimension member for each of those two values, inheriting the member for each of the other three dimensions from the cell in the result grid.

Creating an aggregate member by using a plus sign to add values works fine when you have only two or three values to aggregate, but it's cumbersome if you have multiple values. For example, suppose that you want to create a query that calculates the total for all states other than Washington.

5. Save the query file, copy the entire contents of the query pane, create a new query, and paste the copied query. Change the query to look like this (changed portions are in bold):

```
WITH
   MEMBER [State].[South West].[Non-WA] AS
      'Sum([State].[State].Members)'
SELECT
   [Measures].Members ON COLUMNS,
   [State].[State].AllMembers ON ROWS
FROM Sales
```

The parent is now *[South West]* rather than *[All Product]*. Making the South West region the parent puts the new member at the State level. Since South West is the last region, this puts the new member at the end of the list of states. For the time being, the expression includes all the states and doesn't exclude Washington.

6. Run the query. The states appear, with Non-WA at the bottom of the list. The values of the two Non-WA cells include the total of all the states.

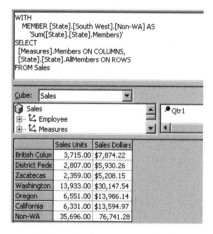

You still need to exclude Washington from the set of all the members of the State level. MDX has a set function that creates a new set by taking all the members of one set *except* those that belong to a second set. The function is named, appropriately enough, *Except*.

7. In the member definition, change the expression *'Sum([State].[State]. Members)'* to **'Sum(Except([State].[State].Members, {[Washington]}))'**, and run the query. While Washington still appears on the row axis—the row axis definition does not exclude the member— the totals for the Non-WA member no longer include Washington.

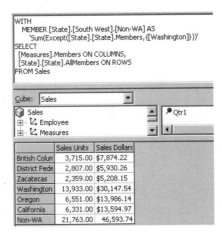

See "Specify the aggregation function for a measure" in Chapter 3, "Dimension and Cube Editors," for details about assigning an aggregation function for a measure.

The Non-WA calculated member uses the same expression for each measure. Since both Sales Units and Sales Dollars have *Sum* as the member's aggregation function, using the *Sum* function in the Non-WA member works fine with either measure. Suppose, however, that the cube contained a measure such as Minimum Price, defined with the *Min* aggregation function. Using *Sum* to aggregate that measure would create an inappropriate value. MDX does have a *Min* function, but it would be extremely unwieldy to create a different Non-WA member for each measure. To resolve this problem, MDX has an *Aggregate* function. The *Aggregate* function simply aggregates each measure using the aggregation function defined for the measure. In general, when you create a calculated member on a nonmeasure dimension, you should use the *Aggregate* function rather than the *Sum* function.

When you create a calculated member on a nonmeasure dimension, you should use the Aggregate function rather than the Sum function.

Note   MDX has three related functions that manipulate two sets (Set1 and Set2) to produce a third set (Set3). The *Union* function puts into Set3 all the members in either Set1 or Set2. The *Intersect* function puts into Set3 only those members in both Set1 and Set2. The *Except* function puts into Set3 only the members from Set1 not in Set2. Each of the three functions strips duplicate values from Set3, unless you include the keyword *ALL* as an optional third argument.

8. In the Non-WA member definition, change the function name *Sum* to **Aggregate** and run the revised query. The values in the result grid should not change. Save the query file.

When you create a calculated member on a nonmeasure dimension, that member will, by definition, intersect with all the members of the Measures dimension. Each of those measures already has an aggregation function defined. Using the *Aggregate* function takes advantage of that previously defined aggregation function.

Create a cumulative total

The *Sum* (or *Aggregate*) function is often used to create a calculated member on a nonmeasure dimension. You can also use the *Sum* function to create a new calculated measure. This is often done to create a cumulative total.

1. Create a new query, and insert the following MDX query statement:

```
SELECT
  [Calendar Month].Members ON COLUMNS,
  [Measures].AllMembers ON ROWS
FROM Sales
```

2. Run the query. This displays all the months as column headings and the two measures—Sales Dollars and Sales Units—as row headings. The *AllMembers* function allows you to see new calculated measures as you create them.

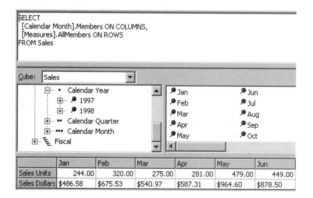

3. Before the SELECT keyword, enter the clause **WITH MEMBER [Measures].[Cumulative] AS** '' and put the insertion point between the single quotes. Then expand the Numeric group of the Syntax Examples tree, and double-click the *Sum* function.

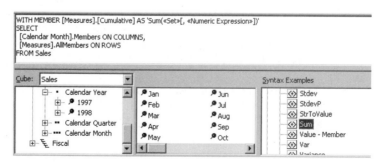

The *Sum* function syntax shows two arguments. The first argument, *«Set»*, is required; this is the argument you used when you created the Non-WA measure in the preceding section. The second argument, *«Numeric Expression»*, is surrounded by square brackets, indicating that it is optional. If you create a member on a nonmeasure dimension (such as Non-WA), you'll almost never use the *«Numeric Expression»* argument. If you create a member on the Measures dimension (such as Cumulative), you'll almost always use the *«Numeric Expression»* argument. The *«Numeric Expression»* argument tells you which measure to use as the base for the new measure.

4. Replace the *«Numeric Expression»* token with **[Sales Units]**, and delete the optional brackets. For the *«Set»* argument, you need a set that begins with the time period of the first column and ends with the time period of the current column. You can use a colon (:) to indicate a range of members.

5. Select the *«Set»* token. In the Metadata tree, select the Calendar Month level of the Time.Calendar dimension. Then double-click the first Jan member in the member name list. Click after the *[Jan]*, type a colon, press enter, and then type **[Time].[Calendar].CurrentMember**. The final definition of the member before the SELECT word should look like this:

```
WITH
    MEMBER [Measure].[Cumulative] AS
        'Sum([Time].[Calendar].[All Time].[1997].[Qtr1].[Jan]:
        [Time].[Calendar].CurrentMember, [Sales Units])'
```

6. Run the query. The result grid shows the monthly values along with the cumulative values.

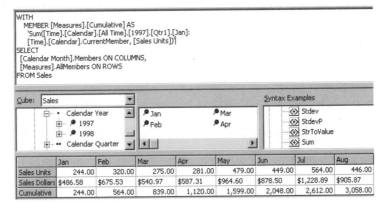

Calculating the cumulative values from the beginning of a particular time period is an extremely common MDX task, so MDX provides functions to simplify the process. The most important is the *PeriodsToDate* function. This function creates a set much like the range you created in the *Cumulative* calculated member: the ending point of the set is the current member of the dimension flagged as a Time dimension (the first

See "Working with Time Dimensions" in Chapter 3 for details about flagging a dimension as a Time dimension.

one, if a cube contains more than one dimension flagged as Time). The default beginning member of the set is the first member that shares the same parent as the ending member. For example, in a normal calendar-year hierarchy with Calendar Year, Calendar Quarter, and Calendar Month levels, a current member of August would produce the set *July:August*. (Qtr3 is the common parent.) A current member of *[1998].[Qtr3]* would produce the set *[1998].[Qtr1]:[1998].[Qtr3]*. (*[1998]* is the common parent.)

If you want to go back to a different common ancestor, simply specify the level of the ancestor you want. For example, with a current member of *[August]*, specifying Year as the level produces the range *[January]:[August]*. You can use the (All) level to go back to the beginning of the entire level.

Note   The *PeriodsToDate* function behaves very similarly to the *ParallelPeriod* function described in Chapter 6. The *ParallelPeriod* function returns a single member, and the *PeriodsToDate* function returns a set of members that can be used in an aggregation function such as *Sum*.

---

7. Change the set portion of the Cumulative member expression to **PeriodsToDate([Time].[Calendar].[Calendar Year])**, run the query, and scroll to see the Cumulative value drop back to match the Sales Units value in January.

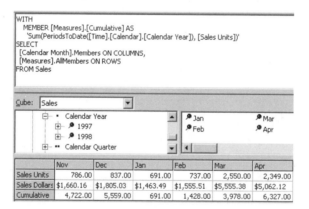

8. Remove the argument from the *PeriodsToDate* function altogether—leaving only the empty parentheses. Run the query, and see the Cumulative value resynchronize with the Sales Units value every quarter.

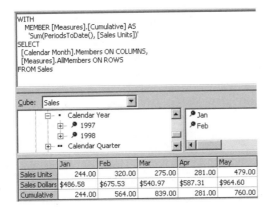

```
WITH
   MEMBER [Measures].[Cumulative] AS
     'Sum(PeriodsToDate(), [Sales Units])'
SELECT
   [Calendar Month].Members ON COLUMNS,
   [Measures].AllMembers ON ROWS
FROM Sales
```

9. Give the query a comment, and save the query file.

You can use functions that aggregate multiple values when you create a new member for either the Measures dimension or for a nonmeasure dimension. On the Measures dimension, specify a Measure member to aggregate; you must use an explicit aggregation function—*Sum, Min, Max,* or *Count.* On a nonmeasure dimension, do not specify a Measure member (since the measure will intersect all the possible measures); you generally use the *Aggregate* function to apply the appropriate aggregation for whichever measure is currently being calculated.

The *Sum* Function Creates a Subquery

Consider how MDX calculates the value for a member using the *Sum* function. For each value, the *Sum* function creates a subquery behind the scenes. The set you provide as the first argument to the *Sum* function serves as the set for the row axis.

When you use the *Sum* function to create a nonmeasure member, the Measure member comes from the main query—from the row or column axis, or from an actual or implied filter. For example, you could use the following MDX statement to replicate the subquery used to calculate the Non-WA value for the Sales Units column in "Create a calculated member of a nonmeasure dimension":

```
SELECT
   {[Sales Units]} ON COLUMNS,
   Except([State].[State].Members,{[Washington]}) ON ROWS
FROM Sales
```

The result grid of that subquery would look like this:

	Sales Units
British Colum	3,715.00
District Fede	2,807.00
Zacatecas	2,359.00
Oregon	6,551.00
California	6,331.00

(continued)

The *Sum* Function Creates a Subquery *(continued)*

The *Sum* function then simply sums all the values in the subquery result grid and returns that single value to the main query. The *Sum* function for the Sales Dollars column creates an analogous subquery to produce its single value.

When the *Sum* function is used to create a member of the Measures dimension, it still creates a subquery, but this time the Measures member cannot come from the main query since the Measures member of the main query is, by definition, the measure currently being calculated. That's why the *Sum* function requires a *«Numeric Expression»* argument when used with a Measures member. The *«Set»* argument to the *Sum* function still serves as the set for the row axis of the subquery. The *«Numeric Expression»* argument serves as the lone member of the column axis of the subquery, and all other dimensions are inherited from the main query. For example, you could use the following statement to simulate the subquery needed to calculate the cumulative May value from the query in "Create a cumulative total":

```
SELECT
  {[Sales Units]} ON COLUMNS,
  {[Time].[Calendar].[All Time].[1997].[Qtr1].[Jan]:
   [Time].[Calendar].[All Time].[1997].[Qtr2].[May]} ON ROWS
FROM Sales
```

The result grid of that subquery looks like this:

	Sales Units
Jan	244.00
Feb	320.00
Mar	275.00
Apr	281.00
May	479.00

Once again, the *Sum* function simply summarizes all the numbers and returns that single value. An analogous subquery is created for each cell of the Cumulative row in the main query. Fortunately, most of the values used in each subquery are stored in the client cache, so each subquery executes quickly.

Calculate discount dollars by using a member function

The Sales Dollars values in the Chapter 7 OLAP database are net of discounts. In other words, if you multiply the Sales Units for a product by the official list price of the product as stored in the Product table of the data warehouse, you'll get a number larger than the Sales Dollars amount. The difference is in various discounts that can be applied. To calculate the Discount Dollars at every level of summarization on all dimensions involves several steps. In this section, you'll learn those steps.

The first step is to retrieve the price for a product. The Product dimension includes Price as a member property. You can create a calculated member that retrieves the value of that member property.

The Price member property was added to the Product dimension in "Create a detail-level member property" in Chapter 3.

1. Create a new query, and insert the following MDX query statement:

```
SELECT
   [Measures].AllMembers ON COLUMNS,
   Product.Members ON ROWS
FROM Sales
```

2. Run the query. This extracts the Sales Units and Sales Dollars for all levels of the product hierarchy. You can now create a calculated measure that retrieves the Price member property.

	Sales Units	Sales Dollars
All Product	35,696.00	$76,741.28
Bread	14,532.00	$30,600.42
Bagels	1,541.00	$3,552.28
Colony Bage	264.00	$308.88
Fantastic Ba	299.00	$1,022.58
Great Bagel:	334.00	$604.54
Modell Bagel	304.00	$994.08
Sphinx Bage	340.00	$622.20
Muffins	6,445.00	$13,081.28

3. Insert the following calculated member:

```
WITH
   MEMBER [Measures].[Base Price] AS
      '[Product].Properties("Price")'
```

This is the same calculated member you created in the cube in "Use an external function to convert a string to a number" in Chapter 6.

4. Run the query. When you retrieve a member property for a dimension, you get a value only for the level at which the member property was defined. At any other level, the member property returns an error value.

	Sales Units	Sales Dollars	Base Price
All Product	35,696.00	$76,741.28	#ERR
Bread	14,532.00	$30,600.42	#ERR
Bagels	1,541.00	$3,552.28	#ERR
Colony Bage	264.00	$308.88	1.22
Fantastic Ba	299.00	$1,022.58	3.69
Great Bagel:	334.00	$604.54	1.86
Modell Bagel	304.00	$994.08	3.4
Sphinx Bage	340.00	$622.20	1.85
Muffins	6,445.00	$13,081.28	#ERR
Colony Bluet	298.00	$739.04	2.65

The Price member property was defined at the product level. A member property is always stored as a text string, even if it is a numeric value such as the price. To use the price, you must convert the string to a number. As explained in Chapter 6, MDX doesn't have a built-in function to convert a string to a value, but you can use the Microsoft Visual Basic for Applications (VBA) function *CDbl* to convert a string to a double (that is, a number that can include a decimal place).

5. Change the expression for the Base Price member to '**CDbl([Product]. Properties("Price"))**'. Run the query. Prices exist only at the Product level. The error values that previously appeared at the higher summary

levels are now some strange large numbers. You can ignore them for the time being. The prices at the product level values don't appear to change, but you can now use them in arithmetic calculations.

	Sales Units	Sales Dollars	Base Price
All Product	35,696.00	$76,741.28	-2147467259
Bread	14,532.00	$30,600.42	-2147467259
Bagels	1,541.00	$3,552.28	-2147467259
Colony Bage	264.00	$308.88	1.22
Fantastic Ba	299.00	$1,022.58	3.69
Great Bagels	334.00	$604.54	1.86
Modeli Bagel	304.00	$994.08	3.4

If you want to calculate the Gross Dollars for a product, you must multiply the Price value by the Sales Units. To calculate the Gross Product for a product category or subcategory, you must sum up the Gross Dollars for all the products in that category or subcategory. For example, suppose that you want to calculate the Gross Dollars for the Bagels product subcategory. You must first find all the products that belong to that subcategory. For each product, multiply the Base Price by the Sales Units to calculate the Gross Dollars for the product. Then sum the Gross Dollars for all the products to get the Gross Dollars for the subcategory.

6. Add the following additional calculated member to the query:

```
MEMBER [Measures].[Gross Dollars] AS
  'Sum(Descendants([Product].CurrentMember,[Product Name]) ,
   [Base Price]*[Sales Units])'
```

The expression for this member uses the *Sum* function. Think through the subquery the *Sum* function generates for the Bagels product. The first argument of the *Sum* function specifies a set for the row axis of the subquery. In this case, you define that set by using the *Descendants* function. The *Descendants* function is like the *Children* function, except that it can retrieve values at any level. The *Descendants* function starts with the Bagels member. It finds all the descendants of Bagels at the Product level—the row axis of the subquery contains all the members of the Product level that are descendants of the Bagels member. The second argument of the *Sum* function specifies the column axis of the subquery. In this case, the subquery includes the Base Price (derived from the Price member property) and the Sales Units (as stored in the cube). The members of the other dimensions are inherited from the main query. The subquery for the Bagels member would look like this:

```
WITH
  MEMBER [Measures].[Base Price] AS
    'CDbl([Product].Properties("Price"))'
SELECT {[Base Price], [Sales Units]} On Columns,
  Descendants([Bagels],[Product Name]) On Rows
From [Sales]
```

And the results of the subquery for the Bagels member would look like this:

	Base Price	Sales Units
Colony Bage	1.22	264.00
Fantastic Ba	3.69	299.00
Great Bagel:	1.86	334.00
Modell Bagel	3.4	304.00
Sphinx Bage	1.85	340.00

The *Sum* function then multiplies the values in the first column by those in the second column and sums the results.

7. Now run the query with the Gross Dollars calculated member.

	Sales Units	Sales Dollars	Base Price	Gross Dollar:
All Product	35,696.00	$76,741.28	2147467259	80,535.43
Bread	14,532.00	$30,600.42	2147467259	31,938.62
Bagels	1,541.00	$3,552.28	2147467259	3,709.23
Colony Bage	264.00	$308.88	1.22	· 322.08
Fantastic Ba	299.00	$1,022.58	3.69	1,103.31
Great Bagel:	334.00	$604.54	1.86	621.24
Modell Bagel	304.00	$994.08	3.4	1,033.60
Sphinx Bage	340.00	$622.20	1.85	629.00
Muffins	6,445.00	$13,081.28	2147467259	13,795.88

As expected, the Gross Dollars are slightly higher than the Sales Dollars at each level of summary. At the Product level, the subquery performed by the *Sum* function is small—only a single row. At the All Product level, the subquery includes all the products in the entire hierarchy. Percolating a member property up the hierarchy can be a slow operation on a large hierarchy.

8. To calculate the Discount dollars, add the following calculated member, and then run the query, add a comment, and save the query file. (Then try varying the set on the row axis—use sets from other dimensions.)

```
MEMBER [Measures].[Discount Dollars] AS
   '[Gross Dollars] - [Sales Dollars]'
```

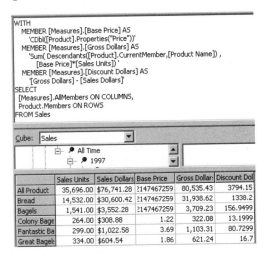

You can use a member property—particularly one that has a numeric value—within calculated members. You must remember to convert the member property to a numeric value before using it in a calculation, and you must use the member property only at the level at which it was created, using aggregation functions to percolate the values up the rest of the hierarchy.

Chapter Summary

To	Do this
Add a comment to an MDX query	Enter double slash characters (//) before the comment.
Include all the members of the Product Name level on the column axis	Use the clause *[Product Name].Members ON COLUMNS*.
Put sets of members on two axes	Use both ON COLUMNS and ON ROWS in a query.
Create a set from explicit members	Enclose the list of members separated by commas, between opening braces ({) and closing braces (}).
Create a set consisting of all possible combinations of two sets	Use the *CrossJoin* function with the two sets as arguments.
Calculate the average of all members of the State level of the State dimension	Use the expression *Avg([State].[State].Members)*.
Calculate an aggregation by using each measure's aggregation function	Use the *Aggregate* function.
Calculate the cumulative total restarting with each new member of the Calendar Year level	Use the expression *Sum(PeriodsToDate([Calendar Year]))*.
Calculate a numeric value of the Price member property of the current member of the Product dimension	Use the expression *CDbl([Product].Properties("Price"))*.

Part 3

Advanced Administration

Chapter 8

Storage Optimization

Estimated time: 1.75 hours

Chapter Objectives

In this chapter, you'll learn when to use each of the three data storage modes, how aggregations work, and how to

- Use the Storage Design Wizard to set storage mode and design aggregations.

- Create aggregations that optimize actual usage patterns.

- Control aggregation levels for individual dimensions.

As you learned in Chapter 1, "A Data Analysis Foundation," an OLAP cube appears to contain every possible summarized value at every possible level of detail for every dimension. For example, the Sales cube created in Chapter 2, "Analysis Manager from 500 Feet," contains Sales Units and Sales Dollars as measures and Product, Employee, State, and Time as dimensions. If you query the cube at the lowest level of detail—for example, Sales Dollars for Bagels by Rebecca Kanagaki in Washington during October 1998—the cube returns the number $3.51 as if it were stored directly in the cube. But at the same time, if you query the cube at a much higher level of detail—for example, Sales Dollars for Bread in the USA by all employees during 1998—the cube returns the number $14,198.45, again as if that number were stored directly in the cube.

The sample Chapter 8 data warehouse on this book's companion CD contains information to support four dimensions: Product, Employee, State, and Time. At the level of detail stored in the warehouse, there are 200 products, 4 leaf-level employees with data values, 6 states, and 22 months. That means there are $200 \times 4 \times 6 \times 22$, or 105,600 possible combinations, which means there could theoretically be 105,600 rows in the fact table. In reality, products, employees, and states were introduced gradually over time and only 6023 combinations actually appear as rows in the fact table. Even though the fact table contains only 6023 detail values, the cube can display up to 105,600 detail level cells—most of which would be empty.

In addition, because a cube appears to contain every possible summarized value at every possible level of detail for every dimension, the cube must appear to contain not only the 105,600 possible detail combinations but also all possible summary values. Counting all the members at all levels of the hierarchy, the Chapter 8 warehouse database has 216 members in the Product dimension, 8 members in the employee dimension, 14 members in the State dimension, 33 members in the Time dimension, and also the 2 measures. The cube must therefore appear to contain $216 \times 8 \times 14 \times 33 \times 2$, or 1,596,672 values. In this small sample database, the cube appears to contain 265 times as many values as the fact table contains rows! This is called *data explosion*. Data explosion is a major issue with OLAP cubes, and all OLAP products must deal with it in some way.

The simplest way to avoid data explosion is simply to not store aggregations at all and, instead, to calculate them on demand. But when you have a large data warehouse, this option quickly takes its toll on performance because requesting a single high level summarized value from the cube would require retrieving and summing hundreds or thousands of values from the source data. The challenge of OLAP is to make queries as fast as possible while avoiding data explosion. Microsoft SQL Server 2000 Analysis Services provides several features that allow the database administrator to control and fine-tune the relationship between the physical size of the cube and the speed of the queries. In fact, Analysis Services provides options in many cases that allow *both* compact data files *and* responsive queries.

Start the lesson

1. Start Analysis Manager, right-click the server, click Restore Database, and restore the Chapter 8 OLAP database.

Specifying Options for Optimizing Storage

The reason to add an OLAP layer to a data warehouse is to make data retrieval flexible and fast. As you learned in Chapter 1, the cube structure, with a hierarchy defined in each dimension, makes interacting with the cube flexible because you can drill up and down the hierarchies and slice or dice by dimension members. To make the data retrievals fast, Analysis Services summarizes selected values and stores them as predefined *aggregations*. You define aggregations in a cube, by first specifying the appropriate *storage modes* for the cube.

Understand Analysis server storage modes

If the cube has the same dimensions at the same level of detail as the fact table, the detail values in the cube match the values in the fact table.

As you learned in Chapter 2, an Analysis Services cube consists of three logical components: a map, detail values, and aggregated values. The map stores hierarchical information about the members of all dimensions used in the cube. The detail values correspond to the lowest-level members of each dimension. (If the cube has the same dimensions at the same level of detail as the fact table, the detail values in the cube match the values in the fact table.) The aggregated values are summarized values for higher levels in dimension hierarchies.

An OLAP cube always stores the cube map within the Analysis server, but Analysis Services allows you to decide where to store the detail and aggregated values. You can choose from three physical storage options: ROLAP, HOLAP, and MOLAP.

- ROLAP, for relational OLAP, leaves detail values in the relational fact table and stores aggregated values in the relational database as well.

- HOLAP, for hybrid OLAP, leaves the detail values in the relational fact table but stores the aggregated values in the cube.

- MOLAP, for multidimensional OLAP, stores both detail and aggregated values within the cube.

If you picture storage in a relational database as a cylinder and storage within Analysis Services as a cube, the three options appear as in the following graphic:

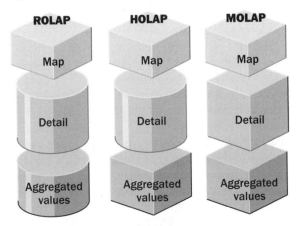

All three storage modes include the cube map within Analysis Services. It's the cube map that makes the data appear as a cube to a person running a query. That means the storage mode is invisible to client applications—that is, applications that query the cube. The client application always sees the cube. The storage option you chose affects only performance.

Because a client application can't tell which storage mode you have chosen, you can change the storage mode without affecting any client applications. Once you specify storage and start using the cube, you can change your mind later and switch to a different storage type. Because a cube appears to the client application as a single, logical entity, you can use different storage modes for different portions of a cube. In order to do that, you must use multiple partitions, which you'll learn about in the section "Working with Partitions" in Chapter 9, "Processing Optimization."

Note   Regardless of which storage option you choose, Analysis Services will never allocate storage for missing values. For example, if you have a database that shows you didn't start selling products in Canada until 1998, Analysis Services will use no storage space for detail or aggregated values for Canada in 1997.

Choose the correct storage mode

Choosing a storage mode is not as difficult as it might seem. In the first place, using Analysis Services to store aggregations in a relational database never makes any sense, so you should *never* choose the ROLAP option. Aggregations in a relational database are both bulky and slow. The purpose of creating aggregations is to improve performance, and relational aggregations defeat the purpose. The only reason you might choose the ROLAP option is if you're learning about aggregations and want to physically look at aggregations. The following section in this chapter uses ROLAP storage to help you understand aggregations. As you'll see when you look at ROLAP aggregations, they're completely unusable by any application other than Analysis Services.

Aggregations in both MOLAP and HOLAP are identical, so the only difference is where the detail-level values are stored. If you count the space required by the original warehouse as well as the space needed for the OLAP cubes, MOLAP does consume more storage space than HOLAP because the MOLAP storage option does duplicate the values from the fact table. Analysis Services, however, is efficient in how it stores data. For example, a freshly compacted Microsoft Access database containing only the SalesFact table from the Market database takes 588 KB of storage space. A cube containing the same level of detail (with no aggregations) takes only 78 KB of storage space! With a very large warehouse database, you could process the data into a MOLAP cube and then archive and remove the original warehouse. By using the MOLAP storage option, you could actually end up using a small fraction of the original storage space.

If you have a large, permanent warehouse, and if using aggregations can satisfy most queries, HOLAP storage is an excellent option. Queries that must go to the detail data will be slower than if the cube used MOLAP storage, but if they're infrequent, the performance gain might not be worth the incremental storage requirements. In addition, processing a MOLAP cube can take more time than processing a HOLAP cube. While developing an OLAP cube—during the time that you might process frequently—you might want to use HOLAP storage simply to speed up processing. Once you have completed the database design, you can switch to MOLAP storage to maximize query performance.

Note   In the Analysis Services documentation and in many presentations about Analysis Services, you might see arguments in defense of ROLAP storage. These arguments actually apply to HOLAP storage, where you leave the detail values in the relational database and store only aggregations in the physical cube files.

Some descriptions of warehouse technology use the term ROLAP to refer to a relational data warehouse that has a fact table and dimensional tables. This is a different meaning of the term than is used within Analysis Services and corresponds most closely to a HOLAP (or ROLAP) cube with no aggregations.

Understand Analysis server aggregations

Aggregations are precalculated summaries of detailed data that enable the Analysis server to answer queries quickly. While you can easily create a cube without aggregations—none of the cubes used previously in this book have any aggregations—aggregations can make a tremendous difference in query time for a large cube. As with storage mode, aggregations are invisible to client applications. Regardless of how many aggregations you design, the cube always appears to contain every possible aggregated value. When you request a value from a cube, Analysis Services uses whatever aggregations are available to retrieve the value as quickly as possible.

You also don't need to store all the possible aggregations for a cube. The Analysis server can use aggregations that do exist to quickly calculate additional values as needed. For example, say you request the total Sales Dollars for 1999 from a Sales cube and that aggregated value is not physically stored in the cube, but the quarter totals are. The Analysis server will retrieve the four quarter totals and quickly calculate the year total.

Don't confuse an *aggregated value* with an *aggregation*. An aggregated value is a single, summary value retrieved from a cube. An aggregation consists of all the possible combinations of one level from each dimension in the cube. The easiest way to understand what aggregations are is to create some simple cubes—designing all the possible aggregations and using the ROLAP storage mode—and then look at the aggregation tables in the relational database.

Inspect aggregations for a single dimension

The simplest possible cube contains a single dimension. Following the steps below, you can create a cube based on the Chapter 8 data warehouse that has only the Time dimension. You'll use the Storage Design Wizard and choose the ROLAP storage option to create all the possible aggregations. Later in this chapter, you'll learn how to use the Storage Design Wizard to refine the choice of aggregations.

The Analysis server must have write permission to the relational database in order to create ROLAP aggregations.

1. In Access, open the sample Chapter 8 database.

    Before creating ROLAP aggregations, the database contains only the fact table and dimension tables.

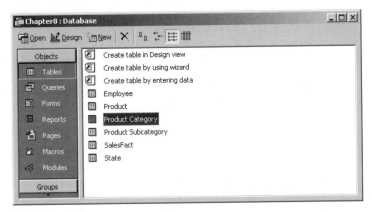

2. Switch to Analysis Manager, and then expand the Chapter 8 database. Right-click the Cubes folder, point to New Cube, and click Wizard.

3. Click Next to skip the welcome screen.

4. Select SalesFact as the fact table, and click Next. Add Sales_Dollars and Sales_Units as the measures, and click Next. Add Time as the dimension, and click Next. Click Yes when cautioned about counting rows in the fact table. Type **Time Only** as the name of the cube, and click Finish.

5. In the Cube Editor, on the Tools menu, click Design Storage. Click Next to skip the welcome screen. Select ROLAP as the data storage type, and click Next.

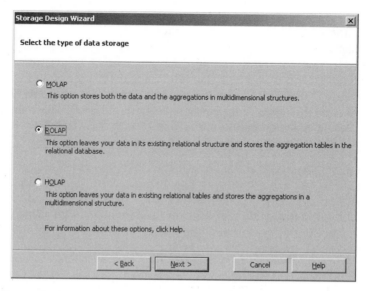

6. When asked to set storage design options, click Start, wait until the Start button changes to Continue and the Next button becomes enabled, and then click the Next button.

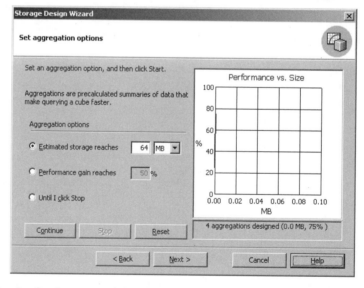

7. On the final screen of the wizard, leave the Process Now option selected and click Finish. If the wizard displays a warning about possible problems with creating ROLAP storage in the data source, click Yes to continue. After the cube finishes processing, close the Process log window.

8. Switch to Access, and press F5 to refresh the Database window. You'll see four newly created tables, each beginning with the prefix TimeOnly_ TimeOnly_, and ending with a number. Each table corresponds to a single *aggregation*.

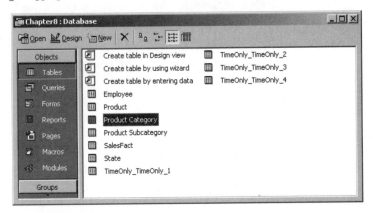

9. Open, inspect, and close each of the aggregation tables starting with TimeOnly_TimeOnly_4 and ending with TimeOnly_TimeOnly_1.

TimeOnly_TimeOnly_4 contains columns for Year, Quarter, and Month, along with columns for the summarized measures—Sales Units and Sales Dollars; the table contains 22 rows, one for each member of the Month level of the Time dimension.

TimeOnly_TimeOnly_4 : Table

Year_L2	Quarter_L3	Month_L4	SUM_SalesDol	SUM_SalesUni
1997	1	1	$486.58	244
1997	1	2	$675.53	320
1997	1	3	$540.97	275
1997	2	4	$587.31	281
1997	2	5	$964.60	479
1997	2	6	$878.50	449
1997	3	7	$1,228.89	564
1997	3	8	$905.87	446
1997	3	9	$917.86	453
1997	4	10	$872.01	425
1997	4	11	$1,660.16	786
1997	4	12	$1,805.03	837
1998	1	1	$1,463.49	691

TimeOnly_TimeOnly_3 contains, aside from the measures columns, columns only for Year and Quarter; the table contains 8 rows, one for each member of the Quarter level.

TimeOnly_TimeOnly_3 : Table

Year_L2	Quarter_L3	SUM_SalesDol	SUM_SalesUni
1997	1	$1,703.08	839
1997	2	$2,430.41	1209
1997	3	$3,052.62	1463
1997	4	$4,337.20	2048
1998	1	$8,574.38	3978
1998	2	$16,918.45	7762
1998	3	$30,062.06	13852
1998	4	$9,663.08	4545

TimeOnly_TimeOnly_2 contains only the Year column, aside from the measures, with two rows.

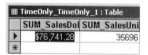

Year_L2	SUM_SalesDol	SUM_SalesUni
▶ 1997	$11,523.31	5559
1998	$65,217.97	30137
*		

TimeOnly_TimeOnly_1 contains only the summarized measure fields and has only a single row because this aggregation corresponds to the All level of the cube.

SUM_SalesDol	SUM_SalesUni
▶ $76,741.28	35696
*	

With a single dimension in the cube, each aggregation corresponds to a single level from the dimension. The following table shows the four levels in the dimension, with each label showing the number of members in the level. The second column shows the actual number of rows in the table over the theoretically possible number of rows for that level. (Because the Time dimension came from the fact table, the actual number is always the same as the theoretical number.) The suffix for each aggregation table is in brackets.

ALL (1)	1/1 [1]
Year (2)	2/2 [2]
Quarter (8)	8/8 [3]
Month (22)	22/22 [4]

Fully aggregated, this cube has 33 aggregated values for each measure, but in the terminology of Analysis Services, it has only four aggregations.

Inspect aggregations for two dimensions

Aggregations get much more complex when a cube contains more than one dimension. Creating a cube with two dimensions—Time and State—and looking at all the possible aggregations can give you a sense of how the complexity of a cube increases exponentially as you add dimensions.

1. In the Cube Editor, click the New Cube button, and repeat steps 3 through 7 of the instructions from the preceding section, but in step 4, add the Time and State dimensions and enter **Time State** for the name of the cube.

   The processing log shows each aggregation as it is created. When you collapse each aggregation entry in the log, the finished log looks like this:

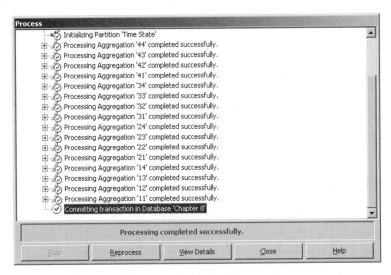

Each aggregation is given a number, with one digit for each dimension in the cube. The value of each digit tells the level number for that dimension in the aggregation. For example, 44 means "the fourth level (Month) of the first dimension (Time) and the fourth level (State) of the second dimension (State)," and 23 means "the second level (Quarter) of the first dimension (Time) and the third level (Region) of the second dimension (State)."

2. Switch to Access, and refresh the Database window.

In the Database window, you see 16 new tables, each with the prefix *TimeState_TimeState_*. The tables end with either a number or a letter. The suffixes aren't as arbitrary as they seem. The first suffix appears to be 0, but if you treat 0 as if it were 10, placing it between 9 and A, the suffixes follow a natural progression (since 5 was the next suffix digit available after the four numbers used for the TimeOnly aggregations). The table names clearly use a different naming scheme for the aggregations than the one used in the Process log window.

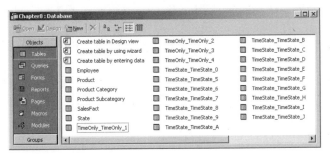

3. Open, inspect, and close TimeState_TimeState_5 (the most summarized aggregation), TimeState_TimeState_J (the most detailed aggregation), and any other tables you want. The most detailed aggregation table contains fields for all the levels of the Time dimension plus all the levels of the State dimension.

Year_L2	Quarter_L3	Month_L4	Country_L6	Region_L7	StateName_L8	SUM_SalesDol	SUM_SalesUni
1997	1	1	USA	North West	Washington	$486.58	244
1997	1	2	USA	North West	Washington	$675.53	320
1997	1	3	USA	North West	Washington	$540.97	275
1997	2	4	USA	North West	Washington	$587.31	281
1997	2	5	USA	North West	Oregon	$395.22	206
1997	2	5	USA	North West	Washington	$569.38	273
1997	2	6	USA	North West	Oregon	$253.54	133
1997	2	6	USA	North West	Washington	$624.96	316
1997	3	7	USA	North West	Oregon	$578.29	260
1997	3	7	USA	North West	Washington	$650.60	304
1997	3	8	USA	North West	Oregon	$295.82	134
1997	3	8	USA	North West	Washington	$610.05	312
1997	3	9	USA	North West	Oregon	$328.71	178
1997	3	9	USA	North West	Washington	$589.15	275
1997	4	10	USA	North West	Oregon	$202.55	104

The Time State cube has 16 aggregation tables because each combination of levels between the two dimensions gets its own aggregation. The following table shows the possible combinations, with each cell showing the actual number of rows in the aggregation table over the number of rows theoretically possible for that aggregation. The aggregation table suffix is in brackets.

	ALL (1)	Country (3)	Region (4)	State (6)
ALL (1)	1/1 [5]	3/3 [9]	4/4 [C]	6/6 [G]
Year (2)	2/2 [6]	4/6 [0]	6/8 [D]	9/12 [H]
Quarter (8)	8/8 [7]	15/24 [A]	20/32 [E]	29/48 [I]
Month (22)	22/22 [8]	37/66 [B]	49/88 [F]	70/132 [J]

In the terminology of Analysis Services, this fully aggregated cube contains 16 aggregations. There are, however, 285 actual aggregated values for each measure, out of a possible (theoretically) 462.

Tip To see the speed difference in creating MOLAP aggregations compared to ROLAP, try creating the same 16 aggregations for the Time State cube by using MOLAP storage.

If the Time State cube were a MOLAP cube, with the lowest level values stored in the cube itself, the sixteenth aggregation (the box marked J) wouldn't even exist as an aggregation because that box corresponds to the detail level of the cube itself.

Looking at the aggregation tables for a cube with one or two dimensions should highlight a number of facts about aggregations:

- Adding a single aggregation can create many aggregated values.

- The number of possible aggregations is the product of the number of levels on each dimension in a cube.

- Adding a new dimension to a cube dramatically increases the number of possible aggregations.

- The number of combinations theoretically possible in an aggregation is the product of the number of members on the corresponding level of each dimension.

- The actual number of summarized values in an aggregation depends on the specific data patterns in the fact table.

- A single aggregation stores aggregated values for all measures stored in the cube. (Calculated members, discussed in Part 2, "Multidimensional Expressions," are not included in an aggregation.)

- Even though the naming of ROLAP tables is not random, it is unpredictable.

You obviously don't want to store all the possible aggregations for a cube of any complexity. Deciding which aggregations will provide the most benefit is a difficult task. In effect, for any given amount of storage space that you use for aggregations, you want the greatest possible gain in performance. Analysis Services contains a sophisticated algorithm for determining the most beneficial combination of aggregations. The Storage Design Wizard is where that algorithm operates.

Use the Storage Design Wizard

The Storage Design Wizard is the tool that you use to decide which of the possible aggregations for a cube will be created. If the cube already has aggregations designed, the Storage Design Wizard offers to add to or replace existing aggregations. In this section, you'll create a Sales cube in the Chapter 8 database with four dimensions. You can use the Storage Design Wizard to add aggregations to that cube.

1. In Analysis Manager, right-click the Cubes folder, point to New Cube, and click Wizard. Click Next to skip the welcome screen. Create the cube with SalesFact as the fact table, Sales Dollars and Sales Units as the measures, and all four existing shared dimensions. Give the cube the name **Sales**.

2. In the Cube Editor, on the Tools menu, click Design Storage. Click Next to skip the welcome screen.

3. Select MOLAP as the Storage Option, and click Next.

For a small cube such as this one, HOLAP is not faster than MOLAP. Even on a small cube, however, ROLAP can be significantly slower than the other two options.

The aggregation options screen of the Storage Design Wizard performs a single task—selecting aggregations from the available pool. The Sales cube has 4 dimensions. The Product and Time dimensions are both standard dimensions, each with 4 levels (counting the All level). The State and Employee dimensions are both changing dimensions, each behaving as if it has 2 levels (counting the All level). Theoretically, there are 64 possible aggregations that could be created for this cube ($4 \times 4 \times 2 \times 2$). The goal of the Storage Design Wizard is to select the best aggregations for a given amount of storage space.

4. Click Performance Gain Reaches, and type **20** as the target percentage. (The default value of 50 percent is unnecessarily high.) Then click Start, and when the Next button becomes enabled, click Next.

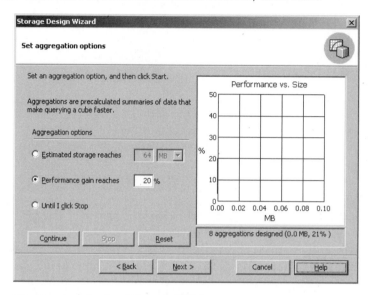

The Storage Design Wizard will try various combinations of aggregations and then (for the sample Sales cube) settle on a specific eight aggregations as the best choices. You have no control over which eight aggregations it selects. For most databases, a 20 percent value for Performance Gain Reaches provides enough aggregation for very good performance. If you later find that queries are executing too slowly, you can add aggregations then. As you increase the performance percentage, remember that the disk space required to reach 10 percent optimization is less, sometimes by an order of magnitude, than the amount required going from 10 percent to 20 percent.

Note   The three aggregation options simply provide different ways of achieving the same result. In a large cube, if you choose the Performance Gain Reaches option and enter 20 percent, you might get 20 aggregations. For the same cube, choosing the Estimated Storage Reaches option and entering 5 MB might result in the same 20 aggregations. Likewise, choosing the Until I Click Stop option and clicking Stop as soon as you see 20 aggregations would select the same 20 aggregations.

---

5. At any time, you can click Reset (and click Yes when asked to confirm) to clear the aggregations and start over.

6. On the Finish screen of the Storage Design Wizard, click the Process Now option and click Finish.

Regardless of the option you choose, Analysis Manager simply stores the definition of the aggregations in the OLAP repository. Storing the definition of the aggregations is different from physically creating them, however. The Storage Design Wizard *designs* aggregations but doesn't create them. The aggregations aren't created until you process the cube. Processing the cube automatically creates any aggregations that have been designed.

7. Close the Process log window and the Cube Editor after the cube has processed.

For a large database with many dimensions, levels, and members, designing aggregations can take a long time. This is because the Analysis server is executing an extremely sophisticated algorithm behind the scenes. The dimensional hierarchies are navigated, and various combinations are attempted, all in an effort to give you the greatest performance benefits for a given amount of disk space. However, designing aggregations is a task that's performed only rarely—when the cube is built, when the cube design changes, or when query performance is less than desired.

If you want to design different aggregations for one part of a cube than for another part—for example, to aggregate the current year at 25 percent but previous years at 10 percent—you must create partitions, which are discussed in "Working with Partitions" in Chapter 9.

Managing the Pool of Potential Aggregations

The Storage Design Wizard selects aggregations from a pool of potential aggregations. As a default, the pool of potential aggregations includes all levels from all dimensions. Analysis Services includes two techniques for controlling the pool of potential aggregations. One option is to use actual usage patterns to affect the rankings within the pool. Another option is to eliminate dimension levels from the pool entirely.

Preparing for Usage-Based Optimization

The algorithm in the Storage Design Wizard is sophisticated, but it can base its decisions solely upon structural factors such as the number of members in different levels of a dimension or the number of rows in a fact table. The Storage Design Wizard can't take into consideration the way a particular type of query actually performs. Fortunately, Analysis Services provides a tool for just that.

One of the most powerful features of Analysis Services is usage-based optimization. It allows you to select aggregations based on actual queries submitted to the server—that is, on the usage of real-world users. The Usage-Based Optimization Wizard behaves exactly like the Storage Design Wizard except that it factors into the equation the actual usage patterns.

Populate the usage log

Usage patterns come from a query log. The query log is an Access database named Msmdqlog.mdb located in the folder containing the Analysis Services executable files (the same folder that contains the default repository database). By default, the server logs one out of ten queries.

If you want to experiment with usage-based optimization, increase the sampling frequency temporarily to make it easier to add entries to the log. To change the sampling frequency, first change a property of the Analysis server. Then stop and restart the Analysis server service for the change to take effect.

1. In the Analysis Manager, right-click the server and then click Properties.

2. Click the Logging tab, and type **1** in the Write To Log Once Per box. Remove old entries in the log by clicking the Clear Log button and acquiescing in the confirmation alert box. Click OK to close the dialog box. Click OK when warned that the change will not take place until you stop and restart the server.

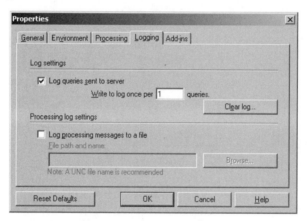

3. Go to Control Panel—click the Start button, point to Settings, and click Control Panel—and double-click Services. (In Microsoft Windows 2000, double-click Administrative Tools in Control Panel and then double-click Services.)

4. Select MSSQLServerOLAPService in the Service list, click Stop Service, and then click Start Service.

5. Switch to Analysis Manager. In the Chapter 8 database, right-click the Sales cube and click Browse Data. Spend a few minutes browsing the Chapter 8 Sales cube.

For example, you might drag over some dimensions, browse members, and perform various queries to add entries to the query log. Each manipulation of the browser layout generates a new query to the server.

6. Close the Cube Browser.

Note   Queries that can be answered by the client cache are never seen by the server and thus are not logged. To clear the client cache, close and restart the client browser application and then reconnect. (When using the sample browser in Analysis Manager, you must close and restart Analysis Manager.)

View usage analysis reports

You don't need to review usage analysis reports before you apply usage-based optimization. However, reviewing these reports will help you decide whether to adjust the aggregations for a cube.

1. Right-click the Sales cube, and click Usage Analysis to start the Usage Analysis Wizard.

2. Select Query Run Time Table, and click Next.

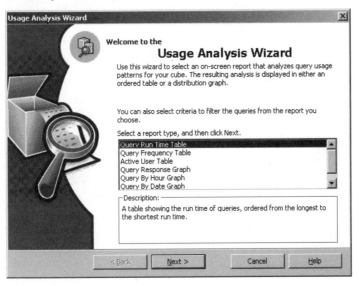

3. Look at the available options for setting criteria, and then click Next without setting any criteria.

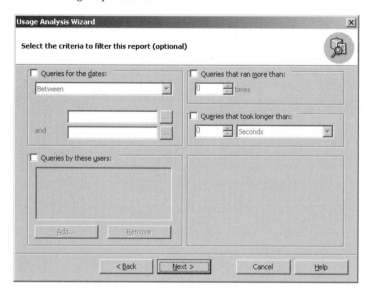

You can filter the report based on the date a query ran, the number of times a query ran, how long it took, or which user executed it.

4. Review the report.

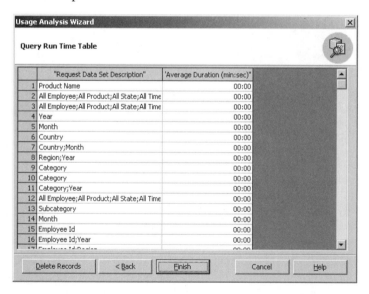

5. Click Back twice, select the Query Response Graph report, and click Next twice to see the graph.

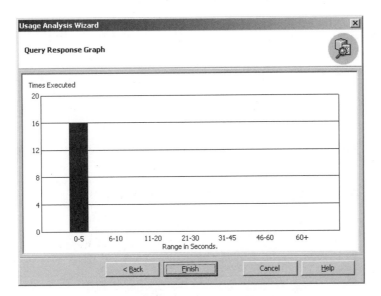

6. Click Finish to close the Usage Analysis Wizard.

> **Note** Because the query log is stored in an Access table in a logical format, it can be read by custom applications to analyze usage. However, one column in the log is cryptic: Dataset. It contains a text string, each character of which is the level number of a dimension in the cube. This is the same format used to describe aggregations, as explained in "Inspect aggregations for two dimensions" earlier in this chapter. Unless you change the number of dimensions in a cube, each log entry for a cube will have a Dataset string with the same number of characters. The column uses a string, rather than a number, because a dimension can have over nine levels. 1–9, 0, and A–N represent the 24 possible levels in a dimension.

Use the Usage-Based Optimization Wizard

Once you've accumulated a set of queries in the usage log, you can use the Usage-Based Optimization Wizard to design aggregations. The Usage-Based Optimization Wizard is essentially the Usage Analysis Wizard attached to the front of the Storage Design Wizard. First you select the logged queries that should apply, and then you design aggregations.

1. Right-click the server and click Properties. Click the Logging tab and then click Clear Log. Click Yes, and then click OK to close the Properties dialog box.

2. Right-click the Sales cube in the Chapter 8 database, and click Browse data. Spend some time browsing the data, and then close the Cube Browser window.

3. Right-click the Sales cube, and click Usage-Based Optimization. Click Next to leave the welcome screen.

4. On the criteria screen, select the Queries That Ran More Than check box and type **0** in the Times box. Click Next to continue to review the filtered queries.

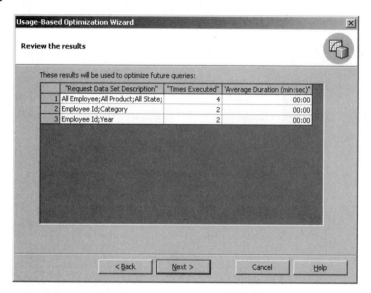

5. On the Review The Results screen of the wizard, click Next.

The wizard automatically proceeds to the screens from the Storage Design Wizard. As with the regular Storage Design Wizard, if aggregations already exist, you can add aggregations or erase aggregations and create new ones.

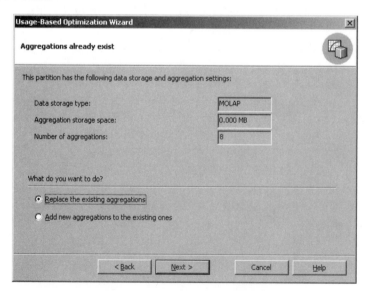

6. Click Replace The Existing Aggregations, and then click Next.

7. Click the MOLAP storage option, and click Next.

8. In the Set Aggregation Options screen, click Performance Gain Reaches, type **20**, and click Start.

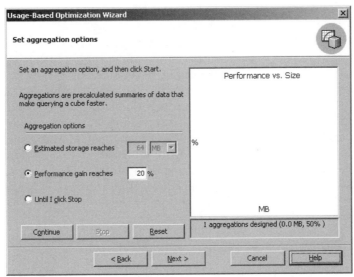

This time, using the selected queries from the log, the wizard concludes that a 20 percent performance gain can be achieved with a single aggregation. (Your results might differ.)

9. Click Next, click Process Now, click Finish, and then close the Process log window.

10. In the console tree, right-click the Server, click Properties, and click the Logging tab. Change the query setting back to **10**, and click OK. Click OK to close the message box, and then stop and restart the Analysis server service.

Consider the server cache

The query you execute most frequently might not be the one that's most in need of aggregations. Both the PivotTable Service and the Analysis server maintain caches, on the client and on the server, respectively. Suppose that a cube has no aggregations and that you frequently review the Product Category by Month query. The first time the query executes, the Analysis server will need to go to the detail level to dynamically assemble the totals, but then it retains those totals in the server cache. As additional people make queries at the same level of detail, the Analysis server is able to respond instantaneously to the request, simply from the cache. Because the Product Category by Month query is so popular, its values are never removed from the server cache.

When you apply usage-based optimization, you must decide whether you want to optimize for the popular Product Category by Month query. If you frequently perform an administrative task that clears the server cache—such as shutting down the server or reprocessing the cube—you should include queries to the server cache in the optimization pattern. If you rarely perform a task that clears the server cache, you can exclude the server cache from the selection criteria.

Remember, however, that queries answered from the client cache never even make it to the log. Your only choice is regarding the server cache.

Manipulate the query log

Suppose that you have accumulated a significant number of entries in the log for a cube. You then change the definition of the cube, which makes the entries in the query log no longer meaningful. Leaving those entries in the log as you perform usage-based optimization could lead to invalid optimization.

The Logging tab of the Server Properties dialog box has a button that will clear all the entries from the log. The server log, however, contains entries for all the cubes in all the databases on the server. If you modify a single cube, you probably don't want to erase the log for all cubes.

If you no longer need the old log data, right-click the cube, click Usage Analysis, and click Next twice. This displays all the queries in the log for that cube. Click Delete Records at the bottom of the report to clear only the log for that one cube.

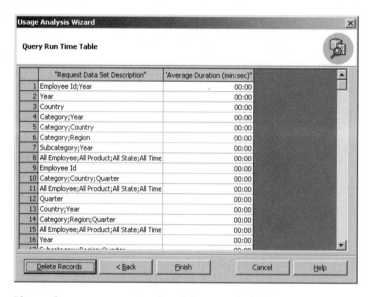

If you do want to retain the old query logs, you can extract them from the log database or you can filter for only new log entries when optimizing aggregations. On the Usage Based Optimization Wizard's criteria screen, select the Queries For The Dates check box, click After in the drop-down list, and select the date the cube structure was last modified in the date box.

Manage aggregations for a dimension

The Storage Design Wizard searches the pool of all possible aggregations when deciding which aggregations to create. Usually, the wizard does a good job of deciding which aggregations will have the most positive effect. Sometimes, however, you know something about a dimension that the wizard can't know. For example, suppose that you're designing a cube that will have dozens of users.

All the users except one need only three dimensions in the cube. That one person needs a fourth dimension, and that fourth dimension is large and complex. All users agree that the fourth dimension shouldn't slow down the rest of the queries. The user making the special request doesn't mind having queries that use that dimension run slowly.

This is an example of a situation in which you as the cube designer know information about the cube that is unavailable to the Storage Design Wizard. The unusual status of this dimension might not even be captured properly by query logs. In Analysis Services, you can control how a dimension enters the pool of available aggregations. Normally, all levels of a dimension interact with all dimensions of all other dimensions. You can specify two other aggregation options for a dimension: Top Level Only and Bottom Level Only.

Consider a table that shows all the possible aggregations for the Time State cube—a cube that contains only the Time and State dimensions. With the default setting for both dimensions, the pool of available aggregations for the Storage Design Wizard consists of all 16 possible combinations of levels. If you flag the State dimension as Top Level Only, 12 of the possible combinations are removed from the available pool. The four remaining aggregations—marked Top Only in the grid—correspond precisely to the pool of available aggregations if Time were the only dimension in the cube.

	ALL	Country	Region	State
ALL	Top Only			
Year	Top Only			
Quarter	Top Only			
Month	Top Only			

In other words, flagging the State dimension as Top Level Only effectively removes the penalty for having the dimension exist. As long as a user doesn't traverse the hierarchy of the State dimension, the value for the State dimension will be the All level, and the All level for that dimension will have aggregations that make responses very fast. That is precisely the example scenario given at the beginning of this section. The fourth dimension—included in the cube only for the benefit of one user—doesn't penalize any users who don't use it, but the person who does traverse the hierarchy of the dimension might experience slower than normal response to queries.

In the two-dimensional Time State cube, if you were to flag both dimensions as Top Level Only, you would end up with only one possible aggregation for the cube—the aggregation with a single row that contains the total value for the measures summarized for the entire cube. Flagging all the dimensions of a cube with Top Level Only would completely defeat the purpose of creating aggregations.

The Bottom Level Only flag has the opposite effect. It prevents any aggregations for a dimension above the lowest level of detail. Consider again the table of possible aggregations for the Time State cube. Flagging the State dimension with Bottom Level Only removes from the pool all but four of the aggregations, the ones marked Bottom Only in the table.

	ALL	Country	Region	State
ALL				Bottom Only
Year				Bottom Only
Quarter				Bottom Only
Month				Bottom Only

Even though the boxes in the table all appear as the same size, aggregations closer to the upper left corner of the table contain few values and aggregations closer to the lower right corner of the table contain many values. Setting a dimension to Bottom Level Only forces all users to pay a performance penalty for a dimension, even those who never use the dimension. You might set a dimension to Bottom Level Only if users are almost always slicing a cube by the lowest level of that dimension. This option is much less useful than the Top Level Only option. For most cases in which you might want to choose the Bottom Level Only option in a dimension (for example, where the bottom level has only a few more members than the top level), the Storage Design Wizard would automatically select the appropriate aggregations even without flagging the dimension.

In the two-dimensional Time State cube, if you were to flag both dimensions as Bottom Level Only (with MOLAP storage mode), the result would be to create no aggregations at all since the bottom right aggregation of the table is the detail level of the cube.

You can set the Aggregation Usage property for a dimension to *Custom* which allows you to enable or disable specific levels within the dimension. In most cases, using the Storage Design Wizard or the Usage-Based Optimization Wizard will give much better results than attempting to control aggregation for levels within a dimension manually.

Setting the Aggregation Usage flags for a dimension merely controls how levels from the dimension will enter the available pool for consideration by one of the Storage Design Wizards. Changing the setting has no effect until you run a wizard to design new aggregations for the cube.

Chapter Summary

To	Do this
Observe aggregation tables	Specify ROLAP as the design mode for a cube; after processing the cube, look at the aggregation tables in the relational data source.
Choose the storage mode for a cube	In the console tree, right-click the cube name and click Design Storage.
Control the number of aggregations used in a cube	On the aggregation options screen of the Storage Design Wizard, select one of the three options for limiting aggregations and click Start.

(continued)

(continued)

To	Do this
Clear all existing aggregations for a cube	On the aggregations options page of the Storage Design Wizard, click the Reset button.
Change the sample frequency for the query log	In the console tree, right-click the server and choose Properties. Click the Logging tab, and enter a value in the queries box. You must then stop and restart the Analysis server service.
Start or stop the Analysis server service	In Windows 2000, click Start, point to Programs, point to Administrative Tools, and click Services. In Microsoft Windows NT, click Start, point to Settings, click Control Panel, and double-click Services. Then select MSSQLServerOLAPService, and click Start or Stop.
View usage reports for a cube	In the console tree, right-click the cube and click Usage Analysis.
Apply usage-based optimization to a cube	In the console tree, right-click the cube and click Usage-Based Optimization.

Chapter 9

Processing Optimization

Estimated time: 2 hours

In this chapter, you'll learn what happens when you process a database and you'll learn how to

- Avoid problems with cubes stored using HOLAP or ROLAP storage.

- Incrementally update a dimension or a cube.

- Avoid problems when incrementally updating a cube.

- Use partitions to manage large cubes.

- Use Data Transformation Services (DTS) to automate processing a database.

Conceptually, the Analysis server is a black box, mysteriously converting the values in a data warehouse into a miraculous object called a cube. And for the most part, you can simply ignore what goes on inside that black box and let the Analysis server work its magic. Knowledge is, however, power, and that adage certainly holds true in the domain of Microsoft SQL Server 2000 Analysis Services. The more you know about what goes on within the black box of the Analysis server, the better you'll be able to troubleshoot unusual situations and find solutions to difficult problems. This chapter explains in broad terms what goes on inside the black box. The explanations are simplified, but they encompass some of the most complex topics in this book. If nothing else, this chapter can give you an appreciation for the sophistication and elegance of the Analysis server design.

Start the lesson

1. In the Analysis Manager console tree, right-click the server and click Restore Database. Then select the Chapter 9 file, click Open, click Restore, and then close the Restore Database Progress dialog box.

2. If you didn't install the files in the default folder, Open the Data Sources folder of the Chapter 9 database and click Edit. Change the database to the Chapter9.mdb database installed from the companion CD.

Understanding OLAP Processing

In this section, you'll learn what happens when you process an Analysis Services database. This includes looking at how the Analysis server processes a dimension as well as how the server processes a cube. You'll learn what happens to client applications while the server is processing a database, and you'll learn what happens when the data warehouse changes and you haven't processed the OLAP database.

How the Analysis Server Processes a Dimension

When you process a dimension, the Analysis server creates a SQL statement to extract the necessary information from the data warehouse dimension table. The extract includes one or two columns for each level in the hierarchy. (If the Member Name Column property for a level is the same as that of the Member Key Column, the Analysis server extracts only the key column. If the name column is different, the Analysis server extracts both.) The Analysis server retrieves one row from the data warehouse for each distinct combination of level keys and sorts the rows using the Member Key Column property of each level. As an example, say you want to process the State dimension in the Chapter 9 sample database. To generate the State dimension from the Chapter9 warehouse, the Analysis server extracts the following rows:

STATE_ID	State_Name	Region	Country
4	British Columbia	Canada West	Canada
5	District Federal	Mexico Central	Mexico
6	Zacatecas	Mexico Central	Mexico
1	Washington	North West	USA
2	Oregon	North West	USA
3	California	South West	USA

The State level has both a STATE_ID and a State_Name column; the Region and Country levels have one column each. The rows are sorted first by Country, then by Region, and finally by State_ID. The retrieved rows represent, if you will, the dimension members from the *warehouse* perspective. The structure of the relational columns does not show that the members of the Region level are children of the State level. The Analysis server needs to create the dimension members from the *hierarchy* perspective. For each member of the dimension, the server creates a unique *path* that contains a component number for each level in the dimension. The State dimension contains three levels, so the path for each member will contain three numbers, one for each level: Country→Region→State.

Starting with the first row retrieved from the relational table, the server creates a new member for each relevant level of the hierarchy. So, for the row containing information about British Columbia, the server starts by creating a member with the path 0→0→0, which corresponds to the All level member of the dimension. (In the Chapter 9 OLAP database, the name of the All level member is *North America*.) The server then creates a member with the path

1→0→0, which corresponds to the Canada country. The server then creates a member with the path 1→1→0, which corresponds to the Canada West region. Finally the server creates a member with the path 1→1→1, which corresponds to the British Columbia state. The server created four members based on the first row from the relational dimension. For the second row, the server creates only three members, since the All level member already exists. By the time the server has finished, it has created a unique path for each member of the dimension. That path contains the genealogy of each member. For the State dimension, the server creates the member names and paths shown in the first two columns of the following table:

Complete Member Name	Member Path	Member ID
[North America]	0→0→0	1
[North America].[Canada]	1→0→0	2
[North America].[Canada].[Canada West]	1→1→0	3
[North America].[Canada].[Canada West].[British Columbia]	1→1→1	4
[North America].[Mexico]	2→0→0	5
[North America].[Mexico].[Mexico Central]	2→1→0	6
[North America].[Mexico].[Mexico Central].[District Federal]	2→1→1	7
[North America].[Mexico].[Mexico Central].[Zacatecas]	2→1→2	8
[North America].[USA]	3→0→0	9
[North America].[USA].[North West]	3→1→0	10
[North America].[USA].[North West].[Washington]	3→1→1	12
[North America].[USA].[North West].[Oregon]	3→1→2	11
[North America].[USA].[South West]	3→2→0	13
[North America].[USA].[South West].[California]	3→2→1	14

To create the path, the server always sorts the children of a member by using the value from the Member Key Column property, regardless of the value in the Order By property for a level. After creating the paths, the server creates a separate ID for each member that does take into consideration the Order By property, sorting by member name as a default. In the preceding table of the State dimension members, the third column shows the ID for each member. In the State dimension, the sequence of the ID numbers matches the sequence of the path numbers, except for Oregon and Washington. The path sequence puts Washington before Oregon because the STATE_ID for Washington (1) precedes the STATE_ID for Oregon (2). The ID sequence puts Oregon before Washington because the State_Name for Oregon alphabetically precedes the State_Name for Washington. The ID numbers sort members into what is called the *hierarchy order*. The hierarchy order is the order for the members if a multidimensional expressions (MDX) query retrieves all the members the dimension.

Note The MDX function *Properties("ID")* displays the ID for a member, but you would rarely need it. There's no way to display the path for a member.

As mentioned earlier, the path for each member contains the member's complete genealogy. The Analysis server combines the paths from all the members to create a *map* for the dimension. The dimension map allows the Analysis server to slice and dice hierarchies very quickly. You don't need to remember (or even really understand) exactly how the Analysis server creates a map for each dimension, but understanding that the family tree is built into each member can help you understand certain behaviors and rules that otherwise might seem arbitrary.

How the Analysis Server Processes a Cube

As explained in Chapter 8, "Storage Optimization," many OLAP products have a problem with data explosion—creating massively large cube files from even moderately large warehouse data. Analysis Services, however, is remarkably efficient in the way it stores data in a cube, often creating a cube that is much smaller than the original data source. The actual physical structure of Analysis Services cube files is proprietary to Microsoft, and understanding it perfectly would not be helpful. But creating a meaningful conceptual picture of a cube can help you both as you design a cube and as you retrieve reports from it.

As you learned in earlier chapters, a cube consists of one or more dimensions combined with one or more measures. Those dimensions form the structure or organization for the data values in the cube. Before the Analysis server can process a cube, it must have already processed each dimension used in the cube.

When you process a cube, the Analysis server executes a SQL statement to retrieve values from the fact table. The SQL statement retrieves enough columns to completely identify each member and the columns for the measures. For each row extracted from the fact table, the Analysis server identifies for each dimension the member that corresponds to that row. It then creates a compound path for the row. For example, the following table contains the first four sample rows extracted to create the first cube in the Chapter 9 OLAP database:

Year	Quarter	Month	Country	Region	State_Name	Sales_Units
1997	1	1	USA	North West	Washington	244
1997	1	2	USA	North West	Washington	320
1997	1	3	USA	North West	Washington	275
1997	2	4	USA	North West	Washington	281

Each row includes two dimensions: Year and State. The server finds the leaf-level member path for each dimension. For the first row, the path for Year 1997, Quarter 1, Month 1 is 1→1→1. As mentioned in the preceding section, the path for the Washington state is 3→1→1. From these two paths, the Analysis server constructs a single path for this combination of members, which you can picture schematically as 1→1→1•3→1→1. This is the internal path for one cell of the cube: Washington in January 1997. In other words, the path for a cell in a cube is an internally generated number consisting of one subnumber for each level for each dimension used in the cube. The cubes in the Chapter 9 database contain two dimensions (Time and State), both of which have three levels (not counting the All level). That means that each cell in the Sales cube has a path consisting of 6 numbers—one for each of the three levels in each of the two dimensions. The Sales cube in the FoodMart 2000 sample database has 10 dimensions actually stored in the cube, with a total of 23 levels between the 10 dimensions. (In Foodmart 2000, the Store Size In SQFT and Store Type dimensions are virtual dimensions, which are not stored in a cube. Virtual dimensions are explained in Chapter 10, "Dimension Optimization.") That means that each cell in the FoodMart 2000 Sales cube has a path consisting of 23 numbers. The more dimensions a cube has—and the more levels in each dimension—the more information is stored in each cell of the cube.

Virtual dimensions are explained in Chapter 10, "Dimension Optimization."

Note Each component number in a cell path is a 16-bit integer (2 bytes). The largest number you can store in a 16-bit integer is 65,535. A member can have only 64,000 children because that is the largest (rounded) number that can fit in a 16-bit integer. Theoretically a path containing 16 numbers should require 32 bytes of storage space, but the path is compressed—typically to about 25 percent of the original size. Thus, each cell physically stored in a cube requires approximately one-half byte for each level of each dimension included in the cube, in addition to the space required for the measures.

When the Analysis server begins processing a cube, it creates a data file to store the cells for the cube. When the server processes a single row extracted from the fact table, it first calculates the path for the leaf-level cell. From the previous table, the path for the first row of sample data looks like this:

$1\rightarrow1\rightarrow1\bullet3\rightarrow1\rightarrow1$ *(1997$\rightarrow$Quarter 1$\rightarrow$January•USA $\rightarrow$North West$\rightarrow$Washington)*

The server checks to see whether a leaf-level cell with that path already exists. If the cell exists, the server adds the new measure to the one already in the cell. If the cell does not already exist, the server creates a new leaf-level cell, storing both the path and the value of the measure. (The leaf level isn't created if you choose HOLAP or ROLAP storage mode when you design storage for your cube.)

After creating a leaf-level cell, the Analysis server creates cells for any aggregations you designed. Now assume that the cube had three aggregations designed: Quarter by North America, Year by Region, and All Time by State Code. The Analysis server simply creates the appropriate three subsets of the original cell path:

$1\rightarrow1\rightarrow0\bullet0\rightarrow0\rightarrow0$ *(1997$\rightarrow$Quarter 1•North America)*

$1\rightarrow0\rightarrow0\bullet3\rightarrow1\rightarrow0$ *(1997•USA $\rightarrow$North West)*

$0\rightarrow0\rightarrow0\bullet3\rightarrow1\rightarrow1$ *(All Time$\rightarrow$•USA $\rightarrow$North West$\rightarrow$Washington)*

Each of these paths corresponds to the path of an aggregated cell. If the cell already exists, the server adds the measure value to it; if the cell doesn't exist, the server creates the cell and stores the measure value. That then completes the processing for one row.

The server repeats this process for each row extracted from the fact table. Because the path for a cell contains the complete genealogy for the member of each dimension in the cell, calculating the path for each aggregate value is relatively straightforward. Along with creating the data file, Analysis Manager creates various index files to facilitate rapid retrieval of the values. Once all the values have been accumulated, the Process log window in Analysis Manager announces that processing has completed successfully.

Watch the server process a database

The Analysis server uses the concept of a *transaction* when processing a database. When the server begins processing the database, it begins a new transaction. When it completes processing, it *commits* the transaction. If, for some reason, processing isn't completed successfully, the server *rolls back* the transaction and the database looks like it did before the transaction started. During the course of the transaction, all changes are made to temporary files so that applications retrieving values from the server are not aware that a transaction is taking place.

When you process a database, all the dimensions and all the cubes are processed within a single transaction. This means that all users can continue to use any cube or dimension with the database—seeing no changes—until the entire database has processed. Also, if anything should go wrong during the processing, all the temporary files are deleted—or *rolled back*—and the database remains as if nothing had happened. You can watch the server create and rename temporary files by looking at the data folder while processing the database.

1. In Windows Explorer, open the Chapter 9 folder within the OLAP Data folder. (You specify the location of the OLAP Data folder when you install Analysis Services. By default, this folder is under Program Files\Microsoft Analysis Services\Data on the Windows drive.) You should see four files for each dimension and one file for each cube within the database, plus a folder for each cube and a few other files.

2. On the View menu, select Details. Make a note of the date and time each file was last modified. (You might want to tile the Analysis Manager and Windows Explorer windows vertically so you can see both at the same time.)

Name	Size	Type	Modified
Sales1 MOLAP		File Folder	6/10/2000 9:08 PM
Sales2 HOLAP Detail		File Folder	6/10/2000 9:08 PM
Sales3 HOLAP Aggregated		File Folder	6/10/2000 9:08 PM
Sales4 Bad Increment		File Folder	6/10/2000 9:08 PM
Sales5 Increment Fact		File Folder	6/10/2000 9:08 PM
Sales6 Increment Filter		File Folder	6/10/2000 9:08 PM
Sales7 Partitioned		File Folder	6/10/2000 9:08 PM
Market.src	1 KB	SRC File	6/10/2000 9:06 PM
Sales1 MOLAP.mdl	2 KB	MDL File	6/10/2000 9:08 PM
Sales2 HOLAP Detail.mdl	2 KB	MDL File	6/10/2000 9:08 PM
Sales3 HOLAP Aggregated.mdl	2 KB	MDL File	6/10/2000 9:08 PM
Sales4 Bad Increment.mdl	2 KB	MDL File	6/10/2000 9:08 PM

3. Switch back to Analysis Manager, right-click the Chapter 9 database, and click Process The Database.

4. As soon as the Process log window opens, switch to the Windows Explorer window that displays the database files. Press the F5 function key to refresh the window.

You'll see new files and folders appear, each with extra characters included in the name.

Name	Size	Type	Modified
Sales1 MOLAP		File Folder	6/11/2000 6:56 PM
Sales1 MOLAP'S		File Folder	6/11/2000 6:56 PM
Sales2 HOLAP Detail		File Folder	6/11/2000 6:56 PM
Sales2 HOLAP Detail'S		File Folder	6/11/2000 6:56 PM
Sales3 HOLAP Aggregated		File Folder	6/11/2000 6:56 PM
Sales3 HOLAP Aggregated'S		File Folder	6/11/2000 6:56 PM
Sales4 Bad Increment		File Folder	6/11/2000 6:56 PM
Sales4 Bad Increment'S		File Folder	6/11/2000 6:56 PM
Sales5 Increment Fact		File Folder	6/11/2000 6:56 PM
Sales5 Increment Fact'S		File Folder	6/11/2000 6:56 PM
Sales6 Increment Filter		File Folder	6/11/2000 6:56 PM
Sales7 Partitioned		File Folder	6/11/2000 6:56 PM
Market.src	1 KB	SRC File	6/10/2000 9:06 PM
Sales1 MOLAP.mdl	2 KB	MDL File	6/11/2000 6:56 PM
Sales1 MOLAP'S.mdl	2 KB	MDL File	6/11/2000 6:56 PM
Sales2 HOLAP Detail.mdl	2 KB	MDL File	6/11/2000 6:56 PM
Sales2 HOLAP Detail'S.mdl	2 KB	MDL File	6/11/2000 6:56 PM

As soon as the database completes processing, you'll see the temporary files disappear and you again see single names for the files in the database. The date and time for these files, however, does indicate that they're the new versions of the files.

Name	Size	Type	Modified
Sales1 MOLAP		File Folder	6/11/2000 6:56 PM
Sales2 HOLAP Detail		File Folder	6/11/2000 6:56 PM
Sales3 HOLAP Aggregated		File Folder	6/11/2000 6:56 PM
Sales4 Bad Increment		File Folder	6/11/2000 6:56 PM
Sales5 Increment Fact		File Folder	6/11/2000 6:56 PM
Sales6 Increment Filter		File Folder	6/11/2000 6:56 PM
Sales7 Partitioned		File Folder	6/11/2000 6:56 PM
Market.src	1 KB	SRC File	6/10/2000 9:06 PM
Sales1 MOLAP.mdl	2 KB	MDL File	6/11/2000 6:56 PM
Sales2 HOLAP Detail.mdl	2 KB	MDL File	6/11/2000 6:56 PM

5. In Analysis Manager, close the Process log window.

You might wonder what happens to a client application that's browsing a cube in the database at the time the database is finished processing, particularly as the client has its own cache and can retrieve some values from that cache while requesting only needed new values from the server. The Analysis Services client component, PivotTable Service, sends a request to the server every 10 seconds asking the server whether the active database has changed. Once the database has completed processing, the server communicates the change to the PivotTable Service, which erases all the old values from the client cache.

Schema, Data, and Metadata

An OLAP cube is a fast and flexible representation of the information stored in a data warehouse. When the information in the data warehouse changes, you must update the cube to make it match. Making an OLAP database match the relational data warehouse is called *processing* the database. Different types of changes can occur in the data warehouse, and the Analysis server provides different techniques for synchronizing the OLAP database with the relational data warehouse.

In the database world, a *schema* is the design or structure of a database. It has nothing to do with the values actually stored in the database. In Analysis Manager, when you work in the Cube Editor or the Dimension Editor, you create the OLAP database schema. In a relational data warehouse, anything that's not part of the database schema is part of the *data*—the values stored in the database. The numbers stored in a fact table are data, as are the keys, labels, and descriptions stored in various dimension tables. Adding a new product or a new month to a relational database has no impact on the structure of that database in any way.

In an OLAP database, the term *data* applies only to the values stored and aggregated in the cube. Information stored in an OLAP dimension—the names and hierarchical arrangement of the members—is neither schema nor data; rather, it's information about the data, or *metadata*. The dimension information—the metadata—is a critical part of the structure of an OLAP cube, but it's a structure that is derived from data in the warehouse, not a structure that you define using Analysis Manager.

Changing Data in a Warehouse

When you process an OLAP database, you make information in the cube and dimensions match the information stored in the data warehouse, using the rules, or schema, you created when you designed the database. If you change the schema—for example, if you add a measure or a dimension to a cube—you must process at least the affected portions of the database. You also need to process at least a portion of the database if the information in the data warehouse changes, as it inevitably will.

The information in a data warehouse is almost always time dependent. That means that, at the very least, you'll continually add new time periods to your data warehouse. In time, you might also add additional products or additional sales regions. When the data warehouse changes, you need to process the database to resynchronize the OLAP database with the relational data warehouse.

The SalesFact table in the Chapter9 sample Microsoft Access database contains data for six geographical areas (states) through October 1998. In the Chapter9 database, the State dimension table includes only the six states that appear in the fact table. The TimeMonth dimension table, however, includes months through December 1998. It is not uncommon in a warehouse to include months in the time dimension through the end of the current year, but to add members to other dimensions only as they are needed.

Included in the same folder as the Chapter9 database is a database named Chapter9a. The Chapter9a database schema is identical to that of the Chapter9 database, and the Chapter9a database includes all the data in the Chapter9 database. It also includes some additions: one new entry in the State table (Vera Cruz, Mexico) and additional rows in the fact table for a new month (November 1998). Switching the data source for the Chapter 9 OLAP database from Chapter9 to Chapter9a simulates adding new values to the data warehouse.

Set storage options for sample cubes

The Chapter 9 database contains seven identical cubes. For each of these cubes, the storage option is set to the default MOLAP with no aggregations. Before changing the data source, assign different types of data storage to two of the cubes, to see the effect that changing the data source has, using different data storage methods.

1. In the Cubes folder of the Chapter 9 database, right-click the Sales2 HOLAP Detail cube, and click Design Storage. Click Next to skip the welcome screen.

2. Select the HOLAP storage mode, and click Next.

3. Click the Until I Click Stop option, and click Next.
   This creates a HOLAP cube with no aggregates.

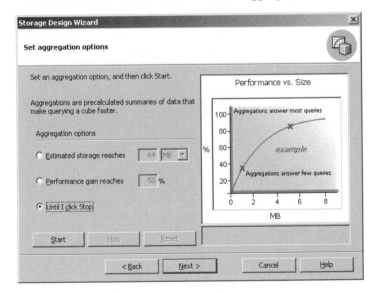

4. Leave the Process Now option selected, and click Finish. Close the Process log window.

Processing with HOLAP storage and no aggregations takes virtually no time because the server doesn't need to even read the fact table.

5. Right-click the Sales3 HOLAP Aggregated cube, and click Design Storage. Click Next to skip the welcome screen.

6. Select the HOLAP storage mode, and click Next.

7. Click the Performance Gain Reaches option, and leave the percentage at 50.

8. Click the Start button, wait until the Next button becomes enabled, and click Next.

The wizard designed three aggregations.

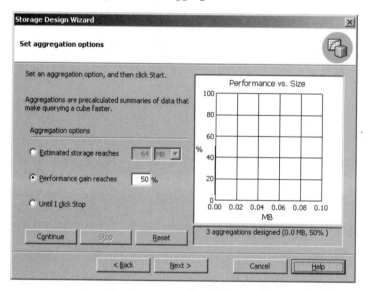

9. Leave the Process Now option selected, and click Finish. Close the Process log window.

With HOLAP storage, if you design aggregations, the server creates cells in the data file for aggregations.

You now have the Sales1 MOLAP cube with MOLAP storage and no aggregations, the Sales2 HOLAP Detail cube with HOLAP storage and no aggregations, and the Sales3 HOLAP Aggegated cube with HOLAP storage and three aggregations.

Browse data before updating the warehouse

In this section, you'll look at the values in the cubes before you change the data source. Each cube has identical contents, but you can arbitrarily browse the Sales MOLAP cube as an example. You can check for key values from that one cube.

1. In the console tree, select the Sales1 MOLAP cube, and click the Data tab at the top of the right pane.

   The grand total for Sales Units is 35,696. The State dimension is in the row area of the data grid. The total sales units for Mexico is 5,166.

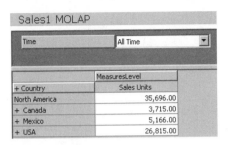

2. In the Time dimension, select the 1998 Qtr4 member.

   The total sales units for Mexico is 1,145.

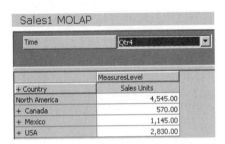

   After changing the data source, you can see the effect that changing values in the data warehouse has on cubes using both MOLAP and HOLAP storage modes.

Change the database data source

Because the internal objects within the database refer only to the data source, you can change the definition of the data source without disrupting the database, as long as you don't change the internal structure of the data source. When you edit a data source, you get the same Data Link Properties dialog box as when you create a data source but with a different tab active initially.

1. In the Analysis Manager console tree, expand the Data Sources folder in the Chapter 9 database.

2. Right-click the Market data source, and click Edit.

3. Adjacent to the Select Or Enter A Database Name box, click the ellipsis (...) button, select the Chapter9a database, and click Open.

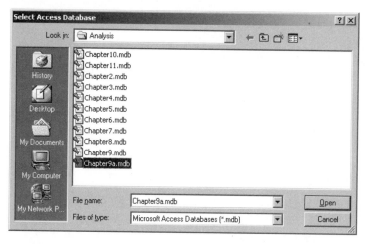

4. Click OK to close the Data Link Properties dialog box.

The name of the data source doesn't change; only the definition changes. By clicking the Provider tab, you could change the data source from an Access database to a Microsoft SQL Server database, for example, or from an OLE DB data source to an ODBC data source. The OLAP database will work the same, as long as the relational database schema remains unchanged.

Note   If you make changes to the structure of an existing data source, you must force Analysis Manager to recognize the changes. To do that, right-click the data source name in the console tree and click Refresh.

Browse data after updating the warehouse

Now that you have effectively changed the data in the data warehouse, the cubes in the OLAP database no longer match the data in the warehouse. The way a cube behaves depends on the storage mode of the cube. To see what values changed, start by browsing the data in the Sales1 MOLAP cube.

1. Select the Sales1 MOLAP cube, and click the Data tab at the top of the right pane to browse the cube. Expand the Mexico and Mexico Central members to see the states.

The grand total is 35,696, and Vera Cruz doesn't appear in the list of states. All these values are unchanged from before the warehouse changed.

Sales1 MOLAP

Time			All Time

			MeasuresLevel
- Country	- Region	State	Sales Units
North America	North America Total		35,696.00
+ Canada	Canada Total		3,715.00
	Mexico Total		5,166.00
- Mexico		Mexico Central Total	5,166.00
	- Mexico Central	District Federal	2,807.00
		Zacatecas	2,359.00
+ USA	USA Total		26,815.00

The Sales MOLAP cube uses MOLAP storage, and it behaves as if you had not changed the data source. When you use MOLAP storage, with or without aggregates, the cube is completely detached from the data warehouse. You can even delete the warehouse database without affecting the OLAP database.

2. Select the Sales2 HOLAP Detail cube, and browse it in the Data pane. In this cube, the Sales Units total is 42,243, which is different from the previous 35,696 total.

Sales2 HOLAP Detail

Time	All Time

	MeasuresLevel
	Sales Units
+ Country	
North America	42,243.00
+ Canada	4,437.00
+ Mexico	6,858.00
+ USA	30,948.00

Because there are no aggregations designed for the cube, all the values are aggregated from the relational data store immediately. Problems arise, however, when you attempt to browse to an area where new members exist in the fact table that aren't represented in the dimension.

3. Double-click the Country level button to display the Region level.

Sales2 HOLAP Detail

Time	All Time

		MeasuresLevel
		Sales Units
- Country	+ Region	
North America	North America Total	42,243.00
- Canada	Canada Total	4,437.00
	+ Canada West	#ERR
- Mexico	Mexico Total	#ERR
	+ Mexico Central	#ERR
- USA	USA Total	#ERR
	+ North West	#ERR
	+ South West	#ERR

The Region list for Mexico still shows only Mexico Central—Mexico West has not yet been added to the dimension—but the values change to show #ERR. The server has recognized a discrepancy in the dimension hierarchy.

4. Select the Sales3 HOLAP Aggregated cube, and browse it in the Data pane. This Unit Sales total is 35,696, unchanged from the original warehouse, as if this were a MOLAP cube.

Sales3 HOLAP Aggregated

Time		All Time ▾

	MeasuresLevel
+ Country	**Sales Units**
North America	35,696.00
+ Canada	3,715.00
+ Mexico	5,166.00
+ USA	26,815.00

Even though this cube uses HOLAP storage mode and uses the relational data source for the leaf level values, some aggregates are physically stored in the cube file.

5. Drag Time to the row area (replacing the State dimension), and expand the 1998 and Qtr4 members.

The total for Nov is 6,547, the new value. This value came from the fact table.

Sales3 HOLAP Aggregated

State		North America ▾

			MeasuresLevel
- Calendar Year	**- Calendar Quarter**	**Calendar Month**	**Sales Units**
All Time	All Time Total		35,696.00
+ 1997	1997 Total		5,559.00
	1998 Total		30,137.00
	+ Qtr1	Qtr1 Total	3,978.00
	+ Qtr2	Qtr2 Total	7,762.00
- 1998	+ Qtr3	Qtr3 Total	13,852.00
		Qtr4 Total	4,545.00
	- Qtr4	Oct	4,545.00
		Nov	6,547.00
		Dec	

The total for Qtr4, however, is still 4,545, the prestored aggregated value. Clearly, 4,545 is not the sum of 4,545 and 6,547. The quarter value doesn't match the sum of the month values. In HOLAP mode (and ROLAP is the same), some cell values are generated from the fact table and use the new values, while other cell values are generated from aggregated values and use the old values.

Cubes that use HOLAP or ROLAP data storage and include at least one aggregation retrieve some cell values directly from the relational source and other cell values from the stored aggregations. This fact makes HOLAP and ROLAP storage modes vulnerable to inconsistencies in cell values. You should always process databases containing HOLAP or ROLAP cubes as soon as the data warehouse changes. In MOLAP storage mode, all cell values—detail and aggregated alike—are oblivious to the data warehouse unless you explicitly process the database. You can even delete the data warehouse without affecting the cube.

Caution If you use HOLAP or ROLAP data storage, process the database as soon as the data warehouse changes to avoid inconsistent values in a cube.

Managing OLAP Processing

The easiest way to make sure that an OLAP database is completely consistent with the data warehouse—and with itself—is to process the entire database. When you process the database, you completely discard all the dimensions and cubes within the database and create new ones. This takes place as a single transaction, which means that client applications can continue to use the existing cubes until processing is complete. It also means that if an error occurs at any point during the processing, the entire change is rolled back, again ensuring that the database is internally consistent.

Processing the entire database is the simplest, cleanest, and best option, provided that you have sufficient time and storage space available. Although processing a large database can consume a considerable amount of time, users can continue to access the existing database while data is being updated in a new version of the database. As an example, suppose that you have an OLAP database that you update every day and that requires ten hours to fully process. Assuming you have sufficient disk space, you could still choose to process the entire database—perhaps by starting the nightly processing after 7:00 PM or as soon as new data is available. Users would then have access to the updated database by the next morning. You would not have to exclude users from the system or wait for them to leave for the day.

Processing a large database can also consume a considerable amount of disk space. The Analysis server not only creates a second copy of all the dimension and cube files created during the transaction, but it also uses additional temporary files to accumulate aggregations, particularly when creating aggregations from a large fact table.

Consequently, some databases are simply too large to process as a single transaction. Analysis Services provides several options for processing individual components of a database. These options allow you to create and manage extremely large databases, but they also require much more work to avoid preventing users from accessing the cubes or, worse, to avoid including invalid or inconsistent values in the cubes.

Incrementally update a dimension

As explained in "How the Analysis Server Processes a Dimension" earlier in this chapter, when you process a dimension, the server creates a map that includes the path for each member of that dimension. Every cube that includes the dimension uses that map. When you process an existing dimension, the map is destroyed and a new map is created. Destroying the dimension map invalidates all the cubes that use the dimension. When you process an entire database, the new dimension is not put into place until all the cubes have been processed as well. But when you process a single dimension, you make all the cubes that use that dimension inaccessible to client applications.

Fortunately, you can make certain changes to a dimension without destroying the existing map. If you don't destroy the existing map, you don't invalidate existing cubes. Analysis Services allows you to *incrementally update* a dimension to make changes that don't destroy the dimension map. The most useful change you can then make is adding new members to a dimension. You can also change member properties, since a member property is not included in the path for a member. With a standard dimension, all other changes to a dimension invalidate the existing map and can't be performed as part of an incremental update. If you want to perform an incremental update on a dimension when you delete or rename an existing member, or change the parent for a member, you can flag the dimension as a Changing dimension. Making those changes to a standard dimension, or changing the dimension schema of any dimension, requires the dimension to be completely reprocessed, which then forces each cube using the dimension to be reprocessed. And the incremental update option is available only if you process a single shared dimension. For example, you can incrementally update the State dimension to include the new Vera Cruz member.

1. In the console tree, open the Shared Dimensions folder in the Chapter 9 database, right-click the State dimension, and click Process.

The dialog box displays two options.

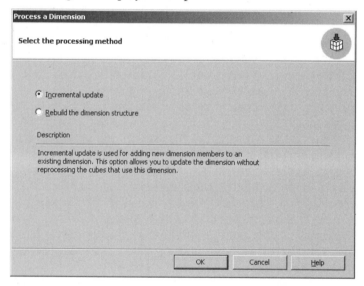

2. Click the Incremental Update option, and click OK. Close the Process log window.

3. Select the Sales1 MOLAP cube, and browse the cube in the right pane. Expand the Mexico and Mexico Atlantic members.

Sales1 MOLAP

Time			All Time	▼

			MeasuresLevel
- Country	- Region	State	Sales Units
North America	North America Total		35,696.00
+ Canada	Canada Total		3,715.00
	Mexico Total		5,166.00
- Mexico	- Mexico Atlantic	Mexico Atlantic Total	
		Vera Cruz	
	+ Mexico Central	Mexico Central Total	5,166.00
+ USA	USA Total		26,815.00

The Sales1 MOLAP cube (with MOLAP storage) does recognize the new members of the State dimension, but the values are empty because a MOLAP cube is unaware of any changes in the fact table.

4. Select the Sales2 HOLAP Detail cube, and browse the cube in the right pane. Expand the Mexico and Mexico Atlantic members.

Sales2 HOLAP Detail

| Time | | | All Time | ▼ |

			MeasuresLevel
- Country	- Region	State	Sales Units
North America	North America Total		42,243.00
+ Canada	Canada Total		4,437.00
	Mexico Total		6,858.00
- Mexico	- Mexico Atlantic	Mexico Atlantic Total	291.00
		Vera Cruz	291.00
	+ Mexico Central	Mexico Central Total	6,567.00
+ USA	USA Total		30,948.00

The Sales2 HOLAP Detail cube (HOLAP storage with no aggregations) recognizes the new members of the State dimension and includes the new values from the fact table. The HOLAP cube with no aggregations does not require any further processing.

5. Select the Sales3 HOLAP Aggregated cube, and browse the cube in the right pane. Expand the Mexico and Mexico Atlantic members. Then select 1998 in the Time dimension drop-down list.

Sales3 HOLAP Aggregated

| Time | | | 1998 | ▼ |

			MeasuresLevel
- Country	- Region	State	Sales Units
North America	North America Total		30,137.00
+ Canada	Canada Total		3,715.00
	Mexico Total		5,166.00
- Mexico	- Mexico Atlantic	Mexico Atlantic Total	
		Vera Cruz	291.00
	+ Mexico Central	Mexico Central Total	5,166.00
+ USA	USA Total		21,256.00

While browsing levels—such as All Time—that can be filled from the aggregations, a HOLAP (or ROLAP) cube with aggregations behaves like a MOLAP cube. When browsing levels—such as Year and State—that can't be filled from an aggregation, a HOLAP (or ROLAP) cube with aggregations displays values from the fact table. Once again, if using a HOLAP (or ROLAP) cube with aggregations, you should process the cube immediately after the warehouse changes to avoid inconsistent data.

When you perform an incremental update on a dimension, the Analysis server uses the same SQL statement to extract information from the dimension as when you rebuild the dimension structure. With an incremental update, the server simply creates new path values for only the new members, and the path for a new member might not be the same as it would be if you rebuilt the dimension structure. For example, the new member in the State table, Vera Cruz, is in the Mexico Atlantic region. After rebuilding the dimension structure, the path for the Vera Cruz member would be 2→1→1 because Vera Cruz (State Code VC) is the first "state" in the Mexico Atlantic region, which is the first region in Mexico, which is the second country. But after the incremental update, the path for Vera Cruz is 2→2→1 because the Mexico Atlantic region is assigned the first unused number for children of Mexico. The next time you rebuild the dimension structure, the paths for the Mexico members will all change. Because the path is used only internally, there are no harmful effects of having the paths change, but you can see why rebuilding a dimension structure invalidates any cubes that use it.

Even after performing an incremental update on a dimension, you want the members to arrange themselves properly in hierarchical order, so as the final step of an incremental update, the server regenerates the member ID values for the entire dimension. Changing the member ID values doesn't invalidate the cube because the cube looks only at the member path.

Incrementally update a cube

When you click the Process command for a cube that has already been processed, Analysis Manager allows you to choose from three options for processing the cube: Full Process, Refresh Data, and Incremental Update.

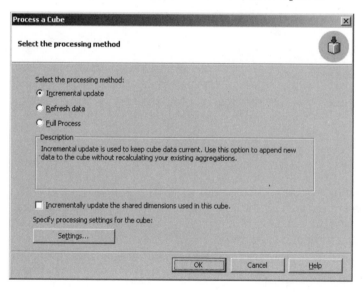

The Full Process option launches the same activity for the cube as when you process the entire database: The server generates a set of temporary files containing replacement data for the cube. Once processing has completed successfully, the server deletes the current files for the cube and renames the temporary files to the permanent names. When you select the Full Process option, the Analysis server checks to see whether any changes have been made to any of the dimension schemas used by the cube. If changes have been made, the server processes the dimension before processing the cube.

The Refresh Data option for a cube is virtually identical to the Full Process option. In both cases the server generates all the files for a new cube, swapping the files into place when the processing is complete. The only real difference is that the Refresh Data option doesn't even check to see whether you have made any changes to the dimension schema. It processes the cube using the existing dimension files, period. Empirically, the Refresh Data option does not seem to be faster than the Full Process option. Even with ROLAP storage, both options delete and re-create all the aggregation tables, and in neither case are you required to redesign aggregations for the cube. Pragmatically, you can ignore the Refresh Data option.

The Incremental Update option is both powerful and dangerous. The Incremental Update option creates new cube files, precisely as if you were using the Full Process option. When the processing is complete, however, the server doesn't replace the old files with the new ones. Rather, it *merges* the two sets of files, creating a third set of cube files. Finally it deletes all but the third set of files and renames those files to become the final cube files. One implication of this procedure is that for a single cube, the Incremental Update option might actually require *more* disk space than the Full Process option, since it creates three sets of files, rather than just two. A more important implication is that if you use the Incremental Update option using a fact table that includes values already stored in the cube, those values will be double-counted after you process the cube.

Watch an incremental update double-count values

The Incremental Update option for a cube is dangerous because it's so easy to double-count values. Use the Incremental Update option with the Sales4 Bad Increment cube to see how easy it is to make a mistake.

1. Right-click the Sales4 Bad Increment cube, and click Process. Click the Incremental Update option, and click OK.

2. In the Incremental Update Wizard, click Next three times and then click Finish. (In other words, run the wizard without specifying any options—a remarkably natural thing to want to do.) Close the Process log window.

3. Select the Sales4 Bad Increment cube, and click the Data tab to browse the cube in the right pane.

   The total for Sales Units is now 77,939, which is the sum of 35,696 (the old value through October) and 42,243 (the new value through November).

Sales4 Bad Increment		
Time		All Time
	MeasuresLevel	
+ Country	Sales Units	
North America	77,939.00	
+ Canada	8,152.00	
+ Mexico	12,024.00	
+ USA	57,763.00	

With a dimension, when you perform an incremental update, the Analysis server adds a member only if the unique path is not already in the dimension. With a dimension, you can never double-count member names. With a cube, it's easy to double-count values because the server adds the values of the measure for each row as it process the fact table data. The server typically adds any one row from the fact table to multiple aggregation cells, and any cell in the cube typically contains values from multiple rows in the fact table.

The Incremental Update Wizard helps you avoid loading the same values into the cube more than once. It uses two mechanisms for isolating the new values you want to add to the existing cube:

- Retrieve values from a different table

- Filter the fact table to retrieve only specific values

Incrementally update by using a separate fact table

You're most likely to choose to update data in a cube by using the Incremental Update option when you're simply adding new values, such as a new period, to the cube. You might find it convenient in the warehouse to store those new values in a separate fact table. The Chapter9a database contains a table named SalesFact_Incr, which includes only the new rows from the SalesFact table.

1. Right-click the Sales5 Increment Fact cube, and click Process. Click the Incremental Update option, and click OK.

2. Click Next on the welcome screen of the Incremental Update Wizard, and then, when given the opportunity to select a Fact Table, click Change.

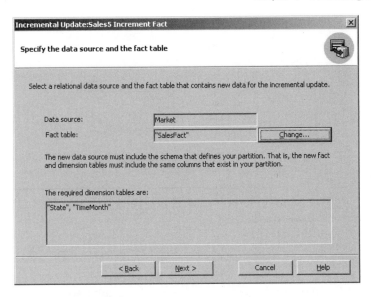

3. Select the SalesFact_Incr table and click OK.

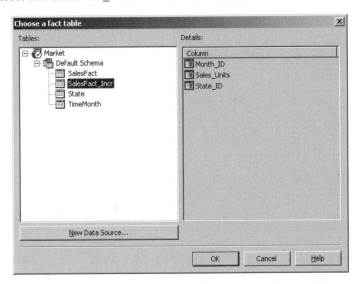

4. Click the Next button twice, and then click Finish. Close the Process log window.

5. Browse the cube.

   The number of total units is 42,243, the total through November 1998.

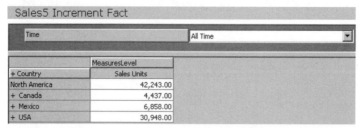

Analysis Manager was able to create the correct total for the cube even though it processed only the rows for the one month. Putting new rows into a "staging" table is often a convenient way to manage incrementally updating a cube. Before incrementally updating a cube, you must first incrementally update all the dimensions used by the cube so that any new members found in the new rows will be available.

Incrementally update by using a filter

In addition to using a separate small fact table, you can also add new rows to an existing fact table. In the Chapter9a data warehouse, the November rows were added directly to the SalesFact table. Because the fact table includes both new rows and rows that have already been loaded into the cube, you must give the Analysis server a filter to retrieve only the new rows. The server attaches the filter expression as a WHERE clause to the SQL statement it generates for retrieving the rows from the fact table.

1. Right-click the Sales6 Increment Filter cube, and click Process. Click the Incremental Update option, and click OK.

2. Click Next on the welcome screen, and then, when given the opportunity to change the fact table, click Next again.

3. On the Create A Filter Expression screen of the Incremental Update Wizard, type the expression **Month = #11/1/1998#**.

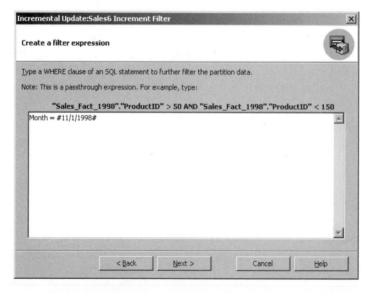

4. Click Next, and then click Finish. Close the Process log window.

5. Click the Sales6 Increment Filter cube, and review the numbers in the Data tab.

The total for the year is 42,243, the same as for the other two cubes.

Sales6 Increment Filter		
Time	All Time	

	MeasuresLevel	
+ Country	Sales Units	
North America	42,243.00	
+ Canada	4,437.00	
+ Mexico	6,858.00	
+ USA	30,948.00	

Once again, the Analysis server was able to create correct values in the cube while reading only the selected rows from the fact table. When you create a large cube, the improved speed of using incremental updates for dimensions and cubes can justify the extra complexities.

Note You must perform an incremental update on each cube separately. Updating each cube is a single transaction. If the processing of a cube fails, the changes to that one cube will be rolled back. However, changes already made to other cubes will remain in the database. When using incremental updates, it's possible for different cubes within a database to contain inconsistent values.

Working with Partitions

Partitions make it possible for you to create extremely large cubes. You can effectively create small, medium-sized, and even remarkably large cubes without using partitions. But partitions are useful when you need to create very large, enterprise-wide applications. For that reason, the ability to manage partitions is available only with the Enterprise Edition of Microsoft SQL Server 2000.

Each OLAP cube consists of at least one partition. You design the measures and dimensions for an entire cube, but you design storage modes and aggregations at the partition level. If a cube contains only a single partition, designing storage for a cube is the same as designing storage for a partition. If a cube contains more than one partition, attempting to design storage for a cube brings up a dialog box (shown on the next page) that requires you to select a single partition before continuing.

If you run Analysis Manager on a different computer than the one on which you run the Analysis server, both computers must have the Enterprise Edition of SQL Server 2000 installed.

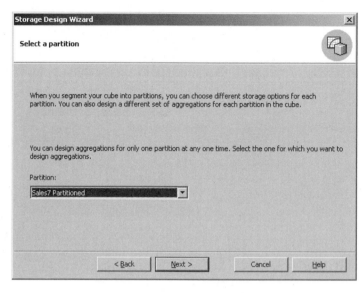

One of the benefits of creating multiple partitions is that you can design different storage for different portions of the cube. For example, say you have one partition that contains information for the current and previous years. You access this information frequently, so you specify MOLAP storage with aggregations to provide a 50 percent performance boost. A second partition contains values for the third, fourth, and fifth years. These years are usually accessed only at a summary level (if at all), and the relational warehouse is also occasionally accessed, so you specify HOLAP storage, with aggregations to the 30 percent performance level. A third partition contains several previous years. Those years are infrequently accessed—the relational warehouse is never used—so you specify MOLAP storage with aggregations to the five percent performance level and then archive the relational warehouse to tape.

A second major benefit of creating partitions is that you can process a partition independently of the rest of the cube. As a fairly extreme example, suppose that you have an OLAP cube used to monitor manufacturing activities and you want to update the information in that cube every ten minutes. You don't have time to completely process the database every ten minutes. By putting the current day into a separate partition, you can process that partition every ten minutes, without having to process the rest of the cube. In effect, creating a partition for the current day is like performing an incremental update on the cube, except that you can completely replace the values in that one partition every ten minutes, guaranteeing consistency with the relational data source.

When you're creating partitions, make sure each partition gets unique data. Otherwise, it's easy to double-count values in multiple partitions. The dangers of creating partitions are similar to the dangers of executing an incremental update on a cube. This similarity is not coincidental. In fact, when you perform an incremental update on a cube, the Analysis server creates a new partition, loads values into the new partition, and then merges the two partitions. Analysis

Services provides three techniques to avoid double-counting. The first two techniques correspond to those options available for incrementally updating a cube.

- Create a separate fact table for each partition.

- Specify a filter (an SQL WHERE clause) to restrict rows from the fact table.

- Specify a data slice, a single member of a dimension, for a partition.

Creating a data slice is the most effective way to avoid double-counting when using a partition, and you should use it whenever feasible. When you use a data slice—that is, specify a single member within a dimension—the Analysis server automatically takes care of creating the appropriate filter for the fact table. Also, the data slice helps the server understand which data is in each partition, so the server can respond more quickly to queries. Imagine that you have a cube with two partitions—one for 1997, and one for 1998—and you use a filter in each partition to restrict rows from the fact table. If the server gets a query for 1998 data, it will still search both partitions for 1998 values. If, however, you use a data slice in each partition, the server knows to search only the 1998 partition.

Note Multiple partitions take advantage of multiple processors. On a computer with four processors, a cube with three partitions can process much faster than a cube with one partition, provided the relational data sources can feed data fast enough.

A client application has no awareness of—let alone control over—partitions used on the server. You can modify the design of partitions without affecting any client application. The most important task when creating partitions is to make sure that each appropriate value from the fact table (or fact tables) makes it into *one and only one* partition.

Note This chapter doesn't cover using separate fact tables to create partitions because the process is identical to using separate fact tables when performing an incremental update, as described in "Incrementally update by using a separate fact table" earlier in this chapter.

Use a data slice when creating a new partition

As mentioned in the previous section, the easiest way to specify a portion of a fact table for a partition is to use a *data slice*. You'll use the Partition Wizard in the following steps to create a partition and create a data slice. When creating a data slice, the Partition Wizard displays the available members of each dimension, so all you have to do is select the data slice you want.

1. In the console tree, expand the Chapter 9 database, the Cubes folder, and the Sales7 Partitioned cube. Right-click the Partitions folder, and click New Partition to start the Partition Wizard. Click Next to skip the welcome screen of the wizard.

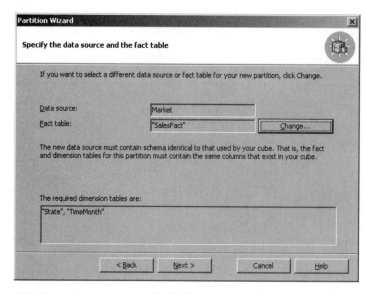

The data source screen of the Partition Wizard looks like the data source screen of the Incremental Update Wizard, as described in "Incrementally update by using a separate fact table," earlier in this chapter.

2. Click Next. The next screen of the Partition Wizard allows you to specify a data slice for the partition.

The option to specify a data slice isn't available when you're performing an incremental update. When you *specify* a data slice, the Partition Wizard creates a filter, restricting the rows that are retrieved from the data source. But when you use a data slice to create the filter, the Analysis server knows which data is in the partition and can make retrievals from the cube more efficient. A data slice can consist of a single member from any dimension. The data slice member can occur at any level of the dimension.

3. In the Dimensions list, select State. Then, in the Members list, expand North America and select USA.

The member *North America.USA* appears in the Data Slice column next to the State dimension.

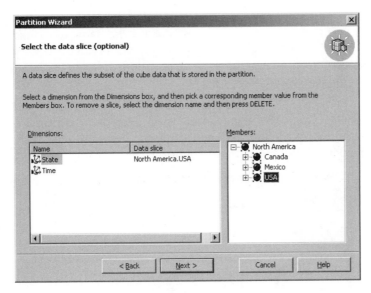

4. Click Next to move to the next screen of the wizard.

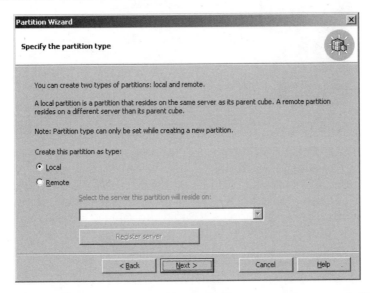

Each partition can reside on a different server. The wizard allows you to specify whether the partition should remain on the local server or be distributed to another server.

5. Leave the Local option selected, and click Next to get to the final screen of the Partition Wizard. Type **Sales USA** for the name of the partition.

You design storage for each partition independently, but if you later want to merge two partitions, the partitions must have the same storage design. The easiest way to get the same storage design for two partitions is to copy the design from an existing partition when creating a new one.

6. Click the Copy The Aggregation Design From An Existing Partition option, select the Process The Partition When Finished check box, and click Finish. If warned about counting the fact table rows, click OK.

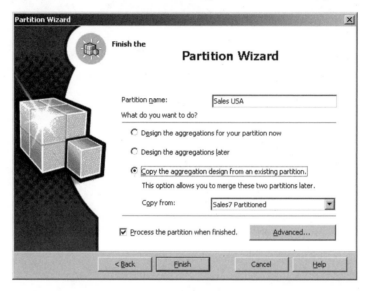

7. In the Process log window, select the statement that begins with a SQL icon and click View Details.

The SQL statement includes both the SalesFact table and the State table. It also includes a WHERE clause with a parameter for the Country column. The server supplies *'USA'* as the value of the parameter when the query runs.

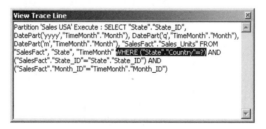

8. Close the View Trace Line window and the Process log window.

9. Select the Sales7 Partitioned cube, and click the Data tab in the right pane.

The total shown for Sales Units is 66,644, which is substantially higher than the correct 42,243 total. The new total double-counts the USA values because they exist in both the original partition and in the new partition.

Sales7 Partitioned

Time		All Time	

	MeasuresLevel
	Sales Units
+ Country	
North America	66,644.00
+ Canada	3,715.00
+ Mexico	5,166.00
+ USA	57,763.00

As mentioned earlier in the chapter, double-counting values is a major drawback of using partitions. Although specifying a slice limits the contents of a partition to that slice and the members that feed into it, specifying a slice for a new partition doesn't automatically adjust the design of any existing partitions. To do that, you must edit the design of the existing partition.

To keep the Sales7 Partitioned cube from double-counting values in the USA slice stored in the Sales USA partition, you must restrict the values of the original Sales partition to exclude values from USA. You cannot use a slice to remove USA from the Sales partition. A slice can consist of only one member from a dimension. To exclude a member, or to include more than one member from a dimension, you must use a filter. When you create a filter, you manually create a WHERE clause for the SQL statement that retrieves values from the fact table. The WHERE clause can be any expression your relational data source will accept.

Use a filter when editing an existing partition

In the Sales cube example, to exclude USA from the Sales partition, you need a WHERE clause of the form *"State"."Country" <> 'USA'*.

1. In the Partitions folder, right-click Sales7 Partitioned and click Edit.

2. Click Next three times: once to leave the data source screen, once to leave the data slice screen, and once to leave the partition type screen.

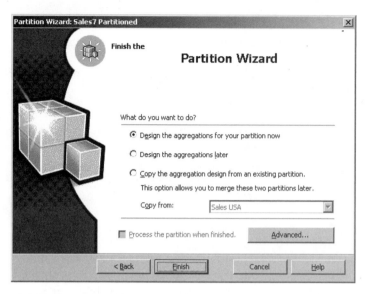

3. On the final screen of the wizard, click the Advanced button.

The Advanced Settings dialog box allows you to enter a Filter Statement.

4. In the Filter Statement box, type **"State"."Country" <> 'USA'**, and click OK.

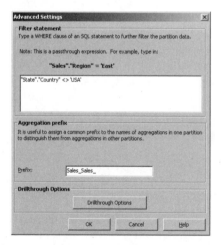

Note   The Aggregation Prefix value in the Advanced Settings dialog box determines what prefix the Analysis server uses when creating ROLAP aggregation tables in the relational data source. If you're not using ROLAP storage, the Aggregation Prefix has no effect. The Drillthrough Options button is useful only when you already enabled drillthrough for the cube, as explained in "Enable drillthrough for a cube" in Chapter 4, "Advanced Dimensions and Cubes."

---

5. Click the Copy The Aggregation Design From An Existing Partition option, select the Process The Partition When Finished check box, and click Finish. Click Yes when warned about counting the fact table rows, and close the Process log window.

6. Select the Sales7 Partitioned cube, and click the Data tab to browse the data. The Unit Sales total for the cube is now the correct value of 42,243.

When you split a cube into multiple partitions, you must be careful to get the appropriate data into each partition. The Analysis server doesn't prevent you from creating partitions that overlap or skip portions of the fact table. The risks involved—and the solutions available—when creating partitions are similar to those involved in performing an incremental update of a cube. In both cases, you can easily put invalid values into a cube. In both cases, you can use separate fact tables or you can filter a single table. With an incremental update, the only way to filter a fact table is to add a filter expression. With a partition, you can filter a fact table either by adding an explicit filter or by specifying a slice, in which case Analysis Manager adds a filter expression for you.

Note One advantage of using an explicit filter is that you have more flexibility than with a slice. You can reference any field in any table used in the SQL query, not just members of a dimension. Because the filter uses SQL, you can use any expression supported by the relational database system. For example, you can use a nested query such as *"MyFactTable"."time_id" IN (SELECT "time_id" FROM "time_table" WHERE "time_table"."year" < 1998)*. In most cases, however, it's hard enough to get the correct values into a partition even without using complex SQL expressions in a filter.

Merge two partitions into one

Consider the situation described earlier in "Working with Partitions," where you create a new partition each day for a manufacturing cube. Each month you would create up to 31 additional partitions in the cube. Simply keeping the partitions straight would be extraordinarily confusing. One solution is to use only two partitions: one for the current day and one for all previous time. Each night, merge the current day partition with the previous time partition, and then create a new current day partition for the next day. Merged partitions don't run significantly faster than separate partitions, but they can be much easier to manage.

You can merge the Sales USA partition back into the Sales partition to see some of the issues involved with merging partitions.

1. In the console tree, right-click the Sales USA partition and click Merge.

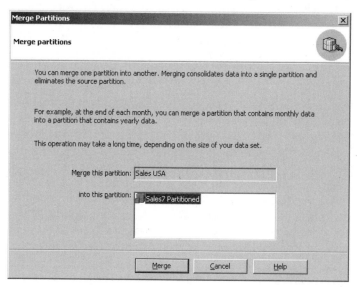

The Merge Partitions wizard displays all partitions with matching storage design, with Sales7 Partitioned preselected.

Note   You can merge a partition only with another partition that shares the same storage design. If you created partitions with different storage design modes, you must edit the partition and, on the last screen of the wizard, copy the storage design from an existing partition. This requires you to reprocess the partition.

---

2. Click Merge to merge the partitions. Then close the Process log window.

The Sales USA partition used a slice to limit the rows of the fact table. The Sales7 Partitioned partition used a filter to limit the rows. Merging the Sales USA partition into the Sales7 Partitioned partition caused the slice to be lost but the filter to be retained. The single remaining Sales7 Partitioned partition retains the filter excluding USA. After merging the two partitions, the values for the cube match the values in the fact table. However, as soon as you process it, the cube will exclude the USA values. You must edit the partition to remove the slice definition.

3. Right-click the Sales7 Partitioned cube, and click Process. Click the Full Process option, and click OK. Close the Process log window, and browse the Sales7 Partitioned cube data.

Sales7 Partitioned

Time	All Time

	MeasuresLevel
+ Country	Sales Units
North America	11,295.00
+ Canada	4,437.00
+ Mexico	6,858.00
+ USA	

The value for North America is very low because USA has been excluded by the partition filter.

4. Right-click the Sales7 Partitioned partition, and click Edit. Click Next three times: once to leave the data source screen, once to leave the data slice screen, and once to leave the partition type screen.

5. On the final screen of the wizard, click Advanced. Clear the contents of the Filter Statement box, and click OK.

6. Click the Design The Aggregations Later option (to create a cube with no aggregations), select the Process The Partition When Finished check box, and click Finish.

7. Click Yes when warned about counting fact table rows, and close the Process log window. Then browse the cube. The total value is again correct.

The definition of the partition is once again clean, so you can process the cube again without getting invalid results.

Merging Partitions with Filters and Slices

When you define a partition, you have three options for avoiding double-counting: you can specify a separate data source for each partition, you can specify a different data slice for each partition, or you can specify a different data filter for each partition. You can also combine options.

When you merge two partitions that have different data sources, the data source for the target partition is kept and the data source for the merged partition is discarded. Analysis Services does nothing to combine the two fact tables; you must combine them outside of Analysis Services.

When you merge two partitions that use different filtering techniques—for example, if the merged partition has a slice and the target partition has a filter—the source filter or slice is lost and the target filter or slice is retained. If you want the remaining partition to include all the data from the fact table, you must edit the partition to remove the filter or slice.

(continued)

Merging Partitions with Filters and Slices *(continued)*

When you merge two partitions that both use a filter, Analysis Services does combine the two filters, using an *OR* expression. For example, if you have one partition with the filter *"State"."Country" = 'USA'* and another partition with the filter *"State"."Country" <> 'USA'*, the filter expression for the merged partition will be *("State"."Country" = 'USA') OR ("State"."Country" <> 'USA')*, which would be equivalent to no filter at all. In a case like this, you could either leave the nonfunctional filter or delete it to improve performance.

When you merge two partitions that both use a slice, Analysis Services behaves in an interesting way. If the slices come from different dimensions—for example, if the slice for one partition is *Product=[Bread]* while that for the other partition is *State=[USA]*—both slices are discarded. If the slices come from the same dimension, the slice of the resulting cube becomes the lowest common parent. For example, if the slice for one partition is *Product = [Bread].[Bagels]*, and that of the other partition is *Product = [Bread].[Muffins].[Colony Blueberry Muffins]*, the resulting slice will be *Product=[Bread]*. In some cases, this might be the effect you want. In other cases, you might see surprising values when you next process the entire cube.

When you merge partitions, be sure to check the data source, data slice, and data filter specifications of the resulting partition.

Automating the Processing of a Database

For most OLAP databases, updating the cubes with new values is a routine process that must be performed on a regular basis—monthly, weekly, nightly, or even hourly. Analysis Manager doesn't provide any direct tools for automating the processing of databases. Manually carrying out routine tasks—particularly if you'll be incrementally updating dimensions and cubes—can be an extremely tedious assignment.

Fortunately, Microsoft SQL Server 2000 has a facility for automating many different types of data manipulation activities, including processing OLAP components. The tool is DTS, which stands for Data Transformation Services. While you can use Analysis Services without using SQL Server, to use DTS, you must install SQL Server.

DTS is a general-purpose application designed to move and manipulate data. DTS can use many different data sources and many different data targets. It can group multiple processing tasks into a *package*, which you can reuse and schedule.

Create a DTS package

To use DTS to automate Analysis server processing, you must create a DTS package. You create DTS packages by using the SQL Server Enterprise Manager.

1. Click Start, point to Programs, point to Microsoft SQL Server, and click Enterprise Manager.

2. Expand Microsoft SQL Servers, the SQL Server Group, the server you want to use, and the Data Transformation Services folder.
   The folder has three entries.

3. Right-click Local Packages, and click New Package.
   The DTS Package window appears. This is where you design the tasks you want to automate.

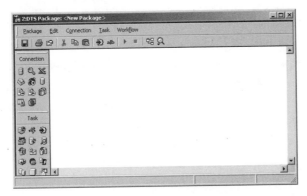

4. Click Save on the Package menu. Type **OLAP Update** as the name of the package, and click OK.

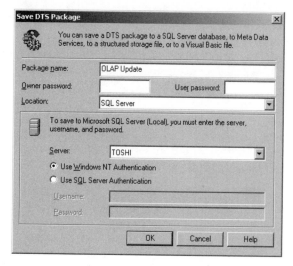

You can now add tasks to the package.

Create an Analysis Services Processing Task

The Task bar at the left side of the DTS Package window contains icons for various types of tasks that you can automate in a package. The Analysis Services Processing Task appears as a cube in the Task pane. This task allows you to process Analysis server objects as part of the package. Suppose that you want to process the Chapter 9 database each night. You can add that task to the package.

1. Drag the Analysis Services Processing Task cube icon from the Task pane onto the DTS Package workspace.

An Analysis Services Processing Task dialog box appears.

If you select a dimension, both the Full Process and Incremental Update options become available. If you select a cube, all three options are available.

2. In the Description box, type **Process OLAP Database**.

3. In the tree view in the left side of the dialog box, expand the server and select the Chapter 9 database. When you select a database, only the Full Process option is enabled.

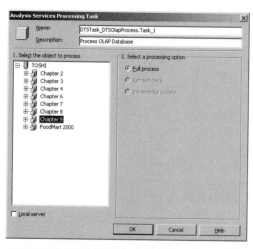

4. Click OK to create the task.

If you understand how to process an object within Analysis Manager, you can easily create a DTS task to automate that processing.

Send an e-mail message if the task fails

A DTS package can contain multiple tasks. You can control the *workflow* between various tasks. For example, you can create a task to send yourself an e-mail message. You can then create a workflow connection that will execute the e-mail task only if the processing task fails. DTS provides three workflow options: On Completion, On Success, and On Failure. To send e-mail if the task fails, you first create an e-mail task and then create an On Failure workflow connection between the OLAP task and the e-mail task.

1. Drag the Send Mail Task icon from the Task pane onto the DTS Package workspace.

2. In the Send Mail Task Properties dialog box, enter your e-mail address in the To box, type **OLAP Process failed** for the subject line, and type **The OLAP task to update the Chapter 9 database did not complete successfully** for the body of the message. Then click OK.

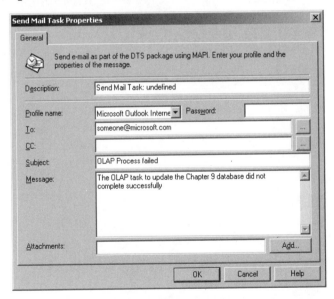

3. Select the Process OLAP Database task. Then press the Ctrl key as you select the e-mail task.

The order in which you select the two tasks is critical.

4. On the Workflow menu, click On Failure.

A red-striped arrow appears showing the relationship between the two tasks.

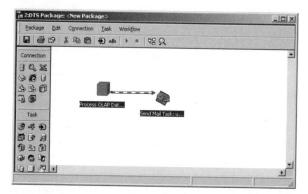

Workflow connections allow you to create sophisticated packages. If you need to create a package that incrementally updates all the dimensions and cubes of a database, you create a single DTS task for each OLAP action and then join them together with On Success workflow connections. From each task, you also create an On Failure workflow connection to the error e-mail message.

Save and schedule a DTS package

Once you have created a package, you can choose to execute it immediately, or you can schedule the task to run at a specific time. Suppose that you want to process the Chapter 9 database each day at 7:00 PM. You can create that schedule for the package.

1. Close the DTS Package window, clicking Yes when asked whether you want to save the package.

2. In the Enterprise Manager window, select the Local Packages folder, right-click the OLAP Update package, and click Execute Package. Click OK to close the success message box and then click Done to close the dialog box.

   This executes the package immediately, displaying an alert message when the package completes.

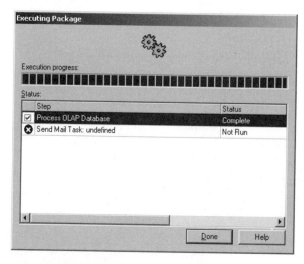

3. Right-click the OLAP Update package, and click Schedule Package. In the Edit Recurring Job Schedule dialog box, click the Daily option in the Occurs group, and select 7:00 PM in the Occurs Once At box.

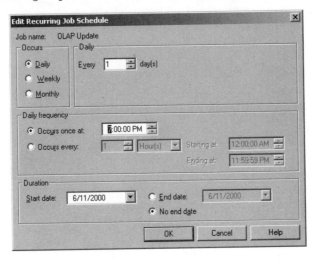

4. Click OK to schedule the task.

The scheduled task becomes a SQL Server Agent job. To edit or delete the schedule, you must go into the SQL Server Agent folder.

5. In the Console tree, expand the Management folder. Then expand the SQL Server Agent folder, and select Jobs.

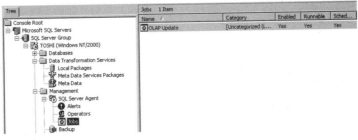

6. Right-click the OLAP Update job in the right pane. Click Delete, and click Yes to confirm the deletion.

The DTS component of SQL Server 2000 is a powerful tool. It's capable of simplifying and facilitating all types of data management tasks, particularly those associated with creating and maintaining a data warehouse. The Analysis Services Processing Task opens DTS capabilities to Analysis Services, but it's only a small part of DTS.

Chapter Summary

To	Do this
Synchronize an OLAP database with a warehouse database	Right-click the OLAP database folder, and click Process Database.
Add new members to a shared dimension without invalidating existing cubes	Right-click the dimension, and click Process. Then click the Incremental Update option.
Add data for new records to an existing cube	Right-click the cube, and click Process. Click the Incremental Update option.
Avoid double-counting values when incrementally updating a cube	Either put new incremental values into a separate fact table or add a filter expression that eliminates fact table rows that have already been loaded into the cube.
Create a new partition for a cube	Expand the cube folder, and right-click the Partitions folder. Then click New Partition.
Avoid double-counting values in a partition	Create a separate fact table for each partition, add filters to each partition to eliminate rows used in other partitions, or add a data slice to automatically filter warehouse rows.
Prepare a partition so that you can later merge it with another partition	In the last step of the Partition Wizard, click the Copy Aggregation Design From An Existing Partition option and select the target partition.
Merge one partition with another	Right-click the partition, and click Merge. From the list of partitions that share the same storage design, select one and click Merge.
Automate the processing of an OLAP database	Launch the SQL Server Enterprise Manager, and expand a server. Right-click the Data Transformation Services folder, and click New Package. Double-click the Analysis Services Processing Task, select the OLAP database, and click OK.
Schedule a DTS task	In the Data Transformation Services folder of the SQL Server Enterprise Manager, select the Local Packages folder. Right-click a package, and click Schedule Package. Select appropriate scheduling options, and click OK.
Delete a scheduled DTS package	In the SQL Server Enterprise Manager, expand the Management folder and the SQL Server Agent folder, and select the Jobs folder. Select the scheduled job, press Delete, and click Yes.

Chapter 10

Dimension Optimization

Estimated time: 1.5 hours

In this chapter, you'll learn how to

- Use unique keys to optimize a dimension.

- Remove joins in a SQL statement.

- Create a single-level virtual dimension.

- Create a multilevel virtual dimension.

- Manage sorting problems within a virtual dimension.

In the mid 1970s, gas prices in the United States increased dramatically, often as much as fivefold. Suddenly, there was a great demand for smaller, fuel-efficient cars. In the 1990s, as gas prices remained stable for a long period of time, the demand for large, fuel-hungry sport utility vehicles increased. A concern over fuel efficiency is directly correlated to the cost of the fuel. Even in the most fuel-conscious times, you want to find the most effective tools for increasing efficiency. As an old saying goes, "Yes, technically, you can improve your gas mileage by emptying the ash tray, but…."

Start the lesson

1. In the Analysis Manager console tree, right-click the server and click Restore Database. Navigate to the folder containing the sample files for this book, select the Chapter10 archive file, and click Open. Click Restore, and then click Close in the Restore Database Progress dialog box.

   An OLAP cube is always associated with a fact table from the warehouse database. A fact table usually contains many rows—at least hundreds of thousands and possibly millions or billions. The size of the fact table clearly has a large impact on the amount of time it takes to process a cube. In contrast, most dimension tables are relatively small. It's a rare dimension table that contains more than ten thousand rows. One would expect dimension tables to have much less impact than the fact table on the time it takes to process a cube. The way you define dimensions within a cube, however, can have a dramatic effect on the time it takes to process a cube. The techniques covered in this chapter can help you design dimensions in such a way that a cube can process up to ten times faster than a cube that has not been optimized.

Optimizing Dimensions in a Cube

The Chapter10 warehouse database has the same general structure as those used in preceding chapters, but it is much larger. There are many more products, the time dimensions go to the day level rather than the month level, the state dimension is replaced by a much larger customer dimension, and there are more employees. Be aware that processing the Sales cube in this chapter—particularly the first time, before you apply any optimizations—might take several minutes.

Process a cube without optimizations

The Sales cube in the Chapter10 database contains five dimensions: Customer, Employee, Product, Time.Calendar, and Time.Fiscal. (Technically, Calendar and Fiscal are hierarchies within a single Time dimension, but separate hierarchies behave the same as separate dimensions.) The dimensions are initially as if you had created them using the basic Dimension Wizard as described in Chapter 2, "Analysis Manager from 500 Feet."

1. Expand the Chapter 10 database, expand the Cubes folder, right-click the Sales cube, and click Process.

2. Click the Full Process option, and click OK. Go get a cup of coffee and relax while the cube processes. Do not close the Process log window.

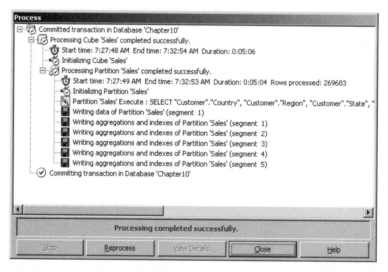

The process log shows the time duration required to process the cube. On my computer, it took just over five minutes to process the 269,683 rows of the fact table. Looking at the SQL statement used to retrieve rows from the database might be informative.

3. Select the line in the list with a SQL icon at the left, and click the View Details button. Scroll or resize the window as needed to see the complete SQL statement.

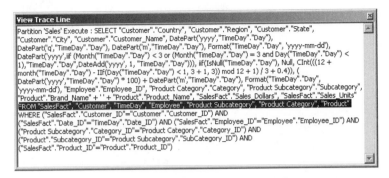

The SQL statement is very long. In the screenshot above, the FROM clause is highlighted. According to the FROM clause, the SQL statement extracted values not only from the SalesFact table but also from the Customer, TimeDay, Employee, Product Subcategory, Product Category, and Product tables. Why does the statement need to retrieve values from all five dimension tables in addition to the fact table?

4. Look at the first five columns retrieved, after the word SELECT: "Customer"."Country", "Customer"."Region", "Customer"."State", "Customer"."City", and "Customer"."Customer_Name".

   These five columns constitute the entire Customer dimension hierarchy. The processed Customer dimension already contains the complete hierarchy. Retrieving the entire hierarchy for each member of the Customer dimension while processing the cube is redundant. The remaining columns in the SQL statement similarly—redundantly— extract all levels of all hierarchy of all dimensions in the cube.

5. Close the trace window and the Process log window.

The first optimization task is to understand why the Analysis server considered it necessary to extract the entire hierarchy from each dimension, and to convince it that doing so is not necessary.

Assign unique keys to the leaf levels of a dimension

In "Allow duplicate names in a dimension" in Chapter 3, "Dimension and Cube Editors," you learned that a dimension level has a Member Keys Unique property, but you didn't learn the full purpose of the property. In this section, you'll learn how the Member Keys Unique property determines the optimization level of a SQL statement.

1. Expand the Shared Dimensions folder, right-click the Customer dimension, and click Edit.

2. Select the Customer Name level—the leaf level of the hierarchy—and look at the Member Key Column property in the Properties pane.

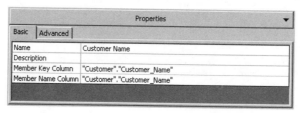

3. Click the Advanced tab of the Properties pane, and look at the Member Keys Unique property.

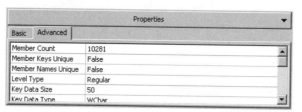

For each row in the fact table, the Analysis server must be able to identify a single, specific leaf-level member of the Customer dimension. The SQL query for the cube therefore includes the "Customer". "Customer_Name" column, which is specified by the Member Key Column property of the Customer Name level. Because the Member Keys Unique property for the Customer Name level is *False*, the SQL query then includes the "Customer"."City" column which is the Member Key Column for the City level—the parent level for Customer Name. That level also has Member Key Unique property set to *False*, so the SQL query retrieves the key column for the next level up in the hierarchy. This process continues to the top level of the hierarchy, whose Member Keys Unique property is *True* by definition.

4. Change the Member Keys Unique property of the Customer Name level to *True*, and press Enter.

Be sure to change the Member Keys Unique property of the leaf level, not of the dimension itself.

5. Click the Basic tab of the Properties window, and select the Member Key Column property. Click the ellipsis (...) button, select the Customer_ID column, and click OK. Then save the dimension. (Click Yes if warned that this change will necessitate reprocessing the cube.)

6. In the Dimension drop-down list on the toolbar of the Dimension Editor, select the Product dimension. And repeat steps 4 and 5, changing the Member Key Column property for the Product Name level to Product_ID. Select the Time.Calendar dimension, and repeat the process, changing the Member Key Column of the Day level to Date_ID. Select the Time.Fiscal dimension and repeat steps 4 and 5 one final time, again changing the Member Key Column for the Day level to Date_ID. Close the Dimension Editor.

You do not need to make any changes to the Employee dimension. The Member Keys Unique property of the leaf level of a parent-child dimension is *True* by definition.

7. Right-click the Sales cube, click Process, and then click OK to fully process the cube. Inspect the log to see how long it took to process the cube.

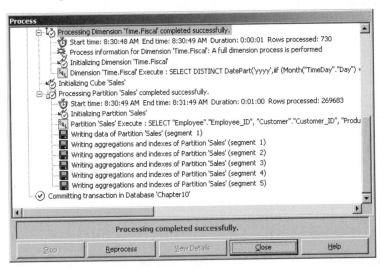

On my computer, processing the Sales partition (essentially, the whole cube), took exactly one minute, which is *one-fifth* the time it required before changing the Member Key Unique properties for the leaf levels of all the dimensions.

8. In the process log, select the SQL statement used to process the Sales partition and click View Details.

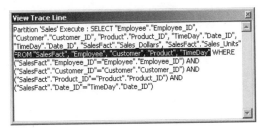

In the preceding screenshot, the FROM clause is highlighted. The SQL statement no longer retrieves values from the Product Category or Product Subcategory tables. The overall SQL statement is also much shorter than the original statement because it doesn't include any redundant levels—particularly the time dimensions levels with complex expressions.

9. Close the trace window and the Process log window.

Removing redundant levels from dimensions is an important way to improve the performance of cube processing.

Optimize a cube

In the preceding section, the FROM clause of the SQL query still includes four dimension tables in addition to the fact table. To identify why those tables are needed, you can look at the columns included in the SELECT clause. The SELECT clause looks like this:

```
SELECT "Employee"."Employee_ID", "Customer"."Customer_ID",
  "Product"."Product_ID", "TimeDay"."Date_ID", "TimeDay"."Date_ID",
  "SalesFact"."Sales_Dollars", "SalesFact"."Sales_Units"
```

Consider, for example, the Customer_ID column. The SQL statement retrieves it from the Customer table. That's why the Customer table is needed in the FROM clause—so that it can be the source of the Customer_ID column. But the Customer_ID column is in both the Customer table and the SalesFact table. The SQL statement could just as easily retrieve the Customer_ID from the fact table as from the dimension table. In fact, it would be much easier to retrieve it from the fact table. The only problem is that the SQL statement uses the value of the dimension's leaf-level Member Key Column property, and that is defined in the Dimension Editor, so it must use the dimension table as the source for the column. Somehow, you must change the definition of the Member Key Column but only within the context of a specific cube.

Star and Snowflake Schema Dimensions

In Chapter 1, "A Data Analysis Foundation," you learned about the difference between a star schema dimension and a snowflake schema dimension. A star schema dimension is simply a snowflake dimension where the levels have been prejoined into a single table to speed up retrievals. When a reporting application retrieves values directly from a relational data warehouse, the performance difference between star schema and snowflake schema dimension tables can be significant. That's because when creating a report from a relational warehouse, retrieving a single value might require retrieving millions of rows from the fact table, and each of those rows must be joined to all the levels of all the dimension tables.

When a reporting application retrieves values from an OLAP cube, the rules are completely different. In the first place, with an OLAP cube, any performance drain from snowflake schema dimension tables occurs when processing the cube, not when retrieving values from it. In the second place, even when processing, if the dimensions are properly designed and unique keys are available at the leaf level of each dimension, processing the cube requires only the leaf level of the dimensions and there's absolutely no difference whatever between a star schema dimension and a snowflake schema dimension.

Also, in an OLAP cube, the difference in processing time between a star schema dimension and a snowflake schema dimension is not very great. In the preceding section, you saw a fivefold improvement in performance, which is dramatic, but very little of that performance

1. Right-click the Sales cube, and click Edit.

2. Expand the Customer dimension, and select the Customer Name level. Then look at the Properties pane.

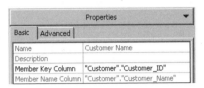

All the properties are disabled except the Member Key Column property. The Cube Editor allows you to edit the Member Key Column property precisely so that you can change it from the primary key of the dimension table to the foreign key of the fact table. You do not, however, have to go change each dimension manually. There is a single command that will convert Member Key Column values from the dimension table to the fact table whenever possible.

gain came from eliminating the joins between the tables of the Product dimension with its snowflake schema. On my computer, where the processing time reduction was four minutes, only ten seconds of that reduction (4 percent) came from the change to the Product dimension. Forty seconds (16 percent) came from the change to the Customer dimension. Forty-five seconds (19 percent) came from the change to the Time.Calendar dimension. Ninety seconds (38 percent) came from the change to the Time.Fiscal dimension. That leaves fifty-five seconds (23 percent) of the reduction that came from the interaction between the dimensions.

In this example—which might not be representative of the cubes you create—the effect of redundantly calculating complex expressions in the Time.Fiscal dimension was far more significant than the effect of joining snowflake schema tables in the Product dimension.

Any joins or expressions in the SQL statement are performed by the relational database. Retrieving values from the relational database is only one part of processing a cube. The other part, performed by the Analysis server, consists of resolving the member definitions, building the data records, and creating any aggregations. Each of these parts is assigned a separate share of the computer's resources, called a *thread*. Assigning the tasks to different threads means that they can occur in parallel. In practice, the second part—the part performed by the Analysis server—is almost always much slower than the first part—the part performed by the relational database system. Optimizing the SQL statement simply speeds up a task that is usually waiting around for the other task to catch up anyway.

3. Click Optimize Schema on the Tools menu.

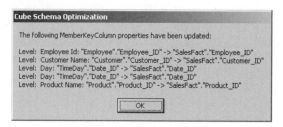

The entire effect of the Optimize Schema command is to make this conversion of Member Key Column properties. Now you can see the effect of the change on processing the cube.

4. Click OK to close the message box. Save the cube, and click the Process Cube button on the toolbar. Choose not to design storage, click Full Process, and click OK. Then look at the process log.

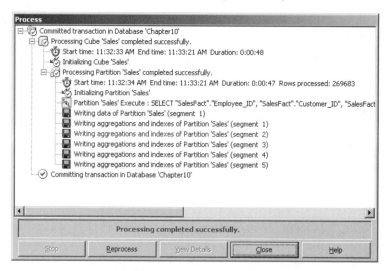

This time the Sales partition required only 47 seconds to process, an improvement of 13 seconds (22 percent) from the previous record of one minute. This is not a trivial improvement, but it's also not earth-shaking and it really is insignificant compared to other changes, such as changing the Member Keys Unique property to *True* for the Time.Fiscal dimension. Looking at the SQL statement is informative.

5. Select the SQL statement, and click View Details.

Once again, the FROM clause is highlighted. The SQL statement now retrieves values *only* from the fact table, not from any dimension table. Loading the fact table into the cube doesn't require *any* joins at all. This is as efficient as you can possibly get when loading a fact table into a cube.

6. Close the trace window, the Process log window, and the Cube Editor.

You can fully optimize loading a cube only when the dimensions are shared because fully optimizing requires that you move the Member Key Column for the lowest level of a dimension to the fact table. With a shared dimension, you can define the Member Key Column for a level differently in the dimension than in the cube since the dimension has an existence independent of the cube. With a private dimension, however, you use the Cube Editor to define the dimension, and there is no way to create dual definitions of the Member Key Column for a level in a dimension.

To fully optimize loading a shared dimension, you must use the Dimension Editor to set the Member Key Column for the leaf level of the dimension to the primary key linked to the fact table; you must set the Member Keys Unique property for the leaf level to *True*; and within the Cube Editor, you must use the Optimize Schema command to switch the Member Key Column for the dimension from the dimension table to the fact table.

Optimizing a Cube When Using Partitions

With very large cubes, you can choose to split a cube into multiple partitions as explained in "Working with Partitions" in Chapter 9, "Processing Optimization." Some of the rules change, however, when you add partitions to a cube. When you partition a cube, you assign different portions of the cube to different partitions, often by specifying a data slice. For example, you might slice a cube by using the Customer dimension, putting the USA member and its children into one partition and the rest of the world into another.

The slicing member is typically close to the top of the hierarchy for the dimension. To divide, or slice, the fact table data, the SQL statement must include all levels of the hierarchy from the leaf level up to the slicing member. This might require joins that would otherwise be optimized away. In a very large database, switching to using partitions might require converting a snowflake schema dimension into one with a star schema.

With either star schema or snowflake schema dimension, you would need to restore the join between the dimension table and the fact table—to "unoptimize" the dimension. If you use a data slice to create the partition, the Analysis server will automatically restore the joins as needed. If you used an explicit WHERE clause to create the partition, you must unoptimize the dimension yourself, using the Cube Editor to change the Member Key Column of the leaf level of the dimension back to the dimension table.

Creating Virtual Dimensions

These settings affect only the efficiency of retrieving rows from the relational data source. To improve the efficiency of building the cube itself, you can create virtual dimensions. Each dimension you add to a cube contributes substantially to the complexity of the cube. Adding the smallest possible dimension—one with only two members—to a cube *doubles* the number of cells in the cube. Anything you can do to avoid adding a new dimension will prevent the complexity of a cube from increasing.

Adding a second hierarchy to a dimension is equivalent to adding a new dimension to the cube. For example, even though Time.Fiscal and Time.Calendar are in the same dimension, and even though they share lowest-level members and the same key column in the fact table, they increase the complexity and size of the cube the same as if they were unrelated. Turning one of two related dimensions into a *virtual dimension* allows it to piggyback on the key values and aggregations of the other dimension.

A virtual dimension can use levels in the base dimension or member properties added to the base dimension. A virtual dimension can have a single level (in addition to the All level) or multiple levels in a hierarchy. Creating a single-level virtual dimension is simpler, so it makes sense to start by creating one of those.

Member properties are introduced in "Create a detail-level member property" in Chapter 3.

Create a single-level virtual dimension

As explained in "Working with a Standard Snowflake Dimension" in Chapter 3, a member property is a column in a dimension table that doesn't fit into the normal hierarchy for the dimension. For example, in the Product dimension, each Product Subcategory is assigned a Category Manager. The Category Manager does not fit naturally in the hierarchy from Product to Product Subcategory to Product Category. You can think of the Category Manager as a single-level alternate hierarchy above the Product Subcategory level. You can create a virtual dimension that gives you a one-level alternate hierarchy without adding to the cube's complexity:

1. Right-click the Shared Dimensions folder of the Chapter 10 OLAP database, point to New Dimension, and click Wizard. Click the virtual dimension option on the Choose How You Want To Create The Dimension screen, and click Next.

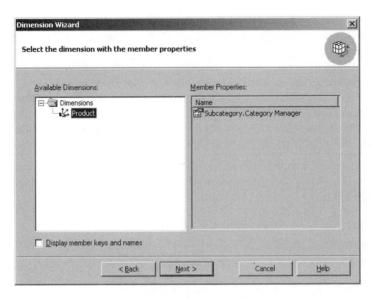

The wizard displays each dimension that has at least one member property defined.

2. Select the Product dimension, and click Next. Then select the Category Manager member property, and click the Create A Level button (>) to create a level from the member property.

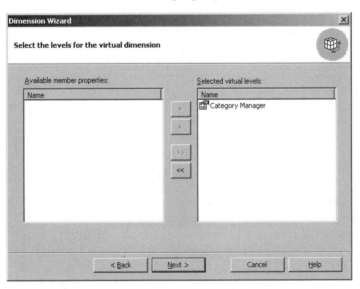

3. Click Next. Then click Next to skip the Advanced Options screen, type **Category Manager** as the name of the dimension, and click Finish. Close the Dimension Editor.

Note   A virtual dimension can be created from a member property, but not all member properties are suitable for creating a virtual dimension. For example, the Product level of a Product dimension might have a Price member property. Because few products share the same price, creating a virtual dimension to aggregate by Price would not be useful.

Once the virtual dimension is created, you can add it to any cube that contains the base dimension. The Sales cube contains the Product dimension.

4. Right-click the Sales cube, and click Edit.

5. In the Cube Editor, click the Insert Dimension toolbar button. Then double-click the Category Manager item to add it to the cube, and click OK.

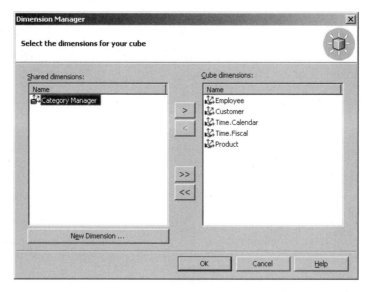

Even though a cube does not store aggregations for a virtual dimension, adding a virtual dimension to a cube does require you to process the cube before using it.

6. Click the Process Cube button. Answer Yes when asked to save the cube and No when asked to design storage. Click OK to accept a full process, and close the Process log window.

7. Click the Data tab at the bottom of the right pane to see the cube data with the category managers displayed as row headings.

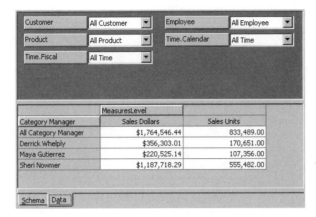

8. Close the Cube Editor.

From the point of view of a client application, a virtual dimension is indistinguishable from a dimension that includes an All level. Using a physical dimension requires more processing time and more storage space than using a virtual dimension, but standard dimensions might be easier to create than virtual dimensions.

Note   You cannot use a virtual dimension in a cube that has disabled the level of the member property used in the virtual dimension. For example, if you had disabled the Product Subcategory level in a cube, you could not add the Category Manager virtual dimension to that cube.

Creating a Hierarchy in a Virtual Dimension

The Sales cube of the Chapter 10 OLAP database contains both Time.Calendar and Time.Fiscal dimensions. Each dimension has four levels in addition to the All level (Day, Month, Quarter, and Year), but the Day and Month levels are identical between the two dimensions; only quarters and years differ between fiscal and calendar dates. You can convert the Time.Fiscal dimension into a virtual dimension. Naturally, you want to retain all the levels of the existing dimension.

Add aggregations to the Sales cube

A multilevel virtual dimension—particularly one such as Time.Fiscal where the levels are built using complex expressions—is not trivial to create. The only reason for creating a virtual dimension is to increase efficiency: to make the cube process faster and take less disk space. So far, the Sales cube has had no aggregations. With a real OLAP database, you will typically design aggregations until the performance gain reaches at least 20 percent. Before converting the Time.Fiscal dimension, add aggregations to the Sales cube to see how long it takes to process with the aggregations.

Chapter 8, "Storage Optimization," discusses how to design aggregations for a cube.

1. In the console tree, right-click the Sales cube and click Design Storage. Click Next to skip the welcome screen. Choose MOLAP as the storage type, and click Next.

2. Click the Performance Gain Reaches option, type **20** in the percentage box, and click Start. In a few seconds, the Start button changes to Continue and you can see the designed aggregations.

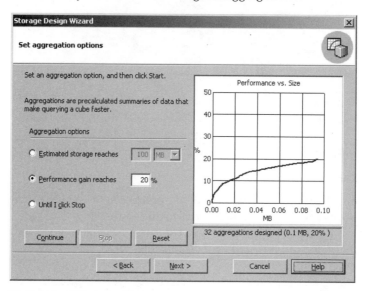

The wizard designed 32 aggregations, requiring an estimated 0.1 MB of disk space.

3. Click Next and then Finish.

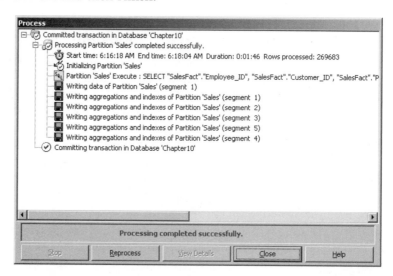

Processing the cube with aggregations took 1 minute, 46 seconds on my computer—more than twice as long as without the aggregations. Aggregations can add significantly to the processing time needed for a cube.

4. Close the Process log window.

Now that you have a base for comparison, you can convert the Time.Fiscal dimension to a virtual dimension and see the performance improvement.

Create a Fiscal Year member property

The first step is to create a new member property for the Fiscal Year in the Time.Calendar dimension, copying the expression from the Year level of the existing Time.Fiscal dimension.

1. In the console tree, right-click the Time.Fiscal dimension in the Shared Dimensions folder and click Edit.

2. Select the Year level, and copy the entire contents of the Member Name Column property.

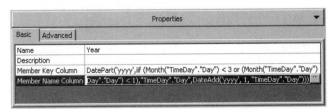

3. In the Dimension drop-down list on the toolbar, select the Time.Calendar dimension. Select the Month level, and click the Insert Member Property button on the toolbar. Select the Day column, and click OK.

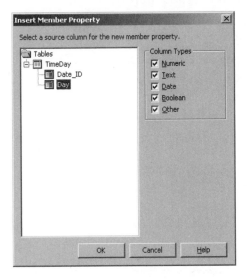

You must add the member properties at the Month level because that is the highest level that will be common between the base dimension and the virtual dimension.

4. Select the Name property, and type **Fiscal Year**.

5. Select the Source Column property (just click the property name), and press Ctrl+V to paste the copied expression.

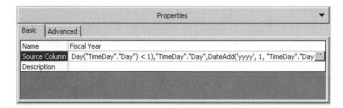

With a member property, the data type of the value stored must match the value of the Data Type property. Since the member property was originally created from the Day column—with type Date—that is its default data type. The expression, however, returns an integer.

6. Click the Advanced tab, change the Data Type property to *Integer*, and save the dimension.

Create a Fiscal Quarter member property

You also need to create a Fiscal Quarter member property—again at the Month level of the Time.Calendar dimension. Once again, you can copy the expression from the Time.Fiscal dimension.

1. Select Time.Fiscal in the Dimension drop-down list.

2. Select the Quarter level, and on the Basic tab copy the entire contents of the Member Name Column property.

3. In the Dimension drop-down list, select the Time.Calendar dimension. Select the Month level, and click the Insert Member Property button on the toolbar. Select the Day column, and click OK.

4. Select the Name property, and type **Fiscal Quarter**.

5. Select the Source Column property, and press Ctrl+V to paste the copied expression.

The expression for the Fiscal Quarter member property returns a string. Once again, the data type of the expression does not match that of the original column.

The Data Type name VarChar stands for variable length character string.

6. Click the Advanced tab, and change the Data Type property to *VarChar*. Save the dimension, and close the Dimension Editor.

Create a Time.Fiscal virtual dimension

You now have the basis for replacing the Time.Fiscal dimension, using member properties for the Fiscal Year and Fiscal Quarter levels along with the original Month and Day level definitions.

1. Right-click the Time.Fiscal dimension, click Delete, and click Yes when warned that this will necessitate reprocessing the dimension.

2. Right-click the Shared Dimensions folder, point to New Dimension, and click Wizard. On the screen that allows you to specify how to create the dimension, click the virtual dimension option and click Next.

3. Click the Display Member Keys And Names check box at the bottom of the wizard. Then select the Time.Calendar dimension

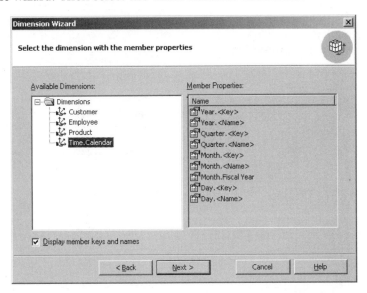

Even though the Time.Calendar dimension was already in the list, you must select the check box to use member names or keys in the next step. The list on the right—somewhat inaccurately labeled Member Properties—displays the pool of member properties, member keys, and member names you can choose from in designing your dimension hierarchy.

4. Click Next. Double-click, in order, Month.Fiscal Year, Month.Fiscal Quarter, Month.<Name>, and Day.<Name>.

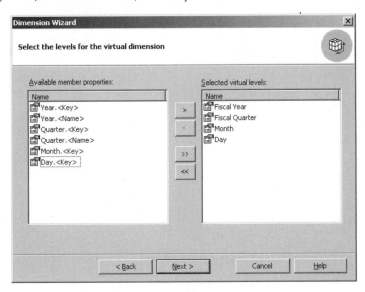

5. Click Next twice, once to leave the current screen and once to skip the Advanced Options screen.

6. In the final screen, select the check box that allows you to create a hierarchy, select Time from the Dimension Name drop-down list box, and type **Fiscal** in the Hierarchy Name box.

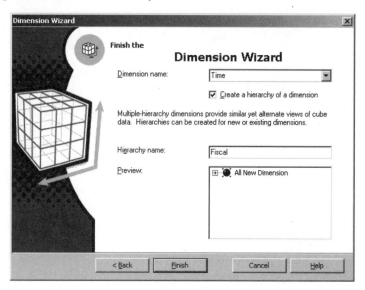

7. Click Finish to create the dimension.

Adjust the sort order of virtual dimension members

The dimension is created, but the members might not all appear in the correct sort order. Controlling the sort order in a virtual dimension is somewhat more difficult than in a standard dimension because both the Member Name Column and the Member Key Column for each level must correspond to names, keys, or member properties in the base dimension.

1. In the Dimension Editor, click the Data tab to browse the dimension. Expand All Time, 1998, and Quarter 1.

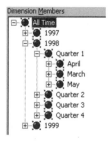

The month names are in the wrong order. They are being sorted alphabetically. The Time.Calendar dimension (as created by the Dimension Wizard) deals with the problem by using the expression *DatePart('m',"TimeDay"."Day")* as the Member Key Column and then sorting the level by key. That expression won't work for months in the Fiscal dimension; it would sort the months of Quarter 4 in the order January, February, December. The now-deleted Time.Fiscal dimension used the expression *(DatePart('yyyy', "TimeDay"."Day")*100)+DatePart('m', "TimeDay"."Day")*, which prefixes the month number with the year number. A simpler expression that gives the same result is *Format("TimeDay"."Day",'yyyymm')*. You cannot, however, enter that expression in the Member Key Column property, because the member name and member key must match a name, key, or member property from the base dimension. The solution is to create a new member property in the virtual dimension.

2. Select the Month level, click the Insert Member Property button, select the Day column, and click OK.

3. Change the name of the member property to **MonthSort**, change the Source Column property value to **Format("TimeDay"."Day", 'yyyymm')**, and on the Advanced tab, select *VarChar* as the value of the Data Type property.

4. Select the Month level, and on the Advanced tab of the Properties pane, select *MonthSort* as the value of the Order By property and press Enter. Then look at the months in the fourth quarter of 1998.

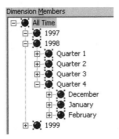

The months are now sorted properly.

5. Expand the December member, and look at the sort order of the days.

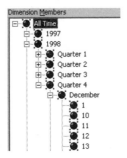

The numbers are sorted as if they were text. With the Day level, you can simply use the same solution as in the Time.Calendar dimension since the fiscal calendar does not affect days within a month.

6. Select the Day level, select the Member Key Column property on the Basic tab, click the ellipsis button, and double-click the Date_ID column.

7. On the Advanced tab, select *Key* as the value of the Order By property and press Enter. Then look at the sorted order of the days.

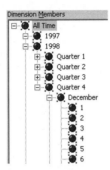

8. Save the dimension, close the Dimension Editor, right-click the Shared Dimensions folder, and click Process All Dimensions. When finished, close the Process log window.

Test the performance with aggregations

You're now ready to add aggregations and see the effect of converting the dimension. Earlier in this chapter, in the section "Add aggregations to the Sales cube," which was before you converted the Time.Fiscal dimension to a virtual dimension, processing the cube required 1 minute, 46 seconds, with aggregations designed to achieve a performance gain of 20 percent.

1. In the console tree, right-click the Sales cube and click Edit.

2. Click the Insert Dimension toolbar button, double-click the Time.Fiscal dimension to add it to the cube, and click OK. Save the cube.

3. On the Tools menu, click Design Storage. Click Next to skip the welcome screen. Click Next to accept MOLAP storage option.

4. Select the Performance Gain Reaches option, type **20** in the percentage box, and click Start. When the button changes to Continue, you can see the designed aggregations.

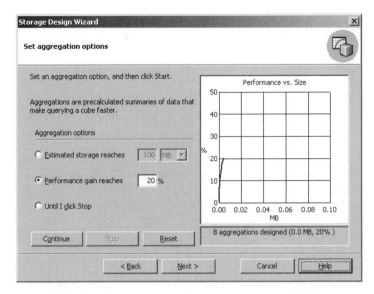

With Time.Fiscal as a virtual dimension, the wizard requires only 8 aggregations in order to reach a 20 percent optimization level. That's because there's no need to even consider all the possible combinations of the levels in Time.Fiscal and Time.Calendar.

5. Click Next, and then click Finish to process the cube.

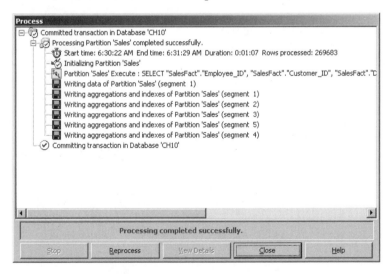

Converting the Time.Fiscal dimension to a virtual dimension cut the time required almost in half.

6. Close the Process log window and the Cube Editor.

If your OLAP databases can process easily within the time you have available, there's no need to bother with converting dimensions into virtual dimensions—or with removing joins in the SQL query. If, however, you have large cubes that push the limits of the available time, the benefits of optimizing can exceed the costs. Fortunately, these optimization changes are completely transparent to any client applications, so you can initially create and deploy cubes quickly and then, as the size of the cubes increase, optimize as needed.

Chapter Summary

To	Do this
Eliminate unnecessary higher-level columns from the SQL statement that builds a cube	Ensure the leaf level of a dimension has unique key values, and set the Member Keys Unique property for the level to *True*.
Eliminate unnecessary joins between the fact table and dimension tables in the SQL statement that builds a cube	Set Member Keys Unique to *True* for the leaf level of all possible shared dimensions,and in the Cube editor, click the Optimize Schema command on the Tools menu.
Optimize a dimension that comes from the same dimension table as an existing dimension	Make the second dimension into a virtual dimension.
Create a virtual dimension by using columns that are not member properties	In the Dimension Wizard, after selecting the virtual dimension option, select the Display Member Keys And Names check box.
Create a multilevel hierarchy in a virtual dimension	Create member properties for all the necessary levels. Then, in the Dimension Wizard, select the dimension containing the member properties. When asked to select levels, move member properties in order, from the most summarized to the least.
Sort the level of a virtual dimension by a column other than the name	Add a member property within the virtual dimension, and change the Order By property of the level to use the new column.

Chapter 11

Security

Estimated time: 1.5 hours

In this chapter, you'll learn how to

- Create security roles in an OLAP database.

- Manage security roles at the database and cube levels.

- Restrict access to dimensions and parts of dimensions.

- Create a custom calculated member for different roles.

- Create multidimensional expressions (MDX) expressions to apply cell-level security.

In most real-world applications, OLAP databases are designed to answer many different questions that might be asked by diverse groups of individuals. For example, a sales representative might be interested in his or her sales in a particular region by product by customer. A district manager might be interested in the total sales in one region by product by customer. And a technical support representative might be interested in the number of telephone inquiries by product by customer.

In many cases, these answers will be found in a series of cubes. In certain circumstances, all this information could reside in one cube. If you'd like the sales rep to be able to see only his or her own sales information and *not* another sales rep's data, security must be implemented. In this chapter, you'll learn about how security works in Microsoft SQL Server 2000 Analysis Services.

Start the lesson

1. In Analysis Manager, right-click the Server folder and click Restore Database. Then navigate to the folder containing the sample files for this book, select Chapter 11, and click Open. Click Restore, and then close the Restore Database Progress dialog box.

Creating Security Roles

Analysis Services security is based on and integrated with the security in Microsoft Windows NT (either Windows NT version 4 or Microsoft Windows 2000). When you define security in Analysis Services, you create roles in the OLAP database. Each role can contain one or more specific user accounts or user groups as defined in the operating system. Once you've created a database role, you can associate that role with cubes or virtual cubes in the OLAP database. In addition, you can fine-tune security within a cube by restricting access to metadata (the members on dimensions) as well as access to data (the values stored in the cubes).

Note   Analysis Services automatically creates an OLAP Administrators group in the operating system. To use Analysis Manager, the active user must be a member of the OLAP Administrators group. Any member of the OLAP Administrators group has complete access to every cube and database on the server. In other words, you cannot create security such that a user can administer one database but be excluded from administering a different database. To protect your Analysis server from being damaged by viruses or macros, user accounts that belong to the OLAP Administrators group should not be used to access Web pages or to use productivity and e-mail applications that support scripts or macros.

Caution   Do not delete the OLAP Administrators group. Without the OLAP Administrators group that's automatically created during the installation of Analysis Services, no one can use Analysis Manager to administer the Analysis server.

Create sample users and groups

Security in Analysis Services depends on operating system User and Group accounts. When a new person is granted the right to use a Windows 2000 or Windows NT server, a server administrator must first create a user account for that person. That user account should be assigned to one or more appropriate user groups. In this chapter, you'll create security by using Windows users and groups. If you have only default users and groups, you should create some sample ones to use as a test. If you already have your own users and groups available in your Windows server, you can use them.

Although the general principles don't change, the detailed steps for adding a new user or group vary depending on whether you're using Windows NT, Windows 2000 with local users and groups, or Windows 2000 with Active Directory Users and Computers. The following instructions are suitable for creating local users and groups in Windows 2000 Server without Active Directory Services.

Note   If you're using Windows NT, click the Start menu, point to Programs, point to Administrative Tools (Common), and then click User Manager. If you're using Windows 2000 to manage Active Directory Users and Computers, click the Start menu, point to Programs, point at Administrative Tools, and then click Active Directory Users and Computers. Within the User Manager, creating new users and groups in Windows NT or in Windows 2000 Active Directory is similar to managing local users and groups in Windows 2000.

---

1. In Windows 2000, click the Start menu, point to Programs, point to Administrative Tools, and click Computer Management. Under the System Tools folder, expand the Local Users And Groups folder.

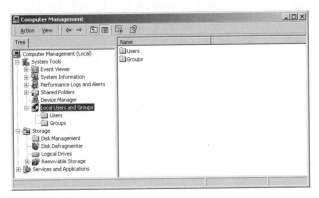

2. Right-click the Users folder, and click New User. Type **_jsmith** in the User Name box. (The underscore at the beginning of the name will make it easy to find and remove the sample users and groups.) Type **Joe Smith** in the Full Name box. Leave the Password box empty, and leave the User Must Change Password At Next Logon check box selected. Then click Create. The boxes in the New User dialog box clear when the user has been created.

3. As a second sample user, type **_mjturner** in the User Name box. Type **Mary Jane Turner** in the Full Name box. Leave the Password box empty and the User Must Change Password At Next Logon check box selected. Click Create, and then click Close.

4. Right-click the Groups folder, and click New Group. Type **_Budget Analysts** in the Group Name box.

5. Click the Add button under the Members box. Select _jsmith, click Add, and then click OK.

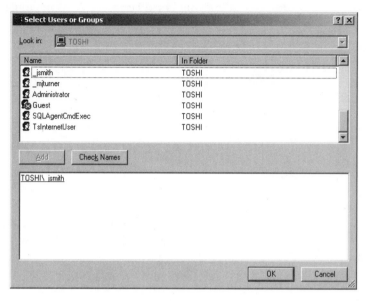

6. Click Create to create the group. Then, to create a second group, type **_Budget Reviewers** in the Group Name box.

7. Click the Add button under the Members box. Click _jsmith, hold down the Ctrl key as you click _mjturner, click Add, and then click OK. Click Create to create the group and Close to close the New Group dialog box.

8. Close the Computer Management window.

Important   After completing this chapter, be sure to delete the sample users and groups from your computer.

Creating a new user or a new group has no effect on Analysis Services until you explicitly add the user or group to a specific database. Of course, adding a user account to the existing OLAP Administrators group would change who could run the Analysis Manager application and browse cubes with no security applied.

Create a role for all users

When you create a new database or cube, it automatically gets a hidden, internal role that gives all power to members of the OLAP Administrators group. This hidden role allows administrators to use Analysis Manager. A client cube browser application can browse the cube provided that the user belongs to the OLAP Administrators group. Any user who does not belong to the OLAP Administrators group has no permission at all—either to administer or to browse the cubes. If you create a cube and make it available to other users in your organization, they will not be able to see anything in the cube.

In many situations, you want to allow all users to browse a cube but not to use Analysis Manager. To do that, you must create a new role.

1. In the Analysis Manager console tree, expand the Chapter 11 OLAP database and the Cubes folder, right-click the Sales cube, and click Manage Roles.

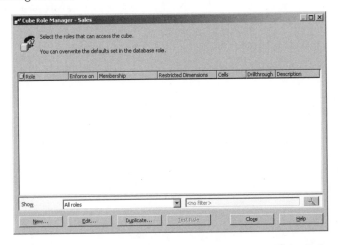

The Cube Role Manager dialog box appears. This dialog box shows all the roles that currently exist in the database. It also allows you to create a new role.

2. Click the New button at the bottom of the dialog box. In the Create A Cube Role dialog box that appears, type **All Users** in the Role Name box.

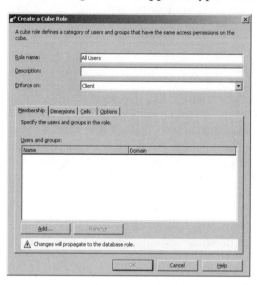

A role comprises one or more users or groups from the operating system. The users and groups must already exist before you can add them to a role.

3. Click the Add button

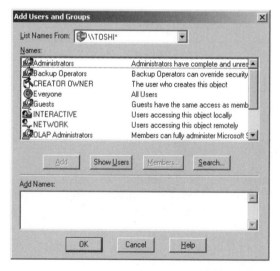

The Add Users And Groups dialog box show all the groups available on the current server. You can use the List Names From drop-down list to select a different server, if necessary. The Names list defaults to show only groups. If you want to show users as well as groups, click the Show Users button. In general, security is easier to manage if you use groups so that you don't need to modify roles each time individual users come or go. For the new All Users role, you want to apply the role to all users. The standard Everyone group refers to any user connected to the server.

4. Select Everyone, and click Add to add the group name to the Add Names list. Click OK.

Note   It's not enough to select the group; you must click Add to move the group name into the Add Names list.

After adding the group, the Membership tab of the Create A Group Role dialog box shows the users and groups that now compose the role. You can use the Remove button to remove individual users or groups; the Add button always displays the Add Users And Groups dialog box.

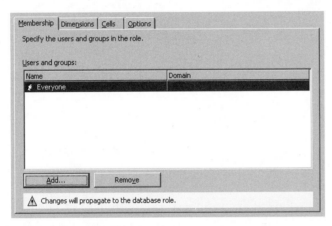

5. Click OK to complete creating the role.

The new role appears in the Cube Role Manager dialog box.

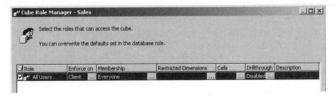

6. Click Close to close the dialog box.

The Sales cube is now available for browsing by any user who can connect to the server. If you intend to make all your OLAP cubes freely available in the organization, this completes all that you need to know about security in Analysis Services.

Create roles at the database level

Some cubes contain information that should not be made available to all users. To restrict access to different users, you must create roles and put specific users and groups into the roles. Roles always exist at the database level. Even when you create a new cube role, you really create a new database role. The role contains the same users and groups (that is, has the same *membership*) regardless of which cube in the database uses it. You can create roles directly at the database level and then apply those roles to cubes as needed. In this section, you'll create roles for budget analysts and budget reviewers.

1. In the console tree, right-click the Database Roles object under the Chapter 11 OLAP database. Then click Manage Roles.

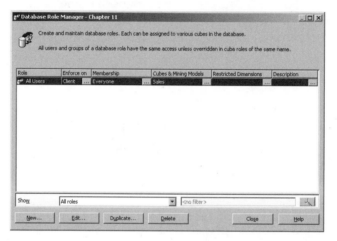

Database Role Manager appears quite similar to Cube Role Manager. They both show all the currently existing roles in the database. As you can see, the All Users role that you created in the Sales cube also appears in the list of database roles. You can use Cube Role Manager to create a new database role, but you must use Database Role Manager to delete one. As you work through this chapter, you'll see additional similarities and differences between the two role managers.

2. Click the New button to begin creating a new database role. Type **Budget Analysts** in the Role Name box, and click Add to add a new group to the role.

3. Select the _Budget Analysts group or any group of your own choosing, and click Add.

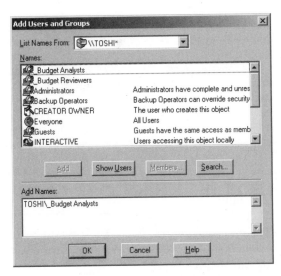

4. Click OK to add the group to the role membership. Click OK to create the role.

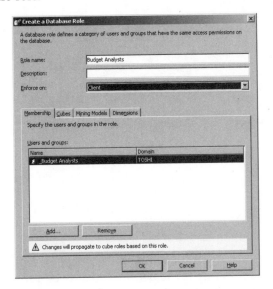

The bottom of the dialog box displays a notice communicating that changes to the role membership will propagate to cubes that use this role. A role is global to a database but can be used by one or more cubes within the database. The membership is intrinsic to the role and will be the same for all uses of the role.

Note   The Create A Database Role dialog box contains a drop-down list labeled Enforce On, with two possible values: Server and Client. As explained in "Analysis Services User Tools" in Chapter 1, "A Data Analysis Foundation," the PivotTable Service component maintains a cache of values on the client computer. This cache makes retrievals fast and minimizes network traffic. When you enable security, some of the values stored in the client cache might be restricted. If you choose to enforce security on the client, the PivotTable Service will determine whether to make values from the cache available to the client. Potentially restricted values will, however, be passing over the network connection, which opens the possibility that some nefarious soul could intercept them. If you choose to enforce security on the server, you effectively disable the client-side cache. Enforcing security on the client is more efficient but slightly less secure than enforcing security on the server.

---

5. Click New, type **Budget Reviewers**, and click the Add button. Select the _Budget Reviewers operating system group (or another group of your choice). Click Add, and then click OK.

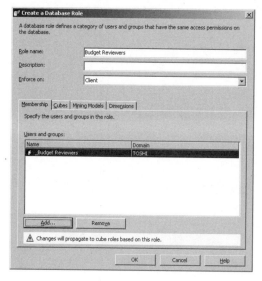

When you create a new database role, the dialog box displays the Membership tab. Membership is the defining quality of a role. However, the dialog box also has other tabs. For example, you can assign a role to cubes as you create it.

6. Click the Cubes tab to show the list of cubes in the database. Click the check boxes next to Finance and Sales.

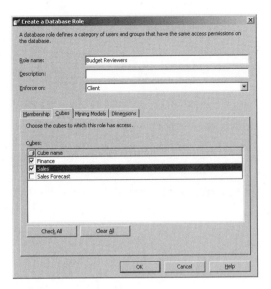

7. Click OK to create the role.

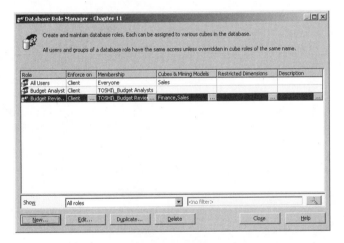

All three roles now appear in the list. As you can see in the Cubes & Mining Models column, the All Users role is currently assigned to the Sales cube, the Budget Reviewers role is assigned to the Sales and Finance cubes, and the Budget Analysts role is not assigned to any cubes at all.

Manage database roles

You can also use Database Role Manager to make other changes to existing roles. For example, if you need a new role that's only slightly different from an existing role, you can make a duplicate copy of the existing role and then modify it.

1. With the Budget Reviewers role selected, click the Duplicate button.

The only thing different between the old role and the new role will be the name, so you'll be prompted for a new name.

2. When prompted, type **Detailed Reviewers** and click OK.

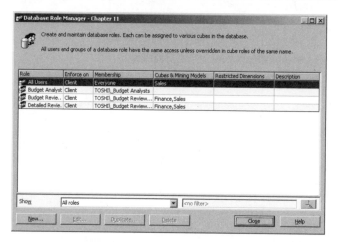

The new role is an exact copy of the previous one. You can edit the role to make changes.

3. Select the Detailed Reviewers role, and click the ellipsis (…) button in the Cubes & Mining Models column. The dialog that appears is identical to the Create A Database Role one, except the caption is different and you can't change the name of the role.

4. Clear the Sales cube check box, and select the Sales Forecast check box.

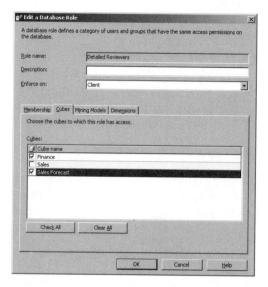

5. Click OK to accept the changes to the role.

You can also change the membership of an existing role.

6. With the Detailed Reviewers role selected, click the Edit button.

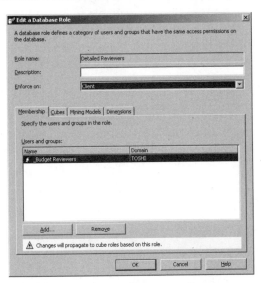

This displays the same Edit A Database Role dialog box as you saw earlier. There's only one dialog box for defining a database role. You can simply get to it from any of several different directions: by creating a new role, by selecting a role and clicking the edit button, or by selecting a role and clicking the ellipsis button in one of the columns. Using the ellipsis button from a column simply preactivates the appropriate tab of the dialog box.

7. Click Add, double-click _Budget Analysts (or a group of your choice), and click OK. Then click OK to accept the revised definition of the role.

From within Database Role Manager, you can also delete a role.

8. With the Detailed Reviewers role selected, click Delete. Click Yes when asked to confirm. Click Close to close the Database Role Manager window.

All databases have an internal role for the OLAP Administrators group, and that role is automatically applied with all power to all cubes in the database. Unless you explicitly create additional roles and assign them to cubes, only members of the OLAP Administrators group can use the cubes. When you use Cube Role Manager to create a new role, the role is created at the database level and automatically applied to the current cube. When you use Database Role Manager to create a new role, you must explicitly add that role to a cube. A default role allows unrestricted access to all dimension information, unrestricted access to read any cell value, and no permission to write back changes to the cube.

Applying Security to a Dimension

When you apply security at the cube level, you simply allow or disallow access to the entire cube. That is often appropriate, but it gives you no flexibility. Often you want managers to see information unavailable to individual contributors, or you don't want individuals in the marketing department to see budget details from the manufacturing department. Dimension-level security provides a powerful, but simple, mechanism for granting partial access to a cube.

Fully restrict a dimension

The simplest—and most useful—option for restricting access to a dimension is to prevent all access other than to the top-level member. Earlier in this lesson, you gave complete access to the Sales cube to all users. Perhaps you don't want all users to be able to see values broken out by fiscal years.

1. In the console tree, right-click the Sales cube of the Chapter 11 database and click Manage Roles.

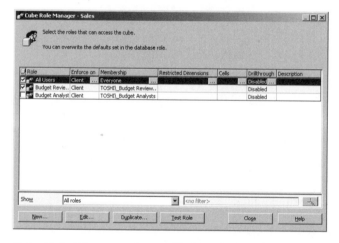

Cube Role Manager shows all the roles in the database, with a check box next to the roles that apply to this cube. If you change the membership for a role, that change will apply throughout the database, but you can change the way the role should be applied without affecting other cubes that use the role.

2. With the All Users role selected, click the ellipsis button in the Restricted Dimensions column.

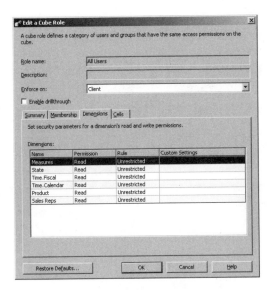

The Edit A Cube Role dialog box shows all the dimensions in the cube. The default rule for each dimension allows unrestricted access. Notice that this dialog box is similar to the Edit A Database Role dialog box. Both dialog boxes have multiple tabs. And both dialog boxes can be accessed either by clicking the ellipsis button in a column or by clicking the Edit button at the bottom of the main role manager window.

3. Select the Time.Fiscal dimension, click in the Rule column, and select Fully Restricted from the drop-down list.

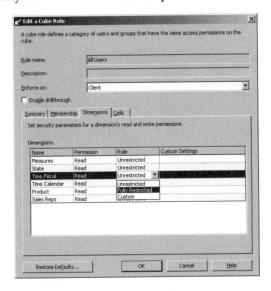

4. Click OK to change the dimension rule.

Cube Role Manager allows you to browse the cube as if you were logged on as a member of the role. This is a tremendous convenience for testing the behavior of a role, since you don't have to work on two computers or continually log on as different users.

5. Click the Test Role button. Resize the cube browser if you want.

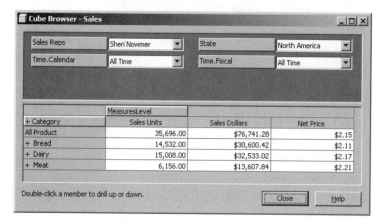

The Time.Fiscal dimension is still available. Using security to restrict access to a dimension does not remove a dimension. If you want to completely eliminate a dimension from a browser, you can use a virtual cube, as explained in "Remove dimensions and measures from a cube" in Chapter 4, "Advanced Dimensions and Cubes." Security does, however, restrict the members you can see in the dimension.

6. Click the Time.Fiscal dimension drop-down list.

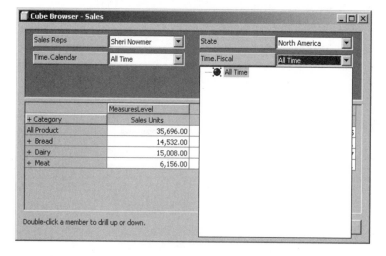

The All Time member is the only one available in the dimension. Dimension security has effectively removed all the other members for users belonging to the All Users role.

7. Press Escape to close the cube browser window.

Restrict the members of a dimension

You might want to allow a group of users to see some parts of a dimension but not all of it. The dimensions of a role allow you to do that. Suppose, for example, that you want all users to be able to see the sales figures only for product categories and subcategories, not for individual products.

1. In Cube Role Manager for the Sales cube, with the All Users role selected, click the ellipsis button in the Restricted Dimensions column.

2. Select the Product dimension, and select Custom from the Rule drop-down list.

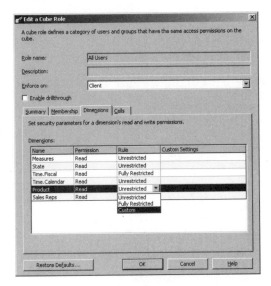

When you chose the Custom option, the Custom Settings box acquires an ellipsis button that allows you to define specific restrictions.

3. Click the ellipsis button in the Custom column. Type **Categories and Subcategories** in the Description box, and select Subcategory in the Bottom Level drop-down list.

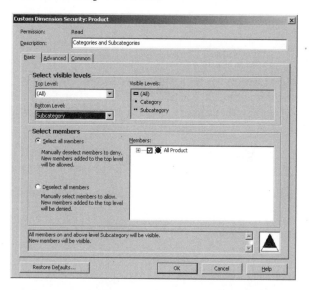

4. Click OK to return to the list of dimensions in the cube.

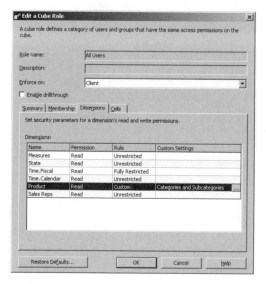

A custom security definition is complex and cannot be displayed in the summary grid for a role. The description does appear and can remind you of the purpose of the custom definition.

5. Click OK to return to Cube Role Manager, and click Test Role to see the security in action. Expand the Category level of the dimension.

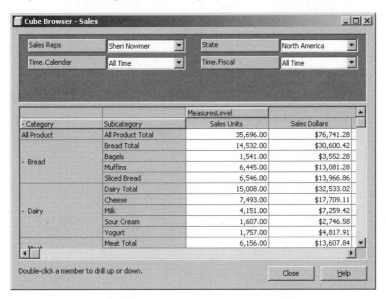

6. Close the browser window.

Control visual totals for a dimension

You can filter dimension members even further—specifically including or excluding individual members. Suppose, for example, that you want to exclude Bread (the Category) and Milk (the Subcategory) from the values that are visible by all users.

1. Click the ellipsis button in the Restricted Dimensions column. Then select the Product dimension, and click the ellipsis button in the Custom Settings column.

2. Leave the Select All Members option selected, and expand the All Product and Dairy nodes. Clear the check boxes next to the Bread and Milk members.

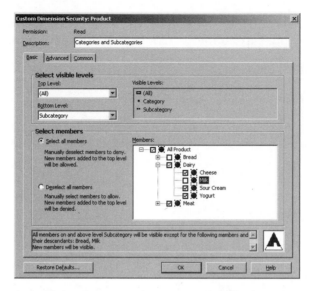

As explained next to the options labels, the Select All Members option means that any members not specifically excluded will be included. The implication is that new members will be automatically included. The Advanced tab of the dialog box shows the effect of choices on the basic tab. Looking at that tab can clarify the behavior of the filter.

3. Click the Advanced tab.

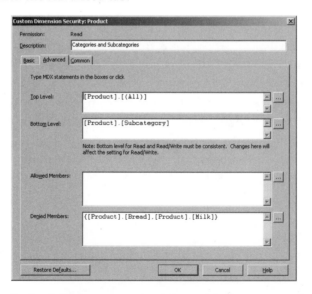

Each of the boxes on the Advanced tab can contain an MDX expression. Selecting values on the Basic tab simply inserts MDX constant expressions into the boxes. In the top two boxes, you can include any MDX expression that returns a valid level of the current dimension. In the bottom two boxes, you can include any MDX expression that returns a valid set on the current dimension.

4. Click OK to close the Custom Dimension Security dialog box, and click OK to close the Edit A Cube Role dialog box. Then click Test Role to see the effect of the changed security.

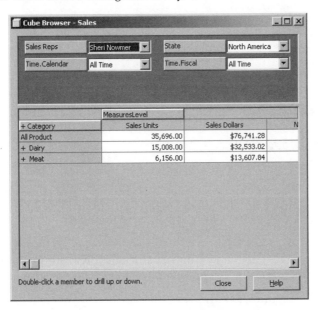

The Bread category simply doesn't exist. Its value, however, can be deduced. If you subtract the Dairy and Meat values from the All Product value, you can calculate the value of Bread. The same is true for Milk but at a lower level. You can deduce the value of Milk by subtracting the other Dairy subcategories from the category total.

The report also looks wrong because the All Product total does not appear to match the values of the subordinate items. The numbers don't match because the All Product total is retrieved independently from the cube, not summed from the detailed values.

Whether because you want to prevent sleuths from uncovering hidden information or just because you want the report to look consistent, you might want to display totals that summarize only the visible values.

5. Close the browser window, click the ellipsis button in the Restricted Dimensions column, select the Product dimension, and click the ellipsis button in the Custom Settings column. Then click the Common tab.

6. Under Visual Totals, click the enable option.

The default is not to show visual totals—that is, to retrieve all values directly from the cube. Enabling visual totals forces summary values to be calculated dynamically, based only on values shown in the report.

7. Click OK twice, and click the Test Role button.

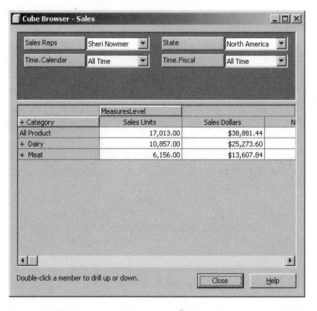

The All Product total now appears as the sum of Dairy and Meat. It's as if Bread didn't exist, and no one—at least no one who is viewing the cube as a member of the All Users role—has access to the information necessary to figure out sales of Bread.

8. Close the browser window.

Create a default member for a role in a dimension

The default member is used for any filter dimension that does not have an explicit value selected. The default default member for a dimension is the member of the All level. As explained in "Specify a default member" of Chapter 3, "Dimension and Cube Editors," you can manually set the default member of a dimension. But what if you need a different default member for different groups of users. For example, suppose that for the Time.Calendar dimension, most users want to see the most recent year but budget analysts want to see the most recent month. By defining the default member in a role, you can give each group the the appropriate default member.

Note   Adding a default member to a role is independent of using an expression to calculate the default member. You can add a constant default member to a role, and you can put a calculated default member directly in the dimension. The only reason for putting a default member into a role is if you want different default members (constants or expressions) for different groups of users.

---

1. In Cube Role Manager for the Sales cube, with the All Users role selected, click the ellipsis button in the Restricted Dimensions column.

2. Select the Time.Calendar dimension, select Custom from the Rule drop-down list, and click the ellipsis button in the Custom Settings column.

3. Click the Common tab, and select the check box for defining a default member.

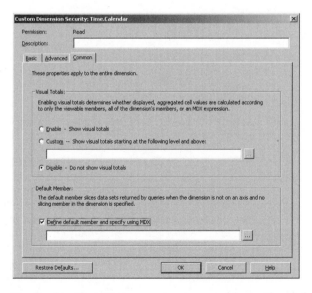

To display the most recent year—and have the default member automatically change as you add new years to the dimension—you must use an MDX expression.

4. Click the ellipsis button, and enter the following expression in the MDX Expression box: **Tail([Time].[Calendar].[Calendar Year]. Members,1).Item(0)**. Then click OK three times.

The Members function retrieves a set of all the members of the Calendar Year level. The Tail function forms a set consisting of only the last member from the level. The Item function then extracts the first (and only!) member of that set. The result of the expression is thus the last member of the Calendar Year level.

5. Click the Test Role button. The default member of the Time.Calendar dimension is 1998. Click the drop-down arrow for the dimension.

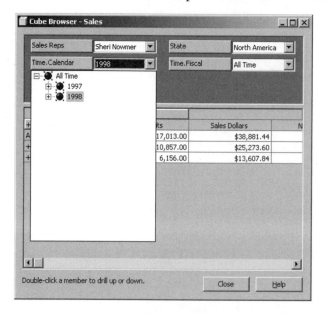

Even though 1998 is the default member, all the other members are still available. Attaching a default member to a role does not add security to the cube; it simply allows you to create a different default member expression for different groups of users.

6. Close the browser window, and close Cube Role Manager.

Note   Dimension-level security applies only at the cube level. You can, however, design dimension-level security for a database role. The dimension security from the database role then simply becomes the dimension security for any cubes that use that role. Within the cube, you can customize dimension security—overriding the dimension security from the database role. This is different from the way the membership in a role works. Membership always applies at the database level. If you change the membership of a role for one cube, you are really changing it for all cubes that use the role.

Applying Cell-Level Security to a Cube

Dimension-level security prevents the user from seeing certain members. Such security does not directly prevent viewing of cell values, but, clearly, if a member does not appear, the values for that member will not be visible either. In short, in most situations, dimension-level security is all you'll ever need. In some situations, however, you might want reports to display all the members but block the values for some of the cells. When you need to secure specific cells without removing members, you need to apply cell-level security to a cube.

Prevent values in cells from being read

The Finance cube contains, among other things, expense information. It includes Headcount, Salary, and Benefits members. Salary information is typically very sensitive within a company. You might want to change a cube so that budget reviewers can see the higher level financial information but not the detailed financial information. You can use cell-level security to do this. Start by reviewing the complete information in the Finance cube.

1. Right-click the Finance cube, and click Manage Roles. Select the Budget Reviewers role, and click Test Role. Expand all the levels of the Account dimension. Resize the browser window as needed.

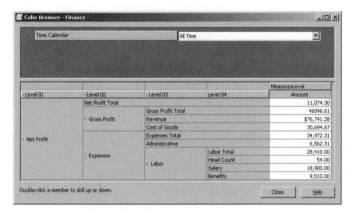

All the cells contain values. You want to prevent the reviewer from seeing the values under the Labor member.

2. Close the browser window. Click the ellipsis button in the Cells column. The default Cell Security Policy value is Unrestricted Read. Select Advanced from the drop-down list.

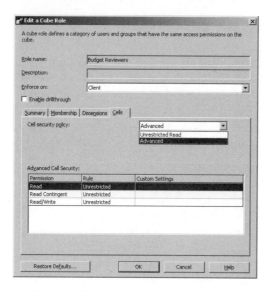

With the cell security policy set to Advanced, the advanced cell security grid becomes available. You want to control the reading of cells but only for some cells, so you'll need a custom setting.

3. With Read selected in the Permission column, select Custom in the Rule column and click the ellipsis in the Custom Settings column. Type **Nothing under labor** in the Description box.

For cell-level security, you need an MDX expression that can be calculated for each cell of a grid. For each cell, before the value is displayed, the expression is evaluated. If, in the context of that one cell, the expression returns the value 1 (*True*), the value is displayed. If the expression returns 0 (*False*), the value is not displayed.

To use the MDX Builder to construct an expression, click the ellipsis button to the right of the MDX box.

4. In the MDX box, type the expression **Account.Parent.Name <>
"Labor"**, and click Check.

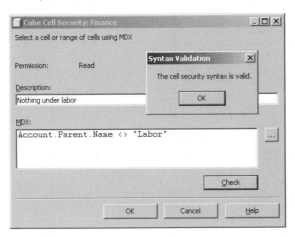

A message box appears informing you that the syntax is valid.

5. Click OK to close the message box and OK to close the Cube Cell Security
dialog box.

Creating a custom security setting automatically sets the Read
Contingent and Read/Write permissions for the role to Fully Restricted.
If you were to set the Read/Write permission to Unrestricted, all users
would have unrestricted access to the cube. That's because Read/Write
permission implies Read permission—even though this cube is not write-
enabled. When you restrict one of the permissions, you must restrict the
other permissions.

*Read Contingent
is an advanced
condition. To find
more about it,
click the Help
button and in
the Cells Tab
(Cube Role Dia-
log Box) topic,
read the descrip-
tion of Read
Contingent.*

6. Close the Edit A Cube Role dialog box. Click the Test Role button, and
fully expand the Account dimension levels, resizing the browser window
as necessary.

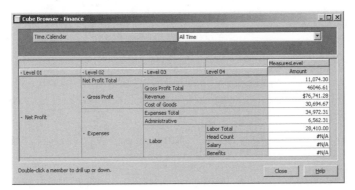

The detailed Labor members still appear, but #N/A appears in all
the cells.

7. Close the browser window, and close Cube Role Manager.

Allow users to write to cells

Cell-level security is particularly important in write-enabled cubes because you might want different groups of people to be able to modify different cell values. The Sales Forecast cube has been write-enabled. As a default, a role gives unrestricted read permission but no write permission even if the cube is write-enabled. To allow the members of a role to write to a cube, the cube must be write-enabled and then the role must be given read/write permission.

1. Right-click the Sales Forecast cube, and click Manage Roles.

2. With the Budget Analysts role selected, click the ellipsis button in the Cells column.

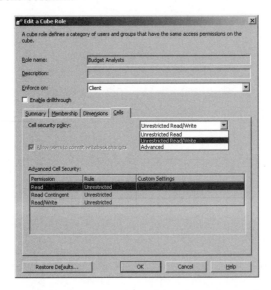

3. In the Cell Security Policy drop-down list, select Unrestricted Read/Write.

Note   The Unrestricted Read/Write policy is available only if the cube has already been write-enabled. A cube that has not been write-enabled has only two options: Unrestricted Read and Advanced.

If you want to allow write permission to only selected cells, you create an MDX expression for the Read/Write permission precisely as described in the preceding section.

4. Click OK to close the Cube Role Editor window, and click Close to close Cube Role Manager.

Security is an important part of an Analysis Services application, and Cube Role Manager gives you tremendous flexibility for applying security. You can apply security with broad brush strokes at the cube level, with small brush strokes at the dimension level, or with single-hair precision by using the full flexibility of MDX expressions.

To	Do this
Allow all network users to see the contents of a cube	Right-click the cube, and click Manage Roles. Click New, type a name for the role, and click Add. Select the Every one group, click Add, and then click OK twice.
Duplicate an existing role	Right-click the Database Roles folder, and click Manage Roles. Select a role and click Duplicate. Type a name for the new role, and click OK.
Change which cubes are assigned to a role	Select a role, and click the ellipsis button in the Cubes & Mining Models column. To the left of each cube name, select the check box to apply the role to that cube or clear the check box to remove the role from the cube.
To restrict access to a dimension of a cube	Right-click the cube, and click Manage Roles. Select a role, and click the ellipsis button in the Restricted Dimensions column. Select a dimension, and in the Rule column, select Fully Restricted from the drop-down list.
Restrict access to specific members of a dimension	After selecting a dimension in the Edit A Database Role dialog box, select the Custom option from the Rule drop-down list. Then click the ellipsis button in the Custom column, and select the appropriate members of the dimension.
See how a cube would appear if you were logged in as a member of a specific group	Right-click the cube, and click Manage Roles. Select a role and click Test Role.
Add cell-level security to a cube	Right-click the cube, and click Manage Roles. Select a role, and click the ellipsis button in the Cells column. Select Advanced from the Cell Security Policy drop-down list. Select Custom in the Rule column, and click the ellipsis in the Custom Settings column. In the MDX box, enter an expression that returns a 1 or 0 for each cell in the cube.

Index

Note: Page numbers in italics refer to figures and tables.

Serve up
powerfully scalable
business solutions

U.S.A. **$59.99**
U.K. £38.99 [V.A.T. included]
Canada $89.99
ISBN 0-7356-0517-3

With the innovations in Microsoft® SQL Server™ 7.0, organizations like yours get a powerfully enhanced tool for turning enterprise information into business results. In this essential companion to version 7.0, two of the most knowledgeable authorities on SQL Server technology step inside the reengineered SQL Server engine to reveal how underlying system structure and behavior affect application development. Use this in-depth, expert investigation—plus the ready-to-load evaluation copy of SQL Server 7.0—to understand how to create high-performance data warehousing, transaction processing, and decision-support applications that scale as far as your vision for the enterprise.

mspress.microsoft.com

About the Authors

Microsoft SQL Server 2000 Analysis Services Step by Step was written by the staffs of OLAP Train LLC and its affiliated company, Aspirity LP, and by Reed Jacobson.

OLAP Train (*http://www.olaptrain.com*) is a curricula development company specializing in OLAP and data warehousing technologies. Its courseware supports Microsoft SQL Server 2000 and other Microsoft products. Microsoft licenses OLAP Train's curricula for worldwide distribution as Microsoft Official Curricula through various Microsoft channels, including Certified Technical Education Centers.

Aspirity (*http://www.aspirity.com*) is a consulting and training company with staff experts in OLAP and data warehousing. Aspirity is the "real-world" link providing experience and case studies for OLAP Train's curricula and book materials.

Reed Jacobson is consulting manager for Aspirity. He is the author of *Microsoft Excel 2000/Visual Basic for Applications Fundamentals* (Microsoft Press, 1999) and other books covering Microsoft Excel, Access, and Office. For more than ten years, he has delivered consulting and training solutions to such companies as Hewlett-Packard, Coca-Cola Enterprises, and Glaxo-Wellcome.

In-depth contributions to the book were made by members of the OLAP Train and Aspirity staffs. **Tom Chester** is a cofounder of OLAP Train and a managing consultant with Aspirity. Tom is author of the *Mastering Excel* book series and creator of Open EIS Pak, Microsoft's groundbreaking EIS/OLAP tool. He has over twenty years' experience teaching and consulting for companies such as Microsoft, Walt Disney, and AT&T. **Sarah Bergseth** is director of development for OLAP Train. Sarah has been a consultant developing OLAP and financial applications for such companies as Abbott Laboratories, Chrysler, and Ford. **Hilary Feier** is Aspirity's president. She has implemented a range of data warehousing, financial, and OLAP solutions for companies such as Amazon, Bay Networks, and Lam Research.

For more information about OLAP Train curricula, licensing, and instructor readiness programs, contact Rand Heer, president of OLAP Train, at (530) 295-1011. For more information about Aspirity and its consulting and training services, contact Hilary Feier at (425) 828-3533.

The manuscript for this book was prepared and galleyed using Microsoft Word 2000. Pages were composed by Microsoft Press using Adobe PageMaker 6.52 for Windows, with text in Stone Serif and display type in ITC Franklin Gothic. Composed pages were delivered to the printer as electronic prepress files.

Cover Designer:	Girvin | Branding & Design
Interior Graphic Designer:	James D. Kramer
Interior Graphic Artist:	Joel Panchot
Principal Compositor:	Elizabeth Hansford
Principal Proofreader:	Holly M. Viola
Indexer:	Bill Meyers

MICROSOFT LICENSE AGREEMENT

Book Companion CD

IMPORTANT—READ CAREFULLY: This Microsoft End-User License Agreement ("EULA") is a legal agreement between you (either an individual or an entity) and Microsoft Corporation for the Microsoft product identified above, which includes computer software and may include associated media, printed materials, and "online" or electronic documentation ("SOFTWARE PRODUCT"). Any component included within the SOFTWARE PRODUCT that is accompanied by a separate End-User License Agreement shall be governed by such agreement and not the terms set forth below. By installing, copying, or otherwise using the SOFTWARE PRODUCT, you agree to be bound by the terms of this EULA. If you do not agree to the terms of this EULA, you are not authorized to install, copy, or otherwise use the SOFTWARE PRODUCT; you may, however, return the SOFTWARE PRODUCT, along with all printed materials and other items that form a part of the Microsoft product that includes the SOFTWARE PRODUCT, to the place you obtained them for a full refund.

SOFTWARE PRODUCT LICENSE

The SOFTWARE PRODUCT is protected by United States copyright laws and international copyright treaties, as well as other intellectual property laws and treaties. The SOFTWARE PRODUCT is licensed, not sold.

1. **GRANT OF LICENSE.** This EULA grants you the following rights:

   a. **Software Product.** You may install and use one copy of the SOFTWARE PRODUCT on a single computer. The primary user of the computer on which the SOFTWARE PRODUCT is installed may make a second copy for his or her exclusive use on a portable computer.

   b. **Storage/Network Use.** You may also store or install a copy of the SOFTWARE PRODUCT on a storage device, such as a network server, used only to install or run the SOFTWARE PRODUCT on your other computers over an internal network; however, you must acquire and dedicate a license for each separate computer on which the SOFTWARE PRODUCT is installed or run from the storage device. A license for the SOFTWARE PRODUCT may not be shared or used concurrently on different computers.

   c. **License Pak.** If you have acquired this EULA in a Microsoft License Pak, you may make the number of additional copies of the computer software portion of the SOFTWARE PRODUCT authorized on the printed copy of this EULA, and you may use each copy in the manner specified above. You are also entitled to make a corresponding number of secondary copies for portable computer use as specified above.

   d. **Sample Code.** Solely with respect to portions, if any, of the SOFTWARE PRODUCT that are identified within the SOFTWARE PRODUCT as sample code (the "SAMPLE CODE"):

      i. **Use and Modification.** Microsoft grants you the right to use and modify the source code version of the SAMPLE CODE, *provided* you comply with subsection (d)(iii) below. You may not distribute the SAMPLE CODE, or any modified version of the SAMPLE CODE, in source code form.

      ii. **Redistributable Files.** Provided you comply with subsection (d)(iii) below, Microsoft grants you a nonexclusive, royalty-free right to reproduce and distribute the object code version of the SAMPLE CODE and of any modified SAMPLE CODE, other than SAMPLE CODE, or any modified version thereof, designated as not redistributable in the Readme file that forms a part of the SOFTWARE PRODUCT (the "Non-Redistributable Sample Code"). All SAMPLE CODE other than the Non-Redistributable Sample Code is collectively referred to as the "REDISTRIBUTABLES."

      iii. **Redistribution Requirements.** If you redistribute the REDISTRIBUTABLES, you agree to: (i) distribute the REDISTRIBUTABLES in object code form only in conjunction with and as a part of your software application product; (ii) not use Microsoft's name, logo, or trademarks to market your software application product; (iii) include a valid copyright notice on your software application product; (iv) indemnify, hold harmless, and defend Microsoft from and against any claims or lawsuits, including attorney's fees, that arise or result from the use or distribution of your software application product; and (v) not permit further distribution of the REDISTRIBUTABLES by your end user. Contact Microsoft for the applicable royalties due and other licensing terms for all other uses and/or distribution of the REDISTRIBUTABLES.

2. **DESCRIPTION OF OTHER RIGHTS AND LIMITATIONS.**

   - **Limitations on Reverse Engineering, Decompilation, and Disassembly.** You may not reverse engineer, decompile, or disassemble the SOFTWARE PRODUCT, except and only to the extent that such activity is expressly permitted by applicable law notwithstanding this limitation.

   - **Separation of Components.** The SOFTWARE PRODUCT is licensed as a single product. Its component parts may not be separated for use on more than one computer.

   - **Rental.** You may not rent, lease, or lend the SOFTWARE PRODUCT.

   - **Support Services.** Microsoft may, but is not obligated to, provide you with support services related to the SOFTWARE PRODUCT ("Support Services"). Use of Support Services is governed by the Microsoft policies and programs described in the user manual, in "online" documentation, and/or in other Microsoft-provided materials. Any supplemental software code provided to you as part of the Support Services shall be considered part of the SOFTWARE PRODUCT and subject to the terms and conditions of this EULA. With respect to technical information you provide to Microsoft as part of the Support Services, Microsoft may use such information for its business purposes, including for product support and development. Microsoft will not utilize such technical information in a form that personally identifies you.

- **Software Transfer.** You may permanently transfer all of your rights under this EULA, provided you retain no copies, you transfer all of the SOFTWARE PRODUCT (including all component parts, the media and printed materials, any upgrades, this EULA, and, if applicable, the Certificate of Authenticity), **and** the recipient agrees to the terms of this EULA.

- **Termination.** Without prejudice to any other rights, Microsoft may terminate this EULA if you fail to comply with the terms and conditions of this EULA. In such event, you must destroy all copies of the SOFTWARE PRODUCT and all of its component parts.

3. **COPYRIGHT.** All title and copyrights in and to the SOFTWARE PRODUCT (including but not limited to any images, photographs, animations, video, audio, music, text, SAMPLE CODE, REDISTRIBUTABLES, and "applets" incorporated into the SOFTWARE PRODUCT) and any copies of the SOFTWARE PRODUCT are owned by Microsoft or its suppliers. The SOFTWARE PRODUCT is protected by copyright laws and international treaty provisions. Therefore, you must treat the SOFTWARE PRODUCT like any other copyrighted material **except** that you may install the SOFTWARE PRODUCT on a single computer provided you keep the original solely for backup or archival purposes. You may not copy the printed materials accompanying the SOFTWARE PRODUCT.

4. **U.S. GOVERNMENT RESTRICTED RIGHTS.** The SOFTWARE PRODUCT and documentation are provided with RESTRICTED RIGHTS. Use, duplication, or disclosure by the Government is subject to restrictions as set forth in subparagraph (c)(1)(ii) of the Rights in Technical Data and Computer Software clause at DFARS 252.227-7013 or subparagraphs (c)(1) and (2) of the Commercial Computer Software—Restricted Rights at 48 CFR 52.227-19, as applicable. Manufacturer is Microsoft Corporation/One Microsoft Way/Redmond, WA 98052-6399.

5. **EXPORT RESTRICTIONS.** You agree that you will not export or re-export the SOFTWARE PRODUCT, any part thereof, or any process or service that is the direct product of the SOFTWARE PRODUCT (the foregoing collectively referred to as the "Restricted Components"), to any country, person, entity, or end user subject to U.S. export restrictions. You specifically agree not to export or re-export any of the Restricted Components (i) to any country to which the U.S. has embargoed or restricted the export of goods or services, which currently include, but are not necessarily limited to, Cuba, Iran, Iraq, Libya, North Korea, Sudan, and Syria, or to any national of any such country, wherever located, who intends to transmit or transport the Restricted Components back to such country; (ii) to any end user who you know or have reason to know will utilize the Restricted Components in the design, development, or production of nuclear, chemical, or biological weapons; or (iii) to any end user who has been prohibited from participating in U.S. export transactions by any federal agency of the U.S. government. You warrant and represent that neither the BXA nor any other U.S. federal agency has suspended, revoked, or denied your export privileges.

DISCLAIMER OF WARRANTY

NO WARRANTIES OR CONDITIONS. MICROSOFT EXPRESSLY DISCLAIMS ANY WARRANTY OR CONDITION FOR THE SOFTWARE PRODUCT. THE SOFTWARE PRODUCT AND ANY RELATED DOCUMENTATION ARE PROVIDED "AS IS" WITHOUT WARRANTY OR CONDITION OF ANY KIND, EITHER EXPRESS OR IMPLIED, INCLUDING, WITHOUT LIMITATION, THE IMPLIED WARRANTIES OF MERCHANTABILITY, FITNESS FOR A PARTICULAR PURPOSE, OR NONINFRINGEMENT. THE ENTIRE RISK ARISING OUT OF USE OR PERFORMANCE OF THE SOFTWARE PRODUCT REMAINS WITH YOU.

LIMITATION OF LIABILITY. TO THE MAXIMUM EXTENT PERMITTED BY APPLICABLE LAW, IN NO EVENT SHALL MICROSOFT OR ITS SUPPLIERS BE LIABLE FOR ANY SPECIAL, INCIDENTAL, INDIRECT, OR CONSEQUENTIAL DAMAGES WHATSOEVER (INCLUDING, WITHOUT LIMITATION, DAMAGES FOR LOSS OF BUSINESS PROFITS, BUSINESS INTERRUPTION, LOSS OF BUSINESS INFORMATION, OR ANY OTHER PECUNIARY LOSS) ARISING OUT OF THE USE OF OR INABILITY TO USE THE SOFTWARE PRODUCT OR THE PROVISION OF OR FAILURE TO PROVIDE SUPPORT SERVICES, EVEN IF MICROSOFT HAS BEEN ADVISED OF THE POSSIBILITY OF SUCH DAMAGES. IN ANY CASE, MICROSOFT'S ENTIRE LIABILITY UNDER ANY PROVISION OF THIS EULA SHALL BE LIMITED TO THE GREATER OF THE AMOUNT ACTUALLY PAID BY YOU FOR THE SOFTWARE PRODUCT OR US$5.00; PROVIDED, HOWEVER, IF YOU HAVE ENTERED INTO A MICROSOFT SUPPORT SERVICES AGREEMENT, MICROSOFT'S ENTIRE LIABILITY REGARDING SUPPORT SERVICES SHALL BE GOVERNED BY THE TERMS OF THAT AGREEMENT. BECAUSE SOME STATES AND JURISDICTIONS DO NOT ALLOW THE EXCLUSION OR LIMITATION OF LIABILITY, THE ABOVE LIMITATION MAY NOT APPLY TO YOU.

MISCELLANEOUS

This EULA is governed by the laws of the State of Washington USA, except and only to the extent that applicable law mandates governing law of a different jurisdiction.

Should you have any questions concerning this EULA, or if you desire to contact Microsoft for any reason, please contact the Microsoft subsidiary serving your country, or write: Microsoft Sales Information Center/One Microsoft Way/Redmond, WA 98052-6399.

Proof of Purchase

0-7356-0904-7

Do not send this card with your registration.
Use this card as proof of purchase if participating in a promotion or rebate offer on *Microsoft® SQL Server™ 2000 Analysis Services Step by Step*.
Card must be used in conjunction with other proof(s) of payment such as your dated sales receipt—see offer details.

Microsoft® SQL Server™ 2000 Analysis Services Step by Step

WHERE DID YOU PURCHASE THIS PRODUCT?

CUSTOMER NAME

Microsoft®

mspress.microsoft.com

Microsoft Press, PO Box 97017, Redmond, WA 98073-9830

OWNER REGISTRATION CARD

Register Today!

0-7356-0904-7

Return the bottom portion of this card to register today.

Microsoft® SQL Server™ 2000 Analysis Services Step by Step

FIRST NAME | MIDDLE INITIAL | LAST NAME

INSTITUTION OR COMPANY NAME

ADDRESS

CITY | STATE | ZIP

E-MAIL ADDRESS

( )
PHONE NUMBER

U.S. and Canada addresses only. Fill in information above and mail postage-free.
Please mail only the bottom half of this page.

For information about Microsoft Press®
products, visit our Web site at
mspress.microsoft.com

Microsoft®